Explore
Mount Kilimanjaro

Jacquetta Megarry

Rucksack Readers

Explore Mount Kilimanjaro: a Rucksack Reader

Second edition published 2002 by Rucksack Readers, Landrick Lodge, Dunblane, FK15 0HY, UK

Telephone   01786 824 696 (+44 1786 824 696)

Fax   01786 825 090 (+44 1786 825 090)

Website   www.rucsacs.com

ISBN 1-898481-16-4

British Library cataloguing in publication data: a catalogue record for this book is available from the British Library.

916.7826
m496
C.1

Designed by WorkHorse Productions (info@workhorse.co.uk)

Reprographics by Digital Imaging, Glasgow

The maps in this book were created for the purpose by Cartographic Consultants of Edinburgh © 2001

Publisher's note

A walk to extreme altitude involves possible health hazards. These have been explained as clearly as possible, and advice offered on how to minimise them. All information has been checked carefully prior to publication. However, individuals are responsible for their own welfare and safety, and the publisher cannot accept responsibility for any ill-health or injury, however caused.

Explore Mount Kilimanjaro: contents

Introduction

A journey to Mount Kilimanjaro is an exploration, not merely a climb. For some, the appeal is simple: it is the highest mountain on earth whose summit is accessible to any committed walker without technical skills or experience. A well-prepared city-dweller may be able to reach 'the roof of Africa'. This is the allure of the highest free-standing mountain in the world.

However, each walker faces a personal gamble, and the stakes are high: altitude symptoms are unpredictable. No amount of preparation can guarantee success. The only certainty is that everyone who takes up the challenge will reach deep down inside themselves during the ascent.

Reaching the summit is not the only goal: success lies rather in the quality of the attempt. Living a lot closer to nature than you are used to, you will explore your own motivation and recognise your dependency on others. On return from Kilimanjaro, whether you 'succeed' or not, you will know more about yourself, your strengths and weaknesses, and your fellow humans, than when you set out. That's why this book's title begins 'Explore ...' rather than 'Climb' Mount Kilimanjaro.

For anyone interested in the natural world, exploring this mountain is fascinating. In a landscape formed by ice and fire, the ascent takes you from tropical rain forest to arctic conditions among the summit glaciers - contrasts that at sea level would be six thousand miles apart. On Kilimanjaro, you walk from equator to pole in four days.

In temperate latitudes, each season takes months to give way to the next; high on Kilimanjaro, winter drives out summer every night. This is a wild place, full of contrasts and extremes. Plants and animals struggle to survive, in severe conditions of drought, arctic cold and blazing sunshine. Your climb is a journey backwards in time, where life-forms become simpler, species are fewer and the struggle to survive is harder.

The mountain rises over three miles above the plain on which it stands, making it an outstanding landmark. Your journey to Kilimanjaro may become an unforgettable personal landmark in your life.

Planning and preparation

When is the best time of year?

Because Kilimanjaro is so near the equator, the sun is always nearly overhead and the seasons are not as we know them in higher latitudes. The two rainy seasons run from late March to early June and from November to December. It's worth avoiding the poorer visibility and slippery paths in the rain forest if you can. Late June to October and January to early March are the best months to aim for, but remember that heavy rain, snow and thunderstorms can affect mountains at any time.

Another factor to consider is the phase of the moon. You will set off on your summit attempt around midnight, and you may prefer moonlight for this walk. If so, time your trip to overlap with a full moon; see page 63 for details. Finally, decide how much preparation time you need before departure (pages 9-24) and choose a reliable tour operator (see page 62). Look for flights direct into Kilimanjaro International Airport (JRO), for example via Amsterdam, rather than via Nairobi (NBO) which involves a long ground transfer.

Combining it with other activities

Since the air fare to Tanzania is likely to be a high proportion of your holiday cost, consider the advantages of spending an extra week or more if you can. You could combine Kili with other activities, such as game safaris, a trip to the spice islands of Zanzibar or Pemba, or climbing Mount Meru (see page 6).

If you have a day to spare, don't miss the chance of a game drive in Arusha National Park. It has a wide range of animals, including baboon, wild buffalo, colobus monkey, hippopotamus and is famous for its giraffes (Tanzania's national animal). Bird life is spectacular, ranging from flamingos, secretary birds and eagles through hoopoes and plovers to sunbirds and bee-eaters: you could see 30–40 species in a single visit.

Giraffe, Arusha National Park

The more famous Tanzanian National Parks (Serengeti, Tarangire and Ngorongoro) are much further away, but Amboseli is just across the border in Kenya (see map on page 26). For all but Arusha, you would have to extend your stay beyond one week.

Committed mountain enthusiasts could climb Mount Meru, a classic volcanic cone which stands in Arusha National Park and last erupted in 1893. The standard route to the summit (4566 metres) takes four days and

Kilimanjaro seen from high on Mount Meru

follows the same pattern as Kili, so it makes an ideal preparation. Climb Meru before Kili, allowing a couple of days between the two. The acclimatisation is valuable, and you may be inspired by seeing the sun rise behind Uhuru Peak.

Which route: Marangu or Machame?

Marangu route profile

Uhuru Peak
(5895)

Gillman's Point
(5685)

Saddle
(optional)

Kibo Hut
(4700)

Kibo Hut
(4700)

Horombo Huts
(3700)

Horombo Huts
(3700)

Mandara Huts
(2700)

Mandara Huts
(2700)

Marangu Gate
(1900)

Marangu Gate
(1900)

1 2 3 4 5

Machame route profile

Uhuru Peak
(5895)

Stella Point
(5795)

(4530)

Barranco Wall
(4330)

Barafu Camp
(4600)

Shira Camp
(3850)

Barranco Camp
(3950)

Karanga
Valley

Machame Camp
(3000)

Mweka Camp
(3100)

Machame Gate
(1800)

Mweka Village
(1500)

1 2 3 4 5

These profiles were created from map cross-sections. They show altitude in metres reliably, but not distances along the ground. No two sources agree about the length in km of the Machame route, and no two-dimensional map can give reliable distances for a route that involves so much movement in the third dimension. On steep, pathless terrain, no two walkers will cover the same distance anyway; in scrambling sections, the notion of distance covered becomes academic.

Although there are dozens of routes up the mountain, the most popular routes for walkers are Marangu and Machame (pronounced Mar**an**goo and Match**am**eh). The route profiles (page 6) and maps (back cover) show how much they differ. The Marangu ascent is described in Sections 3.1 to 3.4, the Machame ascent in 3.5 to 3.9, whilst Section 3.10 covers descent on both routes. On Marangu, you go back the way you came, whereas on Machame, you descend by a different, more direct route, normally via Mweka Camp.

The Machame route is much more strenuous, because

- you walk further
- you do more climbing and descending en route to your summit attempt
- the terrain is rougher so the walking takes more effort.

Sensible Marangu operators arrange an extra night for acclimatisation at Horombo, offering an optional walk in the 'saddle' region. On this basis, both routes involve five nights on the mountain. However, if you are feeling tired or unwell, the Marangu route lets you choose how much or little you do on Day 3, whereas on Machame you have no option.

You should also weigh up the accommodation. On Marangu, you sleep in permanent bunk-bedded huts, with solar-powered electricity. Most huts take up to six people, except Kibo Hut which has 60 beds in five dormitories. People of either sex are allocated to huts on arrival. Most of the toilet blocks have running water and are close to the huts.

On Machame route, you sleep normally two to a tent, with only your sleep mat between you and the ground-sheet, relying on your head-torch for lighting. Sleeping in tents is colder than in the Marangu huts, but gives you greater privacy. If you go with a friend or partner, you will probably share a tent all week. However, the latrines (toilets) are generally more primitive and further to walk to than on Marangu.

Latrine at Barafu Camp, Machame route

For some people, the choice is easy: if you dislike the idea of tented camping or doubt your ability to complete the more strenuous route, choose Marangu. (It is also called the 'tourist' or 'Coca-Cola' route,, because soft drinks and bottled water are on sale in all the huts.) If you regard camping as a bonus, prefer a round trip that lets you see more mountain scenery and are confident of your fitness, choose Machame. If you find the choice difficult, read Part 3 carefully and try to talk to people who have climbed by either route. Visit our website's Links page for first-hand accounts of each.

At one time, Machame was much less crowded, with less litter than Marangu. Recently the authorities have not been limiting numbers on Machame, and the route came under intense pressure. On Marangu, the limited sleeping capacity of the huts sets a ceiling on numbers. Weekend departures are the most popular choice, and everybody walks to the same schedule. However at least on Machame the walkers nearly all travel in the same direction.

The Machame route has the reputation of a higher 'success' rate: a higher percentage of walkers reach the summit. Overall, the average for Marangu may be only 40-50%, although some operators claim 75% or more, and higher still (80-90%) for Machame. This does *not* mean that you will improve your personal chances by choosing Machame. The figures are inflated by the fact that very fit, experienced hikers are attracted to the more expensive, more extended route; they are more likely to succeed whichever route they choose. Also, the Marangu figure is depressed by low-budget, minimum-stay tourists who omit the extra night at Horombo – a false economy.

All the evidence is that exertion is a major risk factor in AMS. If your over-riding concern is to maximise your chance of reaching the summit, choose Marangu. It involves less effort overall, and has only one seriously taxing day. On Machame, your summit attempt comes after four full, strenuous days of trekking, and is immediately followed by a longer descent than on Marangu. Reaching the summit, however, is not everything, and there are good reasons why many people prefer the more scenic Machame route.

Sunset over Mawenzi, taken from Barafu Camp, Machame route

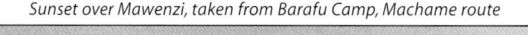

Fitness, exercise and heart rate

Muscles get stronger if they are used regularly, at a suitable level and for a sustained period. This is known as the training effect. As a hiker, you might think the most important muscles to train are in your legs, but in fact the heart is even more vital. If you train your heart muscle, it pumps blood more efficiently and delivers more oxygen. Cardiovascular (CV) fitness refers to your heart and circulation: you can improve your CV fitness simply by exercising in your target zone for at least 20 minutes several times a week.

Your target zone

This table shows how your target zone is calculated from your age; the formula does not allow for individual differences. Exercising above your target zone will not increase your CV fitness significantly further, and may tire you faster. Exercising below it will benefit you in weight loss, increasing your power-to-weight ratio. However, it will not noticeably improve your fitness level.

If you exercise within your target zone for 20-40 minutes every other day, within a few weeks you will notice your fitness improving. You will have to work harder to push your heart rate into your target zone, and it will return to normal faster when you ease off. The guideline is to work hard enough to make yourself pant, but not so hard that you cannot also talk. A wrist-worn heart rate monitor takes out the guesswork by showing you a continuous read-out.

Age range (years)	Target zone (beats per minute)
16 – 20	140 – 170
21 – 25	136 – 166
26 – 30	133 – 162
31 – 35	130 – 157
36 – 40	126 – 153
41 – 45	122 – 149
46 – 50	119 – 144
51 – 55	116 – 140
56 – 60	112 – 136
61 – 65	108 – 132
66 – 70	105 – 128
71 – 75	102 – 123
76 – 80	98 – 119

The fit person climbs more easily, uses less oxygen per unit of work done and is more energy-efficient. When everything takes more effort than usual, as at altitude, it helps progress and morale to know that your heart is pumping the available oxygen efficiently to your tissues. Taken to extremes of altitude, your brain is your most important organ: if your judgement is sound, you may take avoiding action before you run into danger.

Unexpectedly, less fit people may be at lower risk of AMS, simply because they are less capable of ascending too quickly. If you are extremely fit, beware of climbing too fast for your body to adjust. However, if you are unfit and/or overweight, you may fail to reach the summit for other reasons, even if you do not suffer from AMS.

Most people already know whether or not they are overweight. Carrying surplus fat adds to your baggage: if you need to shed some weight, do so gradually and well ahead of your trip. This will reduce one risk factor for altitude sickness. However, don't go to extremes: fat insulates your body from cold, and if you are very thin, you will have to carry more clothing to avoid hypothermia, which is another risk factor.

Where and how to exercise

The answer depends on your preference, your lifestyle and where you live. If you live in or near pleasant terrain for walking/jogging, have considerable self-discipline and you don't mind the weather, suitable footwear may be all you need. Consider getting a heart rate monitor to make your training more systematic. Try going out with a friend who also wants to get fit: if your training needs and pace are compatible, you will motivate each other.

If brisk walking or jogging does not appeal, find a mix of activities that you enjoy and can do often enough (three times per week). If you dislike an activity, you won't stick to it. Anything that puts your heart rate into the target zone is fine, eg energetic dancing, cycling or swimming. Consider joining a gym or fitness centre: their equipment is designed to measure and build CV fitness. A gym makes you independent of the weather and limited daylight, there are trained staff and it's easy to monitor your progress.

Avoid relying on a single form of exercise. The smooth flat surface of a treadmill does nothing to prepare your leg muscles for rough terrain or climbing loose scree. If you use a gym for convenience, try to complement it with some hill-walking expeditions in the weeks prior to departure.

However you exercise, minimise the risk of straining your body, especially at first, by warming up slowly beforehand, cooling down afterwards, and stretching both before and after. Stretching beforehand reduces the risk of injury. After exercise, stretching prevents a build-up of lactic acid in your muscles, which would lead to stiffness later. Take a water container and drink plenty before, during and after your sessions.

When and how often to exercise

You don't have to become an exercise junkie to climb this mountain, nor give up your normal life and pleasures. Just get reasonably fit so you can enjoy the experience. Start well in advance: if you are already fit, a month of special training might be enough, but if you are unfit, try to start at least six months in advance. If you smoke, either give it up or at least suspend it until after your trip.

For CV fitness, you need at least 20-minute sessions for maximum training effect, but build up to 30 minutes, and, approaching your departure date, 40-60 minutes. Better still, spend the odd day walking fast on rough or hilly terrain. During the climb your heart rate may exceed the target zone for hours on end, and on summit day you will be hiking for 15 to 18 hours. Prepare your body for sustained effort.

The best frequency for training is every other day: the body needs a rest day to extract maximum benefit from the training session. Since you may miss the odd session, three times per week is the goal for your main training period. In the month prior to departure, build up to longer sessions and higher target heart rates.

Stop training a day or two before you leave, but if you have a spare day on arrival in Tanzania, go for a long walk. Even at only 3000 feet or so, the airport and village of Moshi give many tourists an altitude advantage over their home bases.

Altitude effects

The challenge presented by the highest free-standing mountain on earth is the ascent of over 16,000 feet (5000 metres) in only four days. This section explains the cause of altitude problems and how to prevent or minimise their effects.

This section is based on several books written by experts on high-altitude medicine (page 61), amplified by personal experience and advice from staff at Explore Worldwide Ltd. The books cited are not for the faint-hearted; we have had to simplify and summarise a large technical literature. Here we try to explain the basics and offer practical advice, using a minimum of medical jargon.

How your body responds to lack of oxygen

The altitude problem for your body is the shortage of oxygen. As you climb higher, the air gets thinner. At 5500 metres (18,000 feet) atmospheric pressure is only half of its sea level value. Approaching the summit, each lungful gives you just under half as much oxygen as at sea level, so your body has to work more than twice as hard to maintain the supply.

In simple terms, your heart is the pump that makes your blood circulate. Your lungs load oxygen into your red blood cells for delivery to your muscles, brain and other organs. These tissues cannot work without oxygen. The demand from your muscles depends on their activity level, but your brain needs a surprising amount of oxygen. Despite being only 2% of your body weight, it needs around 15% of its oxygen. If your brain is deprived of oxygen, your judgement declines, movement control suffers and speech becomes confused.

Your body responds in various ways to needing more oxygen:

- you breathe faster and more deeply
- your heart beats faster in order to maintain the oxygen to your tissues
- your body gets rid of excess fluid and creates more red blood cells, making the blood thicker.

You start to breathe faster right away, and your heart rate rises within minutes. It can take several days before your blood starts to thicken: if you suddenly find yourself urinating a lot that may be a sign that your body is acclimatising well. Making more red blood cells is a much longer process that gets under way within a week or two: on normal Kili schedules, this won't be in time to make a difference.

At altitude, breathe deeply and freely as much as possible. Sleep is an important time for the body's adjustment: avoid sleeping pills and alcohol, which depress breathing while asleep.

Be aware that some people have episodes of 'periodic breathing', a pattern in which the sleeper's breathing becomes faster and louder for a minute or two, then decreases or perhaps even stops. The cycle repeats itself, but if the sleeper wakes up with a start, they may be prone to panic. Simply reassure them that all is well and try to get back to sleep. Periodic breathing is normal for some people even at sea level, but it becomes more obvious at altitude; with acclimatisation, it diminishes.

Acute Mountain Sickness (AMS)

Acute Mountain Sickness is what medical people call altitude or mountain sickness; 'acute' simply means that the onset is sudden. AMS symptoms do not last, and, if mild or moderate, may disappear if the victim rests or ascends no further; if they are severe, the victim must descend. Most people who attempt Kilimanjaro have invested a lot of time and money, so the stakes are high. Learn to recognise whether AMS is mild, moderate or severe.

Mild AMS feels like a hangover and can affect people at any altitude above 7000 feet or even lower. Its commonest symptom is a headache (which should respond to aspirin, paracetamol or ibuprofen) combined with at least one of the following:

- feeling sick
- lack of appetite
- difficulty sleeping
- general malaise (feeling lousy, lacking energy).

Moderate AMS differs from mild in that

- there is likely to be vomiting
- the headache does not respond to pain relief
- the victim may be very short of breath even when not exercising (eg after 15 minutes' rest).

Mild AMS is bearable, and affects most people who attempt Kilimanjaro to a greater or lesser extent. Moderate AMS can be seriously unpleasant, and some sufferers have to give up. Although symptoms may clear if there is no further ascent, very few Kilimanjaro trips have the flexibility to allow individuals prolonged rest or to postpone the summit attempt. In practice the choice tends to be simple: continue the ascent or descend.

Severe AMS is different again:

- there is ataxia - the word medical people use to describe loss of muscular co-ordination and balance, as when somebody stumbles, staggers or falls (but see below)
- there may be altered mental states, such as confusion, aggression or withdrawal
- it may lead to fluid leakage into the brain and/or lungs (see *Complications*, below)
- if untreated, it can cause coma followed by death.

However, there are many other causes of ataxia, such as extreme fatigue, hypothermia, dehydration and low blood sugar. Get the suspected victim to have a short rest, a drink, and a snack, and put on extra clothing if need be: this should take care of other possible causes. If they recover promptly, the ascent can continue. If symptoms persist, or if there is mental confusion and/or extreme shortness of breath while at rest, suspect severe AMS.

Severe AMS is avoidable and treatable, but only if you are aware of the possible risks and look out for yourself and others. Most of your group will have mild AMS at some stage of the walk, but anyone with moderate AMS should be monitored closely in case they worsen. Assess the sufferer's condition first thing in the morning: symptoms that persist after resting should be taken seriously. Severe AMS should be treated by immediate descent, oxygen and suitable drugs.

If you are unlucky enough to have moderate to severe AMS, you will probably feel so ill that you no longer care about reaching the summit. Occasionally, because the stakes are so high, some very determined individuals play down or even deny their symptoms and want to struggle on. The problem is that AMS has affected their judgement, and they do not realise how ill they have become. In such cases the guide or group leader may instruct them to descend, and his or her decision is final. If you are on the trip with a friend, you will know that person better than the group leader can, so you can help the decision process.

Over the millennium holiday between 22.12.99 and 5.1.00, 1180 people tried to climb Kilimanjaro: of these 36 had to be rescued, and three died – one from a heart attack, one from a fall and the third from AMS complications. Casualties on this scale are unusual, and could have been prevented if people knew the basic facts about AMS and were truthful about their experiences.

Complications from AMS (HAPE and HACE)

If you and your group act on the advice given so far, you are very unlikely to meet these complications. Edema (spelled *oedema* in Britain) is medical jargon for swelling. Two serious complications are known as HAPE and HACE: High Altitude Pulmonary Edema and High Altitude Cerebral Edema - swelling of tissues in the lungs and brain respectively. HAPE has occurred at altitudes from 8000 feet and HACE from 10,000 feet, although both are less unusual at higher altitudes.

HAPE is caused by fluid from tiny blood vessels leaking into air sacs in the lungs, and affects perhaps 2% of those at altitude, usually people who already have some AMS symptoms. Cold, exercise and dehydration all increase the risk of HAPE. So does gender: men are 5-6 times more likely to be affected than women, and children are more at risk than adults. (Children under 10 years are not allowed above 2700 m (9000 feet) on Kilimanjaro.) Around 1 in 10 HAPE cases will die unless promptly diagnosed and treated – by immediate descent, oxygen and suitable drugs.

The HAPE sufferer looks ill and

- has extreme difficulty in breathing
- is very weak, unable to sustain any exercise
- has a rapid pulse
- may have a fever
- may have bluish-looking lips and fingernail-beds; this is not unusual at altitude, but, if pronounced, is serious
- may have a cough; if any sputum is pink, frothy or contains blood, the case is serious.

HACE is rarer than HAPE, and results from swelling of the blood vessels in the brain: with no room for expansion, pressure builds up and causes ataxia, extreme lack of energy, incoherence, hallucinations or numbness, followed by coma. HACE may be accompanied by HAPE. Unless treated promptly – by immediate descent, oxygen and suitable drugs – HACE can be fatal.

Less serious side-effects of altitude include high altitude edema (swelling of hands, face and ankles) which is twice as common in women. Remove any tight-fitting jewellery before going to altitude. High altitude syncope (fainting) can affect some people who stand up immediately after eating, but they often recover and have no further problems. Some people become prone to nosebleeds; these can be inconvenient but are not serious. Most folk make more intestinal gas at altitude, which can be a harmless source of amusement.

Contact lens wearers may find their lenses become unbearably painful at extreme altitude, and should take spectacles as an alternative. Snow blindness is a troublesome condition that can involve headaches, double vision and acutely painful eyes; choose good quality sunglasses that block at least 99% of the ultraviolet rays and either wrap around or have sidepieces.

How can you tell if AMS will affect you?

You can't. No amount of training, preparation or medication can guarantee future success. You can reduce your risks by following the advice in this and other books. You can take your fitness to new levels, but this will not of itself reduce your chances of suffering AMS.

There is good evidence that things you cannot change, such as age and gender, affect your chances, although doctors cannot explain why. Females are less likely to experience AMS than males. At moderate altitude, young people are more likely to suffer AMS than their elders: the risk decreases with age in an almost straight line. Whether this reflects the greater enthusiasm of youth for rushing up mountains despite warning symptoms, or whether it is a biological effect of ageing, or represents self-selection among the group who climb high, nobody knows.

AMS is highly unpredictable, both in its onset and recovery. On my first trip (Marangu) I was lucky and had no AMS symptoms at any altitude. A year later on Machame, I had mild to moderate AMS on the afternoon of the third day while *descending* to Barranco Camp at 3950 metres. However, I recovered overnight and had no further symptoms, despite climbing a further 2000 metres over the next 24 hours. This is not what the textbooks lead you to expect, but it seems not uncommon on Machame. Other hikers first suffered AMS only on the steep approach to the crater rim, in several cases so badly that they had to turn back.

No expert nor textbook can predict whether or how any one individual will be affected. If you can't face the possibility that you might 'fail' due to AMS, then choose some other mountain.

Does Diamox prevent AMS?

Many drugs have been tried in the treatment and prevention of AMS. The research literature is large and contains some conflicting conclusions. Here we cover only acetazolamide (trade name Diamox), which has been studied thoroughly over 25 years.

Your blood has to maintain a finely tuned balance for bodily functions to work well. When you hyperventilate (pant), as when over-exerting at altitude, you lose a lot of carbon dioxide which can reduce the acidity of your blood. Diamox blocks or slows the enzyme involved in converting carbon dioxide. As a result, it speeds up acclimatisation by stopping the blood from becoming too alkaline and by smoothing out your breathing: it also reduces periodic breathing (page 12). Many people who attempt Kilimanjaro take Diamox with them because it can help to prevent, as well as treat, AMS. Before rushing off to get a doctor's prescription, however, consider the possible side-effects.

Diamox has been known to cause severe allergic reactions in a few individuals. So you should try it out ahead of your trip to test if you are allergic, to experiment with dosage and to discover whether you can tolerate the side-effects which may include:

- increased flow of urine (diuresis)
- numbness or tingling in hands, feet and face
- nausea
- finding that carbonated drinks taste flat.

Since altitude has a diuretic effect anyway, many people prefer to avoid Diamox, wishing to avoid further interruptions to sleep in order to urinate. This may be a problem only when dosage is too high; individuals vary so much that you may have to establish your own dosage: not easy if Kili is your first high-altitude trek. At one time, the recommendation was to take 250 mg three times a day, starting several days before the ascent. Two recent authorities (Houston 1998 and Bezruchka 1994) suggest starting with 125 mg daily at bedtime starting only on the day before ascent, and increasing this to up to 250 mg twice a day *only if need be*.

These dosages are suggested when using Diamox as a preventive measure. In treating AMS, the higher dosages should be used and descent is strongly recommended. Although the medical authorities tend to favour Diamox, I noticed no difference in acclimatisation between the members of two holiday groups according to whether they used the drug. As many people who were taking Diamox suffered symptoms as did those who took nothing. Because of the small numbers involved, this has no scientific validity, but it shows that taking Diamox doesn't necessarily prevent AMS.

Advice on food and drink

Meals are capably provided by support staff and, despite the difficult conditions for preparation and cooking, most people find the food both palatable and plentiful. The diet is rich in carbohydrates, good for helping to overcome altitude symptoms. Bring some snacks and treats such as dried fruit, trail mix, cereal bars or chocolate. They will boost your energy and morale, and can be

Hot food being carried into the mess tent, Shira Camp

shared with others. On the longest day, you may be walking for 15 to 18 hours in all, and snacks help to bridge the long gaps between meals. Bring also some throat sweets or peppermints as many people suffer very dry throats at altitude.

Few people carry sufficient water, and even fewer keep it handy. You dehydrate quickly when walking: every time you breathe out, you lose moisture, especially when the air is cold. Also altitude makes your body produce more urine (the diuretic effect), and you lose water vapour all the time, especially when exercising, as invisible sweat. Expect to drink two to four litres per day on top of the liquid you take with meals.

Try to drink *before* you become thirsty: a water bag or bladder with tube (eg a Platypus) is ideal as it lets you take sips whenever you need without having to stop or fiddle with rucksacks. If in doubt, check the colour of your urine: pale straw colour is fine, but yellow warns that you are dehydrated.

Keep iodine purification drops or tablets in your rucksack, and carefully follow the instructions about standing time and dosage in cold conditions. If the slight flavour bothers you, use neutralising tablets or fruit-flavoured powder. You may want to take some isotonic powder, at least for an extra boost on summit day: added to water, this makes a drink which replaces minerals that you lose when sweating a lot.

You can limit your fluid loss through sweating by adjusting your clothing. Try to anticipate your body's heat production. Shed excess layer(s) just before you start to overheat, and restore them just before you start to chill (eg for a rest stop or because the weather changes). Because each of these actions means stopping and fiddling with rucksacks, it's sometimes easier to keep a steady pace and wear clothes designed for flexibility. For example, prefer jackets with underarm zippers and pockets large enough to stow gloves and hat, and trousers with legs that unzip to make shorts.

Beyond the last water point, you have to carry all the water you need. On summit day take care to keep your water bladder or bottle well insulated or close to your body heat; otherwise it will freeze during the night hours. If you use a water bladder, the narrow tube is likely to freeze, so either keep it protected or else blow back the water after each sip so the tube remains empty. Dehydration during the night-time climb is a common mistake.

Summary: how to prevent and manage AMS

- prepare well by becoming fitter (and giving up smoking)
- take suitable supplies and pack your gear for easy retrieval
- avoid over-exertion: if possible ascend slowly enough that you can still breathe through your nose
- avoid sleeping pills and alcohol on the mountain
- eat small amounts of food often, even if you don't feel hungry; avoid excessive salt
- drink plenty of fluids (four to five litres per day), especially water
- if you plan to use Diamox, experiment with dosage well ahead of time, under medical supervision
- do not deny any symptoms you may experience and keep the group leader or guide informed.

Other health issues

Your decision to try to walk to extreme altitude carries risks as well as benefits. Before you commit yourself, talk to your doctor (general practitioner or physician). He or she may have no detailed knowledge of altitude physiology so take along your schedule and route profiles (page 6). Unless your medical history involves special risk factors, your doctor should be enthusiastic about the healthy side-effects of preparing for this trip.

Take this chance to check the latest information on which vaccinations are required and recommended for Tanzania, and over what timetable. Ensure that you store your records safely: you may be refused entry without proof of yellow fever protection, for example. Take advice about anti-malarial drugs and insect repellents (eg something with a high percentage of DEET), and follow it carefully. Malaria is a life-threatening disease which is easy to prevent but difficult to treat. Although for much of the time you will be too high to be at risk, you need protection if only for the beginning and end of your trip; a single infected bite is all it takes.

If you haven't taken anti-malarials before, discuss with your doctor whether you need to take an experimental dose ahead of time. Some can cause side-effects, including nausea and other problems which could be confused with AMS symptoms and generally won't help your attempt. You might want to ask his or her views on Diamox at the same time.

Remember to visit your dentist well before departure. Your feet are about to become the most important part of your body, so consider seeing a chiropodist, and obtain blister prevention and treatment. If you are a blood donor, make your last donation at least eight to ten weeks before you leave. (Your blood probably won't be welcomed until one year after your return, as AIDS is endemic in this part of Africa.)

Upset digestion is not uncommon, so consider what remedies to take, including anti-diarrhoea medicine. Some of those who have to turn back do so because of diarrhoea and consequent dehydration. The nature of the latrines and absence of running water in most campsites makes it crucial to keep yourself clean: take a good supply of wet wipes, preferably medicated.

Finally, the sun's rays are far stronger at altitude, because the thinner air screens out less of the harmful radiation. Since the equatorial sun is already much stronger than most tourists are used to, the risk of sunburn is doubly severe. (On this trip you may risk sunburn and hypothermia within a matter of hours.) Bring a sun hat, cover-up clothing and cream with the highest Sun Protection Factor you can find, minimum of SPF 25 for your face and SPF 33 for your lips, which are especially at risk.

Equipment and packing

There is a packing list on page 24. Major items include a well broken-in pair of walking boots, a suitable day rucksack and kit bag, walking poles and five-season sleeping gear for the very cold nights at altitude. Be sure to test anything you buy specially on weekend walks long before you set off.

Boots

If your walking boots need to be replaced, buy new ones well ahead of time. Take or buy suitable socks and consider buying special insoles (or footbeds). They can make a boot feel more supportive and comfortable, but may need a larger size: a common mistake is to buy boots that are too short. This may lead to serious toe trouble, especially on the way down (Section 3.10). Specialist fitters can fix almost any other boot problem.

Rucksack and kit bag

Your day rucksack should be around 35 litres to hold lots of water and spare clothing. If in doubt, err on the large side, for easier retrieval and packing. Either buy a waterproof cover or liner, or use a bin (garbage) bag.

Check that the rucksack

- is comfortable to wear (test it loaded in the shop)
- has a chest strap as well as a waist strap
- is easy to put on and take off
- has side pockets for small items
- has loops for poles (see below).

Everything that isn't in your rucksack will be in your kit bag, which will spend the week being carried on a porter's head. A suitable kit bag must be large, soft and light, without a frame, wheels or dangling straps. Rucksacks and conventional suitcases are unsuitable: either buy a special bag, preferably waterproof, or use a sailing bag or large sports holdall. It should be tough enough to withstand aeroplane baggage handling (or else must be packed inside something which is).

Support team numbering two porters per hiker, plus guides

Trial packing

Long before you depart, do a trial pack using the kit bag, to find out if you are within target weight (15 kg). Refer to the list on page 24, but leave out your hiking boots, as you will either be wearing them or carrying them in your rucksack. Pack also in your hand baggage anything fragile (torches, sunglasses, camera) and any medicines you might need during the flight, as well as your passport, ticket, vaccination records and other valuables.

If your packed bag is too heavy, try again choosing only the bare necessities. If it weighs under 10 kg, and you have included everything essential, congratulations. Most people will end up with between 10 and 15 kg at the outset, perhaps less by the time the snacks have all been eaten.

Take extra care about packaging and organising: clear polythene zip-lock bags are great for keeping small stuff handy and visible, and cling-film keeps moisture off batteries and other delicate items. Time can be short on the mountain and if you are feeling unwell, you will bless the thought you put into such details.

You will probably leave any surplus kit and valuables at your hotel before you set off for the mountain: this might include spare toiletries, a set of clean clothes, aeroplane reading, personal hi-fi and anything you need for other excursions or parts of your holiday. It is only your mountain kit that must weigh under 15 kg (preferably less). You may be allowed up to 20 kg on the international flight.

Walking poles

Even if you don't normally use poles, consider trying or buying them before this trip. They improve your balance, save effort and reduce knee strain, especially going downhill. Telescopic poles can be set longer for downhill, shorter for uphill. A pair is better for rough, steep terrain, but some people prefer to keep one hand free. Poles can be stowed on your rucksack loops, eg when scrambling. If you are serious about photography, consider the kind which unscrews at the top to form a camera monopod.

Alternatively, you can buy a solid wooden walking stick very cheaply at the mountain gate: made of eucalyptus, they are light, long and strong. However, they would be challenging to bring home on the plane and you may find them less comfortable and effective than the telescopic metal type.

Clothing and night gear

Dress in layers, to help control your body temperature. The base should be a 'wicking' fabric, such as knitted polyester. Over that, wear a medium-weight fleece. The outer layer is a waterproof jacket and trousers; choose 'breathable' waterproofs that allow sweat to evaporate. Some people need a down-filled jacket in addition, for cold nights at altitude. Pay special attention to good gloves, footwear and head/face protection, to avoid hypothermia and frostbite.

Don't underestimate how cold you may be at nights, especially in tents on Machame. If you can't afford a really warm sleeping-bag and (Machame only) a good sleeping mat, then borrow or hire them. You can't enjoy your holiday if you are too cold to sleep properly. At higher altitudes, some people need to wear most of their clothes at night, including hat and gloves.

Packing checklist

The checklist on page 24 is divided into essential and desirable. Experienced trekkers may disagree about what belongs in each category, but others may appreciate a starting-point.

You will not see your main kit bag between morning and night: carry in your rucksack everything you need for the day's walk. With the exception of the torches, some spare clothing and sleeping gear, that could mean wearing or carrying everything in the Essential list on most days.

Essential

- well broken-in walking boots
- plenty of suitably warm walking socks
- poles (preferably two for the descent)
- many layers of suitably warm clothing, including underwear
- warm hat and/or balaclava for protection against cold
- broad-brimmed hat for protection against sun
- sun protection for eyes (good quality sunglasses or glacier glasses)
- gloves, glove liners and/or warm mittens (especially for summit day)
- waterproof jacket/trousers
- water carrier(s) (bottles or bladders)
- water purification tablets or drops
- snacks and throat sweets
- first aid kit including blister, headache and diarrhoea relief
- toilet tissue (biodegradable)
- wet wipes and wash bag equipped for skin and teeth cleaning
- head-torch, pocket torch and spare batteries
- very warm sleeping bag and (if needed) pillow
- warm self-inflating sleeping mat (Machame only)
- enough cash for tips (for guides and porters) plus any soft drinks or beer; US dollars are widely welcomed, but take plenty of small notes as you will be given change in Tanzanian shillings.

Desirable

- light and rugged camera; remember spare batteries and film
- waterproof rucksack cover or waterproof liner, eg bin (garbage) bag
- pouch or secure pockets: to keep small items handy but safe
- gaiters (to protect trouser legs on scree and snow)
- thermal sleeping bag liner
- spare shoes (eg trainers or hut slippers), spare bootlaces
- notebook and pen, playing cards or book
- guidebook and/or map.

Code for Kilimanjaro explorers

Keep your packaging to a minimum before setting off. Take as little as possible onto the mountain and leave nothing behind except footprints.

Leave no litter: it takes many years to biodegrade, many decades in the dry, cold conditions high on Kilimanjaro. Take your litter with you and dispose of it elsewhere.

Keep local water clean: avoid using pollutants such as detergents in streams or springs. If no toilet facilities are available, make sure you are at least 30 metres away from water resources, and bury your waste.

Don't pick flowers or pull up plants: especially on the upper slopes, plants struggle to survive in extreme conditions and they grow very slowly. Take only photographs.

Book your holiday with operators who put money back into local communities. Prefer those which support Friends of Conservation or like-minded charities.

Learn at least a few words of the local language. Local people will respect and appreciate your efforts.

(Extracted and adapted from the Traveller's Code and reproduced by permission of Friends of Conservation, see page 62)

2·1 Tanzania, history and Kilimanjaro's 'discovery'

Tanzania is a very large country, more than twice the size of California, with many tourist attractions including its Indian Ocean coastal islands and national parks and game reserves covering one-seventh of its area. Its population was approximately 30 million in 1997; most of its workforce of around 12 million are subsistence farmers. The main port and commercial capital is Dar es Salaam, population 1,650,000.

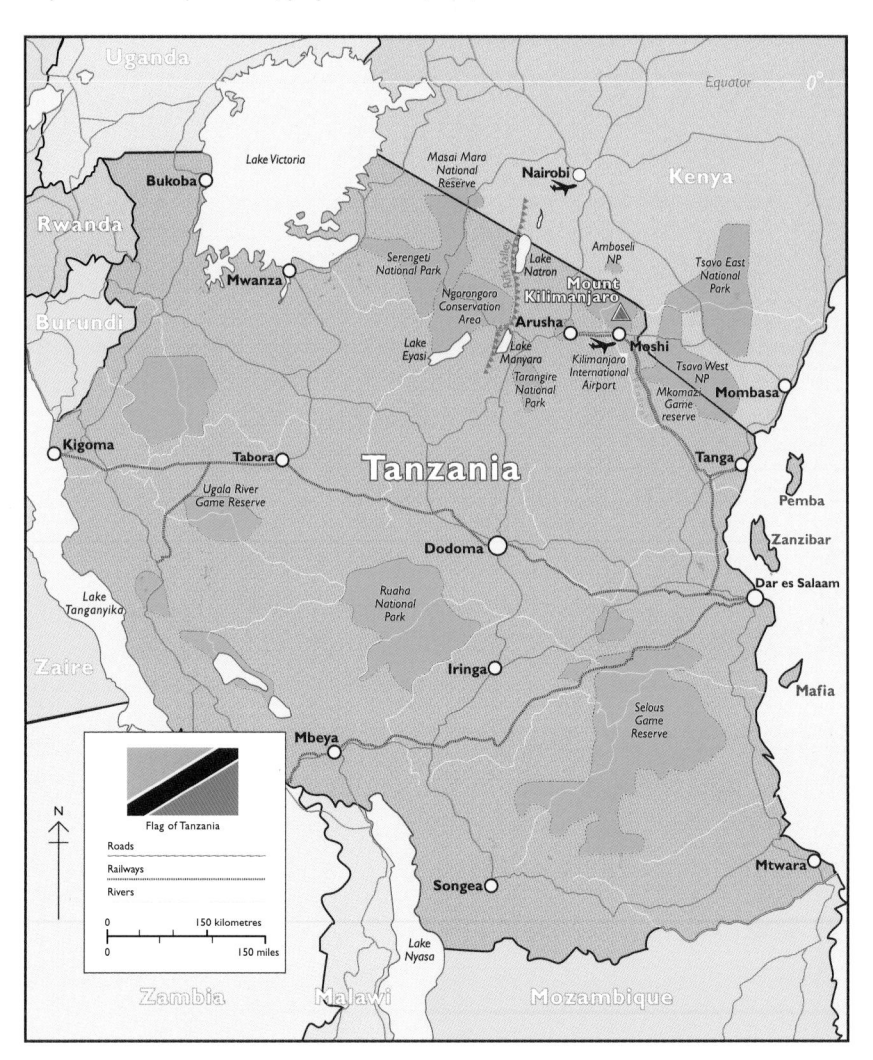

The four colours in its flag symbolise the people (black), the land (green), the sea (blue) and its mineral wealth (gold). The country's motto 'Uhuru na umoja' means 'Freedom and unity' in Swahili, its national language. Tanganyika gained independence in 1961. In 1964 its name changed to the United Republic of Tanzania when it joined with Zanzibar. Julius Nyerere was Tanzania's President from 1962-85.

Mount Kilimanjaro is an important symbol of freedom and appears in the national Emblem. The Uhuru Torch was first lit at its summit in 1961, in the words of Nyerere's famous speech, '[to] shine beyond our borders giving hope where there was despair, love where there was hate, and dignity where before there was only humiliation.'

Although Ptolemy of Alexandria wrote of a 'great snow mountain' in the second century AD, and Kilimanjaro was mentioned by Chinese and Arab writers in the 12th and 13th centuries, Europeans were surprisingly slow to 'discover' and accept the idea of a snow-capped mountain only 3° south of the equator.

In 1848, the missionary Johann Rebmann set out on an expedition to Kilimanjaro, and 'observed something remarkably white on the top of a high mountain'. He soon realised that it was snow, and later identified the twin peaks of Kibo and Mawenzi. He published his account in the *Church Missionary Intelligencer* in April 1849. Bizarrely, the British armchair geographers of the time refused to believe this first-hand account, and it was another 12 years before Rebmann's view was accepted.

Serious attempts by Europeans to climb Kilimanjaro began in 1861, and continued through the 1870s and 1880s, but most groups turned back at the snowline, then around 4000 metres, if not before. Finally, on 5 October 1889, Hans Meyer and Ludwig Purtscheller reached the summit, which they called Kaiser Wilhelm Spitze.

Contrary to a widespread myth, Kilimanjaro was not 'given' by Queen Victoria to her grandson Kaiser Wilhelm. The reason that the straight line of the Tanganyikan border was made to kink southward between the mountain and coast was to place the sea port of Mombasa in Kenya, then British. German East Africa kept the port of Dar es Salaam as part of the carve-up of Africa finally agreed by the European powers in Berlin in 1896.

2·2 Conservation, tourism and the local economy

Hotels in Marangu were running guided ascents of Kili from the 1930s, but visitor numbers were small and grew slowly. In 1959, around 700 tried for the summit, of whom around 50% reached Gillman's Point. In 1997, around 19,500 attempted the walk; by the time you read this, pressure of numbers will have become extreme on both routes, with well over 20,000 walkers per annum.

All land above the 2700 metres contour is included in Kilimanjaro National Park, and the Park regulations are clearly posted. Walking on this unique mountain carries a responsibility to ensure its preservation for future generations. Your Park fees are used to help with maintenance of the trails, huts and campsites, helping the authorities to fight their constant battle against woodcutters, poachers, accidental fire and the scourge of litter. As visitors, we can help in a positive way, not only by never leaving litter, but also by picking up the odd piece we may find on the trail. Follow the Code (page 25) and remember that everyone's behaviour also acts as an example, good or bad, to others.

Exploitation or economic opportunity?

Especially on a first visit to Africa, many Westerners feel uncomfortable about the idea of 'native porters' carrying their baggage and supplies, preparing meals and (on Machame) putting up and breaking down tents. Porters' loads are supposed to weigh less than 18 kilos (Marangu) or 15 kilos (Machame), whereas the average tourist's rucksack probably weighs around five kilos. At one level, this is obviously unfair.

On the other hand, the visitors' holidays pay for the porters' wages, and their tips are an important supplement to low wages. Porters are poorly paid by Western standards, but they are still better off than Tanzanians who are unemployed or subsistence farmers.

Furthermore, after three years' experience, porters may progress to become Assistant Guides, and after a further year or two, reach the rank of Head Guide. Guides are better paid, normally carry only their own equipment, have some training and speak some English.

Both guides and porters are vastly fitter than the visitors, have amazing balance and are well-acclimatised to altitude because of where they live and their frequent experience of ascents. However, they are human, they too feel tired and cold, and occasionally even they experience altitude symptoms. They suffer more from the cold than the better-equipped visitors: porters may have no proper footwear or sleeping bags.

Guides may be better equipped, but because they have to walk at the slow pace of the visitors, they may feel even colder than the porters who are free to set their own pace. Grateful tourists sometimes donate the odd item of clothing or gear at the end of the week, and many Head Guides operate a system for sharing such extras. Such gifts are, of course, no substitute for fair wages and generous tips.

The Chagga people are one of over 100 tribes living in Tanzania. They have lived on and around Kilimanjaro for only three or four centuries, and may have come from the northeast. When Rebmann arrived in 1848 they were divided into over 100 clans, each with its own chief. External force and diplomacy reduced this number progressively to about 50 by 1890 and only 15 when Tanganyika gained independence in 1961. The position of hereditary chief was abolished in 1962.

Most of the guides and porters are Chagga, and many come from the village of Marangu. They are self-employed, within a framework established by the Tanzanian National Parks, and they have a reputation for independence and strength of purpose. The missionary legacy is surprisingly strong, and most guides and porters seem to be Lutheran; you may even hear Christian hymns sung in Swahili. There is no single name for Kilimanjaro in Swahili, but its two peaks are called Kipoo (Kibo) and Kimawenzi (Mawenzi).

2·3 The volcanoes, geology and scenery

The Great Rift Valley reached its present form only between two and one million years ago. Compared with the formation of the earth around 4000 million years ago, this is, in geological terms, very recent. Long before Kilimanjaro was formed there was a gently rolling plain with the remains of a few eroded mountains. About a million years ago, the plain buckled and slumped, sinking over a period to form a huge basin known as the Kilimanjaro Depression.

The Kilimanjaro of today was formed between 500,000 and 750,000 years ago from three volcanic centres: Kibo was and still is the highest at 5896 metres, connected by its saddle region to Mawenzi (5149 metres). Shira, at 3962 metres, is the oldest and was also the first to collapse and become extinct. Eruptions and lava flow raised Kibo to its maximum height of about 5900 metres some 450,000 years ago, and it has shrunk only slightly since that time. Uhuru Peak, Kibo's 'summit', is simply the highest point of a giant oval crater rim, more than three kilometres long by two kilometres wide.

The Shira plateau was later worn down by erosion, but it still has interesting minerals (see page 51). Weathering exposed the jagged crags of Mawenzi, formed from slower-cooling, harder rocks that have resisted erosion. Around 100,000 years ago, subsidence caused a huge landslide that breached part of Kibo's crater rim and scoured out the Great Barranco on its way downhill.

Kibo continued to be active, and even today it is technically dormant rather than extinct. Its most violent eruptions were around 350,000 years ago, producing lava flows up to 50 metres thick. This distinctive black lava filled in the Shira basin and flowed over the saddle area towards Mawenzi.

Kibo viewed from the west, with parasitic cones in left foreground

Later volcanic activity on Kibo formed a smaller crater inside the main one, now known as the Reusch Crater. Over 200 years ago, the last puff of volcanic activity formed the Ash Pit inside the Reusch Crater. There are still traces of volcanic activity there, but very few walking tours include a visit to the crater.

Aerial view of the Reusch Crater, with Ash Pit

Kilimanjaro's extraordinary scenery was formed not only by volcanic fire, but also by ice. The ebb and flow of the glaciers has modified the shape of the mountain over hundreds of thousands of years. In extreme glacial times, an unbroken sheet of ice covered the entire mountain down to around 4000 metres, with finger glaciers reaching down to the tree line at 3000 metres.

You might expect that the overhead sun's rays would melt the glaciers, but in fact the flat, white ice reflects most of the radiation. Instead, the dark, dull lava and rocks absorb the heat, and the warm ground undermines the ice cliffs above, creating overhangs and undercuts. As ice blocks fall off and columns splinter, they create shade and help the ground to absorb further heat, melting more ice. You can hear the cracking sounds clearly if you walk past the summit glaciers in suitable conditions.

Kibo's glaciers are in retreat

Sadly, Kibo is gradually losing its ice cap, as is obvious if you compare modern with older photographs, or read accounts of the snow levels in early expeditions. Although global warming may also have a role, geologists have found that Kilimanjaro has a long history of glacial advance and retreat. At times it has been completely ice-free for tens of thousands of years, perhaps because of volcanic activity as well as climatic change. At other times, the ice cover has been so complete that ascent would have been impossible for walkers. So we are fortunate to be able to reach to the crater without technical climbing skills and yet to enjoy the extraordinary beauty of the summit glaciers.

Zebra Rock

On the Marangu route, in the saddle area you may notice a number of 'parasitic cones': these are small conical hills formed by offshoots of the main lava flow (see photograph on page 30). If you do the optional saddle walk, a mile above Horombo you will pass Zebra Rock, an overhung cliff face marked by light stripes. These were caused by rainwater seeping down the rock-face from above, leaving light deposits on the dark lava.

On the Machame route, you will camp on the Shira Plateau, where there are also many parasitic cones. You will see the Shira Ridge rising 400 metres above the main plateau, with dramatic peaks known as the Cathedral and the Needle. Later you see wonderful views of the Lava Tower and Western Breach Wall, and you walk through the Great Barranco.

Aerial view of Mawenzi (foreground) and Kibo (distance) from the southeast

2·4 Habitats and wildlife

Summit

High desert

Heath and moorland

Rain forest

Lower slopes

▲ Uhuru Peak 5895   6000 m

▲ Stella Point 5795

▲ Gillman's Point 5685

5000 m

▲ Kibo Hut 4700   Barafu Camp 4600 ▲

Barranco Camp 3950 ▲   4000 m

▲ Shira Camp 3850

▲ Horombo Huts 3700

Mweka Camp 3100 ▲

3000 m

▲ Machame Camp 3000

▲ Mandara Huts 2700

Marangu Gate ▲ 1900   Machame Gate 1800 ▲   2000 m

Five zones encircle the mountain for around 1000 metres of altitude, each with its own climate, plant life and animals. The higher you go, the colder it gets and the lower the rainfall, limiting the number of species, and demanding remarkable adaptations for survival.

33

The lower slopes

The lower slopes range from 800 to 1800 metres, with rainfall varying from 500-1800 mm per year. The Chagga people cultivate the rich volcanic soil, especially on the wetter south and west sides of the mountain. Farming activity has replaced the bush and lowland forest by crops: you may notice maize, coffee and bananas as you are driven past. There are masses of brilliant wild

Coffee plantation

flowers and interesting grasses and clovers. These slopes support a wide range of bird life, including the common bulbul (brown with a black crest), the tropical boubou (a black and white shrike), lots of scruffy brown speckled mousebirds and sunbirds (long curved bills for nectar-feeding and iridescent feathers).

Rain forest

The rain forest occurs between around 1800 and 2800 metres, with rainfall of about 2000 mm per year on the southern slopes, half that to the west and north. This is the source of 96% of all the water on Kilimanjaro, some of it dropping through the forest floor, down through porous rock, to create springs supporting farming on the lower slopes.

Because of the moisture, there is often a band of clouds, mist and high humidity. There are many fine tall trees, often decked with streamers of bearded lichen. Mosses and ferns grow huge in these conditions, and wild flowers include violets, the occasional orchid and the unique red-and-yellow *Impatiens kilimanjari*, which are related to 'busy Lizzies'.

Giant fern

Common tall trees include *Podocarpus milanjianus* (photograph at right) and the huge camphorwoods. An oddity is the lack of bamboo, which would normally occur in the upper belt of rain forest on East African mountains. In the upper forest, you start to see giant heather trees with yellow-flowered hypericum (St John's Wort) growing among them.

If you look carefully, you will see many insects, including beautiful butterflies. Watch out for the shiny brown safari ants, which may bite if you step into their marching column. Fruit trees attract many birds: if you hear a bird braying like a donkey, it is probably a silver-cheeked hornbill (black and white). If you are lucky enough to see a large bird flashing crimson at its wings, it could be a turaco.

Although there are many wild animals, you may not see them since they are shy and easily hidden in the thick vegetation, mist and cloud. You might see blue monkeys (which are actually dark grey and black) and may hear the shy colobus monkeys (black with a flowing white mane) leaping through the trees.

Left: Colobus monkey   Below: Blue monkey

Heath and moorland

Between around 2800 and 4000 metres are overlapping zones of heath and moorland, with rainfall averaging about 1300 mm per year on the lower slopes, down to 500 mm on the higher slopes. Above 3000 metres, frost is regular at nights and intense sunshine can leads to high daytime temperatures.

Heather and allied shrubs are well adapted to the conditions: the giant heathers (*Erica arborea*) have tiny leaves and thick trunks. These also occur in the upper forest, where they grow even taller, but heights of up to ten feet or so are common in the heath zone. The varied grasses are important in conserving moisture and retaining the soil.

Three kinds of flowers in this zone are especially striking: *Protea kilimandscharica* is common around Maundi Crater and up to Horombo, but, as its name implies, unique to the mountain. Then there are *Helichrysum*: clumps of everlasting daisy-like flowers of various colours (page 43). Finally, you may be surprised to see huge red-hot pokers (*Kniphofia thomsonii*) standing to attention.

Kniphofia thomsonii

Protea kilimandscharica

The moorland is dominated by giant groundsels (senecios) and lobelias, especially near water courses. Of the various groundsels, the most striking is *Senecio kilimanjari*, which grows into trees of up to 18 feet high. The smaller *Lobelia deckenii* (up to 10 feet) has a hollow stem and spiralling 'leaves' that close over at night. Look carefully inside and you will see their blue flowers sheltering within.

Senecio kilimanjari, probably over a century old

Although there have been sightings of mammals such as elands, duikers and klipspringers, and lions are said to visit the Shira Plateau, the only animals you are likely to see are far smaller: the four-striped grass mouse (*Rhabdomys pumilio*) has found its niche around the Horombo huts, and is surprisingly tame. If you sit quietly while eating a picnic lunch, you may be approached by the alpine chat (a dusky brown bird with white sides to its tail).

Lobelia deckenii

From just above the forest upward, you will often see and hear the harsh croak of the white-necked raven, which scavenges successfully from the huts. I was once lucky enough to see a Lammergeier, a large vulture, just above Horombo in the late afternoon.

White-necked raven

High desert

Also known as highland, montane or alpine desert, this zone stretches from 4000 to 5000 metres high and has low precipitation, perhaps 250 mm a year, with summer giving way to winter every 24 hours. The temperature varies from 35-40°C in the noonday sun to well below freezing every night. Soil is scanty, and what little there is can be affected by *solifluction*: when the ground freezes, it expands and flows, disturbing plant roots. Only the hardiest can survive, and only 55 species are found above 4000 metres.

Lichens are some of the more successful: they do not need soil, but grow directly on the lava rocks. Lichens are a close partnership between fungi and algae. The photograph shows two kinds: red lichen growing flat on the rock surface with grey-green lichen dangling from it. The yellow clump of helichrysum clings to the thin soil in the rock's shelter.

Tussock grasses are important survivors in this desert. The mainly dead tussock retains moisture and insulates new shoots against the intense cold and radiation. Small insect are mainly flightless, and hide or live underground. Still, they provide a diet for spiders. Ravens and birds of prey visit during the daytime, but they cannot live at such altitude.

Hardy lichens grow directly on the rock, while the yellow helichrysum depends on its shelter

The summit zone

Above 5000 metres, the air is colder and drier still, and the precipitation falls mainly as snow. There is surprisingly little, probably under 100 mm a year. Rather than falling from above, much of it condenses from clouds sucked up from below when air pressure drops because of the warming effect of the sun. There is no liquid water on the surface: it disappears into porous rock or is locked into ice and snow.

Living things must not only endure the blazing equatorial sun by day, but also arctic conditions by night, when altitude defies latitude. With deep frosts, fierce winds, scarce moisture and less than 50% of the oxygen available at sea level, this environment is deeply hostile to life.

The few lichens that survive are slow-growing: any you see are very old indeed, so treasure them. The highest flowering plant recorded was a small helichrysum at 5670 metres, down in the crater. Animals are very rare, although in 1926 the Lutheran missionary Richard Reusch found and photographed a leopard frozen in the snow. Hemingway immortalised this animal in his 1938 short story *The Snows of Kilimanjaro* and remarked that 'No one has explained what the leopard was seeking at that altitude'.

The Kersten glacier, seen from the crater rim

Tropical rain forest

3·1 Marangu Gate to Mandara Huts

Marangu

Time (average)	3–4 hours
Altitude gained	800 metres (2625 feet)
Terrain	mainly good path, may be muddy and slippery during or after rain
Summary	a gentle introductory half-day walking through the rain forest

After your kit has been loaded, you will be driven to the Marangu park gate where formalities are completed (registering passport numbers and paying park fees). From Moshi the drive takes around 45 minutes, and it gains you 1000 metres of altitude: the gate is at 1900 m. Expect the gate formalities to take an hour or two: if you are lucky it may be less. Trying to identify birds, flowers and trees (see Section 2.4) may help to pass the time. Also, make sure you have enough drinking water for the day and a packed lunch.

When you meet your guides and porters, try to remember their names and faces. They are about to become very important people in your life. By the end of the week you may think of them as supermen. (As of 2000, all guides and all but one of the porters were indeed male.)

Unless the path is wet and slippery, this walk may seem disarmingly simple. Maintain a slow, steady pace anyway, to help your body to acclimatise. If you need to leave the trail for any reason, be sure that somebody knows you have done so. If walking as a group, you may stop together for lunch, or even postpone lunch until you arrive at Mandara Huts.

Normally this walk is only a half-day, and there is plenty of time to visit Maundi Crater, a 15-minute walk from Mandara. The extra effort is rewarded by brilliant wild flowers and perhaps superb views of Kibo and Mawenzi.

Mandara Huts with (inset) white-necked raven perching on hut

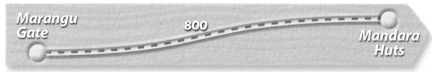

3·2 Mandara Huts to Horombo Huts

Marangu

Time (average)	**5-6 hours**
Altitude gained	**1000 metres (3280 feet)**
Terrain	**good footpath with steady gradients**
Summary	**after clearing the forest, you walk across moorland with some great open views**

After an early breakfast, you will start the day's walk by clearing the forest and perhaps seeing more views of Kibo and Mawenzi. The vegetation is changing markedly now, and at your picnic lunch (usually at the halfway point) you may see the four-striped grass mice, which are keen scavengers.

If it is clear, you will be enjoying mountain views for much of this day's walk, on a good footpath. You may well arrive at Horombo by early to mid-afternoon. If your group is spending an acclimatisation day, you will have two nights here, probably in the same hut (but leave your gear stowed tidily, just in case). Dinner, as at Mandara, is served in the communal dining hut by the support team.

Horombo Huts

Clump of helichrysum ('Everlasting')

On an acclimatisation day, the saddle walk to the north is highly recommended: the views of Kibo and Mawenzi are terrific, the ascent and descent (from 3700 to 4400 m and back) is just what your body needs, and if you set off early you will still have most of a free afternoon. You will also be able to see Middle Red, West Lava and East Lava Hills, as well as Barafu Camp to the west. However, if you are nursing blisters or other problems you can opt out of the walk, or do it in part, to suit your energy level. At the very least, visit Zebra Rock, only a mile or so above Horombo (see page 32).

From the saddle area, note the steep path to Gillman's Point (right)

Mandara Huts

1000

Optional saddle walk

Horombo Huts

3·3 Horombo Huts to Kibo Hut

Time (average)	**5-6 hours**
Altitude gained	**1000 metres (3280 feet)**
Terrain	**good path with steady gradients easing across the saddle (middle of the day)**
Summary	**passing through high semi-desert, you see some good views of Mawenzi and Kibo**

The first part is similar to the optional saddle walk but the path bears off at a more north-westerly angle. Approaching the high desert of the saddle region, notice how the giant groundsel (senecios, see page 37) persist wherever there is a watercourse. Top up your water supplies at the Last Water point (1.5 to 2 hours above Horombo Hut). The path steepens, and the landscape becomes even bleaker, as you approach Kibo Hut.

Giant senecio and heather (foreground), Mawenzi (background)

You may arrive at Kibo Hut by early afternoon for a well-earned rest before the major challenge of the night's summit attempt. Make sure that you purify (or buy) plenty of drinking water for the night's walk, and pack it so your body warmth reaches the water, otherwise it will freeze. The most common mistake people make at altitude is not drinking enough.

This is also the moment to insert fresh batteries and film in your camera and to check or replace your head-torch battery. Pack enough snacks and morale boosters to see you through the night's walking, arrange your warmest clothing ready for action, including gloves, hat and thermals. Then put your head down and sleep for as long as you can. If you cannot sleep, just relax and think peaceful thoughts: your body needs to rest before the very strenuous 24 hours ahead.

High desert, approaching Kibo Hut, with Mawenzi (background)

Horombo Huts   1000   Kibo Hut

3·4 Kibo Hut to Gillman's Point/Uhuru Peak

Time (average)	**6-10 hours**
Altitude gained	**985/1195 metres (3230/3920 feet) to Gillman's Point/ Uhuru**
Terrain	**a steep, rough ascent on loose scree and rocks to the crater rim; gentler gradients thereafter**
Summary	**by far the most strenuous stage of the route, normally attempted between midnight and dawn**

You will be woken around midnight to walk through the night. This is mainly because you need the time to try to reach the summit and still be able to descend in daylight. To reach your next night's accommodation via Uhuru, you need not only to gain 1195 metres of vertical height, on a slope averaging some 27%, but also to lose 2195 metres (Section 3.10). Also, in some ways walking at night is easier as the scree is firmer when cold or frozen and the snow less slushy in the early morning.

On waking, slip into as many layers of clothing as you have: you will be cold, perhaps very cold, to start with, but may need to shed layers after you have been climbing for a while. Alternatively, if a high wind gets up, you may become colder than ever, especially your hands, feet and ears.

Sunrise behind Mawenzi, summit ascent

Eat and drink whatever is on offer. Check that your drinking water and snacks are handy and that the water will not freeze. When your head-torch is switched on, take care not to dazzle others by looking directly at them. If there is moonlight, you may not need the head-torch.

The first half of this ascent is on a steep, winding rocky path. Try to maintain a very slow, but steady pace: this may be less tiring than constantly stopping for short pauses. Shorten your stride if need be, and don't be afraid to hang back if the pace is too fast for you. Many people get into a trance-like rhythm, trudging up rhythmically through the starlight. The halfway point is Hans Meyer Cave (5150 metres) where you may have a slightly longer rest.

After the Cave, the path becomes steeper as it zig-zags up towards Gillman's Point. This is by far the most difficult section of the route: just plod on, don't be discouraged by the way that Gillman's Point mysteriously seems to recede. If you are determined enough, and escape altitude sickness, you will get there in the end. If your feet slip back on the scree, try pushing harder on those poles, and edge in with your boots. As you near or reach the crater rim, the sun will raise your morale and body temperature. Pause to enjoy what is generally considered the finest sunrise on earth.

From Gillman's Point, it takes another 1.5 to 2 hours to Uhuru Peak, although the gradients are much gentler and the terrain easier. There's no point in making a colossal effort to reach the summit unless you are also still capable of getting yourself down: read Section 3.10 carefully ahead of time. You may find that the achievement of reaching the summit gives you a rush of energy that sees you through this, perhaps the longest day of your life.

Summit glacier seen from crater rim

Kibo Hut   985   Gillman's Point   210   Uhuru Peak

3·5 Machame Gate to Machame Camp

Time (average)	**5-7 hours**
Altitude gained	**1200 metres (3940 feet)**
Terrain	**rough path with many tree roots; very slippery and muddy when wet**
Summary	**a straightforward first day, unless wet underfoot, on a path enclosed by rain forest**

As with the Marangu route, the day begins with a drive to the park gate (Machame) and the formalities (registering passport numbers and paying park fees) take an hour or two. From Moshi the drive takes about 35 minutes, and it takes you to 1800 metres. Trying to identify birds, flowers and trees (see Section 2.4) may help you to pass the time. Also, make sure you have enough drinking water for the day and a packed lunch.

When you meet your guides and porters, try to remember their names and faces. They are about to become very important people in your life. By the end of the week you may think of them as supermen. Because the terrain is rough and sometimes steep, on this route porters occasionally fall. Even with your lighter load and poles for support, you may on occasion struggle for balance, especially if it is wet and muddy underfoot. Spare a thought for the people who are carrying your luggage, tents and cooking equipment.

The walk through the rain forest is full of interest, although it feels curiously enclosed for a mountainside. Mist and cloud are common in the late morning to mid-afternoon, and on arrival at Machame Camp you may see disappointingly little. Early mornings are better for views at this height. Get in the habit of looking around the campsite and locating your torch well before darkness falls.

Machame Camp

Machame Gate   1200   Machame Camp

3.6 Machame Camp to Shira Camp

Machame

Time (average)	**5-7 hours**
Altitude gained	850 metres (2790 feet)
Terrain	path mostly good with only one real scramble – the rocky ridge leading to Shira plateau
Summary	steady climb leads to splendid campsite on Shira plateau

After an early breakfast, you set off toward Shira plateau. Leaving the forest, the path heads up into the moorland along a ridge of volcanic rock. About two hours after Machame, there is a short scramble up a rock 'wall', but this is not very challenging (American Class 3, British grade 1) nor high (about 8 metres). The path climbs steadily along the ridge towards a picnic lunch stop, usually at around 3600 metres.

Once you have completed the rocky ridge, you head north, apparently away from Kibo. After crossing some streams, you emerge on to Shira plateau, where the gradients ease and you pass Shira Cave. Shira is the oldest of the three volcanoes that make up the Kilimanjaro massif, and its plateau has many interesting features and minerals. You may notice shiny jet black pebbles lying on the ground: they are made of obsidian.

Continuing north, you soon reach the first of the three campsites. From here you may have splendid views of the Shira Ridge to the west, with its three pinnacles of Shira Needle, Shira Cathedral and East Shira Hill. Looking east, you may see Kibo's Western Breach and its glaciers. Far away, to the south west, you might even see Mount Meru (page 6).

Shira Camp

Machame Camp — 850 — Shira Camp

3·7 Shira Camp to Barranco Camp

Time (average)	**5–6 hours**
Altitude gained	**rising 680 metres (2230 feet) above Shira before steep descent to camp (100 m/330 ft net gain)**
Terrain	**fairly rough path, some scree, some steep sections**
Summary	**through rocky semi-desert with dramatic views of the Lava Tower and Breach Wall**

From above Shira Camp, looking east

From Shira, your route turns sharply east, and at last you are walking directly toward Kibo and its Western Breach. The line of nearby hills to the left of Kibo is the Oehler Ridge. You climb steadily to a high point of 4530 metres (14,860 feet), close to the distinctive Lava Tower. There are impressive cliffs and rock formations all the way, with some interesting colours if the light is good.

Breaking up Shira Camp

The last few hours of the day are spent descending steeply into the Great Barranco (valley), ending at an altitude of 3950 metres, only 100 metres higher than your starting-point. Nevertheless, you will have climbed and descended 680 metres (2230 feet) and may be ready for a hard-earned night's sleep. First, take time to enjoy the spectacular situation of Barranco Camp, which lies below the Western Breach. The front cover photograph shows its tents in the foreground; look closely, and you will see that the white of the clouds differs from that of the snows.

Lava Tower

Shira
Camp

680

Barranco Camp

3·8 Barranco Camp to Barafu Camp

Time (average)	**7–8 hours**
Altitude gained	**rises 380 metres (1250 feet) over the Barranco Wall, then falls and rises to Barafu (650 m/2130 ft net gain)**
Terrain	**after a steep, exposed climb up the Barranco Wall (some scrambling), gradients ease**
Summary	**a taxing day, to be followed by an even tougher night, but with good views**

From the campsite, you head north for a short distance and cross a river before meeting the day's main challenge: the imposing-looking Barranco Wall. Although the Wall is close to vertical in places, your route takes a diagonal line and is not as hard as it appears at first. The scrambling itself is no more difficult than on Day One, but it is more exposed and lasts much longer – a stiff climb of over 300 metres. You will feel a great sense of achievement looking down from the top.

If you aren't used to scrambling, follow behind someone who is, putting your hands where he or she does: your feet will follow. If you are worried by the exposure, don't look down. Think of the Wall as a long, uneven staircase with the odd section of rope ladder. Take comfort from the fact that, unlike the porters, you have your hands free and you're carrying a lot less weight.

After the Wall, the path crosses a plateau area divided by several valleys with superb views up towards the southern icefields (Heim, Kersten and Decken glaciers, in the order that you see them). You descend fairly steeply into the Karanga Valley (4000 m), where most groups stop for lunch and which is the last water point. Water must be carried from here to Barafu campsite and onward. You may be lucky enough to have a cooked lunch al fresco, providing fuel for your night-time attempt on the summit.

Hot lunch, Karanga Valley

About 3 km after the Karanga Valley, the circuit path meets the Mweka trail, which is the normal Machame descent route. You turn left at this junction, heading up toward Barafu Camp. Alternatively, your group may take a more diagonal route from Karanga Valley, in effect cutting the corner to reach Barafu. Once you are settled in, watch out for lovely evening light on Mawenzi: the back cover photograph was taken here near sunset.

As the campsite is exposed and rocky, it is especially important to familiarise yourself with the terrain before dark falls. There have been a number of accidents at Barafu over the years, mainly at night. Read also page 45 for reminders on checking your gear before nightfall.

Rocky descent towards Karanga Valley

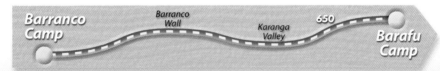

Barranco
Camp

Barranco
Wall

Karanga
Valley

650

Barafu
Camp

3.9 Barafu Camp to Stella Point/Uhuru Peak

Machame

Time (average)	**6–10 hours**
Altitude gained	**1195/1295 metres (3920/4250 feet)** to Stella Point/Uhuru
Terrain	**a steep, rough ascent on loose scree and rocks to the crater rim; more gradual thereafter**
Summary	**the most strenuous stage of a strenuous route, normally attempted between midnight and dawn**

As on the Marangu route, you will be woken around midnight to walk through the night, and you need the early start to try to reach the summit and still have time to descend in daylight. To reach your next night's accommodation via Uhuru, you need not only to gain 1295 metres of vertical height, but also to lose 2795 metres (see Section 3.10). Read the second and third paragraphs of Section 3.4 for advice on preparation.

The steep climb to Stella Point takes you past the Rebmann glacier.

Most people find the climb to Stella Point the most daunting section of the Machame route, mainly because of the dark and the altitude. However, it presents no technical difficulties. It is a long steep slog, very steep in places, but if you are determined and escape altitude sickness, you will get there in the end. If your feet slip back on the scree, try pushing harder on those poles and edge in with your boots; watch the guides. As you near or reach Stella Point, the sunrise will raise your morale and body temperature (see photograph on page 46).

From Stella Point it takes another three-quarters to one hour to Uhuru Peak, although the gradients are much gentler and the terrain easier. There's no point in making a superhuman effort to reach the summit unless you are also still capable of getting yourself down: read Section 3.10 carefully ahead of time. However, you may find that the achievement of reaching the summit gives you a rush of energy that sees you through this, perhaps the longest day of your life.

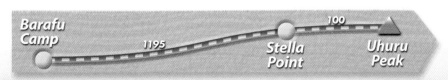

3·10 The summit day descent

Time (average)	**4-8 hours (including rest/lunch stop)**
Altitude lost	**from Uhuru, 2195 metres (7200 feet) to Horombo Huts or 2795 metres (9170 feet) to Mweka Camp**
Terrain	**gradual descent around crater rim, then steep, loose scree followed by rough path**
Summary	**many people find the descent hard on the knees and feet: don't underestimate this stage**

Coming down sounds simple, and most people underestimate it. Some books don't mention this stage at all. On any mountain, your chances of falling are greater on the way down, and on this steep scree they are higher than usual. Older walkers will know that descent can be harder than ascent, with potential damage to knees and toes.

The descent from Uhuru Peak is the second part of your summit day that began at midnight with the eerie climb towards the crater rim in the dark. It differs according to route, but the figures are impressive anyway. On Marangu, you need to lose 2195 metres of altitude to reach Horombo Huts, whereas on Machame you descend 2795 metres to reach Mweka Camp. Even from the crater rim, you have to lose 1985 or 2695 metres respectively. These are serious descents, much further than you would attempt on a day hike at home. Yet your body has to perform this task immediately after a night of unprecedented exertion at altitude, without sleep or rest.

Walkers descending towards Kibo Hut (centre)

Then there's the terrain: although the crater rim walk is fairly straightforward, the steep scree is another matter. You may be especially glad of two poles at this point. The guides have a nifty technique of half-running and half-sliding down the scree: some people copy this easily, others fall a lot. If you fall, try to relax on the way down and watch out for rocks. Don't let yourself be pressurised into descending faster than you want to. The dust may cause serious irritation to your eyes, nose and throat. Either protect your face or hang back (or both): the problem is worst when you follow another walker closely.

However you come down, your knees and toes may find it hard going. Before you start, make sure your boots are tightly laced over the instep: the goal is to prevent your toes from hitting against the end of the boot. This can cause lasting numbness, especially in the big toe, and may lead to later loss of a toenail or two. If your boots were not long enough in the first place, you will find this out to your cost.

Once you have reached your overnight stop safely, you will find beer on sale at Horombo Huts or Mweka Camp. By all means enjoy one or two, but be aware that you are still at high altitude (3700 or 3100 metres) and alcohol will have around double its sea-level effect. It is also a diuretic, and may reduce your chances of an unbroken night's sleep after your summit day.

Descent from Uhuru: yellow line is Marangu, purple line Machame, with altitude drops shown in metres

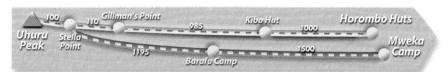

After your well-earned overnight rest at Horombo Huts or Mweka Camp, on your final day (or half-day) you descend further to exit by a Park Gate. On the Marangu route, you repeat your first two days' climb in reverse (1800 metres from Horombo Huts to Marangu Gate), with a lunch stop probably at Mandara Huts.

On the Machame route, the descent is shorter (1600 metres from Mweka Camp to Mweka Gate) mainly through the rain forest. You may be carrying a picnic lunch to eat en route or at Mweka Gate. (At times when the Mweka section of the trail is closed for repairs, you may be diverted to use a different descent route, for example via the Rau Camp which is east of Mweka Camp but at the same altitude.)

Your last day on the mountain is precious, and with the pressure off, it seems a shame to hurry it. However, remember that you will be saying goodbye to the guides and porters at the Park Gate. They will be given their hard-earned tips before returning to their families, and you will not want to delay them unduly. If you are lucky, they may even sing for you – providing a moving memory of an unforgettable week.

Sunset over Kibo

Reference

Get by in Swahili

hello	jambo
goodbye	kwaheri
thank you (very much)	asante (sana)
welcome	karibu
no problem	hakuna matata
sorry	pole
slowly	pole pole
quickly	haraka
let's go (now)	twende (sasa)
yes	ndiyo
no	hapana
danger	hatari
help	usaidizi
toilet	choo
water (drinking)	maji (ya kunywa)
journey	safari
I am tired	nimechoka
my head aches	kichwa kinauma
I feel (much) better	afadhali (sana)
fine, good (very good)	mzuri (sana)
bad	mbaya
hungry	njaa
thirsty	kiu
expensive	ghali
cheap	rahisi
ice, hail	barafu
storm	kipunga
how are things?	habari?
how much/many?	ngapi?
where?	wapi?
when?	lini?
why?	kwa-nini?

Further reading

Bezruchka, Stephen *Altitude Illness: Prevention and Treatment* Cordee 1994 ISBN 1-871890-57-8

Pocket-sized 93-page coverage of the causes, symptoms and signs, with decision trees, tables and interesting case studies; good index but no glossary

Houston, Charles *Going Higher: Oxygen, Man and Mountains* Swan Hill Press, 1998 ISBN 1-84037-097-1

Substantial (272-page) treatment of atmospheric oxygen, mountain sickness and its prevention and treatment; case studies, line drawings and glossary are helpfu, but not easy reading for most; long and authoritative bibliography.

For technical climbing on Kili, a good source (with excellent bibliography) is: Burns, Cameron *Kilimanjaro & Mount Kenya: A Climbing and Trekking Guide* Cordee 1998 ISBN 1-87189-98-5

Kilimanjaro websites

Please visit our website **www.rucsacs.com** and its Links page for direct access to various worthwhile sites: some are first-hand diary-style accounts, others feature specific aspects such as geology or star-gazing. Also try searching online using your favourite search engine: "Marangu" and "Machame" are useful search terms. If you can suggest additions or amendments to our listings, please email us on info@rucsacs.com.

Because the nights are truly black and the air is thin, from Kilimanjaro the stars look unexpectedly brilliant. Near the equator the constellations appear at an unfamiliar angle and appear to move differently. A website was created especially for readers of this book: see our Links page.

Contact details

If phoning from outside the UK, dial the access code followed by the number as shown, ignoring any leading zeros. From within the UK, dial the 0 instead of the +44.

EXPLORE worldwide

Explore Worldwide Ltd was established in 1981, and specialises in small group exploratory holidays. It has been running trips to Kilimanjaro (Marangu and Machame) since 1993. Its UK Head Office details are given below, and it also has offices in six other European countries, Australia, Canada, Hong Kong, USA, New Zealand, and South Africa: check the Explore website for details.

Explore Worldwide Ltd
1 Frederick Street
Aldershot, Hants
GU11 1LQ
UK
Tel: +44/(0) 1252 760 100
website: **www.exploreworldwide.com**
email: info@exploreworldwide.com

Ground agents

Shah Tours is a specialist local operator of Kilimanjaro treks, covering all routes since 1985.

Shah Tours & Travels Ltd
PO Box 1821
Moshi
Tanzania
Tel: + 255 27 275 2998
Fax: + 255 27 275 1449
website: **www.kilimanjaro-shah.com**
email: kilimanjaro@eoltz.com

Kearsley Travel & Tours is a long-established ground operator of Tanzanian safaris.

Kearsley Travel & Tours
PO Box 801
Dar es Salaam
Tanzania
Tel: + 255 22 211 5026
Fax: + 255 22 211 5585
website: **www.kearsley.net**
email: kearsley@raha.com

Friends of Conservation

FoC is a charity that aims to promote a balance between tourists enjoying their trips abroad, conservation of the environments which they visit and the needs of local peoples and wildlife. It publishes the Traveller's Code (see extract, page 25). It is supported by responsible travel operators and individual membership.

Friends of Conservation
Tel +44/(0) 207 731 7803
website: **www.foc-uk.com**
email: info@foc-uk.com

Visas

Most visitors need a visa for admission to Tanzania. Britons should apply to the Tanzanian High Commission, 43 Hertford St, London, W1Y 8DB. American citizens should apply to the Tanzanian Embassy in Washington and others should seek advice from their travel agent or tour operator. The email for British visa enquiries is visa@tanzania-online.gov.uk.

Full moon

Dates of each full moon in the current year are given in many pocket diaries. When full, the moon looks the same from anywhere on earth, although in its other phases the crescent seems to shift around at different latitudes. For future dates, consult an almanack or the website (see Links page).

Acknowledgements

The publisher wishes to thank several people for commenting on parts of the manuscript in draft, and for various other kinds of support; many improvements were made as a result of their comments, but any flaws that may remain are our responsibility. Thanks are due to: Nick Anstead, Travers Cox, Andy Cronin, Dr Carol Darwin, M.B., B.Chir., Dr Maggie Eisner, Katrina Marsden, Sir Robert Megarry, Caroline Phillips, Brian Spence, Chris Thurman and Len Adam. Above all, heartfelt thanks to all the guides and porters without whom neither of the author's ascents would have been possible, let alone enjoyable.

Photo credits

Nick Anstead (p 32 lower), Michèle Cook (p 30, p 32 upper, p 37 upper, p 42 and p 59), Travers Cox (p 31 upper), Rob McSporran (p 6), anon (p 34 upper and 35 middle); all of the foregoing © Explore Worldwide and reproduced from its slide library by kind permission; Craig Smith (p 46); Peter Blackwell/BBC Natural History Unit (p 60); Jacquetta Megarry front cover, p 1, p 5, p 7, p 8, p 18, p 21, p 22, p 25, p 28, p 31 (lower), p 33 (all), p 34 (lower), p 35 (upper and lower), p 36 (both), p 37 (lower two), p 38, p 39, p40, p 41 (both), p 43 (both), p 44, p 45, p 47, p 48, p 49, p 50, p 51, p 52, p 53 (both), p 54, p 55 (both), p 56, p57, p58, back cover (both).

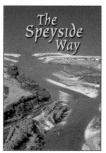

ISBN 1-898481-08-3

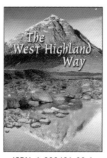

ISBN 1-898481-09-1

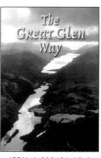

ISBN 1-898481-15-6

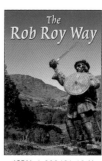

ISBN 1-898481-13-X

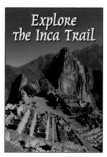

ISBN 1-898481-12-1

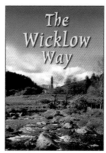

ISBN 1-898481-14-8

Rucksack Readers

Our books on long-distance walks in Scotland and Ireland are printed on waterproof paper. Other books include *Explore the Inca Trail* (three Inca Trails to Machu Picchu, Peru). For more details, or to order online, please visit **www.rucsacs.com**. To order by telephone, dial 01786 824 696 (+44 1786 824 696 from outside the UK).

We welcome feedback on this book and on our list: please email us at **info@rucsacs.com**.

Index

ALBAN BERG
LETTERS TO HIS WIFE

Alban and Helene Berg

ALBAN BERG
letters to his wife

edited, translated and annotated

by

BERNARD GRUN

ST. MARTIN'S PRESS
NEW YORK

AFFILIATED PUBLISHERS:
Macmillan & Company, Limited, London
also at Bombay, Calcutta, Madras and Melbourne
The Macmillan Company of Canada, Limited, Toronto.

CONTENTS

7

ILLUSTRATIONS

9

MAPS

For twenty-eight years I lived in the Paradise of his love. His death was a catastrophe I only had the strength to survive because our souls were long ago joined together in a union beyond space and time, a union through all eternity.

Helene Berg

PART ONE

1907 - 1911

CHRONOLOGY

1846   Conrad Berg, Alban Berg's father, born at Nuremberg (d. 1900).
1849   Franz Nahowski, Helene's father, born (d. 1925).
        Strindberg born (d. 1912).
1851   Johanna Berg (*née* Braun), Alban Berg's mother, born (d. 1926).
1859   Anna Nahowski (*née* Nowak), Helene's mother, born (d. 1931).
1860   Gustav Mahler born (d. 1911).
        Hugo Wolf born (d. 1903).
        Schopenhauer dies (aged 72).
1862   Gerhart Hauptmann born (d. 1946).
        Peter Altenberg born (d. 1919).
1864   Richard Strauss born (d. 1949).
        Frank Wedekind born (d. 1918).
1867   Conrad Berg moves to Vienna.
1870   Adolf Loos born (d. 1933).
1872   Hermann, Berg's eldest brother, born
1874   Arnold Schoenberg born (d. 1951).
        Karl Kraus born (d. 1936).
1875   Rilke born (d. 1926).
1877   Carola (Heyduck), Helene's half-sister, born (d. 1945).
1879   The fragments *Wozzeck* by Georg Büchner (1813–37) published.
1882   Karl (Charly), Berg's brother, born (d. 1952).
        Anna, Helene's sister, born.
1883   Wagner dies (aged 70).
        Anton Webern born (d. 1945).
1885   Alban Berg born (9th February at Vienna 1, Tuchlauben 8 (d. 24th December 1935).
        Helene Berg (*née* Nahowski) born.
        Erwin Stein born (d. 1958).
1886   Oscar Kokoschka born.
1887   Smaragda, Berg's sister, born.

15

1888	Frieda Leider, Wagnerian soprano, friend of Berg family, born.
1889	Franz Joseph Nahowski, Helene's brother, born (d. 1942).
1899	Berg family move to Breite Gasse 8.
	Karl Kraus's *Die Fackel* published for the first time.
1900	Conrad Berg dies (aged 54).
	Nietzsche dies (aged 56).
1901	Berg's first attempts at composition.
	Verdi dies (aged 88).
1902	Hugo Wolf dies (aged 43). Berg attends his funeral.
1903	July: Berg fails in final school examination.
	Autumn: Attempts suicide.
1904	July: Passes examination.
	October: Becomes civil servant—and pupil of Schoenberg.
1905	First performance in Vienna of Wedekind's *Pandora's Box*.
	Berg's first *Lied*, 'In the Room' (No. 5 of the *Early Songs*).
	End of year: Berg family move to Hietzinger Hauptstrasse 6.
1906	Ibsen dies (aged 78).
	Hauptmann's *And Pippa Dances*.
	Berg present at Austrian première of Strauss's *Salome* in Graz.
	October: Berg leaves civil service.
	End of year: First meetings with Helene at Opera.
1907	Spring: Beginning of correspondence.
	Autumn: Berg family move to Vordere Zollamtsstrasse, No. 11.
	7th November: Concert of compositions by Schoenberg's pupils. Berg's *Double Fugue for String Quartet with piano*, and three *Lieder* performed for the first time.
	9th December: Mahler leaves for America, having resigned his post as director of the Vienna Opera.
1908	23rd July: Berg has first attack of bronchial asthma.
	8th November: Second concert of compositions by Schoenberg's pupils. Berg's *Twelve Variations for Piano on an Original Theme*, and Webern's *Passacaglia*, op. 1 performed for the first time.
1909	22nd July: Liliencron dies (aged 65).
	25th July: Blériot flies the Channel.
	August: Berg in Bayreuth.
	September: Berg in Venice.

1910   His *String Quartet No. 1*, op. 3, finished.
      His op. 1 (*Piano Sonata*) and op. 2 (*Four Lieder*) published.
      July: His letter to Helene's father.
      20th August: Helene's parents consent to his marrying her.
      September: Her sister Anna marries Arthur Lebert.
1911   3rd May: Alban Berg marries Helene Nahowski.

(1)

> With your dear hands
> O close my eyes.
> Beneath its touch
> All suffering dies.
> Wave after wave
> Now sinks the smart.
> No ripple more,
> You fill my heart[1]

One good thing about the image in this song, it gives me an
excuse to send you the letter you scorned last night. Again and
again I kiss that hand of yours, my most glorious Symphony in
D Minor!

                                                       Alban

(2)   Undated
                                                       (1907)

Oh dear, I know I'm horrible. I remembered the discussion you
were all having last Thursday, when everybody talked about
profundity and superficiality and 'not being too serious with
people'. Then my heart began thumping away and I couldn't help
thinking: isn't it enough for you, Helene, if one man throws himself
at your feet? A man with a soul—real deep feelings, I mean—and a
body and mind, too, as good as anyone else's. To make your
happiness complete, do you really need a man friend to flatter you
and several boring girl friends? Can't I become everything to you?
Questions like this keep going round and round in my brain and
tormenting me. They cast a shadow over my happiness, and give me
pangs of conscience. I wonder whether perhaps I'm wronging you,
whether you're quite justified in feeling deeply hurt. Oh, how I long

[1] Alban Berg twice set the verses by the German poet Theodor Storm
(1817–88) to music: the first time in 1900, the second in 1925.

to be alone with you for once, for hours and hours, with nobody else around. So that our hearts could open and melt into each other, so that peace and serenity could pervade my being at last, so that I need not for ever feel only the 'suffering of love'.[1]

Good-bye, my incomparable one.

(3)   Undated
                                                             (1907)

Well, I really *am* in love. I can't go to sleep any more unless I first have a little chat with you, even if only by letter. And I need it all the more today when from eight o'clock in the morning till midnight there has been nothing to gladden my heart.

What miserable luck! There I was, sitting at the piano all day, with an idea that you might come round. Then I felt a bit ill and was going upstairs to get a glass of brandy—when the bell rang. Of course André[2] *would* be out just then, so our precious moment had to be made all formal. If I'd only stayed where I was another minute, I should have seen you coming by and rushed out to meet you. That's why it was such miserable luck.

Still, I did get a little card from you, thanking me in a very nice way for the Mahler[3] autograph. And it's very kind of you to worry about my health. I'd be almost ashamed of your being so kind to me —if I didn't like it so much! Also, it makes me more serene in my love (at least for a month, till Raoul[4] comes back).

Don't think, my dearest, that I am already losing faith in you again. Oh no, my faith is built on you, and it's a fine solid structure. Still, I can't help being terribly worried, because even the most impregnable fortress can be in danger from an earthquake, and however solidly built, our love has its foundations in volcanic soil. Oh, may the earth not gape open! Whole cities have been engulfed before now; how much easier for men and women to go under!

So I remain, all day and all night, praying to a goddess: 'Protect our country! Oh Goddess, oh Helene, protect the country of our love!'

[1] 'Minneleide' (the one who suffers from love) is the name of a fairy from the opera *Die Rose vom Liebesgarten* (*The Rose from the Love-Garden*, 1901) by Hans Pfitzner (1869–1949).
[2] The Berg family's manservant.
[3] Gustav Mahler (1860–1911), idol of both Helene and Alban Berg, had been Artistic Director of the Viennese Court Opera since 1897.
[4] One of Helene's admirers.

Reading through the letter I wrote last night, it struck me you wouldn't understand why I was writing all that. That's why I'm writing again now, to tell you it was meant to be a defensive action, so to speak, against any *future* emotional intrigues. I wanted to make it clear how devoted to you I am, how I hope—and believe—that you feel devoted to me as well. For our love is sacred, rooted in our innermost hearts and souls.

I also wanted to tell you that I am no longer strong enough to give you up. You have become indispensable to me, and I cannot yield you to another unless he offers you something like the same love as mine, not just a bundle of feelings. Surely Raoul's feelings for you and yours for him are not the genuine article of love, as I once feared. If they were, but only then, I should be strong enough to retire, no, to vanish, perhaps from life itself.

But I don't want to think of that yet. Perhaps my physical constitution is secretly taking care of this, and I shall be spared having to think of it. No, I will think only of everything splendid and beautiful you have already given me, and perhaps will go on giving me: only of our feelings for each other, untouched by the outside world, contented and happy. I want to know that you too are in the same state, contented and happy. Oh, if you could only reach that state, the most glorious day of my love would have dawned. I wait for it, I long for it—and now good-bye, beloved.

Your own
Alban

(5)   Undated
                                                         (1907)
This afternoon I went through such a gamut of emotions that my heart is still quivering from them. Our first time alone together, and you were so tremendously harsh to me—until a gentler mood gradually came over you, and I then realized how great you were. For only someone like you, after being so harsh, could redeem everything with so boundless a kindness.

I was almost overwhelmed by your greatness—when you sang. The beauty of your voice and the intensity of feeling you put into your singing left me so moved and delighted, I could not speak. I felt almost angry when you stopped, and all this beauty had suddenly come to an end. I felt half angry. It had made such an impression on me, both in artistic and in human terms. To sing like you and even to listen like me—agreed, Helene?—is a profession of true artistic appreciation.

That's why I am writing to you now with my thanks—thanks beyond number. Not only for the two *Lieder*, but also for the feeling you have awakened in me, that I love a woman with great art in her, the art which means everything to me and builds me the finest bridge to exalted humanity: music.

It's now 2.45 a.m.—so sleep well, dearest musician!

(6)   Berghof[1]
                                                                              (Undated, early
                                                                              summer 1907)
And so the days roll on, full of 'pleasures' which deep down I can't enjoy, full of irritation at not finding the time I need for my work, full of sadness to be without you in all this, my sweetheart. How often when I am sailing on the lake with all the others, everybody laughing and chatting, my heart alone is constricted, thinking of you. Or I am on a night drive with Smaragda[2] and her girl friend. The stars flicker through the shifting clouds, all the night's soft sounds are heard, and only an occasional whispered word muffles the clip-clop of the horses. But I keep thinking, Why just me? When everything around is full of love's happiness, and able to bask in the bliss of loving and being loved.

But perhaps I am ungrateful, immodest. For a letter from you, dearest, is surely worth more than any signs of love or favour in the world outside . . .

Good-bye, dear heart

                                                                              All yours,
                                                                              Alban

(7)   Berghof
                                                                              (Undated, June 1907)
Adored Helene,

'High time to tell you again how very much I love you.' That's

---

[1] Berghof, the family estate on the Ossiacher Lake in Carinthia, near Villach, 250 miles south-east of Vienna.
[2] Smaragda Berg (1887–1954), Alban Berg's sister.

the beginning of one of Richard Wagner's most beautiful letters (to Frau Ritter[1]); so let me begin the same way.

It is a kind of *Leitmotif* which has been sounding all through the turmoil of these past days: sometimes joyful and clear, as when a charming card arrives from Trahütten;[2] at other times—alas, too often—heavy and dark, as when no sweet strains from there reach my ear for a long time. I try not to expect too much, make firm resolutions to accept what cannot be helped, not to think of suicide straight away! Now and then, with so much melancholy in the atmosphere, when sky and lake and forest and meadow seem full of tears and heart-ache, a deep sadness comes over me. But the wild fantasies which burst into my mind, though often they torment me with agonizing fears and suspicions, can also build me splendid castles in the air.

I picture the storm sweeping across trees and plains, the sky loud with thunder. As I revel in the cool water lapping around my body and arms, waves breaking over my face and hair, I imagine you coming to share with me these elemental delights of nature. How beautiful you are as the wind seizes your silky hair, and twines round your lovely face, that face with eyes shining out so deep and mysterious. Together we drive through fragrant lime-tree woods, absorbed in silent joy.

Then we are sitting side by side at the Opera, and never before have we listened to the tragic saga of Tristan and Isolde with souls so open, minds so free. Then home! Oh, lovely aircastles!

You smile and think: well, *he's* all right then. But remember that such minutes of bliss are followed by hours of grim 'coming back to earth', when all the rapture dies. I picture you serene at Trahütten, writing to my sister Smaragda, then saying to yourself with a smile: let's send a card to the 'poor kid', to set his mind at rest.

But then I think of your last letter with its saddest of confessions: 'I don't believe in love any more.' A confession so sombre and desperate that I cannot fathom it. I rack my brains wondering how such a thing could have happened. Disappointments? No, they only strengthen one's belief in Love. Should I lose my faith and delight in Music because there is such a mass of musical trash around, or give up my faith in Nature because it takes in so much

[1] Julie Ritter (1784–1869), Wagner's devoted friend and patron from Dresden.
[2] Trahütten, summer residence of Helene's family (the Nahowskis), near the small town of Deutsch-Landsberg in south-western Styria.

23

ugliness? Ask yourself, dearest, how firm your faith is in these two; and can you still say you have no love in your heart?

Again no mail. Since your precious letter ten days ago, all I have had is one nice card which arrived the day before yesterday. I pretend that if I post these lines straight away, I might get a reply from you the sooner; forgetting that there is nothing in them which deserves an answer. But my longing is too much for me, and I still have to post them at once.

Oh, I have nothing new to tell you, except that I love you, love you more than words can say. And if I go on saying that, you'll soon be bored to tears. A reason to end my letter. Good-bye, dearest Helene, and if only for a few seconds let me hold your beloved hands to kiss them.

(8)   Berghof, 2nd June 1907
My adored and dearest Helene,
'It would be a miracle indeed if I could ever believe confidently in love again.' So writes a gay and glorious young being born for love! But we all have our first big disappointments, Helene, and these have left scars on all our souls. But our souls must not sink into such apathy that we are ready to die of these wounds.

We must believe all our lives in the miracle of love, just as we believe in the miracle of death, since 'the secret of love is bigger than the secret of death'.[1] Oh no, my darling, love doesn't happen only in fairy-tales, poetry and music; it is love rooted in *life* which has given poets their inspiration. Right into his very old age Goethe loved with the ardour of youth, and so he could write that wonderful set of 'love works' from *The Sorrows of Young Werther*, through *Tasso*, to the *Natural Affinities*.[2] And even in the last of these he could still describe the power of love as a towering and unbounded force of nature. For the secret and miracle of love had been revealed to him.

To write works like *Tristan*, the *Mastersingers* and *Parsifal* does not demand only a fertile imagination plus subtle harmonies and melodies. Someone who could write *Tristan* must surely have believed in love with the utmost conviction. Would all those who are transported into ecstasy by it, explain their state of mind as the

[1] *Salomé* by Oscar Wilde, 1893.
[2] Johann Wolfgang von Goethe (1749–1832) wrote *Die Leiden des jungen Werther* in 1774, *Torquato Tasso* in 1790, *Die Wahlverwandschaften* in 1809.

effect on their nervous system of the altered diminished seventh? No, my beautiful one, you must surely believe that this music, written in love, will touch strings in you to produce a purer, truer tone—unaffected by the intellect and (in your phrase) 'keeping the eyes wide open'. For, as Beethoven tells us, 'Music is truly a higher form of revelation than all philosophy.'

And then I don't really need to remind you of all the names I could bring up from an age (in your words) 'when we no longer believe in miracles and fairy-tales, an age void of all Wertheresque romanticism.' Names like Ibsen,[1] Wedekind[2] and Peter Altenberg,[3] Strauss[4] and Pfitzner. These great men could not have written such works, produced such sublime ideas, by mere command of dramatic technique or the rules of composition. They 'kept their eyes wide open', yes—but besides, they preserved an ever-green idealism, the belief in love. Oh, you know all this as well as I do, only it has become so much part of your being that you somehow failed to take it into account. So forgive, dearest, a 'kid' like me writing to an experienced 'grown-up', as if I could *teach* you about such things.

We have to stand 'in the midst of life', to get to know it properly. The microscope, not the telescope must become our instrument. Because, if we consider the real springs of action, we shall cease to doubt love's existence and its immense power. However many disappointments we meet in it, we shall still know that absolutely everything is rooted in this love, that love is the condition for everything great and beautiful, that this has been so from time immemorial and will remain so for ever.

Reading through these eight pages of mine, I feel you may laugh out loud in amazement at my quite unwarranted 'address from the pulpit'. Please forgive me, my sweetheart. It's just that my heart is so wide open when I talk to you, that much unsuitable matter pours out, with no thought of how it will be received.

You are right, that's the way with love-letters—if this *is* a love-letter. Couldn't I have written the same to someone else, someone I was indifferent to? Perhaps—except that my heart would not have trembled like this all the time, as if you were standing right by me,

[1] Henrik Ibsen (1828–1906).
[2] Frank Wedekind (1864–1918), on whose plays *Erdgeist* (*Spirit of the Earth*) and *Die Büchse der Pandora* (*Pandora's Box*). Berg based the libretto of his opera *Lulu*.
[3] Peter Altenberg (1862–1919) Viennese poet, a friend of Helene's.
[4] Richard Strauss (1864–1949).

shaking your dear beautiful head. This trembling must surely be love.

Once more a thousand thanks for your letter just arrived, dear and adored Helene. And again the old request, write again as soon as possible, a nice long letter, telling me what you think of all my sermons, and how you are faring all the time, how you are thinking and loving.

Good-bye, my darling

Alban

How happy I was that you ended your letter with just 'Helene'

(9)   Berghof, 17th August 1907

What a day that was yesterday! About noon I was in the throes of composing, with only a few bars left to do, when your letter was brought in to me. 'At last!' I cried, and was just going to open it, when I looked at my song and a sudden burst of self-discipline came over me! Incredible as it may sound, I put your letter away unopened and with racing heart finished the song:[1]

> 'The day was almost frightening in its splendour,
>   The day of the chrysanthemums white.
> And then you came to make my soul surrender.
>   Deep in the night.
>
> I was afraid, and you came softly stealing;
>   You'd just been in my dreams, a vision bright.
> You came; like fairy music faintly pealing,
>   Soft rang the night.'

And so to your splendid letter—your letter at last. How can I possibly thank you for it? Well, my terrific joy could be thanks enough, I hope, for that's all I can offer. Now to answer it.

You talk of 'distrust', but I don't understand that. Distrust of what? Does something look different to you from what it may really be? Are you afraid of suddenly finding that 'drab humdrum follows every happy hour?'

---

[1] *Traumgekrönt* (*Dream-Crowned*) by Rainer Maria Rilke (1875–1926). Berg's setting of it was later published as No. 4 of the *Sieben Frühe Lieder* (see footnote Letter 14).

Hindemith, Křenek, Milhaud, Webern and Schoenberg had also set poems by Rilke to music.

Oh, my adored one, how could people like you and me live in a world where we had no faith in eternal beauty, purity and truth? Would they be ideals if they were so cheap and commonplace? Perhaps ideals are by definition unattainable. Yet who could really *live* without believing in them? Not I, and you least of all. Can you imagine waking up one morning and finding the world without any ideals, so that you had nothing worth striving for, worth aspiring to? But you forget this just because your ideals have once been disappointed—and because, you say, you distrust innovations.

'Oh, life contains its own renewal, let's hold on to that—we leave life soon enough.' That's out of some Ibsen play, Ibsen, your great favourite.

Do you think I'm old-fashioned, making this long defence of 'ideals'? I'm not really. Our present world is not as poor in ideals as it may seem. Admittedly some of the false and obsolete ones have gradually found their way on to the shelf. But our great innovators have instead brought us a mass of glorious new ideals, purer and finer than the old ones now deformed. Nietzsche[1] stares at us from afar with his piercing eyes. Ibsen with wry mouth speaks his harsh truths. And in the shadow of these two, so many names: Strindberg,[2] Oscar Wilde,[3] Gerhart Hauptmann,[4] Wedekind, Karl Hauer, Weininger,[5] Wittels,[6] Karl Kraus,[7] Hermann Bahr.[8] Why should our hearts beat faster just to hear these names mentioned, if we had not in ourselves the same strivings and aspirations, the ideals they clung to, transposed by their pens into real and tangible life?

Oh dear, I'm talking like a schoolmaster again, how horrible! Let's go on to something else.

I don't want to bore you with all my views on friendship, but must tell you that I'm more than your friend, I'm a man who loves you. The difference may not mean much to you, but it means everything to me. Even the best friend does not give his whole heart. So don't measure me, my beloved, by the standards of

[1] Friedrich Nietzsche (1844–1900).
[2] August Strindberg (1849–1912).
[3] Oscar Wilde (1854–1900).
[4] Gerhart Hauptmann (1862–1946), German dramatist.
[5] Otto Weininger (1880–1903), Austrian philosopher, author of *Sex and Character*.
[6] Dr Fritz Wittels, Viennese psychoanalyst and author, one of Freud's early disciples.
[7] Karl Kraus (1874–1936), Austrian poet, essayist and satirist.
[8] Hermann Bahr (1963–1934), Austrian novelist, dramatist and critic.

friendship. A friend, for instance, may be satisfied if he doesn't get an answer to his letter for four or six weeks, or doesn't even get one at all—but you mustn't expect that of me . . .

Don't, my dearest, let me wait for an answer. Really, I am getting more and more modest in my demands every day, every hour. Certainly, that's how I felt after reading that nice, kind, lovely letter of yours. But I'll never become *so* modest. In fact I think, I'd be most offended in my grave if a fortnight after my death your visiting card with messages of sympathy failed to arrive . . .

(10)
Vienna, Hietzinger
Hauptstrasse No. 6[1]
(Autumn 1907)

Your letter of yesterday was balm for me on my sick-bed. I at once began to live again in the happy conceit, darling, that you loved me. How incorrigibly conceited I am!

I felt so full of gratitude for the affection in your letter that I got up in the afternoon and began to change and copy an old song of mine. But the flesh was weak, and I had to stop working. Perhaps it's a good omen that I only reached the first verse, which is a hymn to your beauty. So I'm waiting for you to arrive this afternoon, because I expect to become well very quickly when your dear hand is resting in mine. Meanwhile the medicines will have to do their best. Don't worry, there aren't too many of them, just aspirin, chloroform, veronal and pyramidon—that's all!

Well then, you'll be coming, my only love. Tell dear Anna[2] that my liqueur is waiting for her.

My fondest and deepest love——

All yours

(11)
Thursday night
(Autumn 1907)

This beautiful paper is all I can find in my bedroom, to make the most of the few minutes before midnight, the first free moments I can give completely to you; because things have been somewhat hectic the last twenty-four hours and I feel quite done up.

[1] The Berg family had moved from No. 8, Breitegasse to this address in Hietzing—a 'better district'—in 1905.
[2] Anna Nahowski (b. 1882) Helene's elder sister.

After we left you last night. I had a quick dinner and drove to the Schoenbergs'.[1] Conversation there very serious and lofty at first, but later quite light-hearted. Around midnight some of us walked into town, and went to the *Fledermaus*.[2] Rather boring at first, and afterwards we five (Smaragda, Loos,[3] La Bruckner,[4] Klimt[5] and myself) went to the 'Z-Keller am Hof', where things became fairly confused for the next few hours. In fact, Helene—well, how can I put it? Should I say the left side of my body, where the heart beats only for you, didn't know what the right side was doing? Because that was the side where La B. was sitting, and—oh, forgive me, Helene—that side was unfaithful to you. She has wonderful hands, which I can't help being attracted by, I confess it, and they made me behave in a stupid way, though I'm sure at any other time of day I could have resisted!

Afterwards we went on to the 'Casa piccola',[6] and home at dawn. To Schoenberg in the afternoon, then into town. Home at half past four, drank some tea to revive myself, and in the evening to the concert, where I thought a lot of you and Anna. Among other things they played Charpentier's *Impressions d'Italie*,[7] with its glorious finale commonly called 'Napoli'. When I got back at night, I found the sad news of your not being well, which cast a dark shadow over the joys and fevers of the last hours. So I decided not to go to bed before writing to you. (To bring relief to myself, as it were, and help you pass a few minutes lying in bed.)

One glimpse into the near future—what about Saturday? Will you come? It would be very dull without you.

That's all for now. I'm exhausted, and there's my bed, waiting enticingly to receive me. I want to dream of you, Helene—goodnight!

Alban

---

[1] Arnold Schoenberg (1874–1951) had been Berg's teacher since 1904.

[2] The *Fledermaus* Cabaret, centre of a circle of young Viennese 'Bohemians', had just opened.

[3] Adolf Loos (1870–1933), the great Austrian architect.

[4] A young woman who belonged to this circle.

[5] Gustav Klimt (1867–1918), Austrian painter, founder of the Viennese *Sezession*.

[6] A popular café in Mariahilferstrasse.

[7] Gustave Charpentier (1860–1956), composer of the opera *Louise*, won the Prix de Rome in 1887, and while staying at the Villa Medici composed the orchestral suite *Impressions d'Italie*.

Last day at Hietzinger
Hauptstrasse No. 6[1]
(Autumn 1907)

It's horrible that I couldn't see you today, dearest. But tomorrow, please, do ring the bell when you pass. Perhaps I could fetch you at Madame Brandt's,[2] it would be lovely to talk to you for a little. This is my last day in Hietzing.

Oh yes, thanks to you and Anna for the books. I'm sending them back now, and would like to borrow them again when I've more time. Good-bye, my dear, I wish I could just look into your eyes at this moment, and see that lovely face.

(13) Undated
(Autumn 1907)

'The day was almost frightening in its splendour,
The day of the chrysanthemums white . . .'

Truly, Helene, my dearest and most beloved, I found the splendour of yesterday's joy almost frightening. I have kissed you! I had to join my lips with yours, I was driven, irresistibly, by some inner force I would not escape. So much ecstasy all at once, my eyes were wet with tears, all my body and soul swamped in one great flood of emotion. This is how much I love you.

Dazed with delight, I staggered homewards, feeling only your sweet hand caressing my soul. I was rocked in bliss, bearing home on my lips the most glorious of kisses.

'. . . You came; like fairy music faintly pealing
Soft rang the night.'

[1] The Berg family were moving from the Hietzing district to a new apartment in the Landstrasse district at 11, Vordere Zollamtsstrasse.

[2] Madame Marianne Brandt was Helene's singing teacher. At that time it was Helene's ambition to become an opera singer, and she appeared occasionally at concerts. She gave this up after marrying Berg.

Vienna, 8th November 1907[1]

My dearest and best Helene,

When I came into my bedroom last night, I felt a fragrance which made my heart tremble. At once I found myself thinking of you, and then I saw the three dark red roses amidst the green laurel leaves.

They are from you, that was my first thought—no, my first and only hope, my most solemn wish. Only you could have somehow produced from your heart this symbol—the three roses which, like my three songs, are comparable to gifts of love. Oh, leave me with the lovely dream, if dream it be, that these roses, their colour glowing with love, conceal the sparks of love within them. This thought went round and round in my mind for a long time, and it was very late in the night—or early morning—before I could get to sleep.

My first moment awake, I was already thinking of you again, my one and only love. Then I learnt that my fond hope was no dream, the laurel leaves and roses *were* from you. I can't describe how overjoyed I was at that moment, I could have hugged the pillow and kissed it in my utter bliss. And then, to crown everything, they told me you would be coming today with Smaragda. How am I going to thank you in words, I wondered, when all my thanks are revealed only in the beating of my heart? Could I thank you in front of everybody, or would you be embarrassed, would you even deny having sent the roses?

Alas, I was spared the answer to these questions, for you did not come. And now I am dying of desire for you. I plunge my face into the cool laurel leaves and soothe my sweet sorrow in the fragrance of the roses. But all too soon the blossoms will fade, and I shall have nothing left but the memory of the few moments, I was loved. That makes me unutterably sad.

'What a baby!'

---

[1] Written the day after a concert at the hall of the Viennese Merchant's Guild (Gremium der Wiener Kaufmannschaft), in which works by Schoenberg's pupils were given; including Berg's Double Fugue for String Quartet with piano accompaniment, and three songs: *Die Nachtigall* (*The Nightingale*), *Traumgekrönt* (*Dream-Crowned*) and *Liebesode* (*Love Ode*). All were later published as Nos. 3, 4 and 6 of the *Sieben Frühe Lieder* (*Seven Early Songs*).

(15)   Vienna
(Undated,[1] 1907)

Today, my darling, I have been unfaithful to you for the first time. You know, of course, that my idea of fidelity is different from most people's. For me it means a state of mind which never leaves the lover, follows him like a shadow and grows into part of his personality: the feeling that he is never alone, always dependent on another, that without the beloved he is no longer a whole person capable of sustaining life.

It was in this sense I was unfaithful to you tonight. It happened in the finale of the Mahler symphony, when I gradually felt a sensation of complete solitude, as if in all the world there were nothing left but this music—and me listening to it. But when it came to its uplifting and overwhelming climax, and then was over, I felt a sudden pang, and a voice within me said: what of Helene? It was only then I realized I had been unfaithful, so now I implore your forgiveness. Tell me, darling, that you understand and forgive!

(15a)   To this letter Helene replied:
But there is nothing to forgive, Alban. Far from it. I am glad this sublime music was so magnificent an experience for you. We cannot be grateful enough to God for giving us ears to hear this celestial language—and to understand it.

(16)   Christmas 1907
So that you can come to us, dearest, even if the weather is bad, I am sending you this umbrella. And do use it now, I'm longing for you so much.

All yours
Alban

(17)   May 1908
Only ten more days to the worst separation.[2] Your sister works wonders thinking up ways of seeing her sweetheart,[3] while you

---

[1] Written after a performance of Mahler's Symphony No. 3 in D minor.
[2] Helene was going off with her family to the health resort of Mitterbad in the Tyrol.
[3] Anna's future husband, Arthur Lebert.

won't even take any chances there are to see *me*. I am afraid of Paul's[1] influence over you, he is giving you a different attitude to everything—including me. Have you any idea how I feel when I realize this? You can't have, or you would never have reproached me, smiling so innocently, for my moods and sulks.

Still, if we ever did meet, you'd find me in a state of complete decline and disintegration, much worse than I was a year ago when our love started. This is what's been tormenting me ever since we met at the art exhibition. That's why I sit here in the early hours of the morning, wondering if there's any way out for me, racking my brains what to do about our relationship. I've had so many ideas, but when I think about them they all seem quite mad.

One was to avoid seeing you till after Saturday. Another was to go to the gallery myself when you met Paul there. By the way, I see you're going to the new exhibition three times. First alone, next time just you and Paul, and at last, when it's only a boring duty for you with a flock of aunts and the like, I am graciously permitted to join the party.

Oh dear, I've read through this letter, and see how feeble and futile it is. I was just trying to give you an *im*pression of my *de*pression! I can picture you folding the letter up, shaking your head, and saying: 'But I'm so fond of him, he knows that.'

(18)   Friday morning
                                      (Undated, summer 1908)

Sometimes one really can *enjoy* ill-health! How quickly the patient can recover from all his ailments if there's a little card arriving from his beloved every morning and in the afternoon she's there in person at his beside, and if, even when she's gone, he can feel the sweet press of her lips on his eye. Oh yes, he'll make wonderful progress then. But here in this miserable hole, when he is parted from her, with not a word of love since she left—then the body can never really get better. I am slowly realizing this, and how inevitable it was that my body should break down after those three assaults on my spirit—Paul, Raoul and the parting from you.

Get better? Oh, my Isolde, I could only get *good* through you. Peter Altenberg says somewhere: 'To educate someone means to change his material needs into spiritual ones.' In this sense you have

[1] Berg's schoolfriend Paul Hohenberg, whose poem 'Sommertage' (Summer Days) he set to music.

unwittingly educated me: made me a better person, through the sheer force of your character. But there are still baser elements in me, Helene, not too far from the surface, and all that a year's work of delicious 'education' has built up can be destroyed by a single day of humiliating disappointment.

Oh, save me. Helene. You alone can do it!

Friday evening

Oh dear, I can see tonight's going to be just like last night, which makes it more boring than ever. Smaragda is in a circle of beautiful women enjoying herself with Altenberg and Karl Kraus. And when she gets home at three in the morning with Ida,[1] I expect she'll come into my bedroom and regale me with her conquests and ecstasies. Then I'll lie waiting for the real morning, hoping the postman and the doctor will bring me a cure. But even together they're not enough. If only my Isolde would come!

(19)   Vienna, 1st July[2]

Only one more night for me in Vienna! I'm travelling alone because Smaragda wants to stay here a few days longer—she'll be at Charly's.[3] I've had so much to do in the last two or three days, especially after being ill, that I haven't really much time, but I felt I must write you a few lines about everything.

I spent my holiday in bed, you know. All very dismal, with only one ray of light to brighten things up—your letter.

Yesterday morning I went to see Carola[4] at Hietzing, and that was quite a little holiday or holy-day, the two of us lying in the grass talking about the world and life and man and art, and thinking of *you*.

In the afternoon I went to the art gallery, as witness the picture postcards I wrote you. It was so quiet there to start with, so peaceful —I was entirely with *you*. But then the strumming began on the café terrace, and I had to run away. Then they all marched on, the Altenberg circle, the Klimt group, and the solitary Karl Kraus— we two lonely ones were kindred spirits. In the evening I met Smaragda at Altenberg's table in the Löwenbrau beer-cellar, then

[1] One of Smaragda's girl friends.
[2] This letter was written the day before the Bergs went off to the Berghof for their summer holiday.
[3] Karl (Charly) Berg, Berg's elder brother (1881–1952).
[4] Carola Heyduck (1877–1945), Helene's step-sister.

34

she went home with Ida, while I met Karl Kraus—Dr Fritz Wittels was also there, all very nice. At 3 a.m. we all went home, but I ran into Ida who had taken Smaragda home, and the two of us roistered on for the rest of the night!

I only came home at 8 a.m., and got ready to present myself for my medical examination; that was at ten. In the end I left completely free—exempt! Yes, Helene, you are lucky. Your first sweetheart is a marriage reject, your second an army reject. Nothing but rejects for your love to cure. Except, oh horror, for the one fit man, the strong knight at the court of your love, the wedding-ring-master in your circus: Raoul. But no more of that, you know too well how I feel! You must grasp all the melancholy within me even when I don't express it! Can you, my dearest? Good-bye for now!

Alban

(20)   Berghof, 9th July 1908

Thank God, there are moments like eternity, when the whole world around one is hushed, when our deepest feelings find expression. Such a moment comes when I read your letter and feel that I am with you lying in the grass, at one with Nature, your arms around me, giving me that message of yearning, the same as my own: that we belong together . . .

. . . Tell me, Helene, what are you reading at the moment? Have you finished *Auch Einer*?[1] It's strange how often I think of this book. And I'm glad, so much of this 'old-fashioned stuff' is to my liking, because it's harder for our generation to appreciate and love what's old than it is for the older generation to get on terms with all that's new and modern. Anyhow, I'm very much enjoying Mozart's string quartets just now, and 'old' Rembrandt is quite one of my idols.

(21)   Berghof, 13th July

. . . I was very amused at your description of the people taking the cure at Mitterbad. Oh yes, I know these types, they make their appearance here too every day. But in my present depressed mood I'm more irritated by them than amused, and indeed since I got here I've become more unsociable than ever . . .

In your letter you don't mention at all my coming over to see

[1] *Auch Einer* (*Also One*), a famous German comic novel by F. T. Vischer (1807–87).

you. You merely say your Papa[1] is still with you all, and that you're going to drive up the Mendola[2] with him, I can't make out whether that's for a few hours or if you'll be staying there. Not a word about when we'll 'have the coast clear', how much longer you'll be at Mitterbad, and when your Alban could or should come. If you are staying some time at the Mendola, I could come out there just as well as to Mitterbad. But what about Papa?! . . .

Physically I feel absolutely rotten. Wonder how I shall end up after this year's holiday. Too weak to move about, constriction in my lungs and chest[3] when I'm lying down, colds and catarrh and kidney trouble just like the man in *Auch Einer*. This morning for the first time I tried doing some work.[4] Hope I can put into it all the things I am missing here, testifying to my three great loves, Nature, Music and Helene.

You say you like getting long letters. That's lucky, because I like writing them. But I hope you pick up everything that can be read between the lines, which is more enduring than all the letters or books in the world—the immensity of my love for you.

If you do, I can finish this letter knowing it hasn't been written in vain.

All yours
Alban

(22) Berghof, 18th July 1908
'When someone writes a letter to a very good friend, or even more, to his beloved, he puts on his best attire, as well he may. For in the quiet of his letter, on the tranquil blue paper, he can express his truest feelings. The tongue and the spoken word have become so soiled by their every-day use, they cannot speak out loud the beauty which the pen can quietly write.'

I couldn't help thinking of that passage from Strindberg when I got your letter this morning. . .

My longing for the mountains is roused again by the lovely little flowers you sent. How lucky you are! Only in my dreams can I gaze on the mountain meadows, with their mauve forget-me-nots

[1] Franz Nahowski (1849–1925), Helene's father, an official at the Court of the Emperor Francis Joseph.
[2] La Mendola, mountain pass in the Dolomites, near Bolzano.
[3] Ten days later Berg became seriously ill for the first time, and for the rest of his life suffered from asthma and bronchitis.
[4] Berg was working on the last of his *Seven Early Songs*.

and black bugles and fiery red rhododendrons, and the precipices with their scattered tree-stumps and branches, and the black salamanders in the white boulders, and flocks of grouse under stunted dwarf-pines. All that is your realm, in which you are queen. And we who live in the plains can only look fondly up at those heights in envy or admiration.

Yet I know the paths which lead up there, the less frequented paths too. And somewhere far above, amidst the clouds and winds, I shall be waiting for you, my hand outstretched in greeting—cold as ice yet warm with life in its love.

And woe betide anyone else who crosses my path whistling Wagner! I'll soon strike his top note off his shoulders!

But now out of my best attire (which looks a bit like tourist dress) and into every-day clothes, for the postman waits! More from Strindberg, though, to end up with: 'It is no pose or deceit if lovers' souls show up better in their letters to each other than in real life. Nor is the lover false in his love-letters. He is not making himself out better than he is: he is *becoming* better, and in these moments *is* better. He is truly himself in such moments, the greatest moments life can bestow on us.'

All yours
Alban

(23)   Berghof, 30th July 1908

That lovely card of yours from the Ulten Valley arrived when I was lying in bed with my worst 'aches and pains'. I'd had another horrible sleepless night, so I was staying in bed all day.

Luckily I've had a supply of interesting books, and for the last week or so I've been deep in Schopenhauer,[1] who has a great deal to say that's fine and true ... I'm impressed by his pessimism, of course, because of its link with Wagner. This is the link you delight in so much, darling, the link we find between geniuses in all ages, just because they are so 'universal'; that enables them to find the most valuable sources of inspiration from their own age. Any number of these links occur to me, like those between Kant[2] and Schiller,[3] Spinoza[4] and Goethe, Nietzsche and both Richard

[1] Arthur Schopenhauer (1788–1860).
[2] Immanuel Kant (1724–1804), German philosopher.
[3] Friedrich von Schiller (1759–1805), German poet and dramatist.
[4] Baruch de Spinoza (1632–1677), Dutch philosopher.

Strauss (Zarathustra) and Mahler (Third Symphony). But the wonderful thing is that the great 'disciples' outgrew their models, became emancipated from them. Wagner was haunted by the idea that the world of today is 'the worst of all possible worlds', but unlike Schopenhauer and that school, he was not obsessed by this. He recognized that we can and must look forward to the future with optimism. He's much more *modern* than Schopenhauer, because, like Ibsen and Nietzsche, he 'says yes to life'.

Well, after these four pages, I'm afraid I feel too ill to go on. But to finish on Wagner's ideas, his concept of a 'natural nobility' comes into my mind, bringing me some small reassurance in the constant struggle I have to face daily, fighting for my middle-class honour against the advantages of aristocracy (Raoul)! A struggle I shall lose, as many people believe. But that will be decided by you and the future!

All yours
Alban

(24)   Thursday, 6th August 1908
Several nice cards from you and that 'rascal' Franz.[1] I'm glad you are so happy in the Tyrol. It's certainly very beautiful, but my memories of the weeks I spent there, at Merano, are rather jaundiced. Mother[2] was very upset about my sister's divorce,[3] and it was terribly hot. I remember one day I had to go out with her on a Sunday excursion to the mountains. The funicular was crammed with all the good folk of Bolzano, and up on top the horrible hotel buildings 'with every comfort'. You can imagine the impression La Mendola made on me.

I much prefer the view I enjoy every afternoon, writing to my distant beloved, alone with you, my dearest, and with Nature. Before my mind's eye the long lake extends, deep into the mountains. Where they seem to meet, there is a lovely little village, but all you can see of it is an avenue of poplars, a church and a monastery wall. How serene I feel there, instead of being up on that mountain 'viewpoint', with every view blocked by some pavilion or skittle alley or liveried servant or waiter in tails. Oh, these fashionable places!

[1] Franz Joseph Nahowski (1889–1942), Helene's younger brother.
[2] Johanna ('Jeanette') Berg (1851–1926) *née* Braun, Berg's mother.
[3] Berg's sister, Smaragda, had been married to Adolf von Eger.

Not very good taste on my part running down a place you found so beautiful. But then you know me, don't you! The fault certainly *is* in the eye of the beholder. Heaven knows why I've talked so much about it—quite unsolicited. Perhaps because of your postcard, or perhaps it's an unconscious feeling that I was with *you*, my only love.

At the Berghof we are now putting on the Happy Family act. Mama has her four splendid children[1] round her, her dear daughter-in-law,[2] and dear little grandson[3]—a great lump of a boy. In fact we make an interesting contrast: Mama over 14 stone, Hermann 16 stone, and huge Erich; then Charly, Smaragda and me, pale as lilies, emaciated, looking as if we'd come straight from the famine in Java.

All this intensive family life makes me pretty irritable, and I can't think straight at all for the pain in my wrist. So it's back to my beloved cigarettes again and my brandy. How else could one put up with things like my brother thumping out 'Vera Violetta, your fragrance is such . . .'?[4] *Plus* Erich crying, and my mother on her household duties clattering and squealing about the place like a muted trumpet.

Sorry about this letter! But anyhow I'm still wholly and completely yours.

Alban

(25)   Berghof, 11th August 1908
Again some cards from you, giving me news of your strenuous tour. I needed my encyclopaedia and atlas to find my way to the places where you've been carried by the favourable winds of South Tyrol. And now I certainly envy you all this magnificent scenery. Like us, I expect you'll be having lovely days at the moment. I realize again how much this 'summer season' business depends on the weather, and—which is even more depressing—on the environment, usually consisting of 'kith and kin'. Still, I won't play that old tune again, for even here the glory of a beautiful day sometimes shines triumphantly over my usual pain.

[1] Hermann Berg (1872–1921), Berg's brother who later went to the United States and became a successful business man, Charly, Alban, Smaragda.

[2] Charly's wife, Stephanie ('Steffi') *née* Leska.

[3] Erich, son of Charly and Steffi. Berg sometimes called him 'Awo-Awo'.

[4] Waltz-song from an operetta popular at the time, *Vera Violetta*, by Edmund Eysler (1874–1949).

Yesterday, for instance, I went on the lake for the first time. As I can't use my own hands, I had myself rowed out, and it was a wonderful evening. The clouds glided slowly by, orange streaks on the dark blue sky, and I gazed spellbound across the rippling green of the lake, to the waving reeds on the shore below the shadowy mountains. What a moment that was, I could have said to it: 'Stay, you are too beautiful.'[1]

But the shrieking maidens, who were bathing somewhere in the reeds tore me out of my dreams, and all the beauty of sky and water and setting sun had soon departed. The whole scene went drab and grey before my eyes, and I had myself rowed back to the boat-house.

Night with her thousand longings had begun!

Good-bye for now, my dearest and best Helene. I kiss your lovely eyes.

Alban

(26)   18th August 1908

You may be surprised, Helene darling, by my choice of book for your Saint's day present. But I think you'll understand after reading it, especially if I tell you that there are few things in modern literature I've grown to appreciate so much.

So here are *A Realist's Fantasies*.[2] I saw the book quoted in a philosophical work, but copies have been confiscated by the censor, so I had a lot of trouble before I managed to borrow it. When I read it, I was tremendously enthusiastic. It's by a Viennese engineer named Josef Popper, who died this spring.[3] To give you the chance of reading this brilliant book, I had it sent to me from Germany, where it is not under the censor's edict. I now submit it to you, very much hoping you will like it. Sorry to waste so many words on this, but you know I've never been much of a person for inscribing in books, and that's why I have to justify my choice of gift here. I must waste a few words (not really a waste!) telling you of all my wishes for you. Your Saint's day gives me a chance to express them for the occasion, although you know them all so well already. I kiss your dear hands full of devotion and adoration.

[1] Quotation from Goethe's *Faust*.
[2] *A Realist's Fantasies* (1899) by the Austrian socialist philosopher Josef Popper (1838–1921) who wrote under the pseudonym Lynkeus.
[3] Berg was mistaken—Popper was then still alive.

(27)   Berghof, 19th August 1908

... As I think I've written to you before, there are four ladies at
the Annenheim[1] who are generally considered 'beauties'. One is
the real officer's-daughter type, would-be aristocratic, terribly slim
and *chic*, with quite fine features and gracious-to-stiff movements—
she's the one Smaragda's in love with.[2] The second is the wife of a
district commissioner from Rumania, extremely refined—and
much admired by my brother Hermann.

The other two are both from Vienna. One is a young and very
merry widow, tall and blonde, nice and silly, as one can see from
her lovely stupid eyes! The fourth is very much the Viennese, of
the best sort, in looks and character. *They're* not my type either, as
you can guess. But when boorish people attack them on something
quite idiotic—because the mother of one of them is flirtatious or
the other has black round her eyes—I spring to their defence. I
have been going around with them a bit, trying to moderate their
rather primitive ideas about modern music, and enthuse with them
over Wilde and Kraus. Even if I gaze at this fourth one with the
chestnut-brown face and long eyelashes, my heart is still as serenely
cool as if I were admiring a Madonna by Raphael.

'Through you, Helene, I've grown a better man.' I once wrote
(or said) more or less instinctively; but its confirmed the more I
think about it. Do you realize the change *you* have made in me in one
year? ...

(28)   Hotel Royal Danieli,
                                         Venice,
                                         23rd August 1908

All I wish is that you could be here with me. The wonderful charm of all the famous 'sights', and even more, of the
hidden, romantic, quiet corners—I should only enjoy them to the
full if you, Helene, my beloved, were at my side. Don't think I'm
picturing the ghastly honeymooner types; no, I see two lovers
rightly bound together in the liberating bonds of our boundless
love.

That's my only reason for writing from Venice. Every grocer
sends picture postcards to his customers from this place, and

---

[1] Strand Hotel, Annenheim on Ossiacher Lake.
[2] Berg's sister, Smaragda, had Lesbian tendencies.

41

there have been many fine, 'immortal' letters written from here.
So enough, my darling,

from your longing
Alban

(29)

Berghof, Monday
24th August 1908

Two delightful days I've had. To glide at night in a gondola
through winding lagoons where no sound is heard, far from the
turmoil and thronging crowds, exulting in the night's brilliance—
but no, that's not at all my theme.

I found Venice, and learnt to love it, in the darkest corners
amidst rotting boats and a reek of refuse floating in the murky
waters. I swam out into the open sea, where the deepest peace
reigns, and quietly landed at the house where the Master died.[1]
In my mind I kissed the steps he once walked up before he stepped
into his gondola—ah, what moments of melancholy sweetness! I
still felt joyful on the way home, driving away from the sea and the
plains, up into the mountains, along the romantic banks of the
turbulent Fellach, by glorious places like Chiusaforte, Treviso, and
the rest. No need to go on about my feelings to a mountain-lover
like you. But there's one name I keep thinking of, that stirs countless
memories; Madonna di Campiglio;[2] it is where *she* lived (the girl
I must tell you about) before she moved with her parents to the
Annenheim Hotel. Her name is Ridi R, and she's one of the pretty
Viennese girls I was talking about in a recent letter. In her early
twenties, and doesn't know the first thing about art, although (or
because?) her father is a journalist. Very pleasant, attractive fellow,
by the way. She's a brunette, medium height—and pathetically in
love with your Alban! It's really very sad, and I don't know how it
will end. She has a cheerful temperament and likes having a lot of
people around her—perhaps she inherits this from her father—so
I'm hoping she will get over it as quickly as possible.

This morning she went away very unhappy, reproaching me for
always avoiding her during her last days at Venice. I, poor wretch,
could not even help her, in fact I had to 'plunge the sword deeper',
telling her how enduring and unalterable my feelings were for you.

[1] Richard Wagner died at the Palazzo Calergi-Vendramin on 13th February
1883.
[2] Well-known summer resort in the Dolomites.

No use in such a case talking of how much I admired her beauty, delighted in her gay spirit, was moved to pity by her generous unrequited love. It's just inevitable for her to be unhappy. I simply cannot help her.

Since then she has written me stormy letters, which I've answered along the same lines. Yet she still believes that my feelings for her will develop into the lasting and inextinguishable love she demands —like a true woman!

There! Now I have told you. And although I have not been unfaithful to you once, I somehow feel freer and lighter 'because there should be no secrets between us'. I kiss your dear hands.

Your own
Alban

(30)   Berghof, 25th August 1908
Although I'm not at all in the mood for writing—after another blazing row with Hermann—I find myself starting another letter to you, dearest. It's the only way of relieving my longing for you, which grows stronger every day. And even that is no real relief, because it all begins bubbling up inside me again directly I close the envelope.

Plus the fact that I hate being here, imprisoned in a place without any culture and in the family misery of squalling children and bad-tempered old people. The whole thing got on top of me so much today that I nearly ran away to Vienna. But I realize myself that there is nowhere my soul can find peace except with you, my darling—and as that condition is not so simple, nobody can help me much.

One thing I keep on telling myself as consolation: even if my love life has few high points, at least those few have such a wonderful radiance and intensity they outweigh everything else, my sorrows and despairs included. That's the only thought that keeps me alive!—for I've long ago given up any idea that I am irreplaceable, least of all as lover!

Good-bye, my darling.

(31)   Berghof, 26th August
Last night I saw the *Waltz Dream*[1] again. Presented by a summer-season theatre in Villach, slightly better than a cheap touring

[1] Berg was fond of the famous operetta by Oscar Straus (1870–1954).

43

company. Once more I rather enjoyed it, and it would have passed off smoothly enough but for a rat running through the (5-man) orchestra and the leading lady having a hole in her trousers! But what does that matter? Then we went to a café, I was a little behind the others, and as I went in I met Dr Fritz Wittels. I was delighted, and heard among other things that he and Kraus had just been a week in Venice. Isn't that funny! How nice it would have been if I'd known that when I was there.

(32)   Berghof, Saturday
                                              29th August 1908

Last night I had a beautiful dream. I was the owner of a huge, magnificent dog, which everyone else was so frightened of they wouldn't go near it. He looked at one with mysterious, magnetic eyes—I was quite in love with those eyes. One day when I was alone with him, he turned into a dazzlingly attractive youth who embraced me full of tenderness and asked me to follow him. We walked together arm in arm, he in divine nakedness and I in spreading black garments, to meet the people who had run away from us before and now waited for us full of joy and enthusiasm. At our approach they began to shout joyfully, waved branches of palm, and showed us a path which opened before us strewn with flowers. At the end of the path we came to a gondola, which we boarded; and amidst a great hush it began to rise. We were in an airship, which climbed higher and higher, circled several times over the city, then moved away, far up into the sky, into the realms of infinity.

When I woke this morning after refreshing sleep I felt so cheerful and optimistic that all the anxieties I have felt lately fell away, the fear that you might be annoyed by my confessions or were so completely absorbed by something else that you had no time or thought to write to me for such ages. During the morning I drove to the station to meet the first train from the Tyrol, which might have brought you, and on the way I called at the Hotel Annenheim to pick up post. So then I found your precious precious letter, which again gave me great joy.

Just as I have dreamed of you through all these days and nights, so out of the letter you grew for me in glorious beauty, goodness and passion, to receive with open arms my immense love. Oh, my dearest darling, I am in such a flood of emotion!

I shan't write anything today about the contents of your lovely

44

letter. But tonight I'll drive to Villach again, for at midnight the second express train from South Tyrol arrives here, bringing *you*, I hope with all my heart.

And now good-bye, my best Helene. I kiss you in spirit in all holiness of heart and ardent passion.

All yours
Alban

(33)

1.30 a.m. Sunday morning,[1]
30th August 1908

I am so deeply moved I almost collapsed in the carriage. But even so I must write to you, my pearl beyond price.

Seeing you after such an age. I realized all over again how wretched I am not to be with you. Your heavenly face a little thinner, if anything more beautiful than ever, the sublime look in your eyes—how could I grasp it all in those miserably short eight minutes?

Tears of terrible longing well up in my eyes, and my love has become so enormous it feels like a burden of agony weighing on my heart. Oh, Helene, I can't find words any more, words for the feelings I yearn to express.

Why, oh why, must I love you as I have never loved before—and as you have never before been loved?

Your own
Alban

(34)

Saturday afternoon,
5th September 1908

... They've all gone back except for Smaragda and me, and we'll be setting off about lunch-time on Monday. Autumn usually gives us its finest days around this time, and you feel completely at one with nature. You step down into the dark green lake and swim along—like one of the larger fishes! Here and there a swallow glides across the water, a flock of wild ducks flap about in the reeds, hurry to the middle of the lake, then swim serenely into the distance. Otherwise all is quiet, very quiet.

Every year I look forward to this season, when the summer

---

[1] Written directly after Berg had seen Helene for a few minutes on the platform of Villach station on her way from Mitterbad to Trahütten.

tourists have left the lake. But this year even these days have become hard to bear—I've never seen the rain pouring down like this. The sky is completely overcast, howling storm and rumbling thunder burst through tightly closed windows. Instead of turning joyfully to water, our second 'element', I turn to codeine and like medicaments! I even look forward to breathing the poisoned air of the big city, where I can be master of my lungs again after the summer 'holiday' has taken its toll. As you see, my darling, my complaints are in the same key at the end of the 'holiday' as they were at the beginning.

Luckily there are still things which preserve my faith in life, and allow me to survive the infinite pain of being parted from you. One thing is the reflection that other 'better' people feel as we do, and that, when all else fails, the abysses of common life can be surmounted with the help of art and of a sympathetic soul. Paul Hohenberg wrote to me the other day—although he's a nature lover, 'even the greatest beauties of nature can't help you over the hours of loneliness, produced by being with trivial people, and having no one "whole", to pour out your heart to.'

It's evening now, the sun just setting. A few last rays have pierced the mist and clouds, so I must go out and get some air. It will relieve my lungs, but not my sad heart. I fear it is almost too late for that, the loneliness weighs too heavily upon me. And there is nobody who could console and relieve me—except you, only you.

(35)   Vienna,
                                      9th September 1908

Now I can breathe freely again, you must surely have a few minutes devoted to you, Helene. I really *am* glad to be back. One feels quite proud, after such a long time, to be able to eat an evening meal out of doors without wearing two overcoats or worrying about the after-effects, and to have a good night's sleep without taking any codeine. When I woke up here the first morning, completely rested, breathing fresh air through the open window, hearing the traffic noises outside, I vowed I'd never again 'go away for the summer' as convention demands. You come back weaker than when you left, and even if you gain in health by 'resting' (which of course I doubt) you lose any benefits in the turmoil of travelling—unhealthy railway journeys, struggles with the smell of moth-balls and the shocking food in restaurants.

Anyhow, here endeth the horrible summer of 1908, and this is its epilogue.

Frieda[1] is in Vienna for a few days—actually at Kaltenleutgeben.[2] We went to the exhibition this morning, then home to play some music, from Berg via Schoenberg to Oscar Straus; and in the evening to the station to see her off. She'll come up every day, so we'll have a nice few days going to the theatre once or twice, excursions into the country, eating out with her—and then she'll vanish from our sight again quite soon.

Such a pity you are not here, I'm sure you would like her. Pity? What a pathetic word to express my feelings about your not being here—considering that I am longing, yearning, pining for your presence!

There aren't words enough, either, for the vileness of the social system which keeps *us two* apart. It's quite intolerable. Sometimes I think I'm going mad with pain, sometimes mad with rage. And the atrocious feeling that 'it's all no use'; I've just got to put up with everything.

Oh, give me calm! I travelled on the city railway[3] today, with the usual heat and stifling atmosphere and dirt. Then I thought of my glorious drives to see you, and (whether from a draught or coal-dust!) the tears came to my eyes. I'm not ashamed of it either!

A thousand kisses for you, my one and only darling.

Your own
Alban

(36)   15th September 1908
... I have bought tickets for the first performance of *Siegfried* (Roller,[4] Weingartner[5]) on the 26th. Carola would like to come too, so I took four: for her and Anna and the two of us—yes, you and me together at last! I gather we'll be getting the opera uncut, but even so I hope we'll have the chance, as you say, of 'annoying' Weingartner. I hate him more than ever now after a performance of *Don*

[1] Frieda Leider (b. 1888), the great Wagnerian soprano, was a friend of the Berg family.
[2] A watering place south-west of Vienna.
[3] A local municipal railway from the outer districts of Vienna (like Hietzing) to the centre of the town.
[4] Alfred Roller (1864–1935), chief designer of the Vienna Opera, a close associate of Mahler's.
[5] Felix von Weingartner (1863–1942), Mahler's successor as Director of the Vienna Opera.

Carlos. He was in a box quite near to us, so I had that moronic face more or less in sight for four hours!

But I could write to *anyone* what I feel about that disgusting business,[1] and that's not my idea in writing to *you*. No, I just have to tell you. Oh, the boundless joy I feel, now that I know definitely I can hold you in my arms (with your consent!) in exactly a week, to be precise at 5.30 next Tuesday evening.

Good-bye, my best and most beautiful, most precious Helene.

Your own
Alban

(37)
Saturday
(Undated, 19th
September 1908)

So you are in Vienna, beloved, and may this be the first message of love from outside to greet you in your home. Poor is the pen that still cannot hit on the right words, at a moment like this when the mere thought 'Helene in Vienna' could produce all the bliss of an hour's embrace. But that one thought is enough I need write no more . . . So let me just send a thousand greetings, and say to you and to myself:

Tuesday, six o'clock.
At the thought of that—I am overcome!
Helene, oh Helene—my darling

All yours
Alban

(38)
Undated
(24th or 25th
September 1908)

The old story then, Steffi has just told me: I can't see you tomorrow. You can imagine my feelings, but no, that's just it, you *can't* imagine them. After three months away you've now been a week in Vienna, and I've only had the chance of being with you for two hours. Soon you'll be off again, for six months, so that in the whole year of our love we shall only have had nine or ten hours together. It confirms the fear which has been seething in my brain

[1] The intrigues surrounding Mahler's resignation from his post as Director of the Vienna Opera, when Weingartner became his successor. The *Don Carlos* episode refers to a performance of Schiller's drama at the Burgtheater.

Above left, a photographic jest; *above right*, at the Berghof with his dogs; *bottom left*, Berg in 1904

Above, 46 Maxingstrasse, Vienna XIII, where Helene Nahowski and her parents lived; *below*, the Nahowskis' country house in Trahütten, near the small town of Deutsch-Landsberg in south-west Styria

ever since the day before yesterday: you don't love me any more! Oh, what use words when feelings are no longer the same? But I had to write now, for the chance of hearing from you. Otherwise tomorrow, which I expected to be so wonderful, would be more than I can bear.

Now at least you'll have some idea how sad I feel.

Good-bye, my fickle fair one!

Your own
Alban

(39)   29th September 1908

I am in despair. Oh, Helene, why must everything conspire against me? Of all the hours in a week it had to be just the one time I'm not free. I've had to take over the administration of some of our houses,[1] and my first job is tomorrow at 11 o'clock to see a builder and a painter, etc. and discuss some work. It may take two hours, I can't put them off, and yet it's the very time when I could have been with you again—for our first meeting in a whole week. Oh, it's so miserable I don't think I can bear it.

It doesn't help, either, that you seem so little concerned, Helene. And when you actually deign to write to me, there's not one loving word for me to read in the five or six lines—on which I must subsist for so many weary days and nights. Dearest Helene, please have pity on me. Tomorrow evening I shall be at Carola's railings, look out of the window or let me see you somehow—I *must* see you or I shall go mad. Oh, Helene, this illness[2] of yours has been too much for me, I am out of my wits!

(40)   1st October 1908,
                                                   on the city railway

I keep on feeling how much I love and adore you, so now I have to write it again too. If only I hadn't had to leave so quickly! Please get someone to telephone and tell me how you are. Do plenty of gargling, and remember to change the compresses often, my darling. Oh, if only I could be with you . . .

---

[1] The Berg family had inherited some small blocks of flats, and Berg was given the job of managing them.
[2] Helene was laid up with influenza.

(41)   6th October 1908

Today my longing for you has grown to a new pitch—for I was hoping so intensely that I would see you this evening. And I felt that, as some poet has put it,

> 'If I today your body can not touch,
> Why then my very soul will tear apart.'

You may think that no one really dies of longing, but surely poets should be the best judges in matters of love.

Then the evening came, and after opening the door several times, to the newspaper woman, man with the ice and various tradesmen, I had to admit to myself that there was no hope or chance of seeing you today. I can't help thinking Fate is very unkind to me. First my lesson with Schoenberg stopped me seeing you this morning, and now my hopes are frustrated again this evening —by some unknown power. And I don't know either what you'll be doing tomorrow or where you'll be. In case it is somewhere near me, remember that there is somebody longing for you at all hours of the day and night, somebody you may once have loved, who therefore feels he still has a claim on you for love's sacrifices. I mean the small sacrifices in time and trouble which I think you could make—no, which I hope you *would* make for me.

A thousand burning kisses,

Your own
Alban

(42)   9th October 1908

I can't come to the station at six this evening. The fact is—that last night Smaragda tried to poison herself with gas. Apparently it didn't do her much harm physically, but mentally she's in complete despair, poor soul.

(43)   Undated
                                                          (Autumn 1908)

Why should I go on concealing my greatest, my unfulfillable wish, which I have been carrying round with me for so long? Even at the risk of your rebuking me or at least laughing at me, I have to talk of it. Because our love has now reached a stage where *we two* must be honest and enlightened with each other, even though dreary darkness engulfs us!

Now everything is working to separate us, I want you to know how this wish has been secretly growing within me, the wish I have clung to without ever believing it could be fulfilled, the desire to possess you as a woman. Please, Helene, don't look on it as a mad dream or as arrogance and selfishness, but as the natural, inevitable consequence of my tremendous love. Take this confession, then, as my highest declaration of love.

Several times I've had it on the tip of my tongue, but then kept silent after some teasing remarks from you or from fear of appearing as your 'suitor', who is then bound to be turned down.

I know better than anyone that my wish is all the more beautiful because like all ideals it is unattainable. But it's a question of whether my love for you is merely the conventional 'young love' which stops, because it has to, when it meets an insurmountable obstacle, like your father's will. And now *that* is the question at stake, I had to tell you that it is something higher and holier—no, forgive me, the highest and holiest anyone can offer to anyone else: no longer just love, but a growing into the other person, beyond all obstacles, beyond space and time—

Please, Helene, tell me where I can write to you, in case we can't see each other again for a long time.

And thank you—a thousand thanks—for your most precious letter.

All yours
Alban

(44)   30th October 1908
As once more a letter from our house may reach you, I'm adding a bit to my sister's letter in the few minutes I've got. I've just come from auditions of various pianists who might play my Variations,[1] as they were too difficult for the first one selected. You can imagine that I don't enjoy this sort of thing much, taking all the steps to drag before the public something which really concerns only me— and you. Quite lucky the public don't listen too penetratingly.

[1] On 8th November a concert by Schonenberg's pupils was to take place at the Grosse Musikvereinssaal, with first performances of Alban Berg's 'Twelve Variations on an original theme' for piano (played by Irene Bien), and Anton Webern's *Passacaglia* (under the composer's direction).

Otherwise they'd notice that even if some of the movements sound confident and triumphant enough, the confidence and triumph are pretty fragile . . .

Oh dear, I've relapsed into a style or mood I was trying so hard to avoid, and all my good resolutions come to nothing. You kindly spirits, help me to stick to my resolutions, don't let me be in thrall to the deepest and most sombre basses of this life, so that I completely forget the melody and the coloratura I've already (compared with other mortals) had so much of. Perhaps I shall then reach a state where the days of my life flow on like music above a pedal point, or at most above tonic and dominant.

It's half past seven, and I have to go to Schoenberg again—no wonder this letter has turned out musical! Perhaps tomorrow, Saturday, I shall find an hour that belongs to us two *alone*: from six to seven, when I shall of course be at the station. Just in case I'm not, you'll see me in the foyer of the Opera, unless meanwhile I've been submerged in music!

Good-bye, my wonderful one.

(45)   Undated
                                        (7th November 1908)
Something else to do with the concert robbed me of the whole morning. As everything rests in my hands and Stein's,[1] I've naturally had a lot of running around and 'clerical work' to do these last days—sale of tickets, sending them off, posters, advertisements in the papers, etc. etc.

That means, alas, that even tomorrow evening I can't come to Hietzing[2] to fetch you, because I have to be at the Hall long before the concert starts—so we shall only see each other for a very short time. *Please*, Helene, try to arrange that I can come out to you very very soon.

But you *will* be coming to the concert, won't you! I should only enjoy it half as much without you beside me, and I do want to enjoy it to the full . . . The number of my seat is 9 in the 8th row: so that you can arrange for me to sit next to you and not, say, next to Carola! I can't even start thinking who I'd give the ticket to if you

---

[1] Erwin Stein (1885–1958), Austrian musicologist and editor, a pupil of Schoenberg's.

[2] The Nahowski family lived in the Hietzing district of Vienna, on the corner of Maxingstrasse and Weidlichgasse.

weren't coming, because I can't think of anybody I'd want to have next to me when I was expecting *you*, my only love.

And now good-bye, dearest, and keep cheerful, knowing you are loved more than words can say by your own.

Alban

(46)
Vienna, Wednesday evening,
4th November 1908
Vordere Zollamtsstrasse 11[1]

I've been blushing with pleasure, darling—have never before had such a beautiful scent in my room, whether it's from the undeserved laurel or the love which presented it. The latter, I presume and hope; and so my soul is filled with unimagined bliss.

Good-bye, my kind one.

All yours
Alban

(47)
Undated
(November 1908),

You'll appreciate, Helene darling, that I *can't* come to you tomorrow afternoon. I've already been thrown out 'in spirit' by your father, and I won't give him the chance to throw me out physically! Apart from that, I mustn't deprive your mother[2] of your company, which she needs so much on her walks. I mustn't disturb your father's peace of mind—and I certainly mustn't ruin *your* reputation by association with a dubious character like me (not even a fixed position!), and so rouse to rebellion the whole Weidlichgasse.

Don't think I am writing this in anger, my precious Helene. I am very very calm and see things clearly.

Smaragda will allow herself the privilege of calling at your house tomorrow afternoon. After all, the throwing-out has nothing to do with her. I needn't spout any more about my boundless adoration for you. I'm sure you know it only too well.

I kiss your hands!

Alban

---

[1] The Berg family had moved to the new flat in 1907. See footnote Letter 12.
[2] Anna Nahowski, *née* Novak (1859–1931).

Monday evening
                                                (December 1908)
I wrote the enclosed two pages during the last few days, and now
send them off, hoping they won't annoy you. Please try to put
yourself in my place, then you will understand and perhaps even
approve.

Thank Anna for her letter. I felt so strongly it was coming that
when the bell rang I rushed to the door like a madman and hurled it
open. And when someone held out the letter, I again *felt* it was for
me, without even looking to see who it was addressed to.

Many thanks for your note too. When I think of you with your
illness over, without pain once more—how splendid that is!—a
feeling almost of joy comes into my tormented heart. But now read
last night's letter.

                                                            Sunday
. . . The Allegro furioso e appassionato has been broken up by a
general pause, after which I expect new developments. Frankly,
I was expecting them much earlier, and confidently hoped for a
letter from you through Carola, but she merely told me it would be
'coming soon'.

So I must try to suppress the words of sadness over my disappointed hopes these last days, and let joy win through, the joy
I felt to hear you were better. But alas, amidst my fits of passionate
unhappiness about your illness and your family's attitude, this
long silence has passed into a dismal void, I mean the awareness
of your complete indifference to me.

It's as if I had been on a ship wrecked by violent storms and
breakers, and were now cast up on a reef where nothing grows or
lives, where no one can stay alive; and I wait impatiently, longingly,
for a life-boat to rescue me. But nothing comes. Far away on the
horizon sailors pass, giving no sign, as if they could not see or
hear my efforts and entreaties. Perhaps they are too far away from
this lone survivor of the wreck, and really do not spot me. So I wait
and wait, standing and waving, shouting, lighting fires of my love,
imploring the unconscious, hoping for miracles—but the beloved
does not move. And meanwhile, amidst the wintry night of my
disappointments, a voice is heard from above saying: 'The performance is over.'

I shake the snow from my feet, cover my head, and stagger away, with mocking birds around me, escorting me—until with a shudder I enter the cave of loneliness and there sink to the ground.

Now it is night. Till seven I managed to endure the horrible loneliness. There was no one in the house, and I didn't know a single person with whom I could have shared the loneliness of my thoughts. Is it really possible that at the age of twenty-four I have lost absolutely everything and everyone, that when my soul sounds this sorrowful note, there is no other soul to join in harmony with it? The others had all been away amusing themselves since half past three, and I was abandoned to my own devices. I couldn't bear it any more, dashed out, drank some black coffee, read the advertisement of the Schoenberg concert in all the papers, said nothing to anyone, eventually got fed up with Kokoschka[1] and Oppenheimer,[2] asking what on earth was wrong with me, rushed off home again, only to meet the same cross-examination there. So I hid again, but nowhere did I find any consolation. At such moments Richard Strauss and Maeterlinck[3] and Strindberg mean nothing— one grabs a bottle of wine and swills down alcohol on an empty stomach.

But that doesn't help either, the same horrible thoughts keep rising within me: why didn't Helene write at least a line every day to me, to say that she thinks of me, wants to see me by her sickbed, is being true to me. It wouldn't have given her any trouble, and would have brought me so much happiness and relief. And: why didn't Helene appear when I stood longingly beneath her window, up to my ankles in snow, only to see something of her, a mere gesture, a wave of the hand? She can't be as ill as all that.

The old helpless anger comes over me, that I am not like other people, that I don't belong in this sort of respectable, conventional world. Despair grips me, worse than I ever remember. I turn over the pages of some of my scores, read through them feverishly, wondering whether they are worthy of survival if only two people in the world like them. I am filled with infinite melancholy, could close my eyes and cry to myself until the morning heralds a new day of wretchedness.

[1] Oskar Kokoschka (b. 1886), Austrian painter.
[2] Max Oppenheimer, Viennese painter, member of the Kokoschka-Klimt circle.
[3] Maurice Maeterlinck (1862–1949), French-Flemish poet and dramatist.

Monday afternoon

So one day surpasses another in torment and distress. Again today no letter has come from Hietzing, nobody considers it worth informing me of your condition. From what Carola told me, I imagine you got up for the first time, which meant you were better; so I did expect at least a short note from you. Nothing has arrived so far, and I am bound to fear that you are after all no better. But why am I left in such horrible anxiety? I dare say you are very depressed because you are still so ill, but that's all the more reason to inform me about your condition, to give me a faint hope that you will be well on 25th February. I could hold the joyful thought of that in balance against all the suffering of these dreadful weeks. But now I can do nothing but wait and wait, and gaze with a new understanding into Strindberg's bitter, tormented face. So here's an end, there are no more words for me to say.

Now you have read these pages, you may shake your dear, beautiful, pale head. Don't shake your head, Helene, but rather lower it, as if you were in church, in the forest, or on the sea. For here is someone who has unveiled before you his Holy of Holies.

Amen

(49)   Undated
                                                   (December 1908)

Alas, my darling, I can't visit you this afternoon after all, I'm afraid, because my String Variations[1] are being rehearsed at Schoenberg's tonight, and I have to copy the parts. Please let me know at what time tomorrow I can and should come up—and how your health is.

With all my affection, and full of yearning!

One thing more just to reassure you: I promise I won't 'nag' again, but will try to accept your favour or disfavour, my state of grace or disgrace, with equal gratitude. And so I kiss your dear hands affectionately . . .

---

[1] Apparently an early version of the Fugue for string quartet.
[2] Berg's musical initials.

(50)

Helene, what *happened* today?

I staggered home like a drunkard, feeling as if I were racked with pain. All these last hours I had been haunted by the thought that you didn't love me, and just because I spoke that thought out loud, you completely turned away from me.

Oh, I can picture you walking down the Maxingstrasse, with your eyes full of tears. Crazed as I already am with doubts and anguish, I now have to face appalling remorse as well, that I have hurt you, my only and most wonderful beloved.

Oh Helene, if I *have* done that, please forgive me, forgive me. Don't be angry any more, but please love me as I love you, and forgive, Helene, forgive me.

I can't go on writing. My whole body is trembling in my terrible agitation, and my eyes are full of hot, stinging tears.

Oh forgive me, Helene!

Sunday morning

I really have nothing more to say since last night, everything else must wait till I see you again, Helene. And I am so longing for that time, I can't wait for the afternoon, to lay myself at your feet—and to tell you how infinite is my love and adoration.

Till I see you!

(51)

This afternoon, when I said to you 'Think of me tonight!', you smiled, and I didn't understand why. But now the few lines, I somehow felt you would write me, have explained the smile. How did you guess what I wanted so much—a volume of poetry by the magnificent one![2] You darling!

But I can't find the right words, and would almost tear up this letter, if I only knew whether I should be meeting you tomorrow at noon. So now you shall only have a few words as a token of the joy

---

[1] In Austria, as in Germany, the traditional ceremonies of present-giving, etc, take place on Christmas Eve.

[2] Maeterlinck.

57

which has filled me since I received your most precious and beautiful present.

In my exuberance, I take the unwanted liberty of kissing you by letter!

All yours

An hour later

My joy is running over! 'We are really living,' says Maeterlinck, 'only if we become better people.' When you wrote to me[1] that I 'made you better', I'm sure I did not merit this praise. But oh, if it were true, how wonderful it would be.

(52)   Thursday
                                               (Undated, spring 1909)
There is a delicate scent in my room. I have before me the second of your lovely veils,[2] and when I press it to my face, I can almost feel the sweet warm breath from your mouth. The violets you picked for me yesterday, which nearly withered in my buttonhole, are now blooming anew, and smell soft and fresh. The cushion on the divan and the chair by the window belong to you, Helene, they have become appendages to your presence. Indeed everything in my room is the same: the mirror in front of which you arranged your hair; the window I have seen you looking through so seriously (even in our gayest moments); the last pale rays of sunlight which make your hair gleam with gold; the glowing fire in the stove; and then the laurel wreath, and the dear little cover on the bedside table—everything, everything is yours.

And that's no wonder seeing that I myself have become so entirely your 'creation'. All my possessions and even thoughts are somehow a loan or gift from *you*. Dressing in the morning, for instance, when I get an idea for a theme, a mood, or sometimes even a single chord, at best a whole extended melody—then I always feel it has come flying in from you. It's the same with everything: if I read something out of the ordinary, with difficult parts in it, I imagine myself understanding those parts and penetrating its mysteries only through you, Helene. I mean this reading in the widest sense. If I look at nature with the eyes of a sensitive

[1] Reference to a letter Helene had written that autumn.
[2] To this Helene Berg remarks: 'Veils were then in fashion. I lost my first one and forgot the second one at the Bergs' flat.'

58

reader, when I hear music or see paintings or—but why go on with a list of all the things which have come to life in me only through you?

Oh, Helene, how can I live without you!

I am completely yours

(53)   June 1909, Whit Monday
Whenever I am near you, Helene, or have been with you, all my longings, carried with me every hour of the day, suddenly vanish, and I feel so free from care and desire, striding through the streets and squares of Hietzing, imagining that all who meet me can see my happiness shining in my face. But sooner or later the radiance will fade, when all too soon I wake from the lovely dream state into the grim reality—of being away from you . . .

Even when I am driving through a well-loved valley in the Vienna Woods in the dark of night, quiet hidden wishes rise before me, like the black pines all round. All of a sudden I would give anything to hear you singing, listen to your heavenly voice, which I love as nobody has ever loved it. To me it is the ultimate perception of beauty, which once suddenly came to me and which I have since then irretrievably lost, though I still catch a faint echo of it. But this is only a tiny part I have picked out from the limitless longing I feel.

A thousand buds open within my soul, only to wilt for all my watering. Like your tiger-lily which I see before me. The last bud burst open last night, though the other blossoms on the same stalk have long withered. In *your* garden they would have been the proudest blooms.

Alban

(54)   Undated
(June 1909)
You mustn't be sad. Think of 'Easter'.[1] All the petty trials of fate are nothing, and cannot survive before the exaltation and joy of which our united soul is capable. In all such trials think always of me more than of others. If your father won't speak to you, don't think of his unkindness but of the pain this causes *me*. Instead of

[1] *Påsk* (1900), passion play by Strindberg.

59

making you poorer, these insults will make you much richer—in all those ugly moments which might make you cry . . .

Sleep well and deeply.

(55)   Berghof,
                                                                   12th July 1909
Sometimes I think I am quite beyond help! . . . As for my body, I have been aiming for years at its complete negation, almost proud of my thinness, hollow stomach and narrow chest; feeling that physical weakness is balanced by greater spiritual strength. So how can I now use science to care for the body positively? I am bound to be different from the others, who judge my frailties from the way *their* bodies work; and if I accept their advice, the results will be exactly the opposite of what's intended! When I go to the country for a holiday, I get seriously ill. When I have good regular meals, I feel fat and bloated and constipated. When I give up all the harmful drugs (alcohol, nicotine, caffeine, etc.) I break down. Yet when I stand up to my ankles in snow, eat nothing for half the day, and have only a few hours' sleep, then I blossom and thrive and feel immortal!

Spiritually, I know I can never live without you, that even your body, which you keep healthy by sound sense and intelligence, gives strength to mine. Like Atlas you carry on your shoulders the entire system of my sky and soul, and if you refused to carry it, my whole world would collapse. That's something I'm quite sure about.

But as to my physical health I'm still very doubtful how things will go. So don't be cross with me for talking about my various ailments again. I won't do it any more, I'll just try to get well as quickly as possible *because you want me to*. What has been worrying me is not physical pain, but my unhappiness that I can't fulfil your wish to see me healthy; and as you know, distress of spirit is much more serious for me than physical pain. But you also know how much stamina and endurance I can show when it's a matter of fulfilling one of your wishes. And that I will do everything possible to get well, and will attain that goal, too!

Your own
Alban

(56)   Berghof, 13th July 1909
                                                                Wednesday afternoon
. . . The way things have been going lately is that I've been in

60

dreadful pain at night and in the middle of the day. In the mornings I lie around in a stupor, and one or two afternoons I've felt more or less all right, so that then at least I could write to you ... Now I again feel extremely bad, so short of breath I'm sure my lungs and heart are having to work twice or three times as hard—and my overfilled stomach is pretty hard pressed too. With the whole frame so weak and nerves overstrained, it's small wonder that everything refuses to function, respiratory tract, bowels, digestion, everything, I begin to despair about my health, which is quite a rare thing for me. Still, it's only to be expected if one is sitting up in bed into the early hours of the morning, sweating hard in the effort to breathe, and listening all day to people who say: 'There's nothing wrong with you, it's only nerves.'

... Oh dear, I'm talking about my health again and boring you. One consolation I came across the other day in a brilliant book I've been reading, Balzac's *Physiology of Marriage*.[1] Somewhere in it he remarks that a woman never gives us so much care as when we are ill. Not true, you may say, but I like to imagine it is, and that I am therefore getting all the care just at present!

There are many fine insights in the book, and I particularly like his comments on whether one can love the same woman for ever. To say, this is impossible 'would be as absurd as saying that a great violinist needs several violins to play a piece of music or to produce a beautiful melody'. And again: 'If there are differences between one moment of desire and another, then a man can always be happy with the same woman.'

... Your letter has come. Oh, Helene, I am so full of thanks. What a lovely letter. How clearly I hear in it the dear sound of your voice! Oh, Helene, we can never be parted from each other.

What an extraordinary, unique love this is, which makes us at night shed the bitter tears of hopeless longing *at the same time*. When we are even ill at the same time. When you care for me so loyally and lovingly, giving me good advice about my health!

Several questions in your letter to be answered. Yes, Mala[2] recognized me at once when he came with Mama to fetch me from the station. He is as sweet and excitable as ever, and also, I'm afraid, just as un-house-trained!

No, I'm not much enjoying being at the Berghof, hardly at all in fact. All its beauty and charms say nothing to me, when I feel it is

[1] Honoré de Balzac's (1799–1850) *Physiologie du mariage*, published in 1830.
[2] The Berg family's white dachshund.

61

bad for my health—and when you are not here, my incomparable one. As to Ridi R.—I haven't given her a single thought here until I read her name in your letter. Word of honour! The things you think! I have been past all the spots where she and I were together, and did not have an atom of memory, not a molecule of feeling, that I had ever been there with *her*. What else would you expect, when all my thinking and remembering is absorbed by you? I have not seen any of the Annenheim people yet—there are supposed to be nine of them staying there, by the way, if they were the nine Muses, they'd stir no chord in me!

My passionate love for you is so great, that while I have been writing this, I have all of a sudden felt quite well: without any pain. So perhaps after all it is only mental suffering. Oh, write again soon, my only darling, your letters are better than any medicines.

I kiss you, Helene.

Yours for ever
Alban

(57)   Berghof, Friday
                                                       16th July 1909
. . . Now I can really breathe freely! What a lot of fine things again in your letter. All the lovely figures of my imagination appearing, the countless dream pictures that people the land of my desire. First the kindly nurse-figure, the wise counsellor and help-mate, the dispenser generally of kindness and love.

Then the mischievous imp-figure. How well I can imagine you in that scene with your Papa, so brilliantly described, so splendidly funny—worthy to be immortalized by Busch[1]—I was quite bubbling over with amusement and couldn't help going off to read it out (the whole two pages of your 'scene') to Mother and the Salzgeber woman.[2] They laughed like anything, but of course it wasn't so close to their hearts, and they couldn't be expected to feel the same inner delight, and admiration, as I did. How wrong you were to call this enchanting humour silly nonsense. On the contrary, it's the most superb *sense*, in which the most glorious D minor chords of your soul sound forth in their full magnificence!

[1] Wilhelm Busch (1832–1908), popular German painter and writer of comic verse.
[2] Baroness Salzgeber, a friend of Berg's mother.

Anyhow, with a few bridging sentences your letter leaves the humour and goes on to the 'heavenly miracle', the 'mysterious powers' which bind us to each other, making us more and more unpartable. Yes, you are right about the miracle and the powers. They go far beyond human understanding, beyond scientific knowledge of the 'finely organized nervous system'. And because you understand this, it gives you full right to 'smile towards the sunny autumn', just as it gives me confidence that one day I shall fully conquer all the *Schwarzalben*[1] trying to undermine me and our love for each other.

I can see a sweet teasing smile on your face that I should compare myself with Siegfried, but I think you know what I mean! The comparison goes like this. Here are the *Schwarzalben*, striving for riches, fame and power, while I stand against them with my striving for the highest, for Brünnhilde-Helene, symbol of spiritual and moral perfection. And since I don't even use Siegfried's means to achieve this end, since I even renounce the treasure of the Nibelungs, perhaps I shall be spared Hagen's death-blow, and can live to witness the twilight of the gods— our gods, Maeterlinck, Strindberg, Mahler, Strauss, and so many others . . .

It's dark already, and I'll finish this now so that it can go off tomorrow morning. But before I finish, I shut my eyes and imagine you were by my side, imagine myself embracing and kissing you. But it's no use, Helene, a most horrible sadness takes hold of me, knowing that I can't do it, can't see, hear, feel you, and that all the letters in the world and all my imaginings cannot reproduce an atom of the titanic emotions I feel. How poor I am, how hungry and thirsty for your presence.

Good-bye, Helene

Your own
Alban

(58)   Tuesday afternoon,
                                        20th July
What on earth is the matter?

I went to the post office myself, the first half hour's walk I've dared do since my recent attacks, but then I had terrific hopes to

[1] The Schwarzalben in Wagner's *Ring of the Nibelungs* are Alberich's toiling dwarfs, the wicked demonic spirits of the deep—personifying the principle of evil.

spur me on: if for some inexplicable reason you didn't write at all on Friday, Saturday and Sunday, or didn't sent it off, you surely wouldn't have missed posting me the longed-for letter yesterday. When I got there, no letter—so I went and sat in the woods, half reading, half staring into the void full of fears; waiting for the mid-day post. But that brought nothing either!

I tottered home, broken and despairing, baffled and helpless. So many things went through my mind, so many fears and miseries. I expect Fritz is out there, I thought, and on a lovely day like this she'll be going on all sorts of walks, and at the end of it no time for her to write a letter. Or has the time of great love and fidelity been followed by a time of relaxation, where a letter from Paul, or a nice summer day, or some thrilling chapter of a book, or a good day's singing, are enough to make her forget me?

Then at home I had to pretend the walking had been bad for me, to give me an excuse for not eating anything at all, and for pacing round my room all afternoon instead of having a sleep.

What a world of loneliness! I am the poorest of the poor, paying for a week of riches with long months of poverty. Truly I am starved by Fate, and how can all the art of doctors succeed with me, or all the experience and advice of those who sit at a richly laid table of life? Perhaps my hunger is just greater than the hunger of others, so that I am not satisfied with the ordinary woman of wealth and elegance, but instead I seize greedily on one who is the complete woman: who gives herself to one by her own choice—not because she would otherwise fall to the ground, unsupported, like poor ivy deprived of its oak.

Yet I have seen the branches of an ivy which grew without a tree or wall, which grew bigger and finer, and bore more splendid leaves than its sisters, the hundreds of parasite plants which wither and dry up like old spinsters—if they have nothing to lean on and cling to.

This sounds immodest. Perhaps the trouble is that I lack the cheap veneer with which the noblest woman may be captured by a man who can persuade her that she is nothing without him—that she needs to lean on him, like the ivy on the oak.

In that case I *am* too modest! For I have always given you to understand that you were the noblest, most precious and perfect woman just as you are; and that to achieve a partnership with you gives me a great and meritorious purpose in life.

That means that I abandon every power over you: that I consider

64

Above, Berg's self-portrait, 1909 [see letter 59]; *below*, a water-colour of Helene Nahowski by her step-sister, Carola Heyduck, 1908

Left, Berg in 1911; *below*, the Berghof, the Bergs' country estate on the Ossiacher Lake, Carinthia, two hundred and fifty miles south-west of Vienna

partnership more valuable than domination or authority of one over the other. And surely you are yourself created for such partnership—for walking hand in hand towards the highest goals. After all, the first of your suitors imagined he could make something out of you, if only as a learned man's wife; and he ran away when he realized that a man can never reach his goal in life if his idea of a relationship with someone else, man or woman, is authority or domination.

I can't go on with this letter. Evening is drawing on, and the afternoon post has still not arrived. I'll go and meet it.

7.30 p.m.

Nothing's come! That's all I'll write. I'm going to bed, and won't let anybody in to me. I said I wanted some peace and sleep, because I was feeling pretty sick. And so I am: sick unto death!

Alban

(59)   Wednesday, 21st July 1909

Don't be angry, please don't be angry, dearest Helene, about my letter. I must have again been almost mad with longing, and wrote as I felt in my anguish of soul. I just couldn't explain to myself why you didn't write for such a long time, and thought of all possible horrible reasons. I was in such agitation, I stayed awake until five o'clock this morning and had a shocking attack of asthma as well. I was so carried away writing you that letter yesterday, and didn't even read it through afterwards, that I'd quite forgotten what it said, and in my insomnia it suddenly struck me that you might find my letters boring, depressing and much too long. They might even go the way of the Rovelli[1] epistles and serve for general amusement. And even that, as with Anna, wouldn't induce you to answer them. So don't be annoyed, my very dear Helene, at my writing such grim stuff. Think of it as merely the result of my exorbitant love. Forgive me for feeling that way, suffering that way; and rejoice in it even more, as proof of my love, than if I had waited patiently.

Today I am worse than ever. This morning, as I lay in bed, full of

---

[1] The lawyer Dr Bruno Rovelli was an admirer of Helene's sister, Anna. On occasions Anna read extracts from his letters to the family.

forebodings about death, I tried to do a sketch of myself[1] for joy. But though I'm worse physically, I *feel* much better and easier, since I received your two very fine letters—not forgetting the picture postcard from Glashütten. So my yards and yards of letters haven't been quite futile, you actually enjoy my rantings and don't find them too obnoxious! It's *very* good to hear that. And what loving care you show me. I'll try to follow all your advice and hope I shall eventually get better. But so far all my efforts have been in vain, so you'll understand my being rather pessimistic, and apprehensive about exposing my health to eight weeks' risk. (Summer holiday on the Berghof.[2])

Still it would be terrible if I didn't have the will-power to get well enough to come and visit you in Styria next month. This at least I must achieve.

Tea with butter goes down very well with me. I shan't be bathing anyhow, dearest, much as I should like to. You ask about my medicines. Almost too many to mention at present, including lactose, codeine, sodium sulphate (the nastiest medicine you can imagine), some morphine mixture, a cocaine solution, menthol with oil of paraffin (because the lactose hasn't worked)—and various others! Quite enough to make me well, or ill, I don't know which. The other day I was proud to have had a very good night, till it transpired that 'in all good faith' I'd taken such a big dose of morphine that they'd never dare give it to a patient deliberately.

You're not supposed to take more than one of these medicines on an empty stomach, so it's a knotty problem first thing in the morning to decide in which order to take three of them. Just as I have decided, I hear someone clumping up the stairs, and in comes *ein Berg* of whipped cream, threatening to swallow me. And so the day begins.

How different I'd imagined it. How much I'd hoped to spend a really creative summer, bursting with ideas and melodies, not with fats and laxatives! And how absorbed I seem to be—sorry—by all these physical ills. I have only a few hours left for the great happiness of devoting them to you. I do a bit of reading now and then, often our friend Maeterlinck . . .

Now I'll finish. I've answered nearly everything, I hope, in your dear fragrant letters. I'm going to put them by me on the pillow as a lucky charm, in the hope of having a better night than last night,

[1] Berg, like Arnold Schoenberg, was an accomplished painter (see portrait facing page 64).
[2] The climate at the Berghof was not good for Berg's asthma.

when I hadn't anything loving from you to put there, no longed-for lovely love-letters . . .

Oh, my dearest, dearest darling.

Your own, your very own
Alban

p.s. It's Thursday morning, 5.30. Again I've found it hard to breathe ever since half-past one, and all the morphine in the world can't give me any sleep. Every time I'm so dead sleepy and dropping off, I wake with a start and forget to breathe three times as quickly, so I almost choke.

I've decided not to go out and post this letter myself, but let someone else take it. And I'll send with it my 'self-portrait from the sick-bed'. How lovely you may look just now—lying in your little bed, far away from me! I realize too late that this postscript is quite superfluous. But when I see a little space left in which I can write something more, my darling, I use it.

At least it will show you that I'm thinking of you day and night!

(60)   [Addressed under this cipher]
'Koralpe 999' Poste Restante,
to Deutsch-Landsberg, Styria
22nd July 1909

Once again I write to you after having just posted a letter off. Only hope this will reach you on Monday, I'm desperate enough as it is, having to wait till Tuesday for the chance of finding out why you're feeling sad. For your letter has just come. I can't go into all it says, because I've only half an hour to write to you, but I *must* hear about this desperation of yours. Thank Heavens it's not *my* fault. Or perhaps I wish it were, then I might be able to put things right in a word or two. But I'm utterly miserable and baffled when I think of you trying to solve the problem yourself, whatever it is.

You shouldn't have kept your trouble a secret from me, Helene, such concealment ought to be unthinkable between two people who love each other. There's nobody in the world with more right than I have, and more craving too, to share your joy with you—and your sadness even more. Yet you can simply write saying: 'I can't tell you what is making me depressed. Let's talk of something else.'

Oh, this uncertainty is horrible. I rack my brains guessing all the things that might be wrong, and cannot stop worrying about it. Are you feeling ill? Or in pain? Perhaps it's only a tummy ache—and remember I love that tummy as much as your darling mouth. Is your throat hurting, is there some trouble with your singing? Have you had a letter from Raoul, and you don't know what to do about him? Or has someone new turned up and put your senses in a whirl, so that your physical love for me has disappeared, like the memory of my face? And now you don't know if you love me at all, which one of us to give up—and you're just feeling depressed at the idea of losing either of us.

Oh, I must send off this letter now, but please be honest with me, Helene. You always say you *are* honest with me—so be honest now. It's terribly important for me. Please tell me what the matter is.

Your own Alban
Yours, yours, yours.

(61) Berghof 23rd July

So you *are* angry, Helene. I write two letters in my anxiety at not hearing from you for three whole days, and I guess you might have fallen out of love with me. And that has made you angry.

Not that there are any angry words in your letter. But what I could read between the lines speaks louder than any angry words. Not a stroke of the pen to suggest any tenderness; no, it gives the impression you regret having worried so much about me and my health. Repelled, no doubt, by my continual moaning and groaning, you leave me to my fate, which amounts to leaving me to rot.

You confess you had another of the horrible times when you were suddenly sick of everything and had to withdraw into yourself. But now everything is all right again, you have become reconciled with life and have found yourself once more. And how was this miracle achieved? Through a glorious summer day with deep blue sky and birds singing. In other words, 'Don't believe I've come back to *you*, Alban. The thing which has rescued and released me and made me immensely happy is not you, with your lamentations of love and your invalid chair, but lovely, heavenly Nature. Now I am myself again, resting in Nature's bosom, which has rescued me from you, Alban, and from my melancholy.'

The rest of the letter discusses the Balzac-Strindberg business[1] in a cool, amiable way—not a straw of love there for a drowning man to cling to. I sit miserably and read right through the letter,

---

[1] See Letters 54 and 56.

considering it from all possible angles, searching for a crumb of comfort, but can only interpret it along the hopeless lines I've just imagined. Perhaps you wrote the letter in your first irritation, but surely you can understand how hurt I would be on getting it, the first letter I've had from you for three days.

Listen, Helene, I know I've written too much about my illness. But it wasn't just whining and whimpering, I wanted to let you know how hard I've been trying to get well, and that I was in despair of ever getting well in this damned place; especially of ever getting well without *you*. Oh, they feed me up here, but it's more than cancelled out by my lack of emotional nourishment, my continual craving for *you*. And now you seem to be telling me plainly: 'I relieve you of your promise, live as you wish'—in other words: 'I don't care if you go to pieces.'

Oh, Helene, why are you doing this to me? With your blue sky and bird-song have you forgotten our last days together? The Wachau,[1] the terrace garden, the journey? I thought you were thinking of all these things, but instead you have completely forgotten them, and feel released and rescued and immensely happy, just because the sun is shining. I can't expect you not to enjoy Nature because I'm not there; perhaps no woman can love as fully as that. But I am hurt, more than I can say, to find you can quite do without me because you enjoy Nature. Imagine my despondency and despair, knowing that every shining cloud will put me in the shade, every warbling nightingale, every trilling lark will drown the cry of longing. Imagine how I must stagger and stumble around if your hand is not outstretched to hold mine, because it rests contentedly in the moss and plays in the grass. If you have no eyes for me, but only for the swaying branches in the forest . . .

I must get to you, I can't be without you any more. You'll get this letter on Monday, so I may have news on Tuesday, and will let you know when and where I'll be coming. And please send me a loving word, so that I'll have something to hope for in these three days, and to live on afterwards: until I lie at your feet, to be trampled on, or lifted up.

Alban

---

[1] The narrow gorges of the Danube valley between Melk and Krems in Lower Austria.

(61a)

Trahütten, 23rd July 1909

Alban dear,

When my letter to you had gone yesterday, I was sorry, because I hadn't been quite honest. I was trying, by rather drastic means, to force you into considering what may happen if you don't soon restore your health. I'm sure it must have suffered a good deal from the effects of your not living in a more sensible way. Look, it's all right for Smaragda to drag you off with her carousing all night, and Hermann does the same when he's in Europe. But she has a good long sleep next day, whereas you get up without enough sleep and try to work, fighting your tiredness by drinking all those cups of strong tea. And what with these nights in smoky places, with alcohol and no food, you've reached the point of being nearly six foot tall and weighing only $9\frac{1}{2}$ stone. I can well understand your hating all the 'fattening food', but it's still the most harmless way of growing stronger, instead of taking medicines the whole time without their making you any better.

These last days I've been very unhappy about all this. You are always writing of your great love for me, but you don't seem to care that our future depends on your health improving. From their point of view, my parents aren't altogether wrong to turn you down. They think I should be constantly worrying about you and so wouldn't be happy with you. Any woman who loves is bound to wonder whether her love is going to bring her suffering, even though it may be her destiny to suffer. But won't *you*, Alban, have one more try to get well? It will take some sacrifices, I admit, but surely you will want to do it for my sake—no, for *our* sakes.

I've had a bad night, because I knew my letter would hurt you, saying harsh things to you, as if I weren't interested any more in you and your health. But no, Alban, I am *not* giving you up. Perhaps you will still achieve something 'great' one day, and I want to help you with it, so that you can do your work unhampered by physical frailty, and can also enjoy life without having heart trouble and attacks of asthma.

So that's that, a long long sermon, and a confession too. Take it as it's meant, and please—be patient.

Your own
Helene

70

Four o'clock in the morning, and a good time to have a chat with
you, as I'm feeling absolutely fresh! How does that happen? Well,
I'll confess.

As you'll understand, I was gradually becoming very scared of
the nights, when the attacks were almost inevitable. They were so
horrible I greeted every dawn with as much joy as if I'd been back
at school and it was Sunday morning, so no school. It was such a
terrific treat to find the pain had stopped and there was nothing
wrong with me.

I was ready to take anything for relief in the night, but nothing
helps in the actual moment of danger. Morphia and bromide may
get me over the first hours, but about 2 a.m. the same ordeal starts,
and there's no escape. I go on gasping and panting right to the
morning, and often have a violent cough as well. I can repeat the
medicine, take a nasal compound or codeine, inhale—nothing's any
good.

But the other day Baroness Salzgeber mentioned quite an ordinary
remedy—tell you what it is later—which helped someone she
knows. Something so obvious I'd never tried it! I decided to
take some of it into my bedroom in case I needed it, but I hoped I
wouldn't have to. Then I took a larger dose of my sedative than
usual, and actually managed to sleep till 3 a.m. Though I tried to
deceive myself into thinking I was dropping off again, the attack
came as usual, and the temptation to try the new remedy was too
great. I took it, and quite soon, oh joy, relief had come. Don't be
cross if I name this elixir of life, I didn't take it till all my courage
was gone. Then I seized the glass of—black coffee! You may still
think me weak or unwise, but surely my nerves won't be worse
affected by a little black coffee than they would be by four or five
hours struggling desperately for breath, straining heart and lungs
and everything else . . .

The two days ahead don't really exist . . . time is swallowed up
between the moment yesterday when I got your letter and the
moment on Tuesday (I hope) when I receive the next one . . .
Doesn't matter how I try to fill the blank time—as long as I don't

keep calling out: a letter, a letter from Helene, a sign that you like me again, so that my soul can once more breathe freely . . .

Looking for one of our common bonds (besides our love), I hit on Strindberg, of course, of whom you wrote in that last unfortunate letter of yours. First of all, I wasn't annoyed with Hohenberg for not sharing my taste. I am not even angry when Kraus abuses Strauss, when Webern[1] criticizes Kraus, when Oppenheimer despises Böcklin[2] and praises Puccini[3]—or (to quote the strongest example): when I myself find the relation of Mahler to Strauss, the relation of Strindberg and Nietzsche to Wagner inconceivable and despicable. But what annoys me is Hohenberg's way of covering his ignorance by abusing what he doesn't like or understand. Because Schoenberg's Quartet[4] leaves him cold, it doesn't give him the right to say when a door creaks: 'That would be a theme for Schoenberg!' Or to disparage an outstanding artist like Kokoschka with a remark he made the other day when we saw an unfortunate freak: 'Could have been dreamed up by Kokoschka!' Or because he can't grasp Strindberg's colossal stature as a writer, to revel in finding something to attack like the *Blue Book*.[5] Finally, I'm furious with Hohenberg for calling Strindberg a humbug.

Personally I think the *Blue Book*, though it may be the weakest of Strindberg's great works, it is also the most interesting; it certainly has some flashes of genius in it. A man like Strindberg, who has written such wonderful autobiographical works, five historical novels, eleven one-act plays, tragedies like *The Dance of Death* and *The Father*, historical plays, and all the other works I've not yet read but am sure are just as fine: such a man is obviously one of the most remarkable personalities of our time. We can't condemn any of his works out of hand!

However, my enthusiasm for Strindberg is not meant to decry others, like Knut Hamsun,[6] whom I still admire very much. But after all, though Hamsun wrote five masterly novels as a young man, he has not produced anything since. Whereas Strindberg has striking achievements in all fields, and has never stopped his creative

---

[1] Anton Webern (1883–1945), was Berg's life-long friend, and his fellow pupil at Schoenberg's classes.
[2] Arnold Böcklin (1827–1901), Swiss painter of the romantic-idealistic school.
[3] Giacomo Puccini (1858–1924).
[4] String Quartet No. 2 in F sharp minor, op. 10, composed 1907–8.
[5] *En Blabok* (1908), one of the most important works of Strindberg's last years.
[6] Knut Hamsun (1859–1952), Norwegian novelist and winner of Nobel Prize for literature, 1920.

work, continually coming out with something that surprises the world . . .

But good Heavens, why all this fuss over Strindberg, you may ask, when I really ought to be doing a bit of fussing over myself! Darling Helene, it's to speed me across the abyss which separates me from your next letter. Oh, lift up my sad soul once again, the door to it stands open to you day and night. Because it is *yours*, as it was in the beginning of time, and will be for ever.

Amen

(64)   6 p.m. Sunday 25th July 1909
My love has become so enormous and all-absorbing I can hardly credit others besides you with the right to exist! And I feel as if it's a different person performing all the external actions like breathing, eating, moving, thinking, reading, composing, drawing, etc; all these things only take place *through you*. I begin to doubt if I really exist at all, or whether I am not a mere creature of your imagination! Am I sitting here alone in my room, while the others are amusing themselves at the Annenheim? Perhaps I am lying dead in my bed, and they stand round in mourning, little guessing that my spirit imagines it is writing letters! Or perhaps when I was sitting by the lake a little while ago, I fell head-first into the water; or was that only what I wanted to do? But no, I can see in front of me the poster of the regatta, which I have just taken down from the wall. And next to it a time-table I have been studying, to find out how best to get to you . . .

Mama and the Baroness have now come back from the Annenheim. With their 'too too solid flesh' they recall me to reality. I touch my forehead, which is full of cold sweat, and smile to myself in bewilderment, wondering if I am mad. Has my mind been clouded by the long absence from you and the pain of these last days? How can I tell? All I know is, I must come to you quickly, there is my salvation, life, eternity. Here at the Berghof, away from *you*, I am threatened from all sides, and would like to withdraw from everybody, until the time, beloved, when I can at last embrace you once more . . .

(65)   Monday afternoon,
                                                    26th July 1909
I am in a state of high excitement, what with the hope of seeing

73

you soon, and probably getting a few lines tomorrow, which may decide the date and time for me to leave here, the time when I shall arrive—and see you coming towards me! Once I am there, should your parents hear of it—well, the old man can't do more than refuse to speak to you, and your Mama will no doubt turn a blind eye if I stay a few days longer; she may pretend she knows nothing about it. The only question is, where's the nearest and least dangerous place for me to sleep? . . .

Oh, I go quite mad when I think that I shall be near you, even if it's only for a few hours, that I shall see you and convince myself that you still love me and are not angry, that it was only this horrible interval which has pulled us apart. I know how serenely and happily the days can pass if we are together long enough: unspoiled by being apart, by having no time, or by the intrusion of other people, the *Schwarzalben*. That's why I want to come to you, so that you recognize my love again. A touch of my hand will be so much more convincing than all the closely written pages I write or have written, and I'll see from deep down in your heavenly eyes that I have been wrong, that your angry letter was only a bad dream of mine or of yours, Helene.

I keep reading through that letter, and finding new bits I haven't answered. For instance, your talking about people who would smile at the idea that anybody can love the same woman for a lifetime. More fools they then! Such loves don't happen often, I admit, even with great men. But that does not mean that they never happen. One may not have found the right woman, another that the woman who seemed his soulmate proved faithless and deceiving, and a third might himself have been making love all round the place. But all this is no proof it can't happen. Also, of course, it's rare to fall in love with the right partner straight away; but even the 'little loves' are among the world's joys. So she needn't be the first love, as long as she's the last!

Some never find her (Beethoven), and yet are in raptures over the *immortal* beloved (Brahms, Hugo Wolf), while they somehow keep going. Others really find the right woman, a Mathilde Wesendonck[1] or a Charlotte von Stein,[2] but are torn away by Fate, not by any diminution of their love. Others again are like Strindberg: cheated more than once when thinking they had found such a woman—yet still not despairing, still believing unshakably that

[1] Mathilde Wesendonck (1828–1902), Wagner's great friend.
[2] Charlotte von Stein (1742–1827), Goethe's friend.

74

eternal living together is possible. The thing is a rarity, but no great man will believe it doesn't exist. At worst he may admit that with his temperament he wouldn't be much good, but even that is because he has never met the real partner to whom he has felt irresistibly drawn.

But suppose *you* were to desert *me*, Helene, I wonder what I should do. Never touch another woman, to prove that you were the right partner, or philander with seven wrong ones every week till I give up the ghost? Anyhow, I'm sure it will never happen. For I believe that you have forgiven me and that your love for me is as great as it used to be. What an optimist I am!

(66)   Wednesday, 28th July 1909
This morning I received a wonderful picture postcard. What a lovely mountain lake! It must be quite near you. I must admit, I'd forgive you if you 'looked or could look at such beauties of nature more tenderly and fondly than you look at me', as Peter Altenberg so finely distinguishes. But there is still a big difference between our loves, because for me you are the rarest beauty of nature, you are my mountain lake! And if you were standing beside me, the scenery would pale before your beauty, which is perfect human nature ...

I can't wait to see your unforgettable beauty once more. Oh my Helene, the very thought of it, and this glorious summer day as well, can make an old grizzler like me understand how one can shout aloud for sheer joy!

Your own
Alban

(67)   Thursday morning,
                                                    29th July 1909
Where are they now, the blissful days of peace and solitude? Sometimes in the mornings I've gone outside the house to see heaven and earth motionless before me, so that you could almost hear the stillness, and my heart was always filled with serenity and solemn wonder. But today chaos reigns supreme here—perhaps you can even see it in the shakiness of my writing! Hubbub everywhere; wild confusion in the kitchen, Mama calling and clattering about the house, with the Baroness in tow; Elk[1] giggling away in the room

[1] Elk Miethke, friend of Berg's sister, Smaragda, wife of a Viennese art-dealer.

75

with Smaragda (she came here last night on a visit); my room being turned upside down because Hermann is arriving in the afternoon; and four dogs quarrelling—our two dachs', Mala and Lidi, and Elk's two terriers. And here am I in the midst of all this, needing peace to come safely through love's sorrows and joys. I feel it's a bit like the state of society, bursting with excitement over Blériot,[1] as if he were conquering new worlds, and forgetting all about the death of Liliencron,[2] our greatest poet.

Perhaps I am ungrateful. There were times, and not so very long ago either, when I wanted life and animation. The peace of the Berghof weighed heavily upon me, I called it boring and wished my friends were here, people, amusements, excursions, parties. But now everybody else but you seems an intrusion on my privacy, and all I wish is to spend my days in quietness and solitude, until I can join my existence for ever with yours. But can't the Berghof supply solitude? Oh no, from the cackling hens to the poetic Elk everyone conspires to shatter my nerves, so that I long to shout at the whole lot of them: 'Be quiet, for Heaven's sake, be quiet, don't you realize I need only one voice in the whole world, the voice that sounds like bells—PLEASE BE QUIET.'

Your last letter has just come. You say I can't come to you at Trahütten, you want me to wait for six weeks. Six weeks! All that time before I see you again—how can I bear it? Please HELP ME, in my direct need.

And how can I endure the enormous injustice, the vile cruelty, that sacred things like our love, that love itself should be contaminated by the touch of a coarse and violent hand?[3]

By the way, Helene, before I forget (my thoughts are in such a whirl), give the postman a good bribe. I'll pay for it. And the maid too, you can say it comes from me. Then at least, I hope to God, our letter-writing won't be stopped too.

I've read through the letter ten times, and the things in it have made me so distraught I don't know where to start answering. Look, Helene, perhaps there's still a way somehow for me to visit you, even if it's only for one day, only from 11 a.m. till 4 p.m. I believe—with the help of Anna, who I'm sure won't let us down—

[1] Louis Blériot (1872–1936), made the first cross-channel flight on 25th July 1909.
[2] The great poet and novelist Detlev von Liliencron (1844–1909), had died on 22nd July.
[3] Helene's father had begun to interfere with her relationship with Berg. (See Letter 65.)

it could be arranged so that nobody sees us. (And with the same manœuvre for my travelling home afterwards.)

Oh, when I think it might be possible after all, I grow a tiny bit calmer. Listen, talk it over with Anna. If your mother knew I was coming to see you just for a few hours, I feel certain she wouldn't refuse to help us. That's one good thing about the world's cruelties. It makes those who suffer from them nobler and kinder, more compassionate . . .

Though nothing can penetrate my loneliness, the doors of yours shall burst open from my love, and no jailor of a father will be able to prevent it. But I can understand now the basis of the whole Trahütten system. He wants to be undisputed master of all your personalities, and keep four people as his slaves—defying you to escape if you can! A real Styrian Napoleon I'd call him.

Alban

(68)   Friday, 30th July 1909

Enclosed you find a telegram which reached Hermann this morning.[1] So my ticket for *Parsifal* is safely reserved, and I've got something nice to look forward to. But I feel so low at the moment, I can't weigh the five or six hours of pure delight against the twenty-four hour train journey to Bayreuth sleeping in strange hotels, etc., which always has a very depressing effect on me. And I suppose I can't come to you after all, and then in the autumn I'll be dependent on your parents' favour, and they only let me see you once or twice a week. The thought makes me so miserable that it's hard work trying to look happy for Hermann's benefit, after the money and effort he's spent providing me with this treat.

You'll say I'm pretending to be blasé, and it's one of the things about me you can't bear. But some day you'll really understand, Helene, that nothing does give me joy if you aren't there to share it. For instance, if I had the choice between having our days at the Wachau over again or going to Bayreuth, I'd let the whole of Wagner and his *Parsifal* go hang, and be in ecstasies of joy. Such a fool I am, Helene, such an innocent fool.[2]

Oh, Helene, I am sometimes, as at this moment, so overwhelmed

---

[1] Hermann had bought a ticket for Berg to see *Parsifal* at Bayreuth.
[2] An allusion to *Parsifal*, the 'Reine Tor'.

with desire to have you at my side for even a second, and to die for you the death of love.[1]

Yours
Alban

(69)   Monday, 2nd August 1909
... I sleep a good deal, and when I'm awake I seem to lead the complete writer's life. That's to say I'm writing one or two chapters a day of a vast novel entitled

HELENE AND ALBAN
The Story of a Great Love

Very likely I've finished one volume of it already! We might collect seventy or eighty letters, put them in order, and make them into quite a nice book—a present for your old man? It could even convert him!

Anyhow I'm altogether taken up with the inner life. That's how I can sit or lie for hours, with perhaps no tangible results except a few hasty sketches on some sheets of music, or an hour of sombre, passionate improvising on the piano, or reading a page of a delightful book that has more to say than whole novels—or, of course, endlessly writing my letters to you, often only in my head, but then putting them down on paper, at all hours of the day. No routine there, and certainly no monotony—Fate with all its variations takes care of that. For how very different the day looks when there's no letter from you, or I hear of Liliencron's death, from a day when two letters from you arrive together, or the *Fackel*[2] appears, or new photos from you, etc. ...

The piano is more or less playable, but as I've said before, I use it very little. Smaragda and Hermann accompany their orgies on it, playing and singing all the operettas and songs. But they haven't even got the real spirit for that; any café pianist could teach them a lesson. We had a big argument about that last night, till I showed them how this sort of music *should* be played. Would you have believed I could do it?! ...

---

[1] An allusion to the *Liebestod* in *Tristan und Isolde*.
[2] *Die Fackel* (*The Torch*), a critical and satirical Viennese magazine, edited by Karl Kraus.

Tuesday morning,
3rd August 1909

A blazingly hot day yesterday, followed by a terrific thunderstorm last night. And now the air is icy cold, one might almost be
in some Alpine shelter. The atmosphere is bleak too, adding to my
own bleakness of spirit. I keep thinking how cosy it would be despite
wind and weather, if only you were here. And how the hours would
fly, each full of new diversions and delights.

Imagine one such day. In the early morning our nerves would
be a-quiver as we rushed to meet each other—for the first kiss, the
first embrace. Then into the forest, talking gaily or exchanging
memories sweet or sad. The sun shines ever stronger, bringing
quiet desire for the dark green waves of the lake. Then you come
out of the cabin, with the sheen of your white body, the fragrance
of your warm breath. We swim out into the waves, then back at last
to the shore and our bath-robes. You lie with me in the grass and the
sun's splendour; joy seeps through every pore of my body, that body
which would wither without the power of your beauty. And another
physical faculty, which I have long been without, would again
emerge: my appetite! In the cool, sheltered veranda we should enjoy
Topfenhaluschka[1] or other simple dishes as if they were ambrosia.
Then up into the quietness and peace of the cool room.

How short the rest of the day would seem, to taste everything our
senses and nerves hanker after: music, singing, nature, excercise in
the fresh air, drives, good books, fresh berries, boating, sunsets—
all in a mad jumble to revel in at every chance. Then evening comes,
the lanterns go out, and only the light of a candle shines here and
there through the green shutters. All sounds of man and beast have
subsided, and there seems only a single sound merging from the
noises of the day, the chirping of the crickets, the continuous rippling
of the wall outside the door. Then, when I open the door of your
room, then, oh then, there would be nothing to part us any more.
We should 'blissfully fall asleep in the arms of love'.[2]

In the morning, long after the first cock-crow, as you rubbed your
dear sleepy eyes, a last fond embrace would close the circle of
happiness, of fulfilment: life's purpose attained.

Such a day would be worth the most miserable, tormented life;
worth death itself.

Alban

[1] A popular Viennese potato dish of Czech origin.
[2] Quotation from the poem 'Liebesode' by Otto Erich Hartleben (1864-1905)
which Berg had set to music. Later published as No. 6 of the *Seven Early Songs*.

(71)   Wednesday, 4th August
... So here is *Die Fackel*,[1] another marvel of deep wisdom and brilliant humour. Read the *Glossen*[2] first (I've marked them with a cross). To appreciate the wisdom, and experience the beauty and stylistic subtlety of the 'Chinese Wall', you need complete quiet and concentration. I think it's extraordinarily fine, the finest thing, next to the 'Apocalypse', that Kraus has ever written.[3] I had to read it three times, and every time with increased interest and pleasure. I was delighted, too, that at the end of the magazine Kraus prints the words Dehmal spoke by Liliencron's grave.[4] Reading this whole issue gave me a joy of spirit such as I have rarely known, free from all dross and disappointment. I think of the mediocre productions of Wagner and Strauss at the Vienna Opera, the concerts this year, where Mahler's symphonies are being so wretchedly performed. Against all this mass of disappointments in every field, here is a masterpiece—the latest issue of the *Fackel!* Oh, if only you like it half as much as I do!

Wholly and for ever yours
Alban

(72)   Berghof, 5th August 1909
It's become the regular thing for me to take up my pencil every morning and start writing, even when I've nothing really to say.

One comforting thought shot through my mind today. When we are back in Vienna, we can make ourselves independent of the old man—by playing truant from the long evenings at the Opera House you are allowed to go to. After all, we can have Wagner's music as often as we wish, if we have a piano, your voice and our own unlimited imagination. But we can't have ourselves whenever we want, so let us at least use the rare evenings of happiness—granted us by Weingartner's programme—to stay away from the noisy Opera House, where we are watched from every corner with hatred, malice and treachery, and meet in my quiet room. Surely we'll be more truly inspired there in our consuming love than the

---

[1] See footnote Letter 69.
[2] Karl Kraus's short, biting commentaries on Viennese daily life.
[3] *The Chinese Wall* and *Apocalypse* are two essays by Kraus on the hypocrisy of society's moral code.
[4] See footnote Letter 67. Liliencron's funeral oration was delivered by the poet Richard Dehmel (1863–1920).

Wagnerians, who can only find their inspiration with the aid of ham rolls, cream cakes and Pilsner beer.[1]

And if it's the music you're thinking of, we really don't need a Weingartner. Remember our music-making together those last days in Vienna—how beautiful it was! But there was still a sort of holy shyness between us. When that is gone, it will be even more satisfying and splendid, and you'll be either horrified or sent to sleep by the mechanical, spiritless traversities of Wagner they put on nowadays at the Vienna Opera. Of course the boredom and misery of five hours' *mezzoforte* performance would be out-weighed for me by the happiness of having you beside me—though even then I should be in pain to feel you concentrating on such a performance, only to learn how artistry is *not* achieved; forgetting that there is a heart beating beside you with nobler rhythms and greater strength than the hammer of Mime.[2]

That's why it would be fine if we missed the Opera evenings! Forgive my going on so long about it, but poor separated lovers like us have nothing left but words and again words, until the words come together to make another whole letter! And here it is—my dearest.

(73)   Friday, 6th August 1909
Bad times for me again: no letter from you all yesterday. I wonder if your last letter was a fraction less loving than the one before it. For days Mama, Elk and Smaragda have been pleading with me to let them take me to the Summer Season Theatre, but they had given up hope of my coming. Then yesterday afternoon, when the last post still brought nothing, I was so frightened of a lonely night with a thousand ghosts, that I told them I'd go with them. Oh dear, it was a badly acted farce, hopelessly boring, and only made me more miserable than ever. A great relief to be riding home through the dark night.

The drive in the carriage, in fact, was the only thing that appealed to me. Because I kept thinking of that carriage drive after I had seen you off at Villach Station, one of the most beautiful and poignant memories of our love. When we got home, I read the *Parsifal* score for hours, and then managed to go to sleep.

Now I am in bed, writing this letter, counting the minutes till

[1] Refreshments sold at the buffet of the Opera House during intervals.
[2] In Wagner's *Siegfried*.

the mid-day post. To be sentenced to go to Bayreuth without the comfort of a letter from you—that would be terrible indeed.

Mid-day

Oh joy, oh ecstasy!

Your Wednesday's letter came just now, and a wave of happiness flooded over me, greater than I have ever known before.

So you *will* be coming to the Berghof! Such joy is more than I can grasp. Oh, I could fall at your feet, fling my arms round your mother's neck, do a thousand things to show my gratitude for this terrific happiness.

Anyhow, Helene, please tell her somehow how happy I am. To feel she has brought this about should uplift her, and make up a little for all the wrong she has suffered at the hands of the joyless one, the *Schwarzalbe*.

To think that while your letter was giving me the prospect of all my longings being fulfilled, you were reading my letter, product of those longings, imagining the day I would spend with you at the Berghof. And now this dream can and will come true! Oh, Helene, how shall I endure the days of expectation?

Tomorrow I leave for Bayreuth. I'll be travelling on the famous new Tauernbahn,[1] via Gastein, Salzburg, Munich, Nuremberg, where I stay the night, and on to Bayreuth Sunday morning. *Parsifal* at four o'clock, stay the night in Bayreuth, and then home as soon as possible . . .

Now I have to pack, drive to the Annenheim and weigh myself, then go to bed early, so as to be up at half-past five. Oh, if I had to get up that early because *you* were arriving, it would be no hardship —but merely for *Parsifal* it's quite a sacrifice! That's because my love of nature and music, and all other joys mental or physical, are centred within me, whereas my whole capacity for love itself finds its centre and culmination in you.

Your own

(74)

Nuremberg,
Saturday night,
7th August 1909

So here I am lying in my hotel room, exhausted after a thirteen-

[1] The railway across the Tauern, the eastern part of the Alps, connecting Salzburg with Trieste and Venice, had been opened in 1907.

hour train journey, disgruntled and disconsolate. I wish I were at the Berghof, with all my familiar belongings round me. I am no good at travelling, being torn away from my usual environment. Still, most of my melancholy comes from the fact that I can't have you with me, the only one who could make me forget all discomforts. But you are not here, and I, who look forward as a rule to solitude, now find it hard to bear. How annoying that the train connections from Bayreuth are so bad. It means that on the return journey, unless I travel by night, I probably shan't get here till Monday evening, have to stay another night at an hotel, and not be back at the Berghof till Tuesday. I wonder if you'd feel as dreary as I do, or whether you'd rather be *without me* when away from your familiar surroundings.

I have to get up even earlier tomorrow, so I'd better try to get some sleep. Meanwhile, good-night, dear love.

Your own
Alban

(75)   Bayreuth, 10.30 p.m. Sunday,
8th August 1909

I'm writing straight after *Parsifal*.[1] It was magnificent, over-whelming. I wish we could have shared this stirring, uplifting experience, but as that was not to be—oh, if only you were here now! Words cannot give you anywhere near the tremendous impression, shattering yet life-enhancing, which this work made on me. Futile trying to describe music like that, and all I can say is that I miss you now more than ever. If only I could sit silent at your side, holding your hand in mine, if only—but how much that only would be! Because you are not here, I cannot savour to the full the delight that was mine this afternoon and evening. So I crawled into my room, taking up the *Parsifal* score with me, to have a little extra celebration after my feast of music.

Tomorrow some sightseeing perhaps, or perhaps not; and then to Nuremberg, where I'll have to spend another night away from home. Day after tomorrow off at 8 a.m., arriving at Villach at 10 p.m. Fourteen hours' journey in sweltering heat—how very pleasant! Sorry I'm making such a fuss about it. I just feel rather worn out,

---

[1] Bayreuth had at that time the sole right—granted to the Festspielhaus by Richard Wagner himself—to perform *Parsifal*.

that's why I'm so apprehensive about all the travelling. But what does that matter, so long as my soul is unscathed and thriving. There might not have been people in the audience at *Parsifal* as 'run down' today as I am, but I'm sure there wasn't one, not a single one, whose soul is bursting with health like mine.

Good-night, my darling

Alban

(76)   Nuremberg, 9th August 1909

What a lovely surprise today. When I arrived from Bayreuth, there was a letter from Mama, which she had sent to the Grand Hotel, and when I opened it, I found a letter in it from you, dearest —written on Friday. You can imagine how I immediately saw Nuremberg in quite a different light, the heat much easier to bear, and so on. I'd have liked to go off somewhere quiet with the little letter, and with a full heart, answer everything it said. But I had already spoken to a cousin of mine[1] on the telephone, and promised to visit him. He lives a little way out of town, has a wife and two small children. So I drove out there and spent a real Bavarian evening with them. Good, honest, straightforward folk, laughing heartily at everything—so that I felt a bit solemn and out of place. Still, the evening passed quite pleasantly, and now I'm sitting in the hotel again, writing these few lines to you, my dearest.

As I have to get off very early tomorrow, I want to force myself to go to sleep. So I'll only tell you briefly that this morning while I was still at Bayreuth I went to see some of the town's sights, such as Wahnfried,[2] Wagner's house, the house where Liszt[3] died, the statue of King Ludwig, showing the wonderful head of a boy favourite, which has ivy growing out of it; then the house where Jean Paul[4] lived and died, etc. etc.—what with picture postcards and sights, I spent quite a lot of money!

In the train tomorrow I hope to have the chance of answering your letter. And now quickly to bed, as usual to dream, before I sleep, of the days you will be spending with us at the Berghof.

---

[1] Konrad Berg (1846–1900). Alban Berg's father, originally came from Fürth, near Nuremberg.
[2] The house Wagner built for himself and his family in Bayreuth in 1874.
[3] Franz Liszt (1811–1886).
[4] Jean Paul (1763–1825), famous German novelist and humorist.

I can tell you, if the three or four weeks aren't over soon, I shall go mad with joyful expectation—and trying not to expect too much! One more good-night, my darling,

Your very own!

(77)   Berghof,
                                    Thursday, 12th August 1909
This morning a wasp stung me in my right hand, middle finger. It began to swell and has now become so thick I can hardly move the fingers; quite painful. Well, that's life in the country! Writing slow and painful too, so I'll be fairly brief in answering the rest of your Monday's letter.

La Mildenburg[1] wasn't at Bayreuth. Nobody decent there at all—'except for yours truly'! Altogether, Bayreuth is an empty delusion. I'd never want to set foot in it again, but for the unforgettable *Parsifal*. If Wagner had not long ago turned in his grave, I am sure, he would rise and take flight in disgust at what goes on in and around Wahnfried. And he would recognize that the piece of his soul, which he here imagined to find, was only an imagination—a peace imagination.[2]

Picture the scene. Left and right of the *Festspielhaus* a Festspiel beer-house and a Festspiel restaurant. I arrived at the theatre in devout mood to find the entire audience (mostly Bavarians and Americans) disporting themselves in those places—led by Siegfried Wagner[3] and his friends. After the first act the same business started again, and I could have run off into the fields nearby and wept. People strolled around laughing and chattering, feeling they simply must have a drink, or else ordering supper for the next interval. And again Siegfried Wagner set the tone—wearing a fresh stand-up collar he had put on after the heat and exertion of conducting. He circulated wherever somebody might ask him for an autograph, and certainly did his best to be solemn and festive at once.

Then we were called back to the theatre for the second act. I had some Munich folk behind me, looking like caricatures out of

[1] Anna Bahr-Mildenburg (1872–1947), dramatic soprano of the Vienna Opera House, married to the Austrian dramatist and novelist, Hermann Bahr.
[2] Play on words: 'Wahnfried' might be loosely translated as 'peace-imagination'. 'Wahn' is an illusion or delusion, 'Friede' is peace—'Wahnfried', the place where he imagined he would find peace.
[3] Richard Wagner's son, Siegfried Wagner (1869–1930), was principal conductor of the Festspiel-season in 1909.

Simplicissimus,[1] and heard one of them say: 'Now for the flower scene, nice and sentimental.' *Parsifal* sentimental! And Wagner wrote his music for people like this! Then Cosima[2] appeared, and of course everybody had to turn round in great curiosity to look at Bayreuth's talented business manageress.

After the second act we had a repetition of the first interval, only guzzling was now more or less *de rigeur*. The Bavarians drank beer, the Americans champagne. Siegfried Wagner had changed from his immaculate white tennis kit into a dark suit, and with all the autograph hunters hardly had time to enjoy his 'Parsifal steak' with rice and stewed fruit, before it was time to go back for Act Three. After all those refreshments, people could hold out until ten o'clock! The whole place is a horrible exploitation of the Wagner idea. Extremely distressing, to see what the 'German nation' had done to the greatest of all Germans.

As to the performance itself, it might have been up to the highest standards of those when Wagner was alive, but hasn't quite caught up with the advances made since then. You could compare it to a first-class production in pre-Mahler Vienna. That's especially so for sets and costumes. In the middle of the forest you can still see the smooth boards of the stage, with pieces of rock and grassy mounds for handy seats; also the very unsubstantial wings and side scenes, etc. Cheap and inartistic, in fact. What is Roller against that?

The orchestra isn't top standard either, *nor* his direction. Nor the chorus. But the soloists are fine, first-class singers: all the same, I believe that with Weidemann, Mayr, Schmedes[3] and la Mildenburg, an even more brilliant performance could be achieved—though not with Siegfried conducting!

But I'd rather talk of all this than write, and anyhow *Parsifal* is still a miracle—I'd rather remember that than all the disgusting atmosphere of Bayreuth. ... I've written more than I meant as it is, and strained my hand quite a lot, so an end to this scrawl. Good-bye, dearest, think as much and as often and as fondly as you can of Your own

Alban

[1] Weekly humorous periodical, published in Munich.
[2] Cosima Wagner (1837–1930), Wagner's second wife, daughter of Franz Liszt.
[3] Hermann Weidemann, Richard Mayr and Erik Schmedes were prominent members of Gustav Mahler's Vienna ensemble.

(78)   13th August 1909

. . . My hand is not better yet, I ought really to keep it very quiet,
so that the inflammation won't spread to the arm. But I just must
write to you, to answer such a loving letter . . .

You're surprised about the Bayreuth programme. Yes, they're
trying to save money there all over the place, so as to make the
maximum profit out of the 'Wagner idea'. I noticed afterwards
another programme, without advertisements, with two singers
shown for each part and the one appearing that particular night
underlined in blue pencil!

Strange—time's passing so slowly now. When I first came back
to the Berghof, I was more or less resigned . . . But now, since I've
known you are coming, my longing and joy and impatience have
grown so fast that I feel I'm almost going mad with them. The
thought of the happiness in store is too much for me, I can't think
of anything else. I'm simply living for the great day two months
ahead.

It reminds me of my school-days. I can remember so clearly:
if there was a visit to the Opera, I would come home at lunch-time,
meaning to get down to my homework and get that quickly finished.
But I was so full of anticipation that I couldn't do anything all
afternoon but keep thinking about the great occasion and how
wonderful it was going to be. Well, now I've got a few weeks, such
long weeks, and all I can do is think about a far greater occasion,
and wait and wait.

Yes, I do remember Strindberg's remark about the three big
humbugs, it's quite extraordinary. But I suppose if a man of
Strindberg's intellect—well, even of my intellect, come to that—
were completely unmusical, so that music meant nothing to him, and
he went to a musical holy-of-holies like Bayreuth, he *would* find
the whole thing humbug. For Mahler to consider Richard Strauss
a humbug of the worst sort is also not so surprising when you come
to think of it. All of us are such a strange mixture with unexpected
tastes and reactions . . .

(79)   Berghof, Saturday,
                                           14th August 1909,
                                           morning

. . . Hermann is here again, and as usual there is a good deal of
noise and heat. The heat is mostly generated by my flaunting in his

87

face one of my unpopular statements, for instance that the crowd are always wrong, that our and the world's salvation will not come through Zeppelins and motor cars, that the German emperor is the antithesis of everything I believe in, etc. It's really quite hard, though, to argue with a Philistine like him. He'll say things like 'the motor car possesses the greatest power on earth, no woman can resist it—or its owner'. That leaves me speechless for a bit, and even if I carefully answer all his points afterwards, he still feels he's won the argument. He knows his world, such as it is, so there are a lot of other small ways like that, in which he somehow gets the better of me.

As for the noise, it's not only from Hermann. For Elk's husband has also turned up, and the alcohol makes quite a bond for all these different characters. As a joke I suggested opening a Berghof bar in which I would mix all the drinks from coloured water and similar liquids. Hermann and Elk's husband decided to take the bar idea seriously, and ordered a terrific assortment—and quantity—of whisky, champagne and liqueurs. So you can imagine the alcohol consumption that goes on here. More 'country life' for you. Last night it was Elk's birthday, and the celebrations became pretty noisy. To keep up appearances I had a glass or two of wine, but kept a clear head and remained very calm. I was just going to bed, in fact, when Elks' husband said something I felt I had to take up. This led to a long, serious argument between us at quite a high level—the others took hardly any part in it—and by the time we had fought each other to a standstill, it was three o'clock, in the morning. Going up to bed I noticed that I was the only person who could still walk steadily, and I felt ashamed of having once more wasted serious argument on 'inebriates' . . .

(80)   Wednesday, 18th August 1909
A holiday for all the others[1]—and a sad day for me! . . . I can't remain silent at the idea that you may not come here after all. Helene, you must bring it off, you *must*. Surely your father's sour face doesn't mean more to you than the terrible pain you would cause your beloved? Or are you playing the 'obedient daughter' against your own better judgment? That surely can't give you the

[1] The 18th August—birthday of the Emperor Francis Joseph—was celebrated as a holiday throughout Austria.

same satisfaction as living up to your deepest convictions of truth and beauty.

But I mustn't try to set you against your parents—and I'm not doing that. Those two questions were only a substitute for the much bigger one of how much you love me. And of course that question answers itself without any words, without your even opening your lovely mouth.

I was really only wanting to give you some advice, on how to make your old man give his permission, although you know all that much better than I do—and in case it should be difficult for you, Anna, his favourite daughter, can squeeze it out of him. Please ask her very, very sincerely from me. Although the visit here may not mean much to her, she might do it for your sake and mine. Anyhow, the time should pass quite quickly for her here as at Trahütten, with plenty of music-making which she also enjoys. For quite a time I've been thinking of playing *Parsifal* to you, and now you ask me to do that in Vienna? Couldn't it be at the Berghof just as well? Anna would also appreciate it, and then there are *Elektra*, *Ariane*,[1] Mahler symphonies, Schoenberg's *Lieder* or my own—if any of all that is welcome. With walks and drives and boating trips and swims, the time Anna sacrifices for us shouldn't be too boring for her. Please, darling Helene, tell her of this very great favour she could do us. With her help and your Mama's consent, it should be easy to get your father's too . . .

(81)   Undated
                                       (August 1909)
That was a very interesting review of *Pippa*[2] you enclosed with your Friday's letter. I don't generally care for great works being too much 'interpreted', like the attempts to find hidden meanings behind every character in Wagner's operas. For my part they can stay hidden, I love Wagner regardless of them. Sometimes, I must admit, it can be quite interesting to read the judgment of someone paid by the line on someone writing for eternity. I'm thinking of Ibsen's plays, which are always being symbolically interpreted, although he protested against it—and now it's happened with

[1] Berg was very fond of the opera *Ariane et Barbe-Bleu* by Paul Dukas (1865–1935).
[2] *Und Pippa tanzt* (*And Pippa Dances*), is a romantic fairy-story play, written in 1906 by Gerhart Hauptmann. Seventeen years later Berg considered using it as libretto for an opera.

Pippa. Only the review has confused me about the play's content, which makes me all the keener to read it again. For instance, I like to think that at the end old Huhn dies, i.e. that the triumph of reality over the world of the imagination is ephemeral . . .

I have known such brutal intrusions into the world I have created for myself. Created, though: not merely dreamed of—there's the difference. For even if my aspirations are not yet fulfilled, I am living in a world where 'brutal reality' can do me no harm, for I confront it with my own vision of the ideal reality . . .

Bayreuth couldn't kill *Parsifal* for me, nor could the ghastly horde of homosexual Wagnerians spoil Wagner, nor Karpath[1] destroy Schoenberg, any more than darkness can overcome light. The triumph of all that is great and holy is not something from my imagination, it is from the reality within me which alone is decisive. After all, when Christ died on the Cross, killed on the instigation of his chief critics, the Pharisees, his triumph was not imaginary, but in the reality of his resurrection. And to follow him as best I can, I must seek my salvation in an ideal, pure reality of the spirit, a resurrection from the brutal materialism of ordinary life . . .

(82)   Berghof, 23rd August 1909

Beloved, you ask in your letter: what is our great goal? Clearly it's not the world's titles and honours, which may or may not come; either way this should not matter to us. But a goal there is, of course, and you are certainly on the way to finding it, a way that leads past all the external worldly goals up to the perfection of each human soul. The nearer to this I feel I am approaching, the more I recognize how long the road still is before we arrive at the mountain top, which from the valley of our lowly existence looked so easy to reach: the summit where only the noblest ones dwell, where *Parsifal*, Mahler's Ninth, *Faust*, *Pippa* and a few other master-pieces can alone be created . . .

Here the goal and destination is all-important. Nietzsche uses the image of 'new seas' towards which his ship is irresistibly heading. Unfortunately I haven't got a copy of Nietzsche at hand; to quote him on this vital question would be more convincing than anything I can say.

But I am sure of one thing, and don't need Nietzsche or any other

[1] Ludwig Karpath (1866–1936), an influential conservative Viennese music critic.

philosopher to tell me: the way to the 'new seas' and 'highest peaks' leads *past* all the paltry aims of this petty world, with a single horizon kept always in view, to become a good, honourable, noble character.

Oh, Helene, are we not going to tread this path together—I with you, you with me? Hand in hand, soul to soul, so that we could ask that question from *Rosmersholm*[1]: 'I know not whether it is I, that walk with you, or you that walk with me?'

Alban

(83)   Monday, 23rd August 1909
... I am so very anxious about when you are coming; longing for the day when I can give myself up to utter joy and hope. Carola must certainly have agreed, and with four against one, Papa would surely give in! You've got any amount of time to choose from, and we at our end would arrange things accordingly. We'll even stay at the Berghof till the end of September if it suits you better to come later. By the end of August the house will be clear of all our tiresome visitors, and ready to receive *you*. After that I don't care if the earth swallows it up, for it will never see more wonderful days!

Please let us at last fix the date of your visit. You wrote some time ago so confidently, about how fast the three or four weeks would pass. And now you're making my days turn into years, years of impatient waiting, so that I've changed into an old man. I'll be dead soon if you're not careful! ...

(84)   Tuesday, 24th August 1909
For four hours I lay on my bed, counting the minutes till the post came. After an age I heard a knock on my door, and they brought me your letter. At first I didn't dare open it, but at last I did; and when I read it, I felt as if I had just started to come out of a long illness, the first sign of returning health ...

I would like to stroke your soft hair for hours, hold your dear face in my hands, in deepest love ...

You needn't have any worries about the dates being inconvenient. I'm sure you know—and Anna too—that I'm not the only one

[1] Drama by Ibsen (1887).

looking forward tremendously to your coming. Smaragda and Mama keep on asking eagerly whether anything definite has been fixed.

But can't you arrange to stay longer, Helene, than just these three days? I'm sure your old man won't go to Vienna before the end of September, and you don't need to be there before him. Just imagine what it would mean to me to have you there for three or four weeks, or even for only a fortnight. These two months which are now completely wasted, for body, mind and spirit, would at least be *spiritually* redeemed. Perhaps they'd even bear mental fruit, giving me new creative power and inspiration; and my body and nerves, which have been through so much, would be fortified by having you there for more than a few days, my blossoming flower!

So make sure it will be a nice long stay, my dearest darling Helene. I believe it would do you good too, to get away for a bit from your father's grimness, and the whole oppressive atmosphere ... Tonight I can look forward to my first peaceful night, when I shall perhaps be granted the joy of dreaming of you. And oh perhaps, perhaps, I shan't need dreams any more but shall have you really and truly in my arms. Oh my darling!

Your own

(85)　　　　　　　　　　　　　　　Saturday, 28th August 1909
... Your letter has just arrived—and
I am finished
The appalling news that you aren't coming,[1] and that Fritz is going to be with you that fortnight, leaves me speechless, completely shattered. What on earth shall I do the whole fortnight? Let my body go perhaps, so that great physical pain will help me forget this latest and worst mental pain. Perhaps that will then be the end of it all. Oh, your letter is so terribly sad for me that the loving bits in it can't yet reach my lacerated soul.

And Fritz will be out there—that's almost the worst of it. Is he staying right to the end of your time?

Oh, Helene, Helene—this is the bitterest blow ever——
Till my last breath

Your own
Alban

[1] After long family scenes Helene's father definitely forbade her and Anna to go to the Berghof.

(86)   29th August 1909
    I am alone, the others have gone off to see the village church
festival. They kept nagging me and trying to make me go with them,
but in the end they left me 'at home'. When I still hoped you would
be coming here, I felt this place might yet become a real home. The
Berghof would be converted into a *Friedhof*,[1] where one of my most
sacred relics was buried—a glorious memory which I should tend
lovingly and visit in reverence. But now it's a scrap yard, a place
I would shun, because the disappointments buried there smell
to high heaven, like rotting dogs, decomposing flesh eaten away by
maggots.
    After receiving your letter, my first thought was to get away from
here, right away. But when I'd worked over all possibilities, I
reached the obvious decision, to stay here and travel home with
you! At first I had the idea of going to Deutsch-Landsberg or
Trahütten some days *before*. If you think this can be arranged,
please let me know immediately ... But in case this too is made
impossible for me, then I will be at the station in Graz on the 9th,
to travel home with you alone or with all of you ...
    And if I had the great joy and surprise of being able to meet you
earlier, either for a few days at Trahütten or for the one day at
Deutsch-Landsberg, that would give us still more time. Just think,
Helene, how much every hour means, when we have been parted
for 1440 hours!
    My heart has begun to beat faster in impatience and excitement,
so I close this letter, in which I have talked myself into new hopes.
Which is why it may seem to you quite crazy.
    Well, I *am* crazy! The two months, and now on top of that the
torments of jealousy.
    But darling, stay true to me, then even the worst cloud has the
brightest of silver linings.
                                        Yours, yours, yours

(87)   Monday, 30th August 1909
    In a recent issue of *Simplicissimus* there was a wonderful drawing
by the late lamented Rudolf Wilke,[2] with a good typical caption:
'If only the Lord had had me as His artistic adviser when He created

[1] Friedhof: a cemetery.
[2] Rudolf Wilke, German cartoonist.

93

the world—the sunset sky wouldn't have turned out so cheap and picture-postcard-like!'

I'm very pleased at my spiritual kinship with Wilke, the more so since I found out he was rather like me in appearance, tall and slim, with the same sort of face as mine—except for a huge beard. Everybody can see the similarity, myself included.

There's another outward similarity I've discovered between myself and one of the great ones: Gerhart Hauptmann is a passionate nail-biter! So are Mahler, Lichtenberg[1] and Altenberg—in very good company, aren't I! . . .

(88)   Tuesday, 31st August 1909

The Miethkes have invited me to spend a few days with them in Venice. In this most beautiful of cities, with all its splendid buildings and works of art, the time should pass quicker for me, much quicker than sitting here counting the hours until we see each other . . .

But if today I heard from you that you were coming out here for a few days, or that I might come to Trahütten, or that we had a clear week to go to the Wachau—why, I'd snap my fingers at Venice and the whole of Italy, or anywhere else people travel to, brandishing their Baedekers. Little I care for all the beauties of nature when I compare them to you; for you carry them all with you.

                                          Afternoon

Your letter is so sweet that I wouldn't dare complain again, although the chances of your visiting here seem to be gradually dwindling to nothing . . . As it is, I am madly happy because of that most glorious phrase you ever uttered; 'the chance of our getting married.' Thinking of these words, tears fill my eyes, tears of emotion, release, blissful happiness. I see the sun shining, feel the warm air . . . and know that at last, after two long years, my spring will turn to summer . . .

(89)   Wednesday
                                    1st September 1909,

. . . Yes, I can understand Schoenberg being hurt with me, and I

[1] Georg Christoph Lichtenberg (1742–1799), German satirical writer.

can understand your little rebuke. It does seem rather strange, but somehow I can't help it. I was looking forward to writing to Schoenberg and getting letters from him, but when I started on one, I realized I couldn't write him the ordinary conventional letter, 'I've now been a fortnight in the country, the weather is such-and-such, etc.' I admire him too much for that. I felt I must write him the same sort of deep, intimate letters as I do to you, only not so often, of course. Anyhow, I then found such letters can be written only once a day, and that had to be to you . . .

So I'd intended to write him the most beautiful letters, and now I haven't written to him at all. There was a card from Oppenheimer signed by Stein and Webern, with a note from Schoenberg at the bottom: 'Why don't you write?' No, I haven't even acknowledged that, and my silence must seem very puzzling. I feel sorrier about it than finding myself unable to compose anything—but as I say, I just can't help it . . .

(90)   Thursday, 2nd September 1909
. . . Your letter arrived this afternoon. That firm 'So we meet at Graz station on the 9th' stifles the last 'but' lingering on my lips, in case we could squeeze a few more hours together from miserly Fate . . .

This morning when I went to the post-office, I weighed myself on the scales at the Annenheim. My weight is now 10 stone 4, so I have put on over 2 lbs. My method seems to work . . . I'm sure I shall put on even more in Vienna, if you will only be a little kind to me! . . .

A week from today, and I shall have seen you. I shan't be able to sleep for joy that first night in Vienna, for the joyful anticipation of seeing you again next day in the garden. Perhaps it's just as well that, by not coming here, you made it easy for me to leave the Berghof. But then again perhaps not: what a radiant memory it would have been in my dismal existence.

Your, your
Alban

(91)   Friday, 3rd September 1909
    So I'm going to Venice after all. It was decided this morning, an hour ago; and there's hardly a minute left for me to pack my case.

Puts me off this travelling business again, if it stops me writing to you.

Still, in a few days all writing will become superfluous, and all the words so long unspoken will flow from our lips. Oh, when I think of your sweet lips and our first kiss, I cannot control my excitement . . .

I'm arriving at Graz at 1.26 p.m., while you, I expect, will have got there at 12.34 and had lunch. The train leaves at 2.45 and gets to Vienna at 8.35—I think that's right. Tiresome that there's no earlier train for me, so that I could be at Graz when you arrive . . .

(92)   Venice
                                               4th September 1909
How splendid it was to see Venice again, the first sight of St. Mark's Square, the first night ride in a gondola—and it showed me how much more I love you than I did the same time last year. For I now feel as if I am never alone, because I am thinking of you all the time: at every lovely view (how many there were today!) from the Alpine valleys, so incomparably beautiful, right up to the Venetian night at this moment with the moon shining down on a fairyland. All the time I am thinking of you, and the words I would say to you if you were here with me; and I am feeling the impression all this would make on you. Have you ever had the same experience, my only beloved, so distant and yet so very close to me? . . .

(93)   Venice, night of
                                            5th-6th September 1909
After a strenuous and tiring day, but with such overwhelming impressions, I must somehow write you a few lines—no time for much detail. Starting with people, I've met two friends of the Miethkes, who joined us here. One was the art-historian Meyer-Graefe,[1] whom I haven't found very pleasant, the other was Franz Blei,[2] whom I've been wanting to meet for some time. Lower part of his face strikingly like Mahler's, upper part—eyes, forehead, head —with something of Hauptmann; anyhow, it's a face you'd certainly like very much. Miethke and I had some interesting and stimulating conversations with them . . .

[1] Julius Meyer-Graefe (1867–1935), German art critic.
[2] Franz Blei (1871–1942), Viennese essayist.

Then the place! What a wonderful, miraculous feast for the eyes is Venice, the basilica of St. Mark's like some gorgeous fairy palace, and so many other glories of architecture—one can scarcely take them all in. And the small physical pleasures, the delicious tastes of all the different fish; and the drive to the Lido, the gondoliers' serenades on the water at night, the Corso under the arcades, the terrific activity of the 'locals' and the 'vice-hungry' visitors; and the magnificent air of Venice! At least I know now that I am not incurably ill, but just a victim of the lethal climate of the Austrian Alps; that there is still a pure air which my lungs can inhale. That gives me an unexpected, long-forgotten sense of physical well-being—an air where your throat too would get well, and you would sing as they sing only in Italy (*not*, of course, meaning the Italian method of singing!).

Oh, if I weren't so tired, I could write you pages of rapture on the air here, the life and beauty—and still not exhaust the theme, for miracles are always inexhaustible, unfathomable, eternally new. Nature, art, the sea, Venice, and the highest, most magical of all—

You

(94)   Thursday
(Undated, autumn 1909)

I don't know, my very dear Helene, whether I'll be able to come to Weidlichegasse as we arranged ... the army of bacilli and bacteria has taken possession of my body; or, as the world would say: 'I have caught a cold.' I'm not living in that world, though. My world is one of sound, of your room and mine. Now that I am banished from your room,[1] my world shrinks and shrivels to a mere bed, the bed I lie in ...

Mama may be going out this afternoon ... If she does, I shall be able to leave the house myself, but will arrange to get back home before her, so that she won't realize I've been out. Please look down now and then to the street-lamp in Weidlichgasse—at around half-past five. If I don't come, you'll know that, because Mama stayed at home, I have had to remain in bed. In that case do write me a few kind words, I need them so badly ...

---

[1] Helene too had caught a cold.

(95)   Seven o'clock
                                           (Undated, autumn 1909)
... You know, don't you, that I suffer as much as you or even
more under the burden of unkindness which afflicts you—from your
family and even the servants. It makes me so unhappy that I forget
my own troubles completely for yours. But no, your troubles are my
own, I have no others or I just don't feel them ...

(96)   Thursday
                                           (Undated, autumn 1909)
... Smaragda telephoned to say she wouldn't be home till ten. The
thought of sitting at dinner with Mama in my present state,
talking about our properties or card games or so-and-so's pneu-
monia, was such a ghastly prospect that I took hat and coat and ran
out of the house. By a piece of luck I found an art-magazine in the
café where I landed up, a special Wilke number with a few brilliant
pictures. But then the clique turned up, I made a few polite remarks
and went out into the cold again. So after two hours I was back
home, where there is still this terrible desolation, because for
so long you have not sanctified my room and made it habitable,
because it is still not permeated with the fragrance of a letter from
you ...

(97)   Friday
                                           (Undated, autumn 1909)
    This morning your letter arrived at last—but what a letter.
You are still no better, and I'm not allowed to come. I can well
believe the 'authorities' would prefer that. I might one day tell them
and their brilliant advisers the truth, those moronic Hietzing
doctors who prescribe a cold-water cure in mid-winter for a girl
who needs the sun of Italy to keep her beautiful body in the bloom
of health ... Suppose some doctor said that to keep healthy you
must avoid staying at Trahütten; only then the head forester and the
schoolmaster wouldn't have a partner for their game of cards. Or
suppose that doctor said, no over-exertion or over-strain; but no,
at seven sharp you have to dash uphill to get back home dead
tired and bathed in sweat, because otherwise there would be one
more family scene.
    Well, no doctor who gave such advice would ever become a
                                    98

Nahowski family doctor. It's hopeless, those idiots, I'm so furious and—

Just in the middle of the sentence comes a note from Anna: 'Friday—Helene is a little better.' Oh, thank you, Anna! How can a stroke of the pen bring such happiness? How can the flood of my anger so quickly abate? Can miracles still happen? They do, they do. No harder to turn water into wine than to turn the sea of my fury into the delicious nectar of new hope.

If only my other hope could be fulfilled, the hope of being with you, the hope that through the power of my love you would get well ten times quicker than from all the cures and medicines, that you would never again fall sick but would go on living in eternal health and youth and beauty! . . .

(98)   25th October 1909
                                 [*Berg stuck the following*
                                    newspaper cutting on a
                                              postcard.]

The Maxingstrasse, which leads up a slight slope to the cemetery, has completely preserved its old character on the left side. The low houses are connected by the wall of the Schönbrunn Palace,[1] and a continuous row of chestnut trees provides shade. But on the right side the line of houses has seen big changes already. Once it faithfully kept guard outside Schönbrunn Park, and the houses remained discreetly small so as not to peer over the wall. Now, however, upstairs three storeys high have risen between the modest villas of Old Hietzing. The Maxingstrasse is jagged and full of gaps like badly made dentures. The old houses still enjoy the privilege of tiny front gardens, whereas the new ones are set back to a second row. Red autumnal vine-leaves stream down from many a noble balcony, and the eyes of the houses seem tightly shut. Other houses are inhabited the whole year round and have pelargonium in all colours blossoming on their terraces. The Tirolergasse and the Gloriettegasse open out in their old beauty, with a view of open country and nothing to remind one of the thronging, thrusting metropolis.

The falling leaves rustle under our feet, as we stroll along by the Schönbrunn wall with its many silent doors built in, which open to nobody. Suddenly the wall is behind us, and Maxing Park

[1] The Imperial Palace in the south-west of Vienna.

99

grants free entry. A Greek temple stands in the green coppice to greet us, and after a few steps we are at the entrance to the

> *Here the cutting ends, and*
> *Berg added in his own hand:*

HOLY OF HOLIES[1]

(99)   Undated
                                                         (Autumn 1909)

... There were you, lying on your sick-bed, and I stood under your window, shivering with cold and longing: how incredible that people in your house should actually burst our laughing ... Now, if *I* had been ill in bed, you looked in, and the air was charged with our longing, my mother, down-to-earth as she is, would have been touched and kind, certainly anything but *amused* ... So I consider it monstrous that when people see a love like ours prevailing for two years over all obstacles, prohibitions and separations, they should react to it by inane laughter.

... I have decided to return to the Weidlichgasse tomorrow, and have asked Carola for a *rendez-vous*. At least she will give me some news of you, as she did a week ago; seeing your home from outside, I shall at least feel that everything which has happened during these last two years is reality and not part of one long glorious romantic dream ... Oh, Helene, please try your very best to let me see you at the window of your room ...

I shall be bringing you the score of Schoenberg's String Quartet,[2] which has just been published. It may not be much use to you but I'll still get it for you because it looks rather special and will some day become quite a rarity. For only a hundred copies have been printed altogether, and you should have one ...

(100)   Undated
                                                         (March 1910)

... Despite your wishes I *must* write to you, Helene. These twenty-four hours without you—that is, without the prospect of seeing you—have been indescribably shattering. So I'm not disobeying the 'ban' out of defiance or restlessness; it's my only

[1] Helene's parents' house was No. 46 Maxingstrasse.
[2] String Quartet No. 1 in D minor, op. 7, published by Dreililien-Verlag.

way of showing you my true character, undistorted by the storms and outbursts of these last days . . .

I don't want to talk about my utter and uncompromising love for you, which knows no obstacles because it is the mainspring of my life . . . But you didn't realize that the reason I wanted you to visit me was to prove that you too were unafraid of the greatest sacrifices to show your love for me. Nor can I really think you would suffer psychological hurt, either from the caretaker gossiping or through your entering the same environment as a prostitute, my sister's present friend.

Still, that's where your misunderstanding started, when I said I found a prostitute's position no more or less offensive than associating with people whom you and many others consider quite unobjectionable. I mean the prostitutes of the spirit, generally respected, although they sully themselves for money, for salaries, offices, honours, advancement; hypocrites who pretend to be very upright and worthy but do and say things they are supposed to reject on principle. I also mean the respectable wives who marry for money, selling their bodies and souls for life. Well, that takes in about 90 per cent of the world's population, who accordingly, in my view, are not much better or more respectable than prostitutes . . .

Which of course doesn't mean I am defending prostitution. You know that at twenty-five I have never had anything to do with prostitutes; unlike millions of other men, who are perfectly capable, by the way, of declaring prostitutes the dregs of mankind, after satisfying their revolting sexual urges with the same 'dregs' . . .

I never said you were a Philistine, nor do I consider you one— of course not. I don't consider myself one either, although some of my views may be Philistine and so may some of yours. For instance, you are very fond of *Tiefland*,[1] while I don't care for it, but that's a mere difference of opinion. I wouldn't have made so much of this difference of opinion or called one of your views Philistine, except that the great proof of your love—that you should come to me —seemed to hang on it. But today, after thinking it over for twenty-four hours and becoming a wiser man, I realize how stupid my demand was. So we come to my having reproached you with closing your soul.

People's souls, I believe, are all different, just as no leaf is the same as any other; and different especially in size. When you open

[1] *Tiefland* (*Lowland*), a successful German opera in the verismo style by Eugen d'Albert (1864–1932).

only a part of your soul to me, it is true I gain more than if an ordinary person should offer me the whole of his; because yours is ten times greater. Christ opened his immense soul to all mankind, while the poor tobacco-seller round the corner opens hers perhaps to her pug-dog, or Smaragda after a night full of tears gives her small, stunted soul to one of these women. All are giving the most they possess, and so in a way they are *giving* more than you if you give only a part of yours.

But although I recognize how fully you love me, I can't solve this riddle, that your soul sometimes seems closed to me. This makes me start hating the other things to which it is open, like Nature, people going on their ways, the Sunday concerts, yes, even Wagner's operas. Whereas even when I'm absorbed in difficult scores by Mahler, Wagner and Strauss, I'm sure you must feel my soul still eagerly open to yours. Do you understand now why at times I have been afraid of your soul's excessive reserve. But for Heaven's sake don't think that I want to reduce your wonderful capacity for *feeling*, as you unfortunately assumed, or that because I found a word to say in defence of prostitutes I was putting you on their level!

In fact the most painful and unfair thing is a suggestion of yours that I am depressed at the idea of seeing you now only 'on the street'. The complete falseness of the implication is one great proof of my *soul*'s longing. Otherwise how is it that during the three summers I have been parted from you, I have not thought of physical satisfaction, and always declined opportunities of this sort with others; that I wrote hundreds of pages in letters thirsting for the union of our souls, and was as happy with your letters, even the less loving ones, as if I were celebrating my wedding night, not reading a few lines of handwriting?

Oh, Helene, my mind has stopped working. The evening has come, and I cannot write any more. My broken heart can scarcely dare ask for forgiveness; only a small spark of pity and understanding for all my faults and failings . . .

(100a)   [*To this Helene replied*]
                                          (Undated, March 1910)
Dear Alban,

I am so hurt at your reproaches on 'closing my soul' that I can hardly answer without agitation. Another girl might have deceived you, but I can't pretend or alter, you must take me as I am. My love for other things besides you is part of my spiritual life, just as my heart belongs to my body, without which I couldn't exist. Is it really a sin against you if I do not think solely of you but give myself, for instance, to the miracle of creation, so grand and yet mysterious, where every small flower or leaf has its own secret, which is perhaps its link with divinity? I cannot fathom all this, but I can feel it, so that I become quite devout.

Oh, leave me this sense of 'belonging' to my trees, flowers and stars! You are not losing anything of my love for you, since 'to him that hath, to him shall be given'. Just because of that my love is still growing, deeper and deeper, bigger and bigger, the more it includes. The same with my love for you, as I come nearer to the miracle of creation in you. For you are much favoured of God, or He would not have given you so bright and sensitive a soul. Your love makes me happy and binds me to you for ever. But it would be a lie if I told you: I give my whole soul to you alone.

Please understand that I am really not robbing you of anything if I sometimes 'lose myself' to Music (which is after all God's best understood language), or to the forest or the starry sky. You should not be at once in despair at this, but should try to understand me and *trust me*.

Do I really have to tell you that you are enthroned in my heart over and before everything else? Don't you know this—can't you feel it?

If you come tomorrow, everything will be all right between us. It will, my dearest darling—you'll see.

Your own
Helene

(101)   Evening of Good Friday,
                                              25th March 1910

Well, in future I'll never return home before my bodily needs drive me to trough and stable—dinner and bed! My home is only with you, in your room, in the garden, in my room if you are in it. But the cold dark rooms I entered an hour ago are empty and desolate, with nothing of home about them.

How could you think that in this place I should ever be capable of reading or working? The notes and melodies I had just thought out on the train, born in warmth of heart, now seem absurd, without feeling, cold as the doorknobs in my room. I can't imagine how I ever found pleasure in Maeterlinck and Dehmel, whose works lie before me here.

Never again will I go home before I have to. If I had only stayed in the Weidlichgasse, you wouldn't have been cross with me, and that would have helped me in my distress.

In my distress. After Jesus had been given the vinegar to drink, 'he cried again with a loud voice, and yielded up his spirit'.

But the Resurrection comes, and I will cling to this thought even when I feel most forsaken.

Then they will come, the Jews and the Pharisees and the Anti-Christs, and will find the rock rolled away from my grave, and the words will once more be made true in you and in me: 'So it is written, and therefore Christ had to suffer, and did rise from the dead on the third day.' That third day will come for us too, Helene, though our souls be buried many times ...

But 'behold, I am with you all your days until the end of the world'.

Amen

(102)   Vienna, 8th July 1910

By now, my dearest Helene, you will have arrived![1] Your first impression will have been decisive, leaving its stamp on the whole three weeks. I hope it was a fine and favourable one, which made you think from the first moment: there's nothing lacking to my happiness—except Alban. Just as, at all the beautiful moments of my life, I think they are truly beautiful only if you are with me. That's why I asked you to come to the rehearsals of my Quartet,[2] and on the car drive, etc. But in case you are not so delighted with the place, the surroundings, the spa hotel, etc., then try to think that the beauty of all these things would only be incidental; that in the 'beautiful moments' we only feel happy because of our inner state. The beautiful scenery, the movement from my Quartet, a delicious cucumber salad, are 'extras'. The main thing is that, come what may, we are together and will remain so for always.

[1] Helene went to Tobelbad in Styria with her family to take the waters. Berg joined her there later, after old Nahowski had left.
[2] The String Quartet op. 3, was written in 1910 but had so far only been performed in private. Its first public performance took place on 2nd August 1923 in Salzburg. (See Letters 335 et seq.)

For I love you—as nobody has ever loved before: with a love so strong and wise and true . . .

(103)   8th July 1910
. . . In my sad loneliness I suddenly see you so vividly and *tangibly* before my eyes that I can't think straight for longing. On top of that there is the horrible fear some man might force himself on you—my terrible jealousy. So there is only one thing for me to do—get to you quickly and save what can still be saved!

I'll be at Premstätten tomorrow at 6 o'clock. As a favour to you I shan't come to Tobelbad—until you send for me. But please send for me soon, very very soon, or I shall 'do something foolish' (in your mother's sense, for I no longer know the difference between sense and folly!).

Now I must go on packing—good-bye for now, Helene!

Oh, if only I were with you!

(104)   In the train to Tobelbad,
                                                           9th July 1910
You are the wiser of us two, you knew how painful our separation would be, whereas I comforted myself with the thought: well, we shall be seeing each other again in two days. As if two days were nothing at all! So I felt my sadness only when it was here, while you suffered before by anticipating it . . .

Then there's the dreadful self-reproach that these last weeks I haven't given myself enough to you—and why on earth didn't I at once chuck up this stupid piano-arrangement job?[1] I could have driven out to you every morning; then it would have been just as beautiful as last year, and you wouldn't have had crazy ideas like 'he's unfaithful to me, that's why it's not so beautiful this year'.

Consequently I have now returned the Songs to Schoenberg. He rang me up yesterday and told me they would have to be completely finished within a fortnight, which would have meant eight to ten hours work a day. I half had to return them and half wanted to. Anyhow, although repentant for the past, I now have no worries for the immediate future. Every minute of the day will be free if love's service demands it! And I can still use any unoccupied minutes

[1] Berg was supposed to make a voice-and-piano adaptation of Schoenberg's *Songs for Voice and Orchestra*, op. 8.

for composing. But not the other way round, that just doesn't work. We'd suffer from it a hundred times more than we should enjoy the 100 Crowns I would earn.

Fine wooded scenery is going past outside, but I can't enjoy it. It seems to be taking such an age getting to Graz and my impatience is growing all the time, making me quite unresponsive to the beauties of nature. Oh, when I am sitting with you in Graz, then I shall have solved the mystery of the beauties of nature, then life will have a purpose again . . .

(105)   *[In the following letter to Helene's father, Berg refutes Nahowski's four reasons for considering a marriage ill-advised.]*
Tobelbad, near Graz,
July 1910

Dear Herr Nahowski,

At last I have the chance to write my 'defence' letter, as promised earlier; please excuse the delay, due to urgent work. But now, after convincing you, I hope, of my honourable intentions, I shall try to provide a thorough refutation of all your charges: my 'intellectual inferiority', impecuniousness, continual ill-health, and the 'immorality' of members of my family.

I regret that in this letter I shall have to be talking constantly about myself, and moreover stressing my good points. This may sound conceited, and I dislike conceit, but it is forced on me in self-defence by your attitude. In my view, when marriage is in question, the great decisive issue is love, not such ridiculously petty details as have been brought up. But I must suppress my feelings on this point, and draw comparisons between myself, the rejected suitor of one of your daughters and the man who is welcomed with open arms as bridegroom for another daughter.[1]

I have to ask what outward abilities and inner qualities Herr Lebert has got that I lack, and why I should not pass, like him, as a future son-in-law. Indeed, Herr Nahowski, I can well understand your affection and fatherly love for Herr Lebert; I myself consider him a most amiable and estimable man, and a good husband for Anna. But your dislike of me, bordering on outright hostility, and the result of it, your constant dissatisfaction with Helene

---

[1] Arthur Lebert, a manufacturer of emery paper, was to marry Anna in September.

(who will never leave me), seem so strange and unreasonable that I can easily move away from the natural, understandable ground of love's idealism—no doubt suspect to you as fanciful and irrational —and plunge into the less familiar country of hard-headed logical advocacy.

1. My 'intellectual inferiority'

My 'schooling' is in no way different from that of other, favoured suitors. I matriculated with honours at the normal age of sixteen,[1] and during the next two years worked in the Imperial administration for the crown lands of Lower Austria, while at the same time attending lectures at Vienna University. These two years greatly increased my practical and theoretical knowledge, and also proved that I could fill a 'bread-winning' position—more efficiently, in fact, than many of my colleagues, as shown by the reforms I made in my department, then somewhat neglected. Other colleagues, who have achieved promotion in the service since then, can confirm this. When I resigned the post,[2] obeying what I felt to be a higher vocation, I received a testimonial, signed by the departmental head, Count Kielmansegg, commending my industry and stating that I had given complete satisfaction.

If you will also bear in mind, sir, that at that time I was often working at my musical studies till the early hours of the morning, you will see, I think, that I was not so completely frittering away my life as you often maintain. It is true that during the last three years I have taken 'afternoons off' to be with Helene, squandering precious hours waiting in the street, but that does not justify your assumption that I am idle. It only proves that by a cruel fate we are denied something which is a matter of course with other engaged couples (like Anna and Arthur Lebert), the opportunity of spending our evenings together. Meanwhile I have to administer my mother's eight houses, quite a full-time occupation in itself, and to pursue my own profession—my vocation as a musician.

You may say you don't care a rap for 'vocations' and consider music at best mere frivolous entertainment, not a profession which will earn anyone a living. Naturally my opinion on that is quite different. There are a hundred times more musicians, for instance, than there are emery paper manufacturers; and you evidently don't think Herr Lebert need be ashamed of his occupation, although it is

[1] A slight exaggeration. See Chronology, page 16, 1903 and 1904.
[2] He was able to do this owing to a small legacy.

both less common and less generally recognized than music—which has, indeed, been an honoured profession all over the world for thousands of years.

To say that it isn't a profession because it won't keep a man, is nonsense. A glance at any newspaper will show you that there are musicians who command just as high an income as court councillors, generals, manufacturers and land-owners: not only conductors of orchestras, university music teachers, instrumentalists in symphony orchestras and Court Opera conductors—but also *composers*, who earn a living by their compositions. Conversely, there are failures in every profession, and nowadays especially we hear just as often of destitute land-owners, officers and civil servants heavily in debt, bankrupt manufacturers, as of impoverished musicians. If one works hard at it and has the necessary talent, success is assured ... Now, you are not in a position to judge as to my musical talent, nor will you trust me when I tell you that I have such a talent, which can lead to a distinguished future; so I am ready at any time to have you confirm these facts by reference to any expert you may choose.

I trust I have thus proved to you, Herr Nahowski, that music is just as good a profession as the making of emery paper, and that it will earn a living for those who profess it ...

II. *My 'Impecuniousness'*

Helene tells me of your discovery that our eight houses are heavily mortgaged. I never denied this. Were they completely ours, we should be multi-millionaires—which, of course, I never said we were either ... My two brothers are financially independent, my sister possesses an insurance; my mother is neither a spendthrift nor a stock exchange speculator, nor (despite your charming joke, sir) has she any intention of remarrying. So altogether I cannot see the slightest possibility of our falling into financial distress.

The fact that I myself have no income at the moment does not mean that I am incapable of earning. I could join a theatre orchestra. You may smile contemptuously, but all the great conductors have started in a small way—Mahler, for instance, at Hallstatt.[1] There are musicians who provide for themselves and their families by orchestrating operas and operettas, or earn money by making piano reductions, giving lessons, accompanying singers, etc. I

[1] At the age of twenty Gustav Mahler was *Kapellmeister* during the summer season: in Bad Hall, however, not Hallstatt as Berg states.

could do any of all this, but Helene agrees that I should wait till I obtain one of the many permanent and established posts, e.g. at the Conservatory, for which I have good prospects.

I should have thought that our readiness to postpone marriage until I have a fixed income, progressively increasing, would set a father's mind at rest as to his daughter's future . . . Was not Herr Lebert welcomed at once, his engagement to Anna announced, although they had known each other for only three months, whereas we have loved each other for three years? And he really had no position either, merely the justified expectation of a splendid income because of his specialized knowledge. But the income will be there only when the factory is built, when it starts producing—just as much on the horizon, therefore, as my music. Only, luckily for me, nobody needs to build me a factory: I have my own with all the newest equipment and greatest productive capacity!—in my head . . .

III. *My Ill-Health*

Before discussing my own health, I could again draw comparisons with Arthur and Anna, both of whom unfortunately have had very serious illnesses—and two of Arthur's sisters are still very ill; whereas neither Helene nor I (nor any member of my immediate family) has any such complaint which might be carried on to our children. So the conditions of health for a satisfactory marriage are better in our case than in theirs.

However, I do not need this type of comparison. A certificate from the health authorities which I can supply at any time will prove to you that I suffer from no organic defects, am perfectly healthy and show no trace of any nervous disorder. I do not deny that I am highly strung, excitable and extremely sensitive. But to suggest that I am suffering from some nervous disease would be as absurd as to diagnose a skin disease because my healthy skin reacts to the finest physical stimuli. Do you really think that a man who is neurasthenic or in any way infirm could have been through the exertions of body, mind and spirit that I have, and still put on pounds of weight? That I could stand in the snow up to my ankles, as I have often done—waiting for Helene? Or expose myself all night to the rain and icy storms, as I did just lately; or swim across the Ossiacher Lake every year at its widest place; or endure any weather ill effects; if I hadn't been thoroughly healthy —yes, healthier than today's red-faced, cranky, over-fed health-fanatics?

IV. *The 'Immorality' of Members of my Family*

I feel almost tempted to dispose of this charge by saying that just as I shouldn't care about the past or present way of life of my loved one's family, so I should expect the same from the other side. Even if a suitor's family had the worst of reputations, he himself might be the noblest of characters. (Beethoven's mother, for instance was a depraved drunkard, his brother a fraudulent business man.) But as everywhere in this letter, I will try to disregard my own attitudes and treat it as normal that I should have to defend myself against your cutting question to Helene: 'Is this the sort of family you want to marry into?'

Well—I consider it as little a disgrace to bear the name of Berg as to bear the name of many people *you* are quite happy to associate with. By the way, we were still addressed as 'Baron' until about a century ago, until my grandfather was sensible enough to renounce the title as superfluous nonsense. Like you, we have in our circle high civil servants, judges, officers, industrialists, business men; we have relatives in Germany who own factories and cars. But I have also a brother who married a poor girl, and a sister whose abnormal condition and Lesbian inclination is her family's desperate sorrow. But alas, there is no sanatorium for her (as there is for Arthur's sister); no place where these tendencies could be cured, where she might be saved from the dangers they carry with them, and from other people's malicious gossip.

So we have come to the root of your attacks against my family. Had I the time, I would make this long letter twice or three times as long, and deal in detail with homosexuality: those afflicted by it and those who, because they are not so afflicted, treat these sick people as criminals. Perhaps your slurs, if I hear any more of them, will one day force me to take the matter up. For the moment I only say that there can be few families without at least one 'problem child'. It is not my business to ask which of your children comes into this category, except that you seem to regard Helene as one— because for the last three years she had been 'walking out' with a man she is not officially engaged to. I doubt, however, whether this 'problem child' and the 'disgrace' she brings on your family ever caused Herr Lebert—who no doubt has a strict moral code—to think: 'Can one marry into a family where there is such a daughter who gives occasion for vile gossip?'

... I know that this letter, in which I speak so much of myself and my affairs, which therefore seems full of self-praise, may leave an unpleasant impression; but I cannot help it—I felt obliged to shake off the dirt which has been flung at me for the past three years. I had to do it not only for myself but for Helene's sake and for our 'just cause'. It is a joy to fight for that cause . . . and I have only remained more or less 'passive' till now because she asked me not to disturb the 'domestic peace', out of respect for my elders, and out of confidence that one day my time will come . . . And now, as I hope this letter will have proved to you, the unbreakable bond between Helene and myself gives me the right and the power to consider myself engaged to her, and to overcome every obstacle put in our way.

But in consideration for your peace, sir, which is sacred to Helene and myself, and which would be disturbed by my presence . . . I shall not spend these next weeks at Trahütten but only near it— so that I can see Helene at least as often as the distance permits. She and I refuse to jeopardize our healths, as we did the last two years, by being separated from each other for three months. We hope in this way to have reconciled your need for a quiet summer vacation with our need to see each other.

Apologies once more for the length of this letter, which I hope you will see was highly necessary. I remain yours very sincerely and respectfully,

Alban Berg[1]

(106)   Berghof, Sunday
                                        (July or August 1910)
The first day completely without *you* once more, Helene. How can I bear it? . . . Happily, some kindly god sent me bright, cheerful, deeply joyful dreams last night. First I dreamt of my publisher telling me that the whole edition of my two works[2] had been sold out, and that a new one had become necessary. Then I had a long and exciting discussion with Karl Kraus about Art and the most sacred things; but I can't remember much of it because of the third dream. At last, at last, we had each other. You were in my room here, and we spent a wonderful, holy, 'Arabian night' together . . .

---

[1] This letter was never read by Herr Nahowski: he placed it unopened in his daughter's room.

[2] Op. 1 (Piano Sonata) and Op. 2 (Four Songs).

Helene, do not give in. Even though meanness has defeated us for the moment, it cannot keep us down for ever. We shall rise again, and blast away at the boulders of filth and prejudice till they come tumbling down . . . All the toadying and sycophancy of the Trahüttener and Hietzinger peasants will die away, drowned in a new Eroica Symphony celebrating the triumph of Love over Meanness, as we burst in with a crescendo of trombones and trumpets and furious drum-rolls on four drums. No power in the world, let alone the petty Princeling of Trahütten, shall stop us leading our cause to victory.

But much as we have suffered already, we shall, I fear, have much more to suffer yet, before the terrifying discords melt away into a pure harmony—which can only be achieved by our great, sublime, super-human love . . .

(107)   Berghof, 4th August 1910
. . . Unfortunately I do not have your heavenly gift of escaping to animals when weary of humans. I find that even the animals— dogs, for instance—are all too human for my present tastes. I don't associate any more with Mala, or perhaps it's he that doesn't associate with me; he prefers to go to the stable. I may be too much of a human for him—or not enough? . . .

By the same post I send you my sonata and the *Lieder* with a dedication. I hope they may please my friends, but if not, at least annoy my enemies!

I kiss you, goddess.

Your own

(108)   Berghof, 20th August 1910
. . . Some people are so overwhelmed by music that they almost faint when they hear an E minor chord on the piano. I am like that with Nature. Even as a small boy, when I was out in the country and the surroundings were too beautiful—I just couldn't bear it. I wouldn't join all the others on their excursions every Sunday, and so acquired a reputation for 'not liking the countryside'.

This fear of Nature still clings to me, the knowledge that great beauty in the natural scene drives me into restlessness and dissatisfaction instead of joy. I shun these frightening ecstasies, as I shun sexual or drunken orgies or morphia dreams. I escape into my room, to my books and scores. I feel here that I am in my own element, my own realm; anywhere else I might fall ill, and in Nature I should disintegrate and be submerged.

Yet I know that whereas other pleasures, like alcohol, are bad for the health and bad too for the soul, those who can enjoy fully the beauties of Nature are benefiting their health and their soul. So there is one hope I cherish, and that is this: a man, intoxicated by delicious wine, leaning in rapture on the breast of his beloved, with vine-leaves in his hair, is transformed from a drunken beast to a sublime singer. A man shattered by Mahler's Third Symphony recovers his strength sobbing in the lap of his beloved. A rake obsessed with his need for sexual indulgence looks into the eyes of his beloved and sinks back in holy adoration. The morphia addict tormented by wildest dreams falls into a deep and dreamless sleep when the beloved lays her hand on his brow, and from then on experiences only the good effects of the drug. And I shall one day feel the same, have felt it already, when with Helene, my beloved, at my side, I saw the sunset in the Wachau, unharmed by Nature the drug, yielding at last to Nature as bringer of peace and wonder and joy . . .

(109)   Sunday, 21st August 1910
After a sleepless night I fell into a heavy sleep this morning. Now I am waiting for the postman, and then I shall probably have more to write. There's no more I can suffer, for I passed the peak of suffering when your parents forbade me to see you, destroying all my hopes. I shall never find my path back into the lovely valley, I am drawn nearer and nearer to the sheer and fatal cliff.

Oh, if I only had you with me!

Yours, all yours

A few hours ago I wrote that I had passed the peak of suffering; and now I am falling down, down into the abyss. Today there is not even a letter from you. I try to work it out: Friday my telegram arrived, now you are waiting for my two express letters, and they were late owing to the wretched postal service; they only arrived yesterday afternoon, so you couldn't answer in time to get a letter to me by this morning. But then I give up the struggle, and fear the worst. Your mother was angry about the express letters because her peace too was disturbed. There was another family row, which you couldn't resist any more, and perhaps they didn't even have the kindness to inform me. All these dreadful thoughts are floating through my mind.

Send another telegram? No sense in that. Write another express letter? Impossible on Sunday. The only thing to do is wait for the two mail deliveries, and if nothing comes, to go to Trahütten ...

Oh, I'm on the rack, suffering the torments of the damned—I feel I'm going mad, quite mad. To wait twenty-four hours—for what? For death, revenge, coffee with cakes, a bowel motion, a letter, justice? What do all these words mean? Is there any difference between them? Between earthly and heavenly justice? Aren't they both just a garbage heap with a few idiots poking in it, thinking they'll find gold there? And *if* they find it, the lump of gold is mud and manure, worshipped by mistake!

It's all too much for me, my brain is bursting.

7 p.m.

... Futile to tell you of a few minutes' suffering, when hundreds of such minutes must be left untold.

This afternoon I stood at Villach Station, waiting, staring vacantly. Suddenly my eyes became riveted on a yellowish-brown skirt of coarse cloth, a brown leather belt over it, a blouse with lace and short sleeves. Just the sight brought a wave of overwhelming nostalgia and longing, floating over me, tears began streaming from my eyes, and I had to rush away into the W.C. until I had mastered the first intensity of pain, and become a little calmer.

It only occurs to me now that I hadn't the slightest idea whether it was a girl or a woman, beautiful or ugly, young or old. I saw nothing but the skirt, belt and blouse, and that was enough to shatter me completely and make me forget there was someone *wearing* those things.

When I came out on to the platform, she wasn't there. The place where skirt, belt and blouse had been was empty. Perhaps it was all a hullucination ...

Beloved veronal! You that possess the superhuman power to soothe pain and sorrow, that can bring sleep and oblivion after such a day, receive your most devoted servant. In half-an-hour you will envelope me, and in its last waking moments my poor defeated heart will praise Science, which has for once found a whole man to embrace you, beloved veronal!

114

Monday, 9 a.m.

A man came rowing across the lake. He brought a telegram: 'All settled, letter follows—Helene.'[1]

(110)   Berghof, 22nd August 1910
... Looking out of the window above my desk, my eyes roam across some fields, two roofs, a wonderful deep blue lake with forests full of colour all round—in the direction where I imagine my dear and lonely darling to be. I picture the sun shining there, bright and warm; I picture you talking to your mother, who has been fighting so gallantly at your side. I try to make myself take a more cheerful view of things, to draw new hope and faith in human nature from her splendid involvement in our cause ... Once I know what she has written, I will answer with a letter, she will be happy to read. But first I must quieten my heart, which starts trembling wildly directly I think of your father's behaviour and equivocations. Despite my excitement, though, I would sink down at your feet, throw my arms round your dear soft legs, and thank you on my knees—for finding the courage and conviction, inspired by your highest self, to demand your sacred human rights from him that would rob you of them, your father. I who could only watch the robbery in impotent pain, thank you now. I am proud of my heroic darling, the holy martyr of our rights! ...

(111)   30th August 1910
Again today you have given me great joy. At last the madness of separation from you is over; and your lovely letter fills me with happiness. All day I keep telling myself: 'A week from today, a week from today!'

Of course I shall come to join you at Graz on Tuesday the 6th. Just let me know when you will be leaving Deutsch-Landsberg. I can arrive at Graz at various times, it depends whether we go on from there at 1.34 (the best connection) or take the slow train at 2.45 as we did last year. That would mean we could go first class, costing exactly the same as going second class by the express (about 17 Crowns). Plus the chance of being alone ...

Is the wedding[2] definitely on Monday? What time is the dinner?

[1] Helene's parents had definitely agreed to her marrying Berg.
[2] Of Anna to Arthur Lebert.

115

(Don't upset your stomach before the journey?) Shall I congratulate your mother again, or send a telegram to Nahowski-Lebert, Trahütten? ...

(112)   31st August 1910
... You will be sick of all the festive preparations and the guests. arriving for the great 'peasant wedding'. Your soul, yearning for peace and love, will be tuned down to its lowest pitch; and I fear that every word I write in my painful passion may upset you or make you angry ...

I wonder if there is a single person in the wedding party who reproaches the old man for his abominable unfairness. Oh, Helene, don't be too kind or show too cheerful a face. They must see in your eyes the suffering you have been through—or the idea might spread around that you're quite contented with things as they are, and wouldn't at all mind staying another week or fortnight at Trahütten. That's the only way I can think of to explain your mother actually suggesting we should stay apart even longer. But if you are firm, they'd never get such an idea.

If I were you, I would remain pretty reserved throughout the hullaballoo. Very friendly to everybody, of course, but no more. You have to show them rather obviously that you're not really involved, and are merely joining in 'for the old man's peace of mind' and to stop gossip by the peasants—the two things hang together— but that you have only one thought and one desire, to be united with me on Tuesday!

Please promise me that. It would help our cause more than flattering the various uncles and aunts, who will anyhow start making their petty criticisms and abusing us as soon as they can. We could never please them all, unless we were to become like them —a horrible idea ...

(113)   Friday, 2nd September 1910
... Yes, I'll be at Graz Station waiting for you. I get there eleven minutes before you and can then fidget about on the platform as if I had St. Vitus's dance—St. Vitus's dance for joy! I only hope by then I can get my complexion clear of all the dust and dirt round here that has so sadly marred my 'beauty'—such as it never was, alas— and that you won't be disappointed by me after all. I quite feel I

116

could do something to improve my looks, if only to impress *you* . . .

Do please take very good care of yourself, and don't catch cold in church. I hope the little flowers which leave Vienna for you tomorrow will help preserve you from all harm. As I don't know whether you have to hold a small bouquet in your hands or just put them on the dress, the flower-shop will send them loose—they can easily be tied into a bunch. In any case they should go well with your dress and I hope will please you. But don't give them to anybody else, sooner throw them away! Not that they're as beautiful as all that, or worth my going on about them. Only I don't think you'd find anything better up there or in Graz, worthy to adorn your beauty and make you stand out even more as the star of the whole company! . . .

(114)   Saturday, 3rd September 1910
. . . I found I couldn't write Anna a conventional letter of congratulations. I like her as a friend too much for that; since keeping to convention is after all rather an insult when you have associated with someone on unconventional terms. So this morning I sat for an hour and a half trying to 'compose' the letter to Anna I had started, and couldn't make any headway. In the end I tore it to pieces in a fury, and within a quarter of an hour had written another, which she will receive by the same mail as this to you. I believe that was the best way to do it . . .

And now at last to your dearest letter. If only you don't catch cold, you poor thing. Do take your English leather-lined jacket to wear over your dress, also your warmest underwear and stockings—and boots, not shoes.

I'm rather touched by your description of the preparations. Glad as I am to stay away, there's one reason I'd quite like to be at these 'rural festivities', attending the church ceremony so dignified and solemn; and the Styrian-Swabian eating match afterwards; listening to the conversations and looking at the expressions on those faces. In that junketing, munching crowd you would be more than ever like an angel from heaven . . .

In 72 hours I shall be in the train with you, in a first class half-compartment—and we shall be quite alone together. Isn't that a nobler and more splendid honeymoon, with more passion and ardour, than your sister's trip to the South! Oh, I'm so distracted with happiness at the thought of it, I just can't grasp that it's going to happen. How wrong your old man was to think we should be worn down by a month's separation. Instead we now know and feel all the more how inseparably together we are, and that no power in this world can harm us. After this summer even *his* naïve idea that he can wear you away from me will have perished.

But I don't want to kick up a shindy on a day when everyone will be affectionate, when even your father will embrace his son-in-law, and fond uncles and aunts will be singing the praises of the happy couple. So I must suppress my harsh thoughts, and think only of us two. Directly I do that, I feel as if after a dismal rainy day I saw the pink sunset of a glorious evening. A radiance beyond my dreams spreads over my soul; I have to clutch at my heart, it is thumping so hard: and often have to shut my mouth tight to stop myself shouting for joy—the joy of seeing you again:

That's how I feel!

My eyes fall tenderly on the sweet 'sacred relics' in my room: the little chocolate lamb you gave me for Easter, the squirrel coat, the little picture on the bedside table—and Carola's drawing of you, which in my terrible loneliness I have put up to bring you more within reach! And all the time I am shaking my head dementedly, incredulous at tomorrow's happiness. For the last time, hundreds of paper kisses. Soon, so soon we shall be hand in hand. You — — and I!

(114a)

[*Here follows the letter Berg wrote to Helene's sister Anna.*]

3rd September 1910

A message of joyful greeting from one in banishment. You have reached the end of one play in life's long dramatic sequence; soon after you have laid your hand in Arthur's, the curtain will come down. When it rises again, you will see the happy faces in the front rows, but might miss the friend in the farthest corner of the theatre, whom Fate has not favoured with a seat in the stalls, but who rejoices in your triumph. You hear the audience's applause, eventually the curtain comes down for good, the theatre empties, the great silence of bliss descends, and the life of your dearest wishes starts, independent of all others, pure and deep self-fulfilment.

Can an 'outsider' wish you more? No need for me to add formal 'congratulations to you and Herr Lebert', planting one more tree or bush in the great impenetrable forest of fulfilled love's mysterious happiness. It would be like carrying water into the sea, sand into the desert, oxygen into the air.

If I could be with you on this day like all the others, I would silently stretch out my hands towards you and Arthur, and bow before your bliss. To do more when God speaks would be a sin. And He does speak on such a day, not so much through the priest's words, or the congratulations of parents, relatives and friends, but very quietly yet powerfully in your own hearts. Here is one person who knows this and can prove it to you, as he waits for the day himself with anguished longing: the day when love's fulfilment will make him fall to his knees in joy and devotion, listening for that voice from Heaven.

Alban

(115)   Saturday night,
                                    3rd September, 1910
... As you might guess from this scrawl, I am writing in bed, dead tired. I wanted you to have a few lines from me before you leave on Tuesday; and I'm not writing any more just in case amidst all the excitement this should somehow fall into the wrong hands! We don't want to give certain folk in Trahütten any chance to make fun of our love ...

I'm wearier than I have been for a long time, and two minutes after putting my pen down I shall be fast asleep.

Sleep well, Helene.

Your own
Alban

(116)   Undated
                                        (Autumn 1910)
... A strange softness has come over me, a sort of peace, as in a dream ... I don't 'get cross' any more, but please come, my dearest. I'll be waiting for you full of confidence tomorrow, Wednesday afternoon; and come early, early. Perhaps you can ring me up, I am

longing for your voice, your beauty, your magical white hand, your depth of soul.

So come, beloved!

Enough.

In some music of Schoenberg's[1] I found a passage which truly reflects my mood. I will put it here at the end, instead of a postscript.

(117)   Fürth,[2]

I received your two cards this morning. Very happy, of course, to hear from you and know you are well, but also very sad that I came here and so missed seeing you ... Perhaps you've got something to do in town on Monday morning. It would be lovely to have the chance to talk to you for a bit, for we shan't get any time to ourselves in the evening at the concert, and then of course I have to go revelling with the whole Schoenberg set, so again nothing for us. Please, Helene, do your best to keep the next afternoons for the two of us to meet, and perhaps some evenings for going to operas or operettas. And as for the next weeks, months, years—keep your entire life for me, I need it so badly. I see that even more clearly when I am away from Vienna. You are indispensable to me. Without you I am adrift like a rudderless ship at sea, with no land in sight.

I am writing this letter in the office of a business friend of Hermann's. It's the first half hour here I've had time to breathe, what with sight-seeing, theatres, visits, night clubs, motor drives in the town or its surroundings. As usual when travelling, I can't be really

[1] The quotation comes from Schoenberg's *Gurrelieder*.
[2] See footnote Letter 76.

happy, it's the same feeling of madly dashing about to no purpose. Perhaps tomorrow, when I visit my father's birthplace, that feeling will die down for a bit, and be replaced by a more sensible, serene calm. I long for this, but the more one fancies one is approaching it, the further off it moves, despite—or because of—all the speeding around.

So once more, you see, I have come up against the automobile problem. The more I get used to motoring, the clearer it becomes to me. The motor-car is definitely the best means of transport available, and as such very desirable, in fact essential. But that's all. I can't find anything so wonderful to be said for it, and as long as I have an 'automobile', i.e. 'self-moving', soul, there are no distances for me which I can't cover a thousand times quicker. That's quite a comfort for me as I sit in my room, poring over Sebastian Bach or Dürer,[1] or kneel by the table in the window at the feet of my beloved, oblivious of all the motor-cars rushing past outside and the rest of 'civilization', conscious that I wouldn't change places with anyone in the world . . .

(118)   Nussdorferstrasse,[2]
                                              12th January 1911

I followed you with my eyes as you walked along the street, until you vanished . . . Then I worked out your progress: now the Pfersch[3] has crossed the canal, now she's just by the station, now she's going up the stairs, she's got one hand on the rail, one foot a step up. Now she's half-way up, taking a breather, going on to the top. The ticket collector looks at your ticket, you step on to the platform, the train arrives, and you get on to it. And I am still standing in the window, watching the train crawl across the bridge. But just as I hope to catch one more glimpse of you, another train comes in, blotting everything out. Then I feel how lonely I have suddenly become.

Oh, return, my glorious and incomparable one.

                                              Your own

---

[1] Albrecht Dürer (1471–1528).
[2] In August 1910 the Bergs had moved from Vordere Zollamtsstrasse to Nussdorferstrasse, No. 19.
[3] Berg invented dozens of pet-names for Helene and for himself. Some of them are pure nonsense names, others are variations on Pfirsich (peach), Floh (flea), etc. They are all given here in their original—as Berg used them.

(119)   18th January 1911
You'll have caught the train today, darling, without running or
waiting. Was it a through train? Did you look up at the balcony?

I really don't know what to write. All the time I feel like mutter-
ing sentences like 'You're so beautiful', 'I adore you', 'You were so
nice to me again'.

The longer I know you, the greater is my yearning when you
aren't here, the more I am obsessed with thoughts of you, the more
stirred I am by the sublime beauty of your body, the more I delight
in the purity of your soul: in short, the more I know

THAT I CANNOT LIVE WITHOUT YOU . . .

(120)   Undated
                                                  (Spring 1911)
. . . I think Peter[1] is right in saying, sleep's a cure-all, *however*,
you bring it on—by real tiredness, veronal or alcohol. Just to sleep
is everything.

I wonder how things will look tomorrow. Whether I'll have to
write an express letter again, or can appear at your place in person.
Imagine my joy, after 160,000 seconds of separation!

But don't worry, I promise you I'll really only come if I feel well.
I'll put on a hot compress, and gargle a lot, and think of *you*, my
loveliest Pfersch!

Oh, it's wonderful to be able to say: I'm happy, full of joy, because you're mine.

Do you feel the same, my dearest darling?

                                                      Your own

(121)   Undated
                                                  (Spring 1911)
My love, love, love!
Don't be sad!
Think of someone you love and who loves you writing this
letter with a trembling hand, just to send you one more fond word
to reach you earlier than tomorrow afternoon, my first chance of
seeing you again! Think of the time soon to come when no tears can
fill your eyes without tears filling mine, and all the tears will merge
in bliss on our cheeks, to make a kiss that smiles through the tears . . .

[1] Peter Altenberg.

                            122

Alas, I meant to say a few comforting words which you might use as a charm in dark hours. But no charm has come up. Yet if sadness should come over you again, forget all my words and sentences, simply drink from a crystal clear spring, the pure spring of my love.

For ever and ever
Amen

(121a)

[Helene wrote the following letter to Berg the day before they were married.]
2nd May 1911

My dearest and nearest!

Tomorrow is our wedding day. I am setting out with you into 'the land of marriage' full of confidence and high purpose. I will always be a prop and support to you, a faithful and loving companion, both here and over there 'in the other world'. Gladly and of my own free will I give up everything that made my girlhood so full of beauty, hope and happiness—my modest 'art'.[1] I quench my own flame, and shall only exist for and through you. Now we shall be together for ever.

Amen

[1] See footnote Letter 12.

PART TWO

1911-1920

CHRONOLOGY

1911 18th May: Mahler dies in Vienna (aged 51).
May (last week): Alban Berg and Helene on their honeymoon in Trahütten.
Autumn: Berg and Helene move to their flat at 27 Trauttmannsdorffgasse, Vienna XIII.
Schoenberg moves to Berlin.
20th November: Berg travels to Munich for first performance of Mahler's *The Song of the Earth* under Bruno Walter.
December: Schoenberg's *Harmonielehre* published.

1912 25th February: Berg travels to Prague for a performance of Schoenberg's symphonic poem *Pelleas and Melisande* under the composer's direction.
June: At the Vienna Music Festival Week Bruno Walter conducts first performance of Mahler's Ninth Symphony.
August: Berg finishes his op. 4, the *Altenberg Lieder*.
September: Webern goes as conductor to Stettin.
November: Fire at the Berghof.
Gerhart Hauptmann receives Nobel Prize for literature.
Schreker's *Der ferne Klang*.
Strindberg dies (aged 63).

1913 23rd February: Schoenberg's *Gurrelieder* (under direction of Franz Schreker) performed for first time (Vienna).
Berg's *Guide to Schoenberg's 'Gurrelieder'* published by Universal Edition.
31st March: Concert at the 'Akademische Verband für Literatur und Musik' (Grosser Musikvereinssaal, Vienna). Programme includes Webern's *Five Pieces for Orchestra*, op. 6, Schoenberg's *Chamber Symphony*, op. 9, and Berg's *Altenberg Lieder*, op. 4.
June: Berg visits Schoenberg in Berlin.
Berg finishes his op. 5, the *Four pieces for Clarinet and Piano*.
July: Berg at Trahütten, working on his op. 6, the *Three Pieces for Orchestra*.

1914 January: Berg travels to Prague for first performance of Schoenberg's *Six Songs with Orchestra*, op. 8.

March: Berg travels to Amsterdam for performance of *Pelleas and Melisande* under Mengelberg.

May: Berg sees at the *Wiener Kammerspiele* a performance of Georg Büchner's dramatic fragment, *Wozzeck*.

28th June: Archduke Franz Ferdinand, heir to the Austrian throne, assassinated with his consort at Sarajevo.

3rd July: Helene goes to Carlsbad to take the waters.

28th July: Austria declares war on Serbia.

August: Berg begins work on libretto of *Wozzeck*.

9th September: Schoenberg's 40th birthday.

1915 22nd May: Italy declares war on Austria.

12th August: Berg joins the army.

October: Training at Bruck an der Leitha.

November: Has physical breakdown.

December: Transferred for lighter duties to Vienna.

Schoenberg moves back to Vienna, is called up for military service.

1916 May: Berg transferred to War Ministry for office duties.

September: Schoenberg completes training as Reserve Officer, and is given leave for indefinite period.

1917 July: Berg begins composition of *Wozzeck*.

Founding of Salzburg Festival by Max Reinhart, Hugo von Hofmannsthal and Richard Strauss.

October: Schoenberg finally discharged from army on grounds of physical unfitness.

November: Schoenberg initiates Seminar for Composition.

1918 9th March: Frank Wedekind dies (aged 54).

April: Schoenberg moves to Mödling.

May: Berg's *Guide to Schoenberg's Chamber Symphony* published by Universal Edition.

Schoenberg conducts in Vienna ten public rehearsals of his *Chamber Symphony*, op. 9 (1906).

September: Break between Schoenberg and Webern.

2nd November: Austria surrenders.

December: Berg becomes Musical Supervisor in Schoenberg's Society for Private Concerts.

1919 Summer: Alban and Helene Berg together at the Berghof.

September: Karl Kraus's *The Last Days of Mankind* published.

17th October: First performance of the *Clarinet Pieces*.

1920 January: Berg forced to take over management of the Berghof.

May: Sale of Berghof arranged, Berg returns to Vienna.

My dear, kind Mama,

I am sitting at my splendid desk in my marvellous room. Through the door I can hear Helene running a bath. The flat is beautifully quiet, with no street noises to disturb us, and despite all the things I've got to do, I simply must write to you now, dear Mama, or I mightn't manage it today. And yet, from the moment we entered the flat, I've been longing to write, to tell you how thrilled we are and how full of gratitude. The first evening, although I had a temperature and a bad sore throat, I had to get up and walk round the rooms which you had prepared for us so lovingly and with so many imaginative touches. I had to look at this and that, open the drawers—which you have filled with such wonderful household things; touch the curtains, admire the colours of the wall-paper, and so on ad infinitum.

Now I'm well again, it's a great pleasure settling in. We've all enjoyed taking a hand in it, first Helene, of course, then Auntie,[2] Carola and me. Even now there is still a lot to do. All my stuff is unpacked, the hundreds of books and scores are in their places and look magnificent. Lots of nice little ornaments, but not too many, make the place feel warm and friendly and home-like; so do the pictures, although not all of them are fixed yet. So we are gradually settling down to life in our first home together, rich in beauty, peace and confidence for the future. For years, dearest Mama, you have lightened our sorrows, and now you have crowned your great work of mother-love by founding *our* household. So thank you again for everything with all our hearts and with our boundless love—

Your loving children
Alban and Helene

[1] All through the summer of 1911, except for a honeymoon at Trahütten three weeks after the wedding, Berg and Helene lived apart in their parents' houses, not having found accommodation of their own. In the autumn they moved into a flat in the Hietzing district (27, Trauttmannsdorffgasse), and Berg wrote the above letter to Helene's mother.

[2] Frau Nahowski's sister, Betty.

Oh, Pferschi, Pferschi, now I am away from you, getting further with every minute and mile. I am very sad, and shall be sad all day. I shan't start feeling happier till I wake up tomorrow morning and can tell myself: tonight I'll be with my dear Pferschi again. But there are 24 hours to go before that, ten now in the train, three in talk, two at the concert, nine in bed. All those hours I shall be wondering whether I was right to go, right to leave my dear sick Pferscher on her own, whether it's any good going at all when I'm feeling and thinking like that. Still, I looked for and found a sign from Heaven. My thoughts were still with summer's wretched damp heat and autumn's horrible cold, and then came the first day of winter at its best, dry crisp air, the sort of weather you thrive best in and feel in your element. That decided me that I *could* go, could leave you . . .

So you won't mind, will you, my having taken delight in the beautiful country I've been through. A little unfaithful? No, I think I'm really being most faithful to you by admiring Nature as *you* do, just as I am by enthusiasm for *our* music and fanaticism in *our* beliefs, love and hope for all that is truly sacred.

Anyhow, an hour has gone as I sit in this compartment, my sadness for you mixed with expectations of the concert, and all the time magnificent scenery gliding past: dark forests in the horizon; closer up, the purple-brown strips of woodland with bare leafless trees; and right in the foreground vast frosty meadows; a pale-blue sky above, almost white, with a rare magical radiance. New valleys continually emerging, the mountains receding, till at last the immense plain lies before me, with its towns and villages, factories and cemeteries, the 'blemishes' on the face of Nature. You will understand what I mean, Helene, since God has bestowed on you the gift of appreciating and praising his Creations, a solitary tree, a book by Strindberg, a symphony by Mahler, or anywhere His mysteries can be perceived behind the blemishes . . . This is our Song of the Earth, scoffed at and misunderstood by the materialists,

---

[1] Gustav Mahler died on 18th May 1911, leaving as part of his posthumous legacy *Das Lied von der Erde* ('The Song of the Earth'). On 21st November it received its first performance at a concert in Munich with Bruno Walter as conductor. (Mahler's Second Symphony was performed on the same evening.) Berg was going to Munich for the concert.

who know nothing of life or death being twilight,[1] for whom every-thing on earth has its clear-cut, scientific explanation.

I can sing you *their* Song of the Earth, my Pfersch, for I am right in the middle of it, in this wheezy train—quite like our local line—sitting on seats hard as stone, squeezed between six commercial travellers, with the thermometer in the compartment registering 25° centigrade in its scientific way, but feeling at least twice as much as that! Meanwhile three cigars and two cigarettes are being smoked all the time, and I must count myself lucky that one of the salesmen dropped off to sleep so his cigar went out. The others are reading or staring at the buttons on my shirt, except for the man next to me, who has given up his railway guide and is looking over my shoulder to read my letter to you. In this atmosphere I find it very hard to think clearly, and I am writing very slowly, so I expect he's having a good read if he can make out my illegible scrawl.

So here I sit, case and writing paper on my lap, umbrella between my legs, lost in thoughts of my darling Pferscherl coming down to earth now and then when my eyes are streaming so badly from the tobacco smoke that they refuse to function. From time to time I go out into the corridor, where someone has left a window open by mistake, so there is a little fresh air coming in. Then I return refreshed and fortified—for more punishment. No communication cord would help, you have to howl with the wolves and sing *their* Song of the Earth, in other words smoke something too. But I haven't got a cigarette, so I'll be destroyed—well, symbolically at least—by the stinking fumes of loathsome humanity!

You see, my dearest, kindest Pferscherl, I have started talking utter nonsense. I can't breathe in here, must get outside and eat my first sandwich. Only I'd better finish this letter first, hoping I can post it on the station at Linz, so that there's a chance of your hearing from me tomorrow first post.

Take good care of yourself, Pferscherl. Keep nice and quiet, and don't strain your mind. I'm sorry we played such difficult piano duets yesterday, I think it worried you . . .

Only 33 more hours, and then I'll be more than ever your very ownest

Lunz[2]

---

[1] A quotation from the first part of *Das Lied von der Erde*, 'Life is only twilight, so is death.'

[2] One of Helene's pet names for Berg.

I have just been passing through the glorious country which sent Gustav Mahler into similar raptures so shortly before his death. The mountains completely under snow right down to the foothills, then green meadows, brown fields, and that sky: almost unbearably beautiful, I wish you could have seen it, you'd have forgotten all the trials of the journey. But now I must watch all this magnificence sad and alone, and—as I wrote this morning—the sadness won't leave me till tomorrow. The right mood, really, for The Song of the Earth and Second Symphony.

Apart from that the journey has gone better than it started. My compartment gradually emptied, and at the moment I am lucky enough to be quite alone in it. After posting the first letter to you, which I reckon you might even re-ceive tonight, I wrote to Schoenberg about the piano reduction of his *Gurrelieder*. We stopped at Attnang-Puchheim for ten minutes or so, and I had a meal on the station, roast veal with potato pancake ($1\frac{1}{2}$ Crowns). As I was getting back into my com-partment, I saw Court Councillor Pollak, a friend of Mahler's, at the window of the first-class compart-ment just next to my third-class one. He came straight in and we had a long and interesting talk. He spoke very nicely about Schoenberg, and  also Mahler, of course. He was the person who actually drew Mahler's attention to the Chinese poems,[1] so he must be rather a remarkable man; I'm sure *you'd* like him. He looks pretty ill, though—lung trouble; and yet he's going to Munich today and returning overnight so as to be in his office tomorrow! A little old peasant woman got in just now. I found her rather touching, and for some reason did a sketch of her. I wasn't thinking about it at all, that's why it seems to have come off quite well.

So now I have been looking out of the window for another hour.

---

[1] Mahler's *Das Lied von der Erde* is based on Chinese poems which the German poet Hans Bethge (1876–1946) adapted and translated in a volume called *Die chinesische Flöte* (*The Chinese Flute*), published in 1907.

You dear kind Pfersch, I could cry that you aren't with me. This is *the* most terrific scenery ever. All these different-shaped ranges, these plains with mountains breaking into them so abruptly. I've been trying to draw them, but no good. Monstrous that I didn't take my camera,[1] and now the sun is setting—what a sunset! Oh, Pferscherl, if only you could see it, and all the pines and other trees, some with leaves, some bare, and the fields and meadows looking like wild heath country, and—oh, words are nothing, I can't describe it.

Anyhow I don't want to think of landscapes, but only of you. *Wonder what you're doing now.* Are you merry—or sad like me? Are you singing, or have you gone for a walk in this lovely weather? Take great care of yourself, my darling, my poor sick sweetheart, and *think of me.*

I must finish now, although it's still an hour and a half to Munich. But a farmer has just got in, with a lad who has a rash on his face. The farmer doesn't know what it is, the boy just says he's got a headache and cries. Might be measles, and they're going on to Munich, so I'd better go outside into the corridor and say good-bye to *you.* There's a storm come up outside, the train is passing a long and beautiful lake with huge snow-covered mountains behind it, perhaps only an hour away, and above the whole scene a mass of snow-clouds in giant shreds. To see all that whizzing past in the dusk for two whole hours is almost too much for me. I shall be quite lost having to talk to people at the end of this having to find my bearings in their thoughts and interests, and then to crown everything *The Song of the Earth* and the *Second Symphony*!

You won't hear from me again until I'm back *with* you. And I hope I'll never again have to write to you, because from now on I must never be without you, my all—

With you entirely and eternally yours

(125)   On the way to Prague,[2]
                                          25th February 1912

My dearest,

My anxiety for you is growing with distance, even though I am only a short distance away so far. Heaven knows how anxious

[1] Berg was a keen amateur photographer (see Letter 147).
[2] To attend a performance of Schoenberg's symphonic poem *Pelleas and Melisande* (after Maeterlinck) op. 5 (1903), under the composer's direction.

I'll be later this morning, let alone by this evening. Please take care of yourself, I implore you. In everything you do, think whether I would agree to your doing it if I were there. Then you'll get well!

I have been sitting in the train quite a long time just brooding dismally, feeling sad and apathetic. Might just as well be going through a tunnel on the local railway for all the scenery my eyes are taking in today. I was going through the paper just as indifferently, when I came across this:

'Metaphysics of Love

Lucka[1] started with the premise that there are three stages in the relationship between man and woman, and that our way of experiencing love is the third and probably the final stage. The higher the lover's level spiritually, the harder it is for him to have any other creature replace his beloved. Modern love is inseparably linked with a demand for the unique and the permanent. The lover wants to be united inseparably with his beloved. This is not possible in the earthly sphere, and so leads in the last resort to a death-of-love, as illustrated with such incomparable beauty and profundity in Wagner's *Tristan und Isolde* . . . '

I like that very much, and think you'll like it too. These few lines say more than the thousand pages of *The Sex Question* with all Herr Forell's[2] cheap aphorisms.

I have had another snooze, the time has gone fast, and in three quarters of an hour I shall be in Prague.

Alas, the number of my neighbours has increased, three moustache-wearers have entered the compartment. We are six now altogether, and the place is beginning to stink.

Enough—I must break off. For I can never close or finish my letters, they are unending, like my love.

Your very, very own, silly old

Lunz

(126)   Prague, 25th February 1912

My Pferschi, I was thinking of you already when I was undressing, and of the letter I was going to write to you. Then I started to put

[1] Emil Lucka (1877–1941), Austrian novelist and essayist.
[2] Auguste Forell (1848–1931), Swiss psychiatrist and writer.

on my night-shirt and found it,[1] oh, it's *so* sweet of you, the tears streamed down my cheeks, and now the pain of not having you with me exceeds anything of the sort I have known before. Can't imagine how on earth I am going to bear it all these days and nights. I was very tired already, but know I shan't be able to sleep for ages now because of my longing for you. And this is only the first day. If only I were getting some mail soon! I'm dying of impatience when I think nothing will arrive till the day after tomorrow. Mustn't complain, though, must I, seeing I brought the pain on myself by sticking to this trip even though you weren't coming with me. I'll shut my eyes and hope the kind old sandman will take pity on me!

But first a few lines about today. Webern was at the station, and we went to the hotel together. It's very nice and very close to the Zemlinskys[2] where Schoenberg is staying. We were expected there too. They'd got a big party there already. Don't worry, Pferscherl, mostly men—tenors, conductors and the like—and most of the women elderly and plain, wives or mothers of the other guests (Prague women seem to be on the plump side!). The party had just finished lunch, so I didn't have to sit down at table or exchange small talk with any of the women—except Frau Schoenberg,[3] who asked after you. I didn't even meet any of them, as Schoenberg at once took me aside, asking questions and gossiping for quite a time. Then some of the other men joined us, and we got into a discussion of aesthetics and philosophy which went on right into the night—keyed me up and took all my mental energy. When we broke up at last, I was terribly tired, made for my hotel and there found your darling letter—*that's the most wonderful thing of all.*

Now I'm lying in bed. It's past one, my jaws ache with yawning, so perhaps I can sleep. I'll try anyhow, and know you won't be cross with me for not writing more, for I have to get up at half-past eight tomorrow.

I imagine you asleep, but no, that's too much, tears keep trickling out of my eyes, so let me stop. Good night, my own-liest one.

Morning

I did get to sleep at last, and slept rather well. Now I'm getting up,

[1] Helene had wrapped a letter in Berg's night shirt.

[2] Alexander von Zemlinsky (1872–1942), Austrian conductor and composer, Schoenberg's only teacher, was at the time musical director of the German opera in Prague.

[3] Schoenberg had married Zemlinsky's sister, Mathilde, in 1901.

with my first thoughts of you, darling, and will finish this letter. Then I go to the first rehearsal. Will write again tonight.

Yours today, tomorrow and till the end of time!

(127)   Monday,
26th February 1912
at night

Once more I'm lying in bed, my Pferscherl. Time seems quite infinitely long, and it's still only two days, with two more to come. Oh, if only it were Thursday already, the day of the last rehearsal and the performance itself. Then I could tell myself, 'Tomorrow I'll be seeing my Pferscherl again at last.' Sometimes I'm so overwhelmed with my yearning I would like to dash off at once to go back to you, back to all those glories beyond my fathoming, just to see and touch your hands, to hear your voice, oh God, only to call your name.

O – Stru––li

I don't think I've ever felt such intense longing. Just to think I shan't be seeing you tomorrow either brings me near to madness. For all the fine and stimulating hours, and the delight of the rehearsals. I consider my stay here like a long prison sentence—even though I brought it on myself, or Fate brought on me this conflict of desires and emotions . . .

Anyhow—this morning the rehearsal of *Pelleas* from ten to half-past one. First impression: magnificent beyond all bounds and expectations. The immense middle part (the love scene which ends so tragically) has only one piece of music to compare with it—the second act of *Tristan*. Highest praise for me, as you know.

Webern and I had lunch at the Horwitzes,[1] as Schoenberg is having most of his meals there—good homely food. In the afternoon W. and I went round to Schoenberg, and had coffee there in the family circle. After that we went for a walk—S., W. and I. I had to talk for ages about Vienna, myself and my life.

Unfortunately there was another party in the evening, at the house of one of the conductors who was at the Zemlinskys last night.

[1] Dr Karl Horwitz, conductor and composer, a pupil of Schoenberg's.

138

Apart from the good food it was rather boring, the more so as I was dreadfully tired. We would so much have liked to be alone with Schoenberg, but couldn't refuse the invitation. Company the same as last night, meaning: no danger at all! Though I don't know why I keep repeating that sort of thing, for I swear to you I'd no more think of any other woman than cutting off my hand! Even my thoughts of and desires for you aren't for you as a *woman*, but as a part of myself, without which there is no life for me. What wonderful joy that you are a woman too! And though this is only secondary, the thought of it floods me with the tremendous realization of your femininity in all its 'infinite variety', and further, of your physical grace. Only—this last thought is always being buried beneath anxiety over your physical health.

And even if I have to recount my experiences when still further away from you, it is to you I always return. In the unknown past you were the starting point for my being, so why should you not also be my goal and destination?

So ends my philosophizing, together with my daily report: dinner party, walk home with Webern, go to bed, and re-read your yesterday's letter over and over again.

Now sleep can come. And my last thought will be a prayer to God—and to you: take care of yourself and your health.

Good-night, Pferscherl.

Your own, very own
Swille

(128)

Tuesday,
27th February 1912,
at night

The day started beautifully, it was like in a dream. First your dearest letter, and the news that you are feeling much better—as Mama also informed me. Horwitz brought these letters for me to the rehearsal. You can imagine the new zest with which I listened to the end of *Pelleas*, and perhaps its peak: Melisande's death. Oh, I was so stirred by the music, as the servants go over to her deathbed, as Golo begins to choke on the horrible suspicion that he may be the child's father. This is one of the many tremendous climaxes, and the mood of voluptuous anguish and despair is conveyed with such sublime beauty—that I could have wept you weren't there to hear it.

The *Pelleas* symphony has only one movement and runs without a break for fifty minutes. The rehearsal went on till half-past one. There was another in the afternoon, so that even I felt exhausted. Another supper, this time at Horwitz's, the same company as on the last two evenings. Zemlinsky in high spirits, which made it rather fun at first. But it soon became boring, I could hardly wait for the end, when I could be at long last *alone* with my Pferschi—which always bears fruit in these letters!

Thank you so very much for your letter. In return I want to tell you as much as possible of my experiences here, the concert, etc. But as usual I'm so tired that it's only a stammer, instead of a fine continuous speech with splendid ideas shooting out like blossoms on a tree's branches. And my tale should be like a great wide spreading tree, so that my Pferschi could have a nice long rest in its ample shade. Instead of which it's only a nursery plantation of rather stunted thoughts, though a great thought is hidden in the buds—*my desire* . . .

(129)   Undated
                                                     (28th February 1912)

This morning Polnauer turned up at the rehearsal. Webern and I had lunch at the Horwitz's again, then we hurried to the station. Königer and his wife and Frau Webern arrived and Schmid was also on that train.[1] Back to the hotel, meeting of everyone at a café. Second rehearsal, again at the old theatre,[2] where Mozart conducted the first night of *Don Giovanni*. In the evening Horwitz and I fetched Linke,[3] and everyone met at a restaurant. First intimate evening, the closest Schoenberg circle, apart from the three wives, his, Webern's and Königer's, who sat apart from us. Just as it used to be in Vienna, and as a souvenir of the evening I had the enclosed card signed—only no card can express my continual tormenting sadness at the thought that you aren't here. And now I lie in bed feeling just as dreadfully lonely and desolate.

But it will soon be over. There's only tomorrow, which will be spoiled a bit by Stefan[4] and Hertzka[5] being there. In the evening the

---

[1] Dr Josef Polnauer, Paul Königer (a brother-in-law of Webern's) and Josef Schmid were pupils of Berg's.

[2] The old Theatre of the Estates, where on 29th October, 1787, Mozart's *Don Giovanni* was performed for the first time.

[3] Karl Linke was a pupil of Schoenberg's.

[4] Dr Paul Stephan (1879–1943), a Viennese music critic of progressive views.

[5] Emil Hertzka (1869–1932), Viennese music publisher, head of Universal Edition.

concert—Schoenberg conducting Bach and *Pelleas*, Zemlinsky conducting two 'cello concertos played by Pablo Casals[1]—and then it's finished.

If you don't hear to the contrary by telegram, expect me Friday evening in Vienna.

All and always yours and with you

Buschi

Wednesday evening

Well, what's this now—you're worse again? I'm miserable, and wish I could snatch time from Heaven to be with you. But there's Schoenberg's symphony to hear. It has always been rehearsed in parts, and I do want to hear it once as a whole without breaks or mistakes, which means tomorrow night, so I can't leave here till Friday night. If only time would fly quicker. For that one hour tomorrow I have to endure tonight, the whole of tomorrow, another night and then another day, perhaps not even knowing how you are. It's horrible!

I know you try to spare me and don't write everything or write it in such a way that I shouldn't get worked up. But it's no good, I'm still full of anxiety without any special reason to bring it on, and somehow I'm sensitive to danger, can 'scent' it even when it's quite unexpected.

So when you tell me not to worry needlessly, something in me changes the word, knowing I *need* to worry, even if I'm worrying *uselessly*, because it really doesn't help matters for me to worry. Anyhow, I don't think it was wrong of Anna to write to me about you being worse. I should have guessed as much without any letters——

(130)   Undated
(evening, 16th November 1912)

Pferscherl, I must write a note before I leave.[2] Please do everything I told you. Pepi is sleeping in the next room.[3] Take some vegetables with every meal. Don't feel on edge or get in a state about my

---

[1] Pablo Casals (b. 1876) on this occasion played the 'cello concertos by Dvořák and Haydn.

[2] Berg was on his way to the Berghof, where there had been a bad fire.

[3] Helene sometimes walked in her sleep so Pepi, the housekeeper, had to sleep near her.

journey. When you receive this, I shall be 24 hours nearer to you. Don't think that I am away, just think that I shall soon be back, that the moment of our reunion is coming nearer every minute. I too am sad, but when I wake up tomorrow morning, I shall be able to tell myself: a sixth or a fifth of the time, the bad time, is gone already; only four, three two-fifths, only one-fifth left—and then, ah then, my Pferscherl!

Good-bye. Make our separation easier by doing everything I told you, as I am doing everything you told *me!*

Yours, only and always yours

Fipipipi

(130a)   17th November 1912,
morning

It will soon be five o'clock, and in half an hour I shall be at Villach. Just passing Wörthersee. Still quite dark, but I can see quite a lot of fresh snow lying. I've been able to lie down in this compartment since eight o'clock last night, sleeping soundly part of the time, dozing a good deal, and another part of the time thinking of my Pferscherl, just as I am now. You'll still be fast asleep, looking so dear and kind and true, a picture of utter innocence. That's how I see you now in my mind's eye, and how I love to see you most of all. Not a shadow from the world's ugliness on your face, a reflection, rather, of unearthly joys. The word 'angel' keeps coming to my lips, but it would sound like a conventional 'term of endearment', and I cannot say it. I want to see it at least on paper, though, and you must read it without any scorn, just as God accepts a prayer from a devout heart.

After all, this is also a morning prayer, which I have to pray before I face this eventful day. But perhaps it won't be so strange, as my pleasant night in this small compartment wasn't. (Cost me a tip of four Crowns, but well worthwhile. There were three or four people in the next compartment, and two had to stand in the corridor all night.)

At a quarter past two I woke up, and had a juicy pear 'to wet my whistle'. The snow was glorious, made the telegraph wires look like ropes. Now it all looks more muddy than anything. Anyhow, I'm well provided for, and have a good slice of warmth inside me thanks to the night. Now I'll take a swig of egg brandy. In three minutes we shall be in Villach. Directly the telegraph office opens, I'll send you a wire, dearest Pferscherl. In the evening I'll write to you about the day—as I've just written to you about the night.

After the arrival

Wastl was here to fetch me. Seems Andreas hasn't spoken a word since the disaster, he just lies in bed very tearful.[1]

I'm now having a good breakfast, then I'll drive out there. It's nippy, but not too cold. At eight I'll send the telegram.

My dearest darling, my Pferscherl, I kiss you—

Your Fipipipi

(131)   Sunday,
                                                     17th November 1912,
                                                                  afternoon

... Have just dashed off a long letter to Mama, my dearest Pferscherl, and had a very important talk with the insurance man of a *different* company, so I know what to do. But it's left me feeling quite stupid!

Had to break off again, darling, and write a p.s. to Mama's letter. The affair becomes madder and madder, but I'll spare you the business side. Not too much time before the mail is collected, so I'll just give you a few impressions from the day.

After breakfast—it was still dark—I drove to the Berghof, with day gradually dawning in this incredibly lovely winter landscape. By the time we reached the lake it was already daylight. The stone-grey lake, looking wavy and oily, the browny-grey sedge amidst the wide snowy plains with the delicate silver of the mountain peaks behind them, beneath a melancholy sky: to drive through all that, wrapped in blankets, with the sound of the horses' sleigh-bells—and Wastl telling me his sad tales. I didn't need those to make me feel in all my being the voluptuous pain of Nature's beauty.

Arriving at the Berghof, I comforted Andreas, who had wanted to fling himself into the lake. I inspected the damage, which is pretty bad. The hay is still gleaming in the barn, which looks like a large hall without a ceiling. The sties are empty, but only two piglets dead, they ran straight into the fire. Three chickens were suffocated. I stayed there about three hours, was in the house too, of course—smoke still blowing about unpleasantly—then returned here.[2]

[1] Wastl and Andreas worked on the Berghof. The store-house had burned down and Berg was supposed to assess the damage for the insurance and discuss the matter with the insurance inspector.
[2] Berg was staying in Villach.

But to give you a little relief from this tale of woe, let me say that I had some excellent coffee with bread and butter, then more long discussions (tell you about those when I see you). I've been busy with the insurance thing for seven hours now without a break, and am completely fuddled, not to mention writer's cramp . . .

I am far away from you, and don't even know how you slept. Did you talk in your sleep? To be with you again is my one constant thought, however full my brain is of all the other stuff. Yet I can't say definitely when I *shall* be with you. By Tuesday morning I shall have done all that has to be done with the insurance people, and could start for home that evening. But who knows whether something new won't come up to stop me? Oh dear, I've written so much today, my hand is almost dropping off. One more kiss!

Your own
Fipipipi

(132)   18th November 1912

Dear Pferscherl,

Another strenuous day behind me, but at least I can hope to be back home by 5 p.m. on Wednesday at latest. Spent the whole day at the Berghof, and am now writing there too, in the nice heated kitchen. The weather has become warmer, and I'm not feeling cold at all. For instance, I walked over to Mesner[1] today to inspect some of our cattle, and it was rather unpleasant, snow a foot deep and a snow-storm; but when I got back, my feet were as warm as toast. Really I feel very fit, big appetite, excellent digestion. You've written about that and are anxious over my health, I know— that's why I tell you all this in some detail!

Since starting this letter, I've had a talk with the builder and been back to Villach, where I found a telegram from Charly (or his lawyer)—160 words!—which meant my writing another express letter to Mama. All this business here doesn't really touch me, though; my only thought is of getting home. But the insurance man I was to meet today hasn't arrived, and suppose he doesn't even come tomorrow? I've got to stay here till he comes, and would send a wire to the company in Vienna. But then I would have to stay here till Thursday at least, and you would have to join me here, my Pferscherl.

For I can't bear the separation any longer. If that *should* happen, I

[1] A farmer near the Berghof.

Above, two oil portraits by Schoenberg of Alban Berg, and Helene Nahowski
1910; *below*, Berg with his dogs at the Berghof in 1910

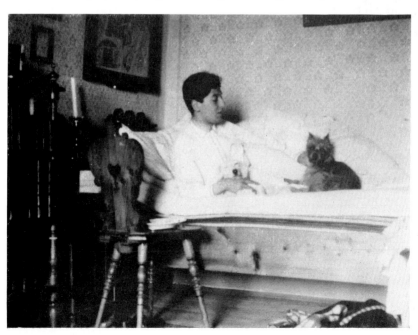

Alban and Helene Berg after their marriage in 1911

Alban Berg and Helene Nahowski in 1908

will send you a telegram: 'Staying here longer come at once.' Then you leave 7.35 a.m. on Wednesday morning, and get to Villach at 3.57 p.m.—where I take you blissfully into my arms. Then we can stay here as long as we like. Nature is wonderful here. Every day I tell myself I must spend the end of my days in the country, having been condemned to spend the first part of my life in a big city.

Today the weather is duller, making the view of the lake even more fascinating. You know my preference for Nature in her more sombre moods. The lake is dark and rough, reminding me of the deep, deep new sounds swinging and swelling in *Pierrot Lunaire*[1]—I always hear them when I see the lake; or the sounds of the Quartets, of *Pelleas* and the George-Lieder.[2] But where is the lake's greeny-browny-grey in summer? Oh, everything beautiful—in nature and Art—is *new*; every day is new, only a Philistine sees always the same . . .

7.00 a.m.—Tuesday

Thank the Lord! The insurance man is here. I must hurry!

Kisses,
Lunz

(133)   Tuesday, 19th November 1912,
                                            morning

I really do have bad luck. I was hoping we could drive out to the Berghof and do everything there that needs doing, then put every-thing in writing in the afternoon, so that I could leave for home this evening. But that hope has been killed. We can't drive to the Berghof yet, as the other man the insurance company needs, a builder—who was promised to me this morning—will only arrive at lunch-time, so we can't go to the Berghof till then. That means we can't possibly finish all the work today, and I have to stay, because after all that's why I came our here.

Just possibly I may be able to travel tomorrow night, arriving Thursday morning at best. Gloomy prospects. So I sit here again, for the third time today in the Café Schacher, while the insurance

---

[1] *Pierrot Lunaire* op. 21 (1912), Schoenberg's setting of twenty-one poems by Albert Giraud (1860–1942), translated into German by Otto Erich Hartleben.
[2] Fifteen poems from *The Book of the Hanging Gardens* by Stephan George (1868–1933), op. 15 (1908).

man does his calculations in his hotel room and makes his preparations for the afternoon. Felt so desperate I bought myself a detective story . . .

(134)   Villach, 20th November 1912
. . . No hope of my travelling tonight, far from it—we have to drive over to the Berghof again tomorrow. These agents are in no hurry, and plague me as much as they can. I have a sort of 'power of attorney', but, if necessary, can feign stupidity and declare that I can't agree to anything. But that can't go on, I'll have to put before Mama the choice of really giving me full authority or else coming here herself . . .
Oh, if I could only hear your voice! My present feelings are indescribable. I can't even say any more that I'm impatient. I am in a state of nausea and despair, like a half-dead horse refusing to move however hard he's whipped. And the misery all the time of putting on an act with these horrible agents, pretending I'm on familiar terms with them, having friendly chats, etc., when my heart is bursting with annoyance and absolutely breaking in desire for you . . .

(135)   Thursday, 21st November 1912
Another letter! When will it be the last? This one chap evidently wants a nice long holiday away from his office, and keeps putting me off. But I've made up my mind to tell him today that I am definitely leaving at half-past nine this evening, as I have six lessons to give tomorrow, Friday, and can't cancel them all. I admit I had to be there yesterday, there were urgent things for me to decide. But this afternoon I shall finish everything on the Berghof, and work it so that he can't detain me any further. This morning when I offered him my help with the inventory, he refused. So I'm sitting here in the café by myself—while he is probably sleeping in his room or writing picture postcards. After he declined that offer, I asked him: 'Anyhow, will you be finished today?' 'Let's hope so,' he grunted—which means he'd like to stay here tomorrow as well; he can too, but alone!
The other chap worked very decently yesterday, and he's sure to be finished today. But I can't bear being separated from you

146

any longer—yet I couldn't ask you to come here, the only way out
for me. You would have had to stay all by yourself all day, and then
sit in the restaurant till eleven at night with people like these
insurance men. If only you had come with me in the beginning, we
could at least have had the first days together ...

So I can't go on any more, Pferscherl ... But of course don't say a
word of this to Mama, she would jump to the conclusion that I've
handled her affair badly and without taking any trouble—whereas
in fact I have worn myself out physically and mentally.

Part of my morning has gone writing this letter, and now I want
to go around this dull town a bit; I might find something suitable for
my Pferschi. I nearly bought you a hat this morning, which I thought
would go well with your light brown coat and leather jacket. But
when I looked at it in the shop, I didn't like it so much as I liked it
in the window, and was afraid you mightn't care for it—so I left it.
I'll describe it for you when I get back, and if you like the sound of it,
I could have it sent. (Don't worry about the price, it's only
11 Crowns.)

At half-past twelve we drive over to the Berghof. In the evening
we return here, have dinner, and then—away! ...

(136)   (Undated, Autumn 1912?)
   I have once more played through Mahler's Ninth. The first
movement is the most glorious he ever wrote. It expresses an
extraordinary love of this earth, for Nature; the longing to live on it
in peace, to enjoy it completely, to the very heart of one's being,
before death comes, as irresistibly it does. The whole movement is
based on a premonition of death, which is constantly recurring.
All earthly dreams up to this peak; that is why the tenderest passages
are followed by tremendous climaxes like new eruptions of a volcano.
This, of course, is most obvious of all in the place where the premonition of death becomes certain knowledge, where in the most
profound and anguished love of life death appears 'mit höchster
Gewalt'; then the ghostly solo of violin and viola, and those sounds
of chivalry: death in armour. Against that there is no resistance
left, and I see what follows as a sort of resignation. Always, though,
with the thought of 'the other side', which we can see in the
misterioso on pages 44–45, as if in the pure air above the mountains,
in the ether itself. Again, for the last time, Mahler turns to the earth
—not to battles and great deeds, which he strips away, just as he did

in *The Song of the Earth* in the chromatic *mordendo*-runs downwards—but solely and totally to Nature. What treasures has Earth still to offer for his delight, and for how long? Far from all strife, in the free, clear air of the Semmering[1] he would make a home for himself, where he could breath in more and more deeply this purest air on earth

where his heart, most glorious of human hearts that ever beat, may expand, wider and wider, before it must stop beating for good.

(137)   In the train, on the way to
                                          Villach, 27th May 1913[2]

Well, Pferscherl, I am alone. Papa has just got out (at Bruck). It was all very *gemütlich*. He was in his jolliest mood, we chatted away all the time, and now he has gone I really miss him. In the past I have often wondered whether he was not as a rule putting on an act. But time and again he seems so genuinely warm-hearted one simply cannot help liking him. I am positive that at such moments he is being honest in his talk and attitudes—so that even if he's telling a lie, he believes the lie himself. The Peer-Gyntish streak in the Nahowskis! (Franzl has it too.) . . .

(137a)   27th May 1913, afternoon,
                                            in the train

After posting my letter at St. Michael, dearest, I returned to my 'empty compartment' to find that a young couple had got in with three little children from six months to four years old, and a nurse. Imagine my delight at this company. The crying, the noise, the anxiety every time the train jerked in case one of the little brats fell out of the window. I tried to read. Hopeless. I tried to join in the 'family life' . . . and watched a dairy being set up in the compartment. The baby was given a feeding-bottle, and goggled all

---

[1] Mountain range in the Austrian Alps, between Lower Austria and Styria, where Mahler (in the village of Breitenstein) had a summer house.

[2] On the way to superintend the rebuilding of the parts of the Berghof, destroyed by fire six months before.

round with his huge eyes, while they tried to keep the squirming little body still. (see drawing)

In the end a chamber pot was put down near me, one of the little dears 'did his wee-wee', and the full pot was carried out in front of my nose. Taking this as a mild insult, I got up, and went to the dining-car, where I gradually recovered, had a very good meal, and am now sitting with a cigarette writing to you, darling Pferscherl. Hope you are not sleep-walking, *I am with you.*

Your own
Pipile

(138)

In the train,
27th January 1914[1]

I'm starting this letter amidst the general interest of my dear fellow-passengers, seven of them. In the three hours since we left Vienna they have been having a continuous conversation, mostly about food, so that I could hardly read. But now it has suddenly stopped as I began writing. I hope their interest will soon revert to food, so that I can write to my Pferscherl without being disturbed; it's almost impossible anyhow with the way the train is shaking. (Which of course is worse, travelling third class than second.)

Well then: at the beginning of the journey I stood outside in the corridor, looking at the scenery. Rather a dreary landscape in the winter. Endless browny-grey fields, snow in only a few places, and the vast grey sky looking just as hard as the soil. It all makes a very sleepy impression, or dead even. The Danube with its cover of

[1] On his way to Prague to the first performance of Schoenberg's *Six Songs with Orchestra*, op.8.

ice looks stagnant, and the only life in the scene is from a few country children, skating here and there, and the mass of flying crows (or ravens). Not very exciting, so I didn't mind when it got dark and there was nothing to see outside. I came back into this hothouse compartment and started to read. By the way, I'd forgotten to take *The Idiot* with me, alas, so I'd got nothing to read for the journey and in bed at Prague. I had thought of buying a detective story, when I suddenly saw Rosegger's *Erdsegen*,[1] which I bought and started to read with great enjoyment. In Gmünd, which is about half-way there, I ate my first sandwich. And there I found your dear note. Oh, you kind Pferscherl, that was so sweet and nice of you. No, I won't catch a cold! At the moment I'm more in danger of roasting, it must be at least 20° centigrade ...

(139)   Prague, the night from
                                        Tuesday to Wednesday,
                                     27th to 28th January 1914

Only a short note, my darling Pferscherl, as it is very late (half-past two). Stein was waiting for me at the station, and we went to Zemlinsky's, where besides Webern, Königer, Stein and myself, Schoenberg and his wife, there were only Keussler[2] and a conductor called Theumann. A lot of talk then, mainly between Schoenberg and Zemlinsky, and that was fine.

My arrival here was well-timed. A rehearsal at ten o'clock to-morrow morning, with stops and repeats, so that I can hear the songs several times. Day after tomorrow last rehearsal and performance.

Schoenberg has got thinner and is in very good spirits. Webern is badly ill. Had a terribly high temperature the last two or three days, and was quite thinking of going back home. Now it's angina, and he can hardly drag himself about.

I am staying near the station, in a simple but very nice room (4 Crowns), hot water, central heating, view on to the theatre. Room number 69, which is three times 23![3] And now I want to

[1] *Blessings of the Earth* (1900), a novel by the popular Styrian author Peter Rosegger (1843–1900).
[2] Gerhard von Keussler (1874–1949), German composer and conductor. He was at the time musical director of the German Choral Society of Prague.
[3] Berg considered the number 23 his fateful and sometimes lucky number. Starting from the first asthma attack (23rd July 1908), many events in his life were associated with that number. In 1931 he was connected with a music magazine in Vienna, called 23, and edited by his pupil, friend and biographer Dr Willi Reich (b. 1898).

sleep, my dearest, kindest darling, or at least close my eyes and think of you.

Your very own

p.s. It's very warm here in Prague—1° or 2° at least—so you really needn't worry!

(140)

A short interval in the day's activity, so I'll use it to write you a few lines, sitting in the café with Königer and Stein, who are playing chess, and Webern, who is feeling much better and also writing to his wife. Schoenberg has gone home, we're meeting him for dinner at the *Blaue Stern*.[1]

So: I slept well, got up at eight, went to the rehearsal at ten. Only three of the songs are being sung, but the most beautiful ones: *Coat of Arms, Full of that Sweetness,* and *When the Little Birds Lament.* There's also Tchaikovsky's *Symphonie Pathétique,* and *Death and Transfiguration,*[2] Manén, who looks very interesting, playing the Mendelssohn Violin Concerto.[3]

The songs for voice and orchestra are very difficult, even for me, knowing them well from the piano as I do. I'm very glad I *have* got to know them beforehand, for if I'd only heard them once or twice as at this rehearsal, I shouldn't be able to enjoy them properly, or rather appreciate them properly. It's certainly a very unusual work, with a special position among Schoenberg's compositions. Winckelmann[4] is quite good, a terrific voice, although it doesn't sound too well trained, no breath anyhow. Or perhaps it's the stage fright he gets. According to Zemlinsky he'll have to wear two pairs of pants for tomorrow's performance!

The rehearsal was very fine. Zemlinsky as conductor even more impressive than before, orchestra remarkably intelligent. Schoenberg wasn't with us for lunch, but in the afternoon the four of us have been strolling around with him till now, almost sinking into the Prague mud—it's thawing. Well, and now I am writing to you, kissing you in my thoughts many thousand times, and thinking that perhaps tomorrow morning a little letter will have arrived,

[1] The Blue Star, a famous old Prague hotel.
[2] The symphonic poem by Richard Strauss (1889).
[3] Juan Manén (b. 1883), Spanish violinist and composer.
[4] Hans Winckelmann, tenor, a son of the first Bayreuth Parsifal, Hermann Winckelmann (1849–1912).

and I'll find out how you are, my darling. Then (at about half-past eight or nine) I'll try to ring you up from Prague, do hope I'll get through. Then the last rehearsal; in the evening the concert, and the following day (Friday) I'll be with you, about lunch-time at the latest . . .

(141)   Amsterdam, 10th March 1914[1]
I am in despair, my Pferscherl, not to have heard from you. Why don't you write, then? You know my address . . . You aren't ill, are you? . . . You can imagine how the day has dragged. Even the terrific impression on first sight of the sea couldn't drive away my miserable thoughts . . .

When I think of these days at Amsterdam now or later, I shan't be able to appreciate the gifts I have received here through Art and Nature. I'm like somebody with stomach trouble who is served with superb dishes and has to leave them untouched. Yes, I know—you're not too fond of that sort of image or simile; so I'll try to keep to the facts.

In the morning rehearsal till 12. Then the wind sextet of the Mengelberg orchestra (piano, flute, clarinet, oboe, bassoon, horn), which gives concerts here like the Rosé quartet[2] at home and plays beautifully, played a new sextet for us by a Dutch composer, which was very nice. I had to promise the ensemble to send them my Clarinet Pieces;[3] the pianist and clarinettist might be able to perform them in one of their concerts. After lunch we had an hour's tram ride via Haarlem (a very friendly place compared to gloomy Amsterdam) to Zandfoort, from where I sent you my card. You can hear waves breaking in the distance, you walk for a bit, and come to the sea. I won't even try to describe it. For an hour or so we stood or walked in the soft moist sand, with huge waves breaking along it, which gradually subsided at our feet, leaving behind them thousands of small mussels—and a border of foam. I took a lot of photographs, though the weather was not good, it even rained at times. But before the sunset in the sea, it appeared once more in full splendour,

---

[1] Berg had gone with Helene to Berlin, and continued the journey to Amsterdam with Schoenberg, Webern and Stein. The occasion was a performance of Schoenberg's *Pelleas and Melisande* given by the Concertgebouw Orchestra under its conductor Willem Mengelberg (1871–1951).
[2] The famous Viennese String Quartet, founded 1883 by Arnold Rosé (1863–1946).
[3] *Four pieces for clarinet and piano*, op.5 (1913).

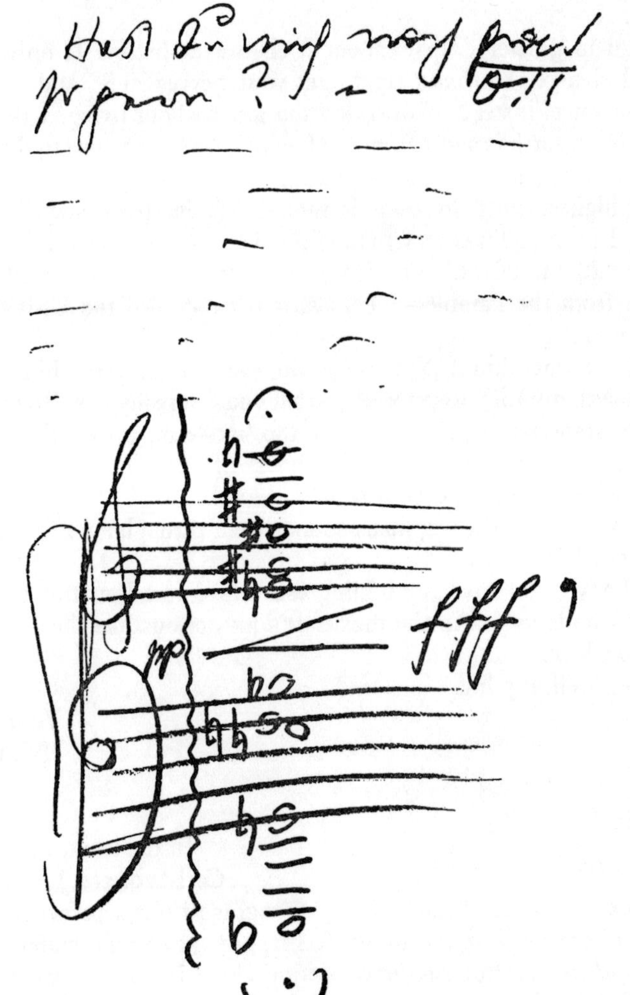

opposite an almost full moon. Then, as the sky gradually got darker, the moon began to light up this landscape; that was indescribable, a miracle, which God had created for *you*—and you aren't there to see it.

I am in greater despair about it than ever before. If only this would change. You *must* try to get your nerves right, and simply live for once, instead of worrying too much about living. I believe that life on earth is a gift from God, which we have to use to the full till it's over; and the gift, above all, is health—it's your and everyone's highest duty to keep it intact! Mahler (who stayed here often, I hear, and was very fond of the place) once said: 'To be ill is to be without talent.' The word talent is used in its old biblical sense, from the Parable—I believe it is called—of the Unfaithful servant...

Believe one thing: You must do everything, everything, my Pferscherl, my Life, to get well, so that you can really live. You must put on some weight ... Don't be too 'modern', my darling; you don't need to be. The natural loveliness of your body has nothing to do with fashion, and your soul is eternal.

Looking out at the sea, many sounds went through my mind. [See page 153.]

Nobody could have any inkling *how* I love you, how my longing for you finds its foil in the music. It's mysterious like the sea, like life, like love.

Sleep well, my life.

Your
Blinus

(142)   In the train, just after
Carlsbad, 3rd July 1914[1]

Up to now, my Pferscherl, my thoughts of our separation have always been on how *you* would feel it, how *you* would suffer from being *alone* ... But suddenly, sitting alone in my compartment, I realize that I am in it too, that the saddest time is now beginning for me, and that I really don't know how I'll come through it without you. You can't imagine, my Pferscherl, the sense of 'bereavement' that has descended upon me. I had to keep warning myself how weak and cowardly it would be to turn back now, as I'd love to,

[1]Helene was ordered by her doctors to take the waters in Carlsbad. Berg accompanied her on the journey, then returned to Vienna.

put aside all my plans for the next weeks,[1] and stay with you in Carlsbad, if necessary borrowing the money (don't laugh, Pferscherl) from you! But it's impossible, and anyhow the train's not going to stop to let me do it. I must just look forward to when I'll see you again in Trahütten and have you all for myself ...

On the station I bought myself a detective novel to deaden my mind. In an hour's time we shall be at Marienbad, and I shall post this. By now you will already have had the mud-bath. Then sleep, then eat! *Please don't try to save money.*

Many kisses, my Schnude. The first half day of the twenty is over. I keep on counting!

Your Schribi

(143)   Again in the train,
                                                              3rd July 1914

A large part of the journey is over. The heat is indescribable. At Marienbad I changed my compartment, and found one in a coach which came from Eger, with only three men in it—although at the moment there are six of us again. Then I got a newspaper. Before that I'd had 'dinner' in the dining-car—have never eaten such abominable muck in my life! In the paper I read all about the arrival of the funeral train[2] at Vienna. On top of everything it had run over and killed a man near Bruck! I also read about the demonstrations in Vienna against the Serbian ambassador ...

At four I had coffee and cake in the dining-car, and that's the end of my money-spending. I'm getting out at Heiligenstadt,[3] taking the local railway to Hietzing, and carrying my case home. That way I'll avoid all the funeral procession business in Mariahilferstrasse.

I must stop. The heat has made me quite dull and stupid ...

(144)   Sunday evening
                                                            (5th July 1914)

Spent the day very simply. Working and telephoning all morning,

[1] Berg was at that time working on his *Three Orchestral Pieces*, op. 6.

[2] On 28th June the Archduke Franz Ferdinand (1863–1914), heir to the Austrian throne, and his wife were assassinated in Sarajevo. Their bodies were brought to Vienna.

[3] Northern suburb of Vienna.

at the piano again after lunch, then went over to see Stein—
I drove, because it started to rain. We couldn't go out for a walk,
so we chatted indoors about music and men, then I drove home.
And here I am in the empty flat, sitting at my desk to write to my
Pferscherl. I don't feel like going to dinner, because my loneliness
would get even worse and I only find a bit of peace, talking to you in
a letter. I keep thinking how very very alone you are, sitting in your
little room. Perhaps you haven't even got a book to interest you and
keep you pleasantly excited over a few hours. Wish I knew something
suitable to tide you over this bad time, one of the 'modern classics',
perhaps. You know what I mean, a book like *The Brothers Karamazov*
would be right. Besides its tremendous depth of thought and its
masterly conception, its story has such grandeur that once started
one could never put it down. The story in *The Possessed*, which is
just as important a book, may not be quite so strong, and if one is
feeling at all muzzy, it might easily leave one cold. That's how I feel
anyhow. Let me know if there's anything in this line you want.
You know just how I enjoy buying books! Or would you like one of
those we've got here that you've not read yet. Perhaps Dostoievsky's
Letters? I'll send it you, just say the word. Enough for today.

(145)   Monday, midday
                                          (6th July 1914)
... How happy I am that you are enduring your lot a little more
easily. If only it stays like that.

I have been working more successfully today than I did yesterday
—all morning, apart from a few interruptions.

The *Gurrelieder* rehearsals in Amsterdam went splendidly.
A great fuss has been made of Schoenberg, dinners and suppers
every day, car rides and motor-boat trips, Stein, of course, included
in everything ...

(146)   Monday evening
                                          (6th July 1914)
Another day gone, my Pferscherl. It went as planned. I drove
to Mitzi Lang,[1] bought the new breeches and jacket, and honestly
they suit me very well. I'm sure you'll be pleased with my purchase

---

[1] Berg's tailors.

for practicality (washable jacket, 'unwearout-able' breeches), and also for fine cut and colour (brown). Here's a drawing of them.

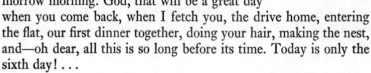

Then I returned to the garden, walked round thinking of various compositions, and finished by indulging in a lot of fruit-gorging: goose-berries, ripe and unripe, sour cherries. They made me so full I don't feel like any dinner!

Wonder what my Pferscherl is doing today. How I'm looking forward to a little letter to-morrow morning. God, that will be a great day when you come back, when I fetch you, the drive home, entering the flat, our first dinner together, doing your hair, making the nest, and—oh dear, all this is so long before its time. Today is only the sixth day! ...

(147)   Tuesday, midday
                                                        (7th July 1914)

... So now I have my Pferscherl with me: thanks to all the precious and beautiful photographs. The little face in the mudbath looks so sweet and *like* you, which comes from this being a snapshot. A face needs time to reach its full expressiveness, whereas a photo-graph is only 'exposing' one moment, out of the millions of moments in a human life. It's giving on one picture what the cinema-tograph repeats in hundreds. On the one hand, it's often only a single expression, a pose even, accidentally seized by the inanimate camera, though it could be a miracle seen through the eyes of an artist of genius; and yet the most important parts of the exposure unite without masking or wiping each other out. On the other hand, it's easy to understand how rarely a photograph gives the real impression of a person. But in your (mud-bath) picture the con-junction of looking, thinking and smiling, which, as you say, happened one after the other, has quite miraculously formed such a picture. I know very few professional photographs as lifelike, perhaps Mahler's picture in my room (Schoenberg's isn't nearly so good). You must tell me in detail what *you* think.

You know my day's work up to lunch-time. In the afternoon I was in the garden with Toni,[1] and we worked hard, picking cherries for

[1] Toni was the Bergs' housekeeper. As they lived nearby, she sometimes also helped out in the Nahowski and Lebert households.

157

jam and liqueur, and gooseberries for jam. Then home, cold bath, into town to fetch the photographs. Straight back to Auntie, who was very nice and admired the pictures. Home, dinner—only my appetite is very small, yet I'm getting fatter every day. Now I must help Toni take out the stones ...

(148)   Wednesday, 8th July
    Had a hard-working day, and a successful one, with lots of important and beautiful ideas coming up in my mind. Only hope I can summon up the strength to put them down just as they occurred to me. But that's still a long way off. Nearly as far as it is from the inspiration of an experience till the moment when it assumes musical form. Of course many experiences never reach that stage at all, or if they do, the form is completely lifeless!
    One more thing to tell you—that I feel terribly lonely, and that you must let me know when you'll be coming back to Vienna. I count the days, telling myself at noon 'another half-day gone' and in the evening 'another full day gone'.

(149)   10th July 1914, evening
... worked successfully. The great piece, the '*March*',[1] is coming along nicely. I keep thinking of it all day long, and even if I am not actually working on it, it is still seething inside me. That's the only way I can explain to myself why some things, the way to solve particular problems, say, don't occur to me for a long time, and then suddenly there they are—for instance, after writing a letter to you, which can't be called 'resting'! But giving lessons is a terrible strain for me, my brain is always quite barren afterwards. I have to think myself completely into my pupils'[2] ideas, to hire myself out, as it were, and it's extremely hard to find my way back from there into my own thinking.

(150)   11th July 1914
... I'd love to finish the little piano piece[3] for you and get it down

    [1] Later to become the third of the *Three Orchestral Pieces*.
    [2] His pupils in these and later years include Gottfried Kassowitz, Hans Erich Apostel, Fritz Heinrich Klein, and Willi Reich.
    [3] Ten years later, at Helene's request, this 'Klavierstückerl' was incorporated into the score of *Wozzeck*, becoming the basis of the famous D minor Interlude before the last scene of Act Three.

on paper, but it just won't take shape at present. Those few bars are really only a beginning, a sort of continuation and end, and of course I could join them up, but it would be just a school exercise, and even you wouldn't like that. I couldn't give my best in it, as I want to do. Perhaps the theme itself is not quite original, somehow derivative in mood and tone, although I can't think of any possible model for it. In all the works I've finished, I have always given the very best of which I was capable at that time, so that I could dedicate them to you, Pferscherl, with a clear conscience as valid self-expression, not derivative: the Piano Sonata, op.1; the Four Songs, op.2; the String Quartet, op.3; the 'Picture Postcards', op.4; and the Four Pieces for Clarinet and Piano, op.5.

I shall be dedicating the new pieces for orchestra to Schoenberg. As my teacher he has long been due for a large-scale work dedicated to him by me. He asked for it outright in Amsterdam as a present for his fortieth birthday. He 'ordered' it, in fact, and was my inspiration for it, not only through my listening to his own pieces for orchestra (but remember, mine don't derive from them, they will be utterly different), but because he urged and advised me to write character pieces.

So if I don't *officially* dedicate these three pieces to Pferscherl, and even if Pferscherl should not like them straight away, I know she will one day love them as she loves me, with all my faults, perhaps even more than that little piano piece, should I ever finish it. I still haven't lost faith in the things I wrote before, even though you didn't care for all of them. I know you would very much like the Quartet if it were performed today. And the Altenberg songs were after all written for you. If you heard them sung properly and all together—in less disturbing circumstances![1] I believe you would enjoy them, even the ones you disliked sung out of context and rather murdered by Boruttau.

[1] Two of the *Five Songs* (*Picture-postcard texts by Peter Altenberg*) were performed in the now-historic concert in Vienna on 31st March 1913 which led to one of the most famous scandals in modern music. The concert presented first performances of Webern's *Six Orchestral Pieces*, Zemlinsky's *Four Orchestral Songs to Poems of Maeterlinck*, Schoenberg's *Kammersymphonie* op.9 and two of Berg's *Five Songs*.
'If the concert was intended to be a memorable occasion, it surely succeeded for it occasioned the greatest uproar which has occurred in a Vienna concert hall in the memory of the oldest critics writing. Laughter, hisses applause continued throughout a great deal of the actual performance ... After the Berg songs the dispute became almost a riot ... Finally the president of the Society came and boxed the ears of a man who had insulted him ... '
—*Musical Courier*, 23rd April 1913

As for the clarinet pieces, they aren't very striking in form, but equally important in intention. You may love them too when you know their content better and hear them well played. That will also be the time for your understanding the works I am writing now. Whether they merit that, I can't say now while working on them. Sometimes everything seems good and flowing, then again I'm so dissatisfied with it I could tear it up, like today, for instance, when progress has been slow and laborious. If I didn't know that a proper judgment can only be formed long after a work is finished, I should despair every second day.

It's a bit the same as with us two, Schnude. As you know, there are days when I am grumpy, or when you feel you've a right to tell me: 'You don't love me any more.' But you haven't got that right, it's the only right you do not possess. You know quite well that you are a piece of me (one of my pieces?!), and that there is no variation in our belonging together, at most a sadness if you should be cross with me, a cheerfulness, happiness, when you are nice to me . . .

(151) Vienna, 12th July 1914

After five hours sitting at the piano, completely absorbed in my work, until my back aches, it's like a big reward when I turn to my desk and write to my Pferscherl. But don't think, my only one, that I have become so modest in my demands that I'm content to be just writing to you. No, you can't imagine the furious pain which sometimes grips me. Only sometimes? Yes, my Pferscherl, this mixture of fury and pain sometimes flares up out of the constant sadness: the pain of being so lonely without you, the fury that I can't change it. I worked out today how much it would cost if I came to you for a day—but it's too much. Even if I do it on the cheap, third-class, no dining-car, without staying overnight, it would be fifty Crowns, which I haven't got. I've got just about half that, to live on for ten or twelve days. Also, I should certainly get asthma if I were in the train for two days. Although I feel perfectly well now, no asthma at all, I had a bad attack four or five days ago, and a lot of trouble the next day. But it's completely over, thank God, so I can tell you about it.

Tomorrow I meet Linke, perhaps we'll go for a long walk. Oh, it will be very different walking in Trahütten—and looking for mushrooms. Towards evening I'll go out into the garden and take work with me, I'll copy what I have composed today, and so the

With Schoenberg, 1914

Berg and Anton Webern in 1912

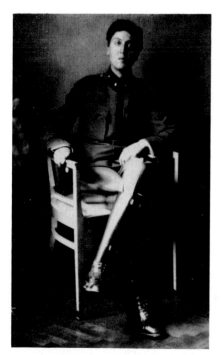

Left, Berg in military uniform in 1915; *below*, (left to right) Helene Berg, Alma Mahler-Werfel, Franz Werfel and Alban Berg

evening will come. Reading the *Fackel*, thinking all the time of Pfersch. Of your dear dear voice, which I heard today, though only from afar on the telephone.

Sweet of you to telephone me, Schnude, even though we couldn't talk much and I didn't catch everything you said. But it was still a piece of *physical* contact, much more than it is with letters . . .

Work went better today. But now comes the big cliff. Pferscherl must pray that I can sail round it safely. Will you do that? And always think lovingly of me, and write me everything? . . .

The singers of the *Gurrelieder* at Leipzig are all unknown to me —apart from la Mildenburg. One's a Dutch tenor. Tove is a soprano, surname Siegl, I think. Polnauer is very sad that Winternitz is not singing. La Freund won't be singing either.[1] (I know somebody who will be pleased!)

. . . The new *Fackel* is marvellous again, and very long, nearly a hundred pages. But I promise I won't read at night, though I haven't finished it yet. So Schnude will have to wait a bit longer, till I can send it to her, with several passages marked.

What do you think of, before you go to sleep? Do you still pray, my darling?

(152)
Monday morning,
13th July 1914

You have never given me more joy than with your last letter. It almost brings tears to my eyes when I think of it and try to find words to thank you for it. Now my work[2] will really thrive. And if it is worth anything, that will be thanks to you, because I so much want to write something for you, and also because I believe you will like what I am writing. Why haven't I talked to you about it before? The urge to do so has often been strong, but one feels terribly shy about baring one's innermost feelings, even if one has already done so in music . . . Still, I would have overcome that shyness long ago, if you had given me a nudge in that direction. But you didn't say you wanted to hear more about the work. In fact, I felt very flattered and honoured and in one way deeply pleased by your saying (my proud little girl!) that you didn't want to 'intrude on

[1] Marya Freund (b. 1876), Polish-Czech soprano, was famous for her performances in modern music.
[2] The *Three pieces for Orchestra*, op.6.

me'. So I too kept quiet about it, though in another way just as 'sad', or even sadder, than you, dearest.

That's why I am now so happy. Thank you from the very bottom of my heart, where I usually get my tunes from!

The *March* will be ready soon, but I shan't orchestrate it till I'm in Trahütten. Here I just want to finish the first of these three pieces for orchestra. The *March* is the third. I've done very little on the second yet, which is to be called *Reigen*,[1] but it's the piece Pferscherl will like most of all—it will be a very tender but also cheerful dance-type piece.

The *Fackel* has gone to you today, please confirm arrival! The letter to Katzerl[2] is very good. I have written a sort of continuation to it—which you can fill out and make more personal. Anyhow the letter must make it clear that the only reason we didn't follow up the invitation straight away was modesty, and that we leave it to her whether she would still like to see us towards the end of the month. Send it off *very soon*, putting your address (clearly!) at the back of the envelope.

Mama's[3] letter is dreadful, something *must* be done for this poor woman. It's quite pitiful that somebody who has (nearly) every reason to be content, or at least to make life pleasant for herself, should go into a decline and live in such misery . . .

I have lost my good Koh-i-noor pencil, including the nice top, perhaps while picking the gooseberries. Might this be an omen? I am growing more and more superstitious!

Webern also wrote to me today. He spends a lot of time at his father's mine.[4]

(153)   14th July 1914

A strange day! After lunch I went back to work, and wrote the end of the *March*. I felt it was not quite right. After tea (I read the evening paper in the café) I tried to rectify the small fault in construction, but in the end was not too sure what needed changing. One loses 'ear' and judgment. It won't occur to me what's wrong

[1] 'Round'.
[2] 'Katzerl' is one of the Bergs' pet names for Alma Mahler (1879–1964), the composer's widow, who was a great friend of theirs. Another such name was 'Almschi'—not to be confused with 'Antschi', their pet name for Helene's sister, Anna.
[3] Helene's mother.
[4] Webern's father was a mining engineer.

162

till tomorrow, or perhaps it's right as it is after all. The *March* has become pretty lengthy. Once again a long movement after so much short stuff. It's longer than the five orchestral songs together. While I'm still here[1] I want to finish the first draught of the so-called Präludium. I'm using for it a good deal of the musical material which I intended to use in the symphony I began last year in Trahütten—it evidently wasn't meant to become a symphony! It didn't develop much beyond the Prelude, so that might introduce the Pieces for Orchestra instead of the symphony. What does Pferscherl say to that? It's eleven o'clock and I'm off to bed. Only hope my work will let me sleep, at present my head is buzzing. I'm looking forward to tomorrow's little letter. You darling! Good night—in my thoughts. I consulted the calendar about the music I have done today. It gave a good answer, though like the Delphic Oracle, not too encouraging.[2]

14
Dienstag
Ratḥ. u. Prot. Bonaventura
Die Kritiḱ ift leicḥt,
die Kunſt ift ſcḥwer.

(154)   15th July 1914
. . . You know my two warts. The one on the sole of my foot is completely healed. The other one on the big toe had begun to hurt again, so I started squeezing it. Soon it lost quite a lot of its core, and last night I scooped out the crater very professionally, as learned from the chiropodist. I went right down to the bottom, where the blood-vessels show. To make a thorough job, I also put some drops of glacial acetic acid into it. At night I woke up  with great pains. They kept me awake for a while, till the pain subsided thanks to my bathing the big toe—in a tumbler. Now I think this wart has also completely healed. Will be very interesting to see what happens . . .

[1] In Vienna.
[2] Here Berg stuck a leaf from a tear-off calendar. On it was the aphorism: 'Criticism is easy, art is difficult.'

You mustn't think your cure has been no use. First, you can't say anything *now*. Wait a few weeks, months even, and see if everything—intestines and rheumatism—hasn't improved and disturbs you less. Of *course* you won't be completely healthy yet. But I believe the progress of your conditions has been checked ... One can't get well in such a short time after being ill for years. How long is it since you've taken *real* action for your health? Not quite three weeks! All these household medicines and remedies from newspaper advertisements haven't been anything worth mentioning.

How I'm looking forward to tomorrow morning, and your telephone call. 'Who is speaking?' 'Oh, how lovely!'—hm, hm, hum, How good that will sound, and how good the kisses will taste! So different from writing down on dead paper 'love and kisses'. Now I want to write to Papa and to Jeanette,[1] while the people in the flat above keep playing:

Pleasant, isn't it!
If only my Pferscherl were here!
Once more kisses from
                                 Prep

I don't enjoy working just now. I'm so restless I almost have to force myself to work. Anyhow, everything I wanted to do *before* Trahütten is finished. But whether it's any good I don't know. You are right, time must pass before I can judge it. Perhaps a few days will be enough.

Now the day of your return is approaching. But so slowly, so very slowly. If only Saturday and Sunday were over ...
p.s. My photograph by D'Ora[2] has been published in a photographic magazine.

[1] Berg's mother.
[2] Well-known Viennese society photographer.

18th July 1914,
                                       Saturday, midday

Am I looking forward to seeing you again!? How can you ask
such a question? I am thirsting for it. I believe I would die of thirst
if you don't come soon, if I hadn't good hopes of seeing you soon,
of touching you, hearing you sing, caressing you. And on top of
this violent longing, there is a vague feeling, half joy, half anxiety,
which keeps me in a state people like to call nerviness. But what has
it got to do with nerves? They are only the conductors to head and
heart—which are sick when you are not with me. So that's my answer
to the first question . . .

Have I been faithful to you? I'm almost ashamed to answer 'yes'
to that. For if I were scoundrel enough not to have been, I should
also be shameless enough to deny the fact now. So it's almost like
praising myself for something which should be taken for granted.
But I fancy my Pferscherl might become suspicious if I took no
notice of the question—so I've answered it!

(158)   In the train,[1]
                                          4th November 1914

My Pferscherl,

I spent the first part of the journey reading newspapers, and
know two of them nearly by heart! I recommend the article in
today's *Neue Freie Presse*, which is particularly interesting, about
wounds in war. The most horrible example was a kind of arrow,
dropped from an aeroplane which fell straight down on to a soldier,
entered his collar-bone, pierced his lungs, diaphragm and intestines,
and came out at the hollow of his knee—death after a few minutes.

Otherwise—an ebbing tide everywhere. Belgium: futile savage
battles, and deliberate inundations which stop our advance there.
Retreat in Polish–Russia. But soon the flood tides will set in, and
with one of them the end of the war and our victory. Can I be of any
use? I had to run for a tram today, and had asthma all the time I
was on it. This damned getting up in the morning. I shall join the
army as a volunteer, on condition they fight only in the afternoon,
and let me sit down all morning!

In the tram I began to read Rosegger's novel *Martin the Man*,[2]

[1] The First World War had begun three months before. Berg was on his
way to the Berghof to hire staff, after Andreas, the steward, had been conscripted
into the army.
[2] *Martin der Mann* (1891) by Peter Rosegger.

and that soon made me forget my asthma. Now we are crossing the Semmering, in glorious sunshine—it gets better and better, the higher we go. Perhaps it's raining in Vienna, while here we are travelling with windows open. In the ditches below me there are patches of fog, lit so dazzlingly by the sun you can hardly look at them. On top of the Rax there is a bit of old snow lying in the furrows. If only I could see you, Pferscherl. How I wish you could soon come up here as Katzerl's guest, although Gucki[1] is now with you, and you will probably be visiting Katzerl in the afternoon. If I knew you were doing that, I should feel much happier. You must write to me at once—but now I'll go on reading for a bit. Oh, by the way, passed a goods train with a lot of young soldiers on the way to Serbia, and twenty or thirty new motor cars (privately owned).

I've eaten the three sandwiches with the greatest relish, they were excellent. You did them beautifully, Pferscherl. Now we're descending the Semmering. Fog increasing, it's getting cold and dull. One can only live at three thousand feet above sea-level!

Half-past twelve, lunch. Everything very good and plenty of it. Only twelve people in the dining car. The train's very empty, and at the moment I'm alone in my compartment. Now and then somebody comes in for one or two stops. And yet, although the people don't bother me and are quite nice, I breathed more freely in the better surroundings of the dining car. Two very nice old men were sitting next to me, and a wounded officer, who had a lot of very interesting things to tell us. He was at the battle of Tarnopol (Army Corps Auffenberg).[2] Near Knittelfeld[3] we passed a huge prisoner-of-war camp, a whole town of wooden huts for about 15,000 Russians.

It's not snobbishness that I don't like the common people. Perhaps it's only the appearance and smell of the third-class. I am sitting in the most horrible car. An axle or something like that must have broken. You feel as if the wheels were jumping across the sleepers, not gliding along the rails. And then the dirt, and the constant smell from the W.C. I don't feel well at all! The weather has improved again, and Villach is not very far now. So, my

[1] Gucki was the second daughter of Gustav and Alma Mahler: Anna (b. 1904) who later married Ernst Křenek. Maria, the elder daughter, had died in 1907 at the age of five. Berg and his wife were often guests at Alma Mahler's villa in Breitenstein on the Semmering.

[2] General Moritz von Auffenburg had defeated two Russian armies in a battle in Galicia on 26th August.

[3] Town in Styria.

Pferscherl, good-bye for today. Write to me soon, a nice long letter. And please, for Heaven's sake, for the sake of our love, don't try to save money on food—you really mustn't.

Kisses
Swibi

(159)   Evening, 4th November 1914,
Villach

Four o'clock, got in to Villach. Had a cup of coffee in the Café Streit, talked for a while with the café proprietor, and now have clearer view of the tasks ahead of me. I believe we can arrange things so that the farm stays as it is, and that I shall be able to find a manager. At least there are several ways I can try to do that. Please tell Mama this; I don't want to write to her till I know something definite.

At six o'clock, after the café proprietor wouldn't listen to me any more and vanished, I went to the cinema, to pass the time. For sixty hellers[1] I saw an excellent programme. Newsreels and an American war film (with marvellous naval battles). It was half, empty, by the way, like the whole of Villach, which looks pretty well extinct! Rather dreary.

Just fancy: the newspaper only appears in Villach three times a week. You have to wait till five in the afternoon for the papers from Vienna or Graz to come. Fine state of affairs!

At eight o'clock I went to my room, ate a rissole, and now I am sitting in the Post Restaurant drinking two or three glasses of very good new wine and writing to you. I want to go to bed early, as I have to get up in good time tomorrow morning and drive up to the Berghof as early as I can. I feel very, very lonely. I hope to get news tomorrow at the post office—and good news! Another thing—shall I buy some stores here if they are much cheaper than in Vienna? For that I would have to know the Vienna prices. As they are anyhow sending some corn on the cob from the Berghof, it could be sent at the same time . . .

5th November 1914

I slept well, and am now at the café reading the latest news. In Poland we have retreated quite a way, and the Russians are hot on our heels. Have you looked at the places on the map? Take the map

[1] One Crown was worth 100 Hellers.

of North West Russia, and go south west from Warsaw and Ivangorod. Now I go quickly to the post office, to pick up a thousand paper kisses! ...

Nothing in the post for me. So you didn't write the night before last. Now I have to go up to the Berghof without news, that's bad!

(160)   Evening, 6th November 1914

Listen to the events of today. I hired a bicycle, tried to see whether after fourteen or fifteen years I could still ride one, found I could, so rode off to the Berghof on it in the morning. But I hadn't thought of the mud. Rode through a morass, and ten minutes later was covered in spots of muddy white slush. No way of turning back, so on I went. In about forty minutes I was at the Berghof, arranged various important things successfully, and as I longed to get something warm in my tummy, and as the cycle hire is cheaper for half the day, I wanted to get back to Villach for lunch. Outside the Annenheim I met with a minor disaster: the chain broke, and there I was. I walked, pushing the cycle in front of me—up to St. Ruprecht the last station before Villach. But the train only goes in the afternoon, so I decided to 'dine' at St. Andrä, where I anyhow had things to discuss—and that was the best thing that could have happened to me. An excellent little inn with delicious food: local fish in butter—just like trout—with creamed potatoes, then apfelstrudel, also quite good, but I left half of it on the plate, being full up—although I had been *very* hungry. That cycle trip was more strenuous than I'd expected. Makes all the difference whether you have to push 70 to 80 pounds—or 150! I walked to St. Ruprecht, mounting the cycle when it was down-hill; then by train with the cycle to Villach ...

Now I am sitting at the Café Streit, having cleaned off the mud, and am dipping into the Rosegger book. It's the strangest of all his books, quite different from the rest—as *Swanwhite* is different from the rest of Strindberg's. There is something of Maeterlinck in it, but I don't mean that it has been influenced by Maeterlinck—I'm sure Rosegger doesn't even know him. So we don't need Maeterlinck.[1] Rosegger can strike the fairy-tale note just as well, and brings up hundreds of clever ideas, whereas in Maeterlinck there is such a hazy mood all the time. It's the same in music: take their hazy

[1] Maurice Maeterlinck had become very unpopular in Germany and Austria by violently opposing the German occupation of Belgium. Hence Berg's sudden hostility to his pre-war idol.

harmonies from Debussy, Ravel, Scriabin and the rest, and what is left? (In Debussy's case, two or three five-note motifs.) But in Schoenberg's works, particularly where there are rather similar harmonies—whole-tones and fourth-chords—you can also find his unprecedented melodic style which is not limited to one melodic line but progresses in a continual counterpoint of many beautiful themes. Anyhow, I hope you'll read this Rosegger novel, *Martin the Man*, and look forward to our having a talk about it.

Just as I was thinking of ending this letter, something happened which produced an interlude! The proprietor was playing cards at the table of the regular customers quite near me. When he came over to my table, I remarked on this, and he found out that I knew the game. So he offered to play me 'double or quits' for the new wine I was drinking. In a quarter of an hour I had scored terrific wins, and didn't have to pay for my drink! . . .

(161)   Saturday evening,
                                          7th November 1914

. . . Your lovely long letter made up for the post I've missed these last two days! I loved the way you told me about your visit to our friend Alma's. The style was so beautiful I could feel all you felt, and that's the finest compliment to any style, including musical style—that one can feel the growth of the composer's own feelings.

If only I had found a steward, I shouldn't need to remain here— or be at the Berghof. But I haven't got one. There are prospects of a foreman, but I am afraid he'll have to join up, and then in January we shall be in the same spot as today . . . I do hope I can travel on Tuesday, I'm longing for you so much, my dearest.

And I'm so horrified by the *milieu* I'm stuck in. These café-tables for 'regulars'. Villach has less than 20,000 inhabitants, but I'm sure there are 20,000 regulars at café-tables. There's one table here which is in grave danger from me, one of these days I'll throw a bottle at it. It's the table of the local worthies, six to ten bearded gentlemen: the orator, the silent listener, the thinker, the man-of-the-world, the smoker, the drinker, the argumentative character, the phlegmatic one, and so on . . .

I'm so looking forward to our own cosy table and the mushroom soup.

Can't keep my eyes open. Good-night, my dearest.

                                          Yours, yours, yours.

I'm thoroughly depressed after this lonely week, and if the good
of the Berghof didn't mean a lot to me, I couldn't bear it here . . .
Before engaging the man I chose, I had to obtain references at a
farm. I drove across country for about an hour (and got very cold),
along by a castle through an avenue of linden trees hundreds of
years old—must look splendid in spring. On my drive back I passed
a military hospital, with wounded soldiers looking out of a window.
There was a nurse with them who looked familiar to me, and after
I'd passed, I realized it was Webern's sister—I knew she was a
nurse. A few minutes later I met Webern's father, to our mutual
pleasure. He was on his way to his daughter, who is detained in the
hospital with some soldiers suspected of having cholera. He wanted
to talk to her through the window, and had brought her some
sweets.

Today I saw a long column of wounded soldiers—horrible.
And soon afterwards a company of soldiers shouting and singing, on
their way to the front. These are memories that won't be wiped out
in a hurry. I sometimes feel here as if I were living outside this
world. My pretty interests amidst the extraordinary maelstrom of
war. My head is just not big enough to take it all in. You read
'Tsingtow fallen', and five minutes later you've forgotten about it,
instead of rushing off into the mountains or swimming far out into
the lake to weep one's heart out, which would be more appropriate.

All these minor events in the war seem more overwhelming than
any we've ever experienced before or perhaps shall ever experience
again. Yet they are only tiny fractions in this piece of world history,
and in the end you take no more notice of them than of some war
you learnt about at school. How important the human spirit is!

(163)   12th December 1914

Well, Pferscherl, to tell you about the journey.[1] At the beginning,
as usual, reading the papers, don't want to look out of the window.
I don't much care for the scenery before Gloggnitz. And even after
that, when the Semmering begins, I'm always reluctant to look out
—from a sort of aversion against 'sight-seeing'. But it's no good, I'm
gradually drawn towards the window more and more, and in
the end my heart seems to be bursting at the sight of all this

[1] Five weeks after the first journey Berg had to travel to the Berghof once
more.

magnificence, ever fresh and ever more beautiful. It was again the most glorious autumn up there, with a fine snow-cap only on the tops of those wooded, rocky mountains. The Rax and the Schneeberg were indescribably beautiful in their infinite purity. By the time we were approaching Semmering Station fog had come up as if from a chimney behind the ridge.

It was quite strange, and wonderful.

In Styria I realized where the fog came from. It was deep winter there, everything wrapped in snow and fog. At Mürzzuschlag I walked along the platform, and looked greedily at the people eating sausages. Suddenly—who should be standing behind the counter, selling hot sausages—but the trumpeter Stelwagen![1] We recognized each other. I walked past him, not saying anything, but whistling.[2]

Lunch-time, dining-car: uneatable soup, very good carp with creamed potatoes, good roast veal with rice and spinach, very good sweet Gorgonzola with butter, black coffee. Near Knittelfeld, where there is a prisoner-of-war camp, they had just had lunch. Very interesting.

Now I am back again in my compartment, alone, continuing my correspondence! . . .

In an hour's time I shall be in Villach. Now I want to have a bit of peace. All this travelling and smell has made me feel quite sick. Otherwise I am right . . . I am so glad your little throat has stayed all right. And now kisses.

---

[1] Principal trumpet player at the Vienna Tonkünstler-Orchester. He gave up his job when he married, and became the owner of the station-restaurant at Mürzzurhlag.

[2] In the following facsimile Berg quotes from the first trumpet part of Schoenberg's *Gurrelieder*, which was first performed in 1913.

11./12. 14 Also Pfeffer mußte meine
Reize zu bringen! Anfangs – wie gewöhn-
lich – Zeitung lesen. Ich mag sie auch
hinausschauen Ich liebe diese Instlschaf-
tgen bei flaggens nicht und dann
wenn die Dämmerung gegen beginnt,
widerstrebt's mir noch immer hinaus-
zu schauen. So eine Art Aversion gegen
die "gewissen Sehens- wirdigkeiten" aber
es nützt nichts. Möglich zieht's auch
immer mehr und mehr zum Fenster und
schließlich geht's und mir das Herz über in
einer neuen- in immer stärerauffiarende
Inbilck dieser Pracht. So war früh
wieder der fröhliche Sonnenaufgang. Da
oben wird die schützen dieser felsigen
Wasberge war zart benebeint. Wie
schön aber die Rax u. der Schneeberg
dalagen in ihrer unendlichen Rein-
heit. Kann ich sie nicht sagen. –
Schon in der Nähe der Seinaglestation

welote fic Nebel. Er zog mi
aus einen Schlot hinter einen
Berg wirken heraus

Ware ganz ngeautemlig; wunterbar.
In Nenemarkt würde mir Klos-
wafer der Nebel kom. Dort war
tieften Winter. Alles in Schnee u
Nebelgehüllt.
In Müggzotgen promenierst
ist an Perron u. joch hierzu

Schicke den letzten Vorspielen
... zur. Nor --- wer steht
dahinter der Bühne und
vielleicht heiße Wünsche ---?
: der Trompeter Stellungen !!!
Wir sehen uns ! Heimlich
geh ich an ihr vorüber und pfeife :

[musical notation]

etc ......

Mittag Speisewagen :
... Suppe (Gerstel — nach
dem Verschnitt Gerstel benannt)
sehr guter Karpf mit Schwarz - Ritter

Unter Kalbsparadeischnitten ist
Reis und Spinat. Faberkeres
Schweinskotel ist Salat (Vofait-
tet Kässl) Crème schnitten ref gut
Gorgon - Zola mit Butter u.s. Mocca
Am Knittelfell nur Gefangenenlager
ist, würde gerade überspritzt.
Sehr interssant. Da ein Hügel
darvor ist fuch ich mir folgentes:

- - - - besätt müssle Zeller mögen
- - - Baguette der Wolga
Kamin Fer - Kürke

(164)   In the train,[1]
                                     29th December 1914
    Today we parted without the usual goodbye note. I meant to write
it in the bathroom, but when I came back into the sitting-room and
you called me, I forgot, and only remembered it in the tram. But
I have *said* everything—more than everything—which I wanted to
tell you for the time I am away. Above all, despite your diet, *eat
enough.*
    Nothing much for me to report, except that I had dreadful
fellow-passengers up to Semmering. A gang of toboggan-racers, who
talked all the time and all at once . . .
    The air in the compartment is indescribable. My ears hurt
because of the smell and the airlessness. First I read the papers, then
Bismarck's *Memoirs.*[2] Like all great men he had a lot to suffer from
his own people. To call him a traitor is as great a sin as calling
Schoenberg a fool.
    Out there nothing but snow, and rain on top of it. I don't look out
at all. One becomes apathetic. People are quite unreceptive in this
period—to art or nature. Even though I have a growing desire for
both inside me, as long as this intoxication lasts, this dream-like
state in which the war has put me, there is no chance for people like
us to enjoy art or nature. And we shall always be disappointed when
we try—unless we're a Weingartner or a toboggan-racer! . . .

(165)   Evening, 31st December 1914,
                                                  Villach
    . . . A quick note so that you get this express letter tomorrow, New
Year's Day, and I don't have to send a telegram: to tell you that I am
travelling to Vienna the day after tomorrow. Tomorrow I am having
one more meeting with the new steward and his wife at the Berghof.
And his wife. Anderl's sister had already been engaged as the new
housekeeper, but because of the steward's wife, I had to send her
home again. Today of all days, when all the jobs for 1915 have
already gone. She left her very satisfactory job only because the
Mendel women[3] asked her to do so, and meanwhile her old job has
gone too. She's a very nice person as well, so it was a horrible thing

    [1] Once more Berg had to go to the Berghof to engage personnel.
    [2] The first two volumes of Bismarck's *Memoirs* were published after his
death (in 1898); the third volume only after the First World War, in 1919.
    [3] The proprietress of a farm near the Berghof.

to have to send her away, and it'll take me a long time to forget. Of course the simple peasant girl didn't dare to make a fuss with the master from the city. I felt quite wretched and guilty, but couldn't help her. I was obliged to give her a fortnight's wages, but in fact gave her a whole month's wages as compensation. She walked off with her bundle, going home for the moment anyhow . . .

(166)   New Year's Eve 1914
                                                      Villach, 31st December,
                                                                          night
Last letter this year. To my Pferscherl, of course: as it's the first New Year's Eve we are not together and I am not at home. I'm feeling very much alone. Understandable, then, that my thoughts turn again to the war. It frightens me more than ever, now I've realized it is going to last for ages longer.

I couldn't imagine that its task would be fulfilled all that quickly: the task of making the world clean! Everything is very much as it was before. There are still people, families, cities, that don't feel the war at all. Our corrupt condition—by which I mean the aggregation of stupidity, avarice, journalism, business spirit, laziness, selfishness, capriciousness, deceit, hypocrisy and all the rest—hasn't changed at all. Sometimes there are things which look or sound like an improvement, but they turn out to be merely a set of clichés that would go well into cheap lyrics for singing, howling or spitting by our society of operetta enthusiasts.[1] In fact I offer this as a suggestion to Herr Leo Fall—to produce a patrol march based on the tune 'In the Park', Herr Lehár to fart a waltz 'Shoulder to Shoulder', Herr Eysler to sick up a sentimental number 'Our Poor Soldiers in the Trenches'. Herr Oscar Straus should have first option of a 'Gavotte for Cripples'. A public that did not shudder at these gentlemen's peacetime output is still ripe for such masterpieces.

Yes, the war has to continue. The muck-heap has been growing for decades, and in its midst there is still no trace of cleanness to be found. Believe me, if the war ended today, we should be back in the same old sordid squalor within a fortnight. As the shares rose, the spiritual values would fall. It is not enough that shrapnel is knifing through the ranks of poor soldiers and even slitting up the moneybags of rich non-combatants. The war's great surprise will be in the

----

[1] In his violent outburst against the Viennese operetta and its composers, Berg includes two, whom he usually appreciated, Leo Fall and Oscar Straus.

guns, which are going to show a frivolous generation their utter emptiness. Perhaps the truth will dawn then—that there exist different values from those which up to now have been taken as the only salvation.

No, not enough has happened yet. How fervently I wish for peace, for the end of this intolerable horror and suffering! But I still cannot ask for this wish to be fulfilled. I know the war must go on until its true task is completed.

These are the thoughts which burden my heart now and make me greet with trembling the New Year that starts in a few minutes. All around me smug Philistinism, so I retire into my most private being and celebrate its arrival by sending a telegram to my Pferscherl.

1st January 1915
Ten minutes after midnight

Suddenly I was in darkness, a clock struck twelve, and when the light went up again, I found on my table a glass of punch sent me by Paltinger,[1] which reminds me very much of your father's New Year's Eve drink. Then a very fat chimney sweep appeared, carrying under his arm a sweet little piggy. Everybody stood up and drank toasts to each other, while I alone sat there quietly, thinking of my Pferscherl, who will be safe and sound in bed, slumbering happily into the New Year . . .

(167) Station Restaurant, Graz[2]

(Undated, 12th August 1915)

Have read your dear long letter, my Pferscherl, which has made everything so much easier for me than I should otherwise have found it. How sweet of you to write me such a long letter so early in the morning, and think of everything. Don't worry, I'll always do everything properly and write you all about things. So: no more worries in the cool, blissful regions of Trahütten.

Sitting at lunch here in Graz, I am horrified at the physiognomies all round me. Much much worse than those of our dear rustics!

(167a) 13th August 1915

Journey to Vienna went well. Met Bummel[3] on the train. He told

---

[1] The hotel-keeper in Villach.

[2] On his way from Trahütten to Vienna to join the No. 1 Militia Rifle Regiment.

[3] A holiday acquaintance of Berg's.

me his brother was at Fort Nensel near Malborget, which the Italians have been shelling heavily. He had distinguished himself, was promoted, and mentioned in dispatches. In the cellars, right down in the fortress, the officers were celebrating his promotion when an Italian bomb exploded, killing the lot, including Bummel's brother.

At the station in Vienna I couldn't get any transport. Walked round with my two bags for three-quarters of an hour, till I at last found a one-horse carriage. At home everything all right ...

Medical inspection at half-past eight. I was passed fit, like everybody else, without even being examined. When asked if I had any ailments, said 'no'—again like all the rest. So I shall enter the service on Monday morning, for the moment in Hütteldorf. There I shall be told which battalion I'm being drafted to.

Am still a bit tired, but otherwise well and no asthma. It's nice and cool here, so how lovely it must be at Trahütten ... The chicken was wonderful. Please enjoy your time at Trahütten. Ten million kisses!

Your own
Alban

(168)　　　　　　　　　　　　　　　　　　14th August (1915)
My dearest Pferscherl,

Today I'm treating myself to one more good day. Am in bed, having breakfast and writing this. Not much to report. Oath-taking took quite a long time. Then I drove to town, paid for my books (Büchner[1]), got a new book by Rosegger, *Stories from Styria*.

Then to Almschi, who was as charming as ever. This morning I met Stein and Steuermann,[2] who is on a week's leave. Perhaps like him I'll get light duties. My tiredness yesterday showed me how little stamina I have. At Höchtl's restaurant I ate corn on the cob and black pudding with horse-radish. At the risk of going down to posterity as a terrible glutton—in case my letters should ever get that far (have taken a great dislike to posterity already!)—I have to inform you that the best way to prepare black pudding is this: cut it raw in slices, and only fry it then. It's heavenly. I'm sure this must

---

[1] George Büchner (1813–1837), whose fragment, *Wozzeck*, Berg had seen for the first time in May 1914 on the stage of the Wiener Kammerspiele.

[2] Eduard Steuermann (b. 1892), Polish pianist, pupil of Schoenberg's.

have been Seraphita's food,[1] although Balzac doesn't tell us anything about it. I would simply call it Pud' à la Swedenborg.[2]

Your first letter has arrived. You are a darling, but not sensible! There is no reason for you to come here earlier. I promise you I'll write at once should I have practical reasons for wanting you in Vienna next week—if I needed nursing, say, or it was essential in my new profession! But if there are no such reasons, I'll gladly put up with my longing and loneliness in order to keep you in the conditions which are so important for your health. So: be sensible, my dear kind Pferscherl. I am always with you, and if you can't manage to feel that all the time, then feel it when you're reading my letters. Feel that I'm sitting right by you and that the only way we can write is by holding hands, that's to say being very very close to each other.

Was at Auntie's place by a quarter-past nine. Asked her for an apple, and she had one fetched from the pantry, where there were some stored beginning to rot. Declined with thanks, went out into the garden, ate five of the most beautiful ones straight off the tree, and wrote to Papa about the brilliance of this year's fruit harvest! Vegetables also very plentiful, two ten-pound parcels will be going off to Almschi on Monday.

Then I went to find out about our 'reversion'.[3] It's extremely simple. We go along one day to the priest, who is a very nice chap, with our Protestant marriage certificate (which I've got), and everything will be arranged in ten minutes.

Then I went to see Stein. He told me a terrific amount about Schoenberg, and things on the Semmering. Apparently there were wild scenes there, ranging from great violence to quite unintentional farce. A tremendous quarrel between Schoenberg and Frau Lieser,[4] so that Schoenberg suddenly wanted to go back to Berlin. In the end she apologized, and he stayed. He has behaved rather

[1] In the winter of 1912 Berg had planned to write a symphonic poem on Balzac's novel *Seraphita*. The work never materialized.

[2] Emanuel von Swedenborg (1688–1772), the Swedish philosopher, was one of Berg's idols.

[3] Berg and Helene were both Catholics originally, but Herr Nahowski made it a condition of his consent to their marriage that they should become Protestants —because divorce would be easier. Shortly before Berg joined up, they returned to the Catholic faith and went through a Catholic marriage ceremony.

[4] Lilly Lieser-Landau, a friend of Alma Mahler's. Schoenberg and his family spent the summer as guests at her house on the Semmering. When the war started Schoenberg was living in Berlin. He stayed there until the summer of 1915. From December 1915 to September 1916, and then from July to October 1917 he served in the Austro-Hungarian army.

badly to her, but on the other hand she is extremely mean over food —for instance, one stuffed kohlrabi as main course. (She herself has always eaten properly by herself before the meal!) Also pretty drastic scenes between L. and Almschi. After refraining for a long time Schoenberg finally went to Almschi, who was charming to him and also abused L. all the time. So that Schoenberg, who had been very irritable all through the week and justifiably in a bad frame of mind, suddenly became a changed man—Almschi certainly knows how to handle him.

Schoenberg and wife were with Almschi for lunch and stayed all afternoon. At seven o'clock, green with jealousy, L. went over there (with Stein), and Almschi greeted them with the words: 'Herr Schoenberg has made me three-quarters well again.' Afterwards he was at her house again, but unfortunately never managed to get through any work all this period. He actually left Vienna without saying good-bye to L., etc. etc. Lots of other amusing gossip I'm dying to tell you.

On 26th January 1916 Stein will probably be performing Mahler's Third. When I went to see him, he and Steuermann had just played the third movement: 'Cuckoo has fallen to his death.' Imagine it—after an age without hearing any music!

After my long talk with Stein I did some shopping, for things I'll need when I'm in the army. Clothes brush, blacking brush, shoe brush, tooth-brush, comb, eating utensils, soap. Brushes first-class, the rest simple and practical—twenty Crowns altogether.

I think of everything! Your name-day is on the 18th (Catholic Helene, Protestant Hellena, Malayan 'Schnude'). I would like to give you something really nice, but don't know what. I'll send some small thing, and you'll get your real present in Vienna if you tell me what you would like or what you need. And now kisses and more kisses . . .

(169)   14th August 1915, evening
. . . I want to catch up with several things I didn't tell you yesterday—in the Schoenberg-Almschi-Frau L. saga.

The Schoenbergs go with the L. family to Breitenstein. They get out at the station, S., plus wife and two children, servant girl and dog, L. with children, servants, four dogs. At the same time Almschi alights from her compartment—she had been a second time in Vienna without visiting S. Outside the station she has to wait for her luggage. In the end she has no alternative but to greet the adjoining party. I gather it was very terse and cool on both sides. Stein says S. felt very hurt by this and by Almschi's behaviour generally, as she had already received Stein and not him. S. also said it was no wonder she is constantly plagued by illnesses and depressions if she, Mahler's widow, becomes Kokoschka's wife.[1]

However, she was charming to Schoenberg later on when he visited her, which wiped out these bad impressions. At Stein's vist her main complaint was that Schoenberg had a wife whom he even has to accompany to the dentist, for instance. True, her Gustav had once suggested going with *her* to the dentist, but she had refused *as a matter of course*. Frau Schoenberg should shield her husband from all financial worries, instead of insisting that he shouldn't bother her with them.

Stein also found it strange that Frau Schoenberg egged him on even more, after the big quarrel with Frau L. was over, and Frau L. had sworn by her children's life (on Schoenberg's insistence) that she hadn't meant to insult him. His wife seems to enjoy working her husband up. Almschi also kept presenting her own mother as a model housewife, whereupon I emphasized Almschi's own talents in that direction from my own experience and as I have heard from you, who understands these things.

Before Schoenberg went to stay with Almschi, there had been quarrels too between Stein and Schoenberg. Once Schoenberg wanted Stein to promise to give a message word-for-word to Almschi, and Stein refused unless he knew what the message meant. Schoenberg was furious, 'Now you have betrayed yourself' (perhaps as no friend of his?). The message, as later transpired, was that as she wasn't very well she should cease to bother with his affairs. He then gave Frau L. the same commission, which she evidently didn't carry out ...

Can't think of any more gossip, so I shall go home. Tomorrow afternoon I am meeting Stein, in the evening Arthur.[2] Day after that—'soldier'.

Have a terrific longing to sit down at the piano and work. Yesterday I played for five minutes—well, only chords, sounds. Another world!

---

[1] Alma Mahler and Oskar Kokoschka for some time thought of marrying.
[2] Arthur Lebert, the husband of Helene's sister, Anna.

You mustn't be cross if I don't write you a long letter today and in the next few days. But I'm incredibly tired, and tomorrow I have to get up at a quarter to four. So here's my daily despatch. Half past four made my tea, back to bed with that and a sausage. Up at half past five, bath etc. Left at six, and was outside barracks at half past. Half an hour early, so went to a café to read morning papers. Happened to be a soldier sitting at next table. He talks to me, says he can help me get into what they call the 'artists' company'. All the actors from the court theatres are in it, and writers, doctors, lawyers. The whole thing was settled in the café!

Stand about in the barrack yard, and in the end a corporal calls me. He is surprised at my name, recognizes me—as he is a pupil of Watznauer's.[1] As his protégé I can at least have a quarter of an hour's rest in a restaurant. Eat a goulash, then we march off at half past eleven—well, not exactly march, we go by tram . . . Back to barracks at 1.15, came across a former school-friend, more waiting. A second school-friend turned up, one I used to get on very well with; Huber,[2] now part owner of the clothes drapers, Bohlinger and Huber. Two hours pass, chatting, before I get my uniform. Who goes there? Linke—what a coincidence! I pay a tip of two Kronen and get a uniform.

You can't imagine it—the smell! Still, thanks to the two Kronen it's at least fairly clean, though trousers are too short. But the great thick cap, and the haversack—someone must have bled all over that! More waiting now, another soldier recognizes me, introduces himself as a bassoon player from the Concert Society (he played at the performance of the Altenberg Songs). Later someone else says, 'I know you from Hietzing.' He's one of the young people who lived in the Wolter-house, and keep on playing the piano—his brother owns the house.

6 p.m.—dismissed at last. Retire to a café half dead. Write a card to Mama, 7 p.m. to Hietzing for dinner with Arthur (assorted cold meats, corn on the cob, warmed up vegetables). Sheer physical enjoyment of sitting down and eating; almost indescribable. By the way, I carried the uniform away wrapped in paper because we haven't yet learned saluting! But tomorrow I have to go to the barracks in uniform, that'll be something when I meet an officer!

[1] Hermann Watznauer, friend of the Berg family, Berg's mentor after his father's death.
[2] Hans Huber, later Kommerzial-Rat (Councillor of Commerce).

In the evening at Maxingstrasse[1] your people thought I looked quite nice in uniform. Others laughed. Your aunt, naturally, said: 'Oh, you poor, poor thing' . . .

(171)   17th August 1915
Darling Pferscherl,

I'm well, and have nice educated people as my superiors. We are quite apart from the others. This morning we went to the Schmelz.[2] Drilled there with half an hour's break until a quarter to eleven. Back to the barracks, free till 1.45. Would like to be left in peace now, but we have to go back to the Schmelz this afternoon. At least there is a nice cool breeze there, though unfortunately it always smells of horse-dung. Today an officer cadet introduced himself, he knows me by reputation and is himself a composer (performed by the Musicians and Concert Society, and therefore trash). I'll find your letter tonight, then I'll continue.

Right. Back to the Schmelz to drill, and again that constant horse-dung zephyr. Back after four, singing students' and soldiers' songs. Endless standing about in the barracks. At 5.30 finish, to the Café Gropl for a black coffee and reading the evening papers and special issues, then home: to find your dear letter, and one from Mama with her blessings and good wishes on my enlistment. Dinner at Maxingstrasse, then home, writing to Pferscherl in bed, re-reading your letter. Am free of asthma again, so don't be afraid, my darling, that I am sitting up in bed and suffering. I've never slept so well . . .

(172)   Undated
                                          (Sunday, 3rd October 1915)

We are at the East Station, my Pferscherl, and have an hour to wait. A great depression has come over me. How will it all go? I long for you so terribly. We have come here by tram, had our food in the school: boiled beef and cabbage . . .

(173)   Sunday, 3 p.m.

The train will soon get in to Bruck.[3] I feel so sad. Many, many

[1] Helene's parents' flat.
[2] Vienna's military parade grounds.
[3] Bruck an der Leitha (*Kiralyhida* in Hungarian), a town in Lower Austria near the Hungarian border, where Berg was drafted for further training.

184

kisses. If only we could have been together for half an hour. When shall we see each other again?

(174)   Undated
                                       (Monday, 4th October 1915)
   First moment I've had a chance to write: midday 4th October in the Bruck camp during dinner break. Still don't know train connections, nor when and where there's chance of our meeting. Hope to be able to write to you tonight, so that you can get here early enough on Wednesday. If not, I'll give you a time for Thursday. It will be in the evening anyhow, at 5 or 5.30, till the evening train back (leaves Bruck 5.45, I think, getting in to Vienna at 9). I shall be free Saturday afternoon and Sunday till the evening. I am quite all right apart from my great longing for you, my darling. Hundreds of kisses, perhaps I'll send you a telegram when and where to come.
   My address: Volunteer Alban Berg,
                  Militia Group 3 Company, 1st Platoon,
                  Reserve Officers' School, Old Camp,
                  Hut 14, Bruck-Kiralyhida, Hungary.

(175)   Undated
                                           (4th October 1915)
Darling Pferscherl,
   This is Hell in the truest sense of the word. Please come on Wednesday, then I'll tell you everything. Each new bad experience makes you forget the ones before. For instance, yesterday's military transport already seems far in the past.
   Just imagine, though. Standing outside the train for a whole hour in pouring rain, then crammed into the compartment soaking wet at half past one, then seven hours for a distance any local train would do in an hour and a quarter. From half past six till nine we sat in darkness, the train was at stops most of the time. Then half an hour at the double to the camp, where they gave us black coffee for supper—and we hadn't had any food since 10.30 a.m. in Vienna. If you hadn't given me the two sandwiches, my kind, thoughtful darling! Then freezing to bed with half our clothes on. Our bags hadn't come yet. But all those physical trials are nothing to today's moral ones. So come soon, Pferscherl, I need you more than ever—
185

I've lost my roots! If I don't meet you at the hut tomorrow or on the way or in the café, I'll wait at the coffee-house till eight o'clock. And if you don't come by then, I'll assume you didn't get my letter in time and won't be coming till Thursday. In that case we'll have the same arrangement.

If you feel like bringing some edible matter, darling, it would be much appreciated. Even if they give one more than black coffee, dinner still isn't very filling! Today, for instance, potatoes and sauce. Now I'm sitting with a few friends in a little restaurant, and have ordered a piece of sausage with oil and vinegar and a glass of beer. Ploderer[1] is sitting at the next table writing. I am very glad to have him here. We sleep next to each other in a vast hut with eighty people. The beds are like rock, the sanitary arrangements highly primitive. Today we didn't wash at all, only hope we get a chance tomorrow, that's the most important thing. The lavatories are revolting, too. But as I said, these are external things, which one can easily get over. If you come, take a carriage at the station, as it's about three quarters of an hour's walk to the hut . . .

(176)   Bruck, 12th October 1915
Dearest Pferschi,
    I'm going to the sick parade today. The pain in the back of my neck has become unbearable, I can hardly turn my head. Meanwhile many kisses.

                                                    Your own

(177)   13th October 1915
    The sick parade went like this, darling. M.O.: 'What's the matter with you?' I describe my condition (completely naked). M.O. squeezes my shoulder slightly. I say: 'A bit lower down.' His interest is not very great. He says: 'Aspirin, go to the hospital, a nurse will give you a rub.' (He didn't say what with.) I let things be, just swallow two aspirins. That was that, and the sergeant let me leave my pack at home. Anyhow after that treatment the pain has got much better already. Also the strain has been much less this week than it was the first week. So don't worry, dearest—take care of yourself and go and listen to Mahler's Second on Thursday. I don't need any food, perhaps a bit of drink and some fruit. Oh

[1] Dr Rudolf Ploderer, lawyer, and friend of Berg's.

186

yes, and the books I asked you through Ploderer to get me. I'm very glad Alma Mahler has written you such a nice letter—can you copy it out for me?

(178)   Undated
                                                      (October 1915)
   We had such a strenuous exercise today, my Pferscherl, that this will have to be a shortish letter. From seven in the morning till one in the afternoon we were marching, running, charging across hill and dale, through the swamps and marshes, down on the ground, up again, and so on. I've got a crust of mud all over me. Afternoon out again, but at least without pack or rifle.
   Stein sent me a card, asking about Schoenberg, his military service, etc. In the present circumstances I can't telephone Schoenberg, must wait till I can talk to him.
   Sunday—we'll be alone and at home. The main thing is that we'll be together! And that's the very opposite of being alone-lonely.

(179)   Undated
                                                      (October 1915)
   Although I haven't much time, my Pferscherl, I must write to you. It was all so brief yesterday, the parting so quick. On the way back I worked quietly on the sketch map, then walked back to camp. Afternoon went fairly smoothly. In the evening Ploderer and I stayed in our quarter's and put things in order. I sewed my coat, tidied up my case and the boxes under my bed, practised a bit of rifle drill, supped on some of your lovely things, read the newspapers, and went to bed at half past nine, thinking of you all the time, my darling.
   This morning again with pack, rifle and equipment up the 'Hospital Mountain'. Now at dinner break, very tired, writing to my Pferscherl. Why aren't we together? It's simply monstrous! . . .

(180)   Monday, 25th October 1915
   What a journey back[1] yesterday! First the No. 57 tram, then a long wait till a No. 18 comes. When it does come, it's crammed full, with people hanging on to the sides. Same with the next one

   [1] Returning to Bruck after weekend leave at home in Vienna.

five or ten minutes later, and with four or five more. Hardly any time left to catch the train. No car there, the driver of an empty carriage refuses to take me. Then another tram. Military police appear, ask for our papers. By this time the tram has come up, and others have stormed on to it. In dire straits I manage to occupy *minute* space on steps. To the East Station at a gallop, just catch train. Train so crowded, we are squashed so tight, even standing room hard to find! Endless journey. I try to work, but almost fall asleep on my feet. Friend in same compartment lets me have his seat for last quarter of hour. I take Ploderer on my lap. Destination reached at quarter past midnight. Hurry back to camp in moonlight, unpack, prepare everything for next day. Into bed.

Waking up horrible! I always get up a bit earlier than the rest, so that I can do something *alone* and don't have to merge into the crowd first thing in the morning. Then I went to the dairy for breakfast. Mean to do that quite often now, especially if I find myself as depressed as today by getting up! For the sake of the whole atmosphere there: the warm room, sitting at a clean table, feeling of relative freedom, chance to prepare oneself for the day. And, instead of having to queue in the mud so that they can pour the slop half over one's fingers, half into the cup, to be served with proper coffee, which freshens you up for the physical and mental efforts of the day. You return to the hut feeling lighter, put on your belt, haversack, pack and rifle, and off you march.

And another such week ahead of us. Day after tomorrow is Wednesday, and then I'll see you again, my darling . . . you don't need to bring anything with you, only yourself . . .

(181)   Hut 3b, Reserve Hospital,[1]
                                                          Bruck, Sunday
                                                 (7th November 1915?)

My own, my only one, now everything's far, far easier to bear . . . your very appearance yesterday was enough. I was so sleepy that in the first moment I just couldn't take in your being there, standing by my bed. It was as if I suddenly heard the sound of beautiful music, which I only recognized gradually as being the dearest and most familiar music (perhaps like my own Pieces for Orchestra, which are *as* beautiful in my imagination at least). So it was only

[1] In November 1915 Berg had a complete physical breakdown as a result of overstrain in his training.

188

gradually when I saw you from my bed that I realized this heavenly picture was my very own Pferscherl, so dear and so familiar, and that I could have you round me for a few hours, a few precious hours.

By talking to Dr S. you did so much good not only for my immediate well-being but also for our future fortunes, the first turn of the tide from *mis*fortune to fortune. Of course your doing that was as natural as the way the appearance of such a noble person in such surroundings had an ennobling effect, all the greater from the gap between 'apparition' and background. In this case infinite, as infinite as my good fortune, dearest, in having you. God, if I didn't have you! Since I have been in Bruck, I have thought of this at least once every quarter of an hour—with an ever greater intensity. That isn't due to our separation or my unhappy environment, as could easily be assumed, but to a realization which becomes clearer all the time: it's the complete renewal of our marriage on an *even higher* level. A renewal symbolized by the second marriage ceremony in the church at Hietzing.[1]

Dr S. has just been here. When he asked me how I was, I told him I had slept better, and that last night the constriction had grown more painful, so I had taken the powder, after which it got better. He gave me another thorough examination, asked me to go on keeping my sputum, and inhaling, and I must have X-rays taken of my heart and lungs. But he had quite a smile on his face, which suggests that he doesn't think my state of health gives any cause for alarm . . .

(182)   (8th November 1915)
    Telegram:

                    BEING EXAMINED
                    TOMORROW ALBAN

                                Here follows the report
                                after medical examination:
Bronchial asthma, swelling of lungs, air-cells of lung, deadening of tips of lungs, lobes of lungs over four inches across the—[a few illegible words in Latin]—stomach. Also sore. Heart too small. Patient complains of shortage of breath during violent exercise.

[1] See footnote Letter 168.

189

Has suffered from asthma since childhood, with violent expectoration. Non-smoker. No prospects of cure. In hospital since 6th November. One sick parade. Suitable for orderly duties. X-ray results enclosed.

(183)   18th May 1916[1]
Have to write to you on this mucky bit of paper, Pferscherl, in the dinner-break before I go and eat. So not much time, and this will be very short. So glad you're having lovely weather.[2] How wonderful it must be up there, and even if you forget about me. I couldn't really blame you. Can't compete with the Semmering, can I! (Or can I?) . . .
Not much of interest to report. First because nothing has happened, secondly every thought gets lost on the way from head through eyes and fingers to typewriter keys! So only chronological order of events: telephoned the Semmering number yesterday, but Pferscherl was out. Then plodded on in office, home 7 p.m., composed for $9\frac{1}{2}$ minutes, Gusti[3] arrived. He was extremely sorry not to see you, of course, but understood why you weren't there. He stayed till 11.30. We both ate a big meal, everything very tasty and plenty of it. (Would like to see my Pferscherl's face at this bit!) We had a very good talk; well, he's a very nice listener anyhow!
Right, back to the office again soon, so I must get something to eat quickly . . .

(184)   Vienna, 19th May 1916
Another magnificent day! Delighted you've found everything so satisfactory. Am expecting a letter from you today. Too bad I shan't be home before evening, as I'm to have dinner with Mama—some business to discuss with her. So I can only get Toni to 'phone me and say whether anything's come, and if it has, I shan't get it till tonight. Will perhaps post off an answer tomorrow morning, so don't be worried if the answer is late.

[1] Following the medical report (see Letter 182) Berg had been transferred to garrison duties in Vienna. As these duties were also too much strain on his health, he was once more transferred, this time to clerical work in the War Ministry. There, in Department X, room 15 on the second floor, he spent the rest of his military service.
[2] Helene was staying with Alma Mahler on the Semmering.
[3] Gustav Göttel, a friend of the Bergs'.

Now to my daily report. Talked to Frau Schoenberg on the telephone yesterday. He has been with his company in Vienna for two days—has to be at the barracks at 6 a.m. and doesn't get home till about half past seven at night . . . By the way, L. was here yesterday afternoon, and asked where we were. Rather sarcastic, says Toni. I came home late, had a lot of work in the office, and after dinner went to the Ploderers, about nine. We played some music— first movement of my Quartet. It went—badly! Hence not much appreciated by 'audience'. Then some stimulating conversation over a glass of brandy. Home at quarter to eleven. Read the paper and Rosegger. And had no Pferscherl at my side! How I long for you, my darling. But my joy that you are having such glorious weather, that everything round you is so exquisite and unique, that you love it and appreciate it so much—outweighs my desire to have you with me . . . What do you think of our victories in the Tyrol? Or are you all so happy up there that you don't hear anything about the war, even the cheering things? . . .

(185)   Vienna, 1st August 1916
My darling,

In a day where one job follows another and I've already been weeks without my Pferscherl,[1] I can just about bear it. But when the afternoon arrives, when the evening is approaching—an evening without the normal end I so much long for every day—then I feel *immensely* miserable. I'd sooner stay in the office and work till sleep comes, and can now almost understand these petty officials for who evening means nothing but the end of their stupid day's work, who can't see a single glimmer of light at the end of that vast tunnel.

So at eight o'clock last night I went to see your Mama and Auntie. Both in good spirits, and they fed me very 'properly', you needn't worry about *that*. At a quarter past nine I went home. It was so empty and lonely. But then I found your note by the telephone. And the eiderdown! Oh, my Schnudoa! It was so sweet of you. Then I found the mail you'd enclosed.

Please keep my mail for me. Almschi asks: 'When are *you* coming, Helene?' not 'when are the two of you coming?'

This morning I made myself tea and a hard-boiled egg with

---

[1] Helene spent the summer with her parents at Trahütten.

bread and butter. So don't worry about my physical needs. And my spiritual ones? Well, that's something different! ...

(186)   Saturday, 5th August 1916,
                                                          midday

... I feel very well, and am not going without anything. I eat more than enough, the sandwiches are twice as big as they used to be! I look all right too, am not at all exhausted, and it's so gloriously cool, even cold. Only 12° centigrade this morning. Last night I covered myself up thoroughly with eiderdown and quilt, for the window is wide open, even the blinds are up. My outward existence is splendidly simple and regular. The flat is kept impeccably ... Only trouble is with my clothes. The old uniform is beginning to show signs of wear and tear, it has already got a fine old hole in it. Went to the tailor's the other day about my trousers, but there was nobody there, so I just left a message. Anyhow the trousers would probably be too warm for now. Then I tried on the shoes, but am not happy with them. They seem a perfect fit, yet I'm convinced that if I walked in them for five minutes, I should be finished. They are tight and narrow everywhere, with no clearance at all. I'm letting them stretch for a few days, and will fetch them then.

Delighted, my darling, that you have all the food you want. Which means you can recover on that side too. And also that everything is all right with you psychologically, with no friction, complete tranquillity. I keep reminding myself of that when I begin to feel despondent because I'm so lonely.

You've redecorated my room at Trahütten, have you? Do you think I'll be coming out there, then? I don't get any leave, you know. The only people who do in our lot are those who've been a year in the War Ministry already—like Dr Wernisch, Hellin and Hofmann, they get a fortnight each. Sad thing is that the last two are always making plans for their leave in my presence (a walking tour somewhere in Styria), and that they are understandably light-hearted, while I am down-hearted. But then I keep telling myself to shut up, remembering the trails and tribulations of Bruck, Reindlgasse, Bisamberg[1]—and how far better and more tolerable things are now...

---

[1] Reindlgasse and Bisamberg, where Berg had been on guard-duties.

I quite went to town yesterday, darling, as you shall hear. Was on duty till half past eight, then went to Hietzing, and at about 9.30 in proud and venturesome mood entered the Restaurant Klein—where the trace-kicking began:

First a portion of fried paprika with egg	Cr. 1.20
then mixed vegetables	Cr. 1.20

Both excellent but not filling, so then I was really hungry. They had done the paprika like mushrooms with egg. Delicious. I had the feeling there was something else in it too. The paprika was cut just like *sauerkraut*, with scrambled egg in between. The whole thing very fatty, almost oily. The vegetables—a bit of everything, spinach, cabbage, red cabbage, tomato sauce round it, and in the middle three half potatoes.

So now I wanted to eat some small dish, something with meat in. According to the menu they had only goulash (Cr. 2.50), the rest cost more than that, well over Cr. 3—and the goulash was 'off'. That's where our Austrian 'individual service' came in handy. The waiter saw my trouble, and 'recommended' me some *Krenfleisch*[1] which was still 'on', though not on the menu. It was just the thing for me, delicious, plenty of it, and costing only   Cr. 2.50

With it a pint and a half of Pilsner, also 'first-class'	Cr. 0.70
A roll	Cr. 0.04
Altogether	Cr. 5.64

It all seemed to me like a banquet, so rare and unexpected these days. On the way home, when I passed various terrace restaurants and heard the raucous blaring music, I couldn't help thinking of the thousands of poor devils out at the front helpless and bewildered in their suffering.

I've developed a stye on my left eye, felt it coming on yesterday. Hope it won't get any bigger. Curious enough, a lot of people seem to get these things, eye inflammations, pink-eye, etc . . .

. . . Fetched the repaired trousers yesterday. They are all right, and I had to pay another Cr. 1.60, and then the shoes. They are also all right now, and seem to be a good fit, I'm wearing them today:

[1] Boiled beef with horse-radish sauce.

Cr. 40. Tonight I am with Charly and Mama, who is well again,
by the way, and is going to Waldegg on Saturday. We ate at the
'Pelican', the fine big restaurant behind the *Karlskirche*.

Now something important. They are requisitioning all metal.
I have read the various regulations thoroughly. We have to hand in
the pot we use for preserving fruit, as we are not professional
'canners'. Then I think we've got a few stove bits and pieces in the
music room. Where are they? I'll give them to Thekla on the 17th,
the day we are supposed to deliver the stuff, with a certificate for
the 'copper and bronze works of art' we are retaining, and the
certificate that we sold the pestle and mortar . . . My eye is all right,
my mood medium to bad, but I enjoyed the enclosed newspaper
cutting with some lines from Wagner: 'Oh, heavens, to be close, to
belong to one another; 'tis still the only thing, yet oh, so difficult.
Nor can you do it with the heart alone, you must have wisdom too' . . .

(189)   Saturday, 12th August 1916
Have somehow collected a sore throat. Had been wondering
where on earth I could have picked it up, stupidly thinking of all
sorts of possible infections and colds, when I suddenly had a
brainwave: don't look for *physical* reasons, which as a rule you
don't set much store by anyhow; there must be some psychological
ones. How could I have forgotten that? In the last ten or twenty
years, perhaps thirty even, a complaint in any part of my body has
almost invariably followed immediately on some emotional distur-
bance or distress. I told you how last Saturday, exactly a week ago,
I was extremely depressed, the day after doing a little composing to
get another smell of what 'life and work' mean. And then back again
away from all that, back into the yoke, into this futile routine, to
which I have had to submit for a year now . . . Then the nagging
anxiety that you were somehow upset, my hurt feelings that you
didn't come to Vienna[1] (I know now, of course, it was all quite
unjustified), my hours of waiting at the station for nothing, the
uncertainty—'will she come, or won't she?'—all that was throbbing
in my nerves . . .

No wonder that a few days afterwards the first signs of a throat
inflammation came up. They became steadily worse until last
night they reached their peak. I don't know whether it's angina or
a catarrh of the larynx, but anyhow the pain in my neck and throat

---
[1] Helene was supposed to go to Vienna for a weekend visit.

194

was unbearable. Eating was a torment, too, because it was so painful to swallow anything. Then last night I had a headache and a temperature as well, so today I've stayed in bed the whole time, snoozing till about four o'clock, and now writing to my Pferscherl. But I shan't post the letter till I'm well again, so as not to worry you.

I have arranged the room in the best 'home nursing' style. The table pushed right up to the bed, all the medicines together: eucalyptus bottle, and a menthol pencil to paint my throat, instead of an ice-bag or cold compresses, which are too much trouble applying; thermometer, lozenges, aspirins. And the gargling! I couldn't find anything at first, but—Ah!—there's a bottle of Formamint, 'substitute for gargling', you put a tablet straight into your mouth—and spit it out again at once! It was agony. Then I saw on the bottle 'Brokamint' in Pferscherl's writing—so that was no good. Then I discovered some drops, which I remembered one could gargle with. Put a few of them into mouthwash glass, gargle, spit, all night, all day. And it really does seem to have got better. At least the pain has moved from the larynx up into the top of the throat. It still hurts when I swallow, but it's bearable. My temperature is normal and I feel hungry again.

Hope to go back into the office tomorrow, and have lunch at your mother's. I sent her a message that I would be coming, but will stay in the garden as I don't want anybody to catch my ailments. (This is the danger, of course, if somebody is *afraid* of getting ill: another 'psychological moment', so that A. could quite well tell B. he was ill when he wasn't really, and B., through being *afraid*, actually catches the illness—for the bacilli, of course, are always present in vast quantities . . .)

(190)   20th August 1916, in the
                                                  train from Deutsch-
                                                   Landsberg to Graz[1]
My darling,
   I don't know what words to use to set your mind at rest about my health. I know how ill I felt the other day at your place. But even from that, with all the pain gone, I still have left my feeling of happiness with you three women[2] caring for me so fondly and thoughtfully and skilfully; the glorious feeling, as I leaned on your shoulder,

[1] On the way back to Vienna from Trahütten after a weekend with Helene.
[2] Helene, her mother and aunt.

of being at home and safe and loved like a small child. So you see how I myself turn even misfortune into a source of good fortune. The fact that I lost some sleep and had a night's asthma is something which really shouldn't make *you* despair.

(191)   Graz, 20th August
Well, I'm sitting in the Café Kaiserhof again, in the same place as I sat about a year ago and also wrote to you.[1] It was before joining up! Again two or three hours in Graz, looking back with a similar feeling of inner hollowness and forward into the immediate future with uneasiness and impatience . . .

The journey to Graz wasn't too bad. At first I read, and ate peaches, afterwards I talked to a sergeant and a gunner. One was quite a pleasant well-educated chap, a schoolmaster's son; the other was Körner, the well-known big businessman from Preding. Both have been at the front since the beginning of the war, both pretty tough. They were on the way back to the front (South Tyrol) after a fortnight's leave. So this part of the journey went fairly quickly and for short periods I had my mind taken off my nostalgic thoughts. But they returned more intensely than ever on the station, as I swallowed the inevitable boiled beef. I hurried off by tram to here, where I can at last have a little letter-chat with you again.

My Pferscherl, it was so pleasant and peaceful those thirty or forty hours in beloved Trahütten with my dearest Schnudoa. I will think of them all through this fortnight, if things are going specially badly; and that will be a real 'retreat' for me. I shall be able to bear the weeks ahead so much more easily thinking of that, and of the time which is bound to come when we two can live up there in peace, when I shall get better again—quicker than you think —and shall be able to work. That's a thought which almost overwhelms me, so beautiful it is and so sure I am of its fulfilment. And I implore my Pferscherl, please, please help me in that by doing everything you can to recover properly yourself and get strong . . .

(192)   Tuesday, 22nd August,
                                      morning, in the tram
Slept well, and now back into harness again, with a visit to

[1] See Letter 167.

Almschi in the evening, when I'd really rather have stayed at home . . .

You can't imagine how difficult I find it to pull myself together for such a simple matter. 'To sleep, to sleep, and nothing but to sleep!'

For months I haven't done any work on *Wozzeck*.[1] Everything is smothered, buried. And this state may last—no, will last—for years. Will tell you about the visit tomorrow.

P.S.   Midday, 22nd August

Had a long talk with our Captain[2] this morning for the first time. He called me in about a rather complicated file I had been working on, and I had to explain it to him for a whole hour, as he is going to the Colonel with it. Everything all right, he was really nice. Of course I was lucky to find him in a good mood. This 'coming forward' has its advantages, certainly: he gets to know me, and sooner or later will find me indispensable, which may mean his helping me get leave later on, in the winter or even late autumn. On the other hand, of course, there are disadvantages: staying-late-in-the-office, evenings and Sunday afternoons, and extra worries and responsibilities, which might be bigger than one expects.

So one never knows whether it'll help—or hinder.

Finally, hundreds and thousands of kisses!

Your own

(193)   Undated

(22nd August 1916)

Just to tell you about it, my darling Pferscherl: I'm on my way home from Almschi, and have got to be careful not to be caught by the Military Police in Hietzing, as my leave is only till eleven o'clock, and it's that now. I got to Almschi's at a quarter past seven. Mother Moll was there and Maria,[3] both were just going. I was thinking of leaving about eight, but you know what it's like, I had to stay. The conversation rather dragged at first. Gucki was playing the harmonium, Almschi the piano, and they had dug out Hugo Wolf, her latest acquisition: his *Geistliche Lieder*. But before that

[1] Berg had been working on the libretto for *Wozzeck* since July 1914. He did not start with the composition until July 1917.

[2] Captain Steiner, Berg's C.O. at the War Ministry.

[3] Alma Mahler's mother was married to the well-known Viennese painter, Carl Moll. Maria was Alma's step-sister.

I had to tell them everything about you and Trahütten. She was in ecstasies over the bilberries, which—unusually for her—she had been immodest enough to ask for. She said they were bigger than anywhere else, and she and the others were still eating them. The flowers you sent her were also in the room. I had the impression she was feeling a bit guilty—she asked, anyhow, when you would be returning to Vienna. I said, 'I don't know for sure, probably in a week or a fortnight.'

Then the 'improvised' supper: cold chicken, which she had had given to her—and that's why Gucki and Maud[1] wouldn't touch the pieces she gave them for all her urging. I had to eat two pieces, and on top of that the remains of some spinach, a lot of tomato salad, two eggs, cheese, warmed-up plum dumplings and your bilberries (stewed). I noticed your tablecloth on the table. It was really quite cosy during the meal. Almschi is slowly losing all her hair, she looked like a Red Indian squaw. Her stomach is like a ball,[2] otherwise nothing exorbitant. Only, her feet—I couldn't believe my eyes—were sometimes sticking out under her dress: in straw sandals, with no stockings!

Before supper I had to play my sonata,[3] and that set the tone for the evening, one might say. After supper I had to repeat several bits, talk about them, explain the musical forms. She proved very interested in all that and appreciative, quite excited, in fact. Then came the songs, of which she liked the second particularly (*Schlafend trägt man mich*),[4] but also the last. We kept on saying how sad it was you never performed them. I had to tell her about your voice, and I really do wonder whether you won't sing for her some time (it needn't be my own stuff). We also spoke a lot about Zemlinsky, she with great enthusiasm. I have to lend her *Kleider machen Leute*.[5]

At around half-past nine Gucki was sent to bed, we looked through my songs, talked at the piano of my other compositions; then she lay down on the divan, drank coffee liqueur, and we chatted for a while. It was only then I realized it was late, especially for someone in an advanced state of pregnancy. But she maintained

---

[1] Maud was Anna Mahler's English nurse.

[2] Alma Mahler had in the meantime married Walter Gropius (b. 1883), the architect. She was pregnant, and six weeks later her daughter Manon was born, whose death, at the age of eighteen, became the inspiration for Berg's Violin Concerto (1935), dedicated 'To the Memory of an Angel'.

[3] op.1.

[4] op.2, No. 2 ('They carry me asleep').

[5] *Clothes Make the Man*, comic opera by Zemlinsky (1910).

it did her good to go to bed late, at least she would sleep better; her heart condition was sometimes bad. 'Well, first of all the whole thing is no joke, and secondly with an old hag like me . . . ' Those were about her words.

I got up to go rather abruptly. She thanked me for my visit and asked me to come again very soon. We had already more or less decided that she would get together a string quartet to play Zemlinsky's quartet in manuscript. But it will have to be sooner rather than later; later may be too late! I shall have to ring her up about it one of these days.

I think that takes care of the most important things in the evening. In case anything more occurs to me, I'll let you have it. I know how tremendously interested you are in all this, that's why I've gone into such detail . . .

(194)   Sunday, 27th August 1916

. . . But what do you think I told Almschi about your voice? Only the truth. That's all anybody will hear from me. Even when I'm talking to people like Almschi, who are inclined to 'invent' a bit. I told her how *beautiful* your voice is, how much I love it, and that she would certainly like it too; then how musical your singing is, and what a crime it was that you hide this gift of God, hide it from her of all people.

At the quartet evening in Almschi's house, I shall be only a listener, of course—as it's a quartet by Zemlinsky. I'll 'phone her tomorrow or the day after, only to ask how she's feeling.

Pferschi, I've been terribly worked up about your latest sleep-walking. *Please* get yourself a night-light. No, really — or I'll die of worry. And the business with the feather! Do you still feel something in your eye? And this 'admirer' of yours! That's horrible too. Why do you go out alone, and not accompanied by Papa. That way you're asking to be followed by someone like this stupid oaf exempt from service.

Today, Sunday, I was at the Ministry till nearly two. Marvellous lunch at your Mama's. Chicken soup, fried chicken with salad, a plum sweet made with potato flour. Then we rested for an hour. Tea at five, then to Schoenberg's till half-past seven. He is in a much better mood. We talked almost entirely about the war, and then about what should happen to Europe after it. He thought there was only one solution, the *Republic of Europe*, just like the United

199

States of America. Schoenberg wants to go on this course where one can become an officer for base duties. He thinks one can stay here afterwards as an officer; which I don't. He might be exempted till then, I fancy. At the moment he is trying to become an Austrian citizen.[1] First he has to get on to the register of some municipality, however small and remote. In Vienna it's impossible, because he hasn't lived here for ten continuous years, and in some other big town it would cost too much.

Polnauer and Frau Pappenheim[2] turned up at his place later on. The papers had just brought the news . . . that the new Poland will come in on our side with an army a million strong which is supposed to be in process of formation. It will all last a long time yet. Till spring anyhow, but perhaps for years more. The Allies' conviction that they can defeat us must be based on the idea of our being exhausted, as we might well become, though not enough for two or three years to admit we are beaten.

Schoenberg seems to be on bad terms with Frau Lieser—some disagreement has occurred there anyhow . . .

(195)   Vienna, 31st August 1916,
                                                          evening
My Pferscherl,
Your Tuesday's letter brought me the greatest joy I have had for years. I was submerged in a stream of happiness beyond anything I could have hoped to experience. I could repeat every one of those beautiful words, so full of holy truth, telling you how much each meant to me in happiness. I think it is the most beautiful letter I have ever received, with that sentence so permeated with all that is lovely and poetic: 'I sometimes feel as if we two were drifting in a shabby little boat, that people laugh at, further and further out, and were already far from the shore.' This image of a beautiful voyage across a lake towards a better destination, a symbolic voyage, significantly in a shabby little boat that people laugh at, is such a wonderful poetic inspiration that it gives me the pure delight in perfection of artistic *form*, quite apart from my happiness at the love and faith you speak of and at everything else you say in this letter. I shall keep

[1] Schoenberg's Austrian citizenship seemed for some time in question, as he had (although born in Vienna) been resident for several years in Berlin.

[2] Marie Pappenheim, author and doctor of medicine, wrote the libretto for Schoenberg's monodrama, *Erwartung* ('Expectation') op. 7 (1909), his first work for the stage.

it always with me. With it you have made me infinitely happy. It means today, after five and a half years, no, after nearly ten years, more than you could ever guess when you wrote it . . .

I want to switch off the light, and am almost tempted—to pray. But formal praying seems unnecessary, for my thoughts tonight are anyhow one great prayer of thanks, for the hour this evening when I received your letter, the hour when my good spirit (you) rescued my soul so deeply cast down, when my guardian angel (perhaps nothing but my good spirit too) saved my life.

(196)   Friday, 1st September,
                                                     morning

Must tell you of last night's experience. I was riding home on the No. 59 tram near the Sezession, where the No. 60 goes from Schwarzenbergplatz. Both trams were speeding like mad, one trying to overtake the other. I was working out quite coolly where the No. 60 would hit ours, so I wasn't surprised when it happened. The usual banging, our tram jumped the rails and staggered along the pavement, still being pushed by the No. 60, whose driver had completely lost control of it. In the end with both trams derailed and smashed up, they stopped together in a heap, completely wedged into each other, across the rails. I soon hurried off to Eschenbachgasse, where I caught a No. 57 tram to Hietzing. Both trams were pretty empty, so nothing much seems to have happened. At most some injuries from broken glass and cases of shock. No, nothing happened to me, I wasn't even particularly frightened. And half an hour later I found your precious, lovely letter—and was happier than ever!

The day is coming nearer and nearer when at last, at last, I shall have you with me.

God, how I'm looking forward to it! Countless kisses,

                                                     Your own

(197)   6th June 1917
Only a brief note, my darling Pferscherl, as there is a terrific lot of work to do (I even had some business with the Colonel today). How beautiful it must be for you just now.[1] I am so glad that you at least, my darling, have freedom and can live a little according to your

[1] Helene was again on a visit to Alma Mahler.

201

inclinations. I didn't know for years, for decades, what freedom was. But now when the thought of it and desire for it is constantly with me, I help myself to carry on by making plans for the immediate future, how to provide myself with some hours of freedom and how to use them profitably.

My most immediate plan is to come up to the Semmering next Sunday, assuming you will still be there. I shall arrive around noon, and would drive home again in the afternoon. All too short, but it would be beautiful beyond all measure. You know what lures me up there, my darling: everything that's up there just now—right to the things that have been there from all eternity, the mountains, the Rax.

Heaps of good wishes to Almschi and her family, perhaps I can soon give her my greetings in person. The words 'everything that's up there' apply to her first and foremost. No, second and nearly foremost! (First is reserved for my Pferscherl.)

Write at once to say whether you'll still be at Almschi's on Sunday. If so, I'll come, unless something unexpected happens to stop me. Till then a thousand kisses—no, one long kiss.

(198)   11th June 1917, on the
                                   way to the War Ministry
Well, that *was* a jolly Sunday! Hofmann and I were with the Captain from 9 a.m. till 7 p.m. without even a lunch-break. In the evening I went to Mama's—she had expected me for lunch—home at night, and now back into the pit!

It was like a dream yesterday. Rather an absurd simile, no doubt, but I think it will do, so long as the world, for all its advances and its World War, is still absurd enough to dream, and has carried this last remnant of fantasy into our most realistic of all ages.

Well then, my few hours in the Mahler house yesterday were like a dream. An aggregation of beauty, light and sunshine, of being far away from everything which today is so close to me, which is always treading on my feet—no, on my face, my brain, my heart. An aggregation that could only be produced in a dream. It is almost beyond me to see it as a reality, something *attainable*. As well, perhaps; for otherwise how could I bear any longer the two-year imprisonment of body and soul?

Perhaps you will come today, my dearest and very own one.
                                                  Your own
p.s. My regrets to all.

I had a slight hope, suppressed but still most satisfying, that I might have you with me by yesterday evening. It has not been fulfilled. Perhaps today! If I didn't know what a lot of good life on the Semmering with Almschi is doing you physically and mentally, I should be utterly unhappy in my loneliness. But at least I want to hear from you every day!

If this letter still reaches you, darling, write to me or send a telegram answering this question. I spoke to Schoenberg on the telephone, and he can at once let us have his four shares in the Communal Restaurant in Hietzing[1] (as *they* are eating at Frau Schwarzwald's).[2] Would we like to take them over? I am all for it, as we could have a famine here soon owing to the drought, and as our reservation for meals after July 1st is by no means guaranteed. Schoenberg also told me that his *Glückliche Hand* has already been published,[3] and that his poem *Die Jakobsleiter* (which he will be setting to music) will be published soon.[4] Schmid wrote to me that he had received from Zemlinsky in Prague the piano score of *Traumgörg*.[5] So that's also out!

Well, even if I haven't had a single note of music published, my 30-pages long Ordinance was printed yesterday. 20,000 copies! That's some sort of substitute for creative work, don't you think?—and looks like it too. Anyway, by this Ordinance some hundred thousand soldiers, aged fifty-one and fifty-two will be able to go home. Let me comfort myself with that for the time being.

The Kraus-Schalek[6] lawsuit has been adjourned. The Schalek woman did not appear in person, and also Kraus has demanded the calling of fifty or sixty witnesses as evidence of the proof of his

[1] Communal Restaurants (*Gemeinschaftsküchen*) had by then been set up in most districts of Vienna.

[2] Dr Eugenie Schwarzwald, a most remarkable woman of her day, was founder and headmistress of a progressive girls' school in Vienna. Schoenberg was on friendly terms with her and had taught Musical Theory at her school from 1903 to 1908. During the war she organized cheap restaurants for Viennese intellectuals. (See also Letters 209 *et seq*.)

[3] Schoenberg's second opera *The Lucky Hand* op. 18 (1910–1913).

[4] *Jacob's Ladder* (1913); its composition remained unfinished.

[5] *Traumgörg*, an opera by Alexander von Zemlinsky.

[6] Alice Schalek was Austria's most prominent female war-correspondent during the First World War. The extravagant patriotic fervour of her reports aroused the fury of Karl Kraus, who was a thorough-going pacifist. He attacked her violently both in his *Fackel* and in his satirical drama, *The Last Days of Mankind*.

assertions. They are all at the various fronts la Schalek visited, and they are all to be heard.

Last night, after waiting for you in vain, I went to see your Papa and was in the garden with him—a substitute for the Semmering. Lord, it must be beautiful up there, to have the Rax in front of you at all times of day and night. I think of all this, whenever I look up from my files. Give my regards to everybody, and you yourself, my dearest, will you come soon?

Your own

(200) Vienna, 5th July 1917

... Another very wearing day yesterday, my dearest. In the office till 8 p.m., then in Mama's flat, where I helped Charly.[1] During the day I had felt rather ill, with a frightful upset in stomach and intestines, which grew worse in the evening as I drove home—so that I couldn't enjoy properly the wonderful eclipse of the moon. (I was in Gloriettegasse at the full eclipse—you must have seen it too.) I had unbearable griping pains which I could hardly put up with even after taking my trusty camomile drops and putting on hot compresses. Altogether I didn't get much sleep last night.

You can hardly imagine what I felt like in the morning, darling, after such a night. Completely exhausted. However, I went to the office as usual, and to a sick parade at 9. The M.O. wanted to send me to hospital, but on my protesting gave me three days off duty on grounds of asthma and general debility. I shan't take them, of course, as I hope to get a longer leave on those grounds later on. When I reported to Captain Steiner, he must have seen how ill I looked. At any rate he couldn't help realizing I wasn't fit to tackle some pressing work we had on. He told me to leave it till tomorrow morning and sent me home. So now it's twelve o'clock, and I'm on my way home.

Toni had a milk pudding waiting for me. I'm feeling a good deal better generally, and with a day's dieting I'm sure I shall be quite all right again. I'm just needing sleep, and mean to revel in that this afternoon and tonight. So you need not worry at all. Toni will take care of the diet side, she is *very* solicitous. I'm so glad I didn't have this wretched night when you were here, it would have robbed you of any bit of sleep you managed to get. You were looking so ill these last few days that I was secretly very worried. I can only tell you this

[1] With the administration of the houses belonging to the family.

today when you are surrounded by all the conditions for health and well-being!

And one more secret thought during these last few days: again the idea of visiting you on my free day (Saturday or Sunday). But owing to this stupid 'indisposition' I have rather dropped the idea, it would be too much. Tomorrow I'll write again. Till then many kisses from your

Alban

Regards to all in the Mahler house, especially Almschi.

(201)   Friday, 6th July 1917,
midday

I feel much better, quite all right really, only tired still . . .

Postscript to yesterday's letter (with all culinary details so that you won't worry). At 2 p.m. I went to bed, ate a large plate of semolina pudding and went into a very heavy sleep, woke around six, without any idea of the time or where I was. Gradually 'coming to', I read Morgenstern's *Palmström*,[1] just the right sort of reading. (Does Almschi know anything of Morgenstern's? I'd like to have her read something by him and hear what she thinks of it.)

Toni, who was up with your people, brought me some rusks from your Mama, which I ate for supper with a night-cap; also a little cocoa for this morning, and a bottle of red wine from Anna, which I didn't drink, however. Went to the office this morning as usual. Thousands of kisses

Your own

(202)   Undated
(24th July 1917)

I'm very fit, no asthma at all thanks to continual fresh air. I sleep with two windows open, and generally have everything I need.

We always get a good piece of meat in the evening—though the price is incredible. Was with Kassowitz last night at the Weingartl Restaurant; fine helping of stewed beef for four Crowns[2] . . .

As I worked so late in the office last night. I wanted to go in a bit

---

[1] A collection of philosophical and humorous poems (1910) by the Munich poet Christian Morgenstern (1871–1915). Hindemith and Reger are among the many composers who set his texts.
[2] About 3s 6d.

later today, but unfortunately my C.O. slept in the office (he doesn't dare go home at night, because there's always a prostitute lying in wait for him; he threw her over, and now she can't be bought off even for 100 Crowns, and she kicks up rows). By the way, he is just being promoted.

Well, yesterday was the 23rd—could it pass without something important happening?[1] Not quite anyhow! First, I had an idea for Schoenberg's immediate future: to write to Skoda[2] asking him to provide for Schoenberg, as being one of the country's great men, who can do very little for the war effort *and* hasn't made anything out of it. That should be expressed in such a way that Skoda, who had become a multi-millionaire during these last two years, feels obliged to help generously. I told Grünwald[3] about this idea, and it fell on good soil—he's going to take the matter in hand. He is in contact with people who in their turn know the very richest financiers: people representing the type of business men interested in the arts or men of the arts concerned with business.

He as good as promised me that something will be arranged on a really generous scale (perhaps including upkeep of a flat). Also that it will be handled in a dignified way and very discreetly . . .

(203)   Vienna, 26th July 1917
                                              War Ministry[4]
Your birthday the day after tomorrow, my dearest and best of Pferscherls, and I'll have to write today wishing you many happy returns, or you wouldn't even get a loving word from me on the day itself. For the last three days I've been chasing round in my lunch-break to get some really nice chocolates for you. But I can't even have the pleasure of giving you that pleasure. Most of the sweet-shops (like Gerstner's, for instance) are closed, and in the few that are open you don't get a single ounce—nor did my attempts to obtain something under the counter come off. So there's nothing doing with that, and you'll have to be content with a few kisses from afar. The actual present will follow when you happen to let out something you need and so would really like. Otherwise I'd only buy something stupid again! . . .

[1] See footnote Letter 139.
[2] Viennese industrialist.
[3] A brother-in-law of Berg's friend Paul Hohenberg.
[4] Helene has once more gone to Trahütten.

206

At seven o'clock this morning Schoenberg rang me: yesterday a 'gentleman from America' had sent him a telegram, asking us to meet him at seven last night at the Café Pordes. S. was detained, I couldn't be reached, so the man waited in vain ...

(204)   Vienna, Friday,
                                              27th July 1917
Yesterday was the opposite of the day before, when everything went wrong. It was a day when everything went right.

At lunch I fixed the matter between Schoenberg and the 'gentleman from America'. His name is Köhler, an Austrian but completely Americanized, speaks terrible German and is very much the type of elegant-American. He has been given safe conduct by the embassy over there, and so has only just arrived in Vienna, incredibly enough, travelling from America via Norway. He is on a sort of trade mission to establish export possibilities from America to Austria immediately after the war. This, of course, is tremendously important. He's in the Army at the moment, but will soon be released in view of the much greater services he might render to his native land.

Things don't look too bad for Schoenberg. The music publishers over there, Breitkopf and Härtel, guarantee him ten performances of the *Gurrelieder*, at 500 dollars each. He needn't go over in person, all he has to do is send a full score. To make this possible, Herr Köhler persuaded the band-leader of the ship which brought him over, for money and good-will, to take the score to New York as one of his band parts. So there's some risk, but anyhow a good chance that the performances may take place with a nice fee of 5,000 dollars, which means about 60,000 Crowns today (in peace-time 25,000 Crowns).

I don't know how much of that Hertzka pockets, but Schoenberg should have plenty left over!

In the evening when I went to Schoenberg and reported the whole thing to him, he wasn't as optimistic about the business as I am. He doesn't want to send the music until he has received the money, being doubtful whether the money would be paid out immediately. We had a bit of an argument about it. I said that the great value of the music and the difficulty of replacing it should form part of the publisher's risk, one they ought to accept for a deal going into tens of thousands.

On the other question, the securing of the money directly the music has arrived over there, I didn't see any occasion for doubt, considering the whole conduct of the matter and the American standards of the firm of Breitkopf and Härtel in contrast to the Jewish standards of Universal Edition. But Schoenberg wouldn't go along with this. If he agrees to the deal, the fee is due to him. Whether and how the firm obtains the music, so as to make its performance possible, is their business. They want to perform the work, and it was they who approached Universal Edition.

In a few days Schoenberg (perhaps with me) might meet the gentleman from America to continue the discussions. It's too bad that at the moment Schoenberg is again annoyed with Hertzka . . .

(205)   Monday, 30th July 1917
   I'm nearly desperate, my Pferscherl, about your being ill. Perhaps it's even worse than you write, and you're just trying to spare me. For heaven's sake, why don't you consult a doctor? If it's too expensive for your old man, when your health is at stake, and if he doesn't want to spend an amount Frank would pay for a single meal, then you must see to it yourself. I implore you, Helene, if you are still as sick when you receive this letter, arrange that the doctor from Deutsch-Landsberg comes up immediately. And you pay him —that is, I pay. It will be my birthday present. Pferscherl, I beg you, do everything humanly possible to cure yourself—in our present age that means doctors and medicines. One can't go on for weeks haphazardly dosing and treating oneself with all sorts of teas and compresses. Don't your people know that, except for the ordinary household stuff, medicines can't be obtained without prescriptions, and for prescriptions a doctor is needed . . .
   Anyhow, please tell them that your illness is not the result of 'running round' but of under-nourishment—as can be medically confirmed—since you are not in a position to stay in some clinic or like Frank live in luxury in Switzerland. Secondly, it's the result of freezing for months last winter when Papa begrudged you every bucket of coke, whereas Carola without any fuss demands and gets enough fuel to heat a whole villa. Thirdly, it's the result of many years of worry for me, the only member of your family—and the one in the worst health—who has served his country in the armed forces, for which the others draw all the profit and my only compensation is in being laughed at. *That's* why you are ill,

208

not from 'running around'. Such is my message for your parents! . . .

(206)   Tuesday, 31st July 1917,
                                                              morning
Thanks be to God. At last, at last, you are better. I was at the Leberts' last night, and heard even then that Mama had written to Auntie you were better and lying out in the sun. Then I got home to find your express letter, which cheered me up a bit. So the thing lasted so long only because you didn't have the right medicine! But this is incredible, you know. You should all have done something about it much earlier . . .

That's as far as I got with this letter on the tram. At eight sharp I was in the office. Steiner was ringing already (which has never happened before). He wants me to go with Hofmann to the Colonel. Hofmann wasn't there, nor was anybody else, so I had to go by myself, not knowing any shorthand. (Imagine!) But it all went quite well. Now it's eleven, and quite a long file done. More work waiting for me, so I've only got time to finish this, with hundreds of kisses, and get really better, my dearest.

(207)   Vienna, 30th August 1917
. . . At lunch in the café I told Hofmann that I had met Danka and her husband the day before. He put it in my mind to work on Arthur[1] for my possible promotion. Since Steiner has been away, its fate has become doubtful again, because the application has apparently not been forwarded—it can't be found anywhere. Hofmann knows from military circles how common it is to exploit such connections all the time, and after much persuasion from him I decided to telephone Danka. It was successful. Arthur will certainly take the matter up and go to the Colonel. Danka was extremely warm and sympathetic throughout our conversation, wrote everything down, and I am sure will exert the right influence on her husband! Anyhow my suggestion seemed to her quite normal and natural.

At 8.30 p.m. I went to see Schoenberg. He was understandably feeling rather depressed, as the money from America hasn't

---

[1] Danka was a cousin of Helene's married to Major-General Arthur Pongracz, an *aide-de-camp* to the Emperor.

turned up yet, and this mood of his still weighs heavily on me today, although we talked about all sorts of quite different things and about our mutual affairs . . .

p.s. 30th August
Danka has just rung me up here at the War Ministry. Arthur has already been with the Colonel, and she only wanted to tell me that her husband heard terrific praise for me there. She is going to write to you about it at once. I was so staggered I could only stammer a few words of thanks and surprise. She didn't tell me anything about the actual success of Arthur's mission, and I didn't like to ask, as she merely said she wanted to let me know about the above (that eulogy). Longing to know what she writes to you.[1]

(208) 3rd September 1917
. . . Arrived safely in Vienna.[2] Unpacked, spread the mushrooms out, and read the post. Your letter and a card from Schreker:[3] 'Dear friend' (how quickly one becomes a friend!), 'I'll be in Vienna on Tuesday evening, will ring you up, and we'll discuss matters and means in detail. Sincerely yours, Sch.'
Stein has just rung me with very bad news. Schoenberg has been notified that his exemption from military service is now withdrawn (cancelled) and that he will shortly be given further information (probably when to enlist). Appeals made to various ministries which have hitherto supported his exemption, but all to no avail. It's appalling. And no answer yet from America. How will it end? —Nothing to do in the office, the others are playing cards . . .

(209) 6th September 1917
But Pferschi, I don't drink any black coffee! Because you can't get any in the whole of Vienna, except at Göttl's. I feel pretty well, apart from the lumbago.
Frau Schwarzwald rang me in the office, she wants to talk to me about Schoenberg. At half past six I went along to her with Stein.

---

[1] The mission was evidently a failure, Berg was never promoted.
[2] After a weekend at Trahütten.
[3] Franz Schreker (1873–1934), the distinguished Viennese composer and teacher. (See Letter 233.)

She has now completely taken over Schoenberg's case, the military business as well as his financial difficulties, and seems to be settling everything with great energy, vigour and admirable readiness to put herself out. (Otherwise, I must say, I don't find her at all a pleasant person.) . . .

(210)   8th September 1917
Went last night with Göttel to Tolstoy's *The Living Corpse*[1] starring Moissi.[2] Magnificent. Today, Friday, off duty.

Stein rang just now to give me the latest news on the Schoenberg situation. Among other things that Webern, hearing of Schoenberg's distress, quite spontaneously offered 1,000 Crowns from his private means. Jalowetz[3] is giving 2,000. He'll refuse the first in accordance with Schoenberg's views, unless it is absolutely necessary, but might accept Jalowetz's offer, also a monthly subsidy of a few hundred Crowns from Stein, because he and Jalowetz aren't serving in the army. But actually Frau Schwarzwald's and our plan is, to induce a few capitalists to give large donations. Perhaps also the Artists' Provident Association, the Musicians' Guild, the Ministry of Education. Oh yes, and the Mahler Foundation. The last is Stein's idea, and he has written to Almschi on the subject. Don't mention to Almschi that you know anything about it, or she will certainly believe that I am behind it all, exploiting my knowledge that she is on good terms with Schoenberg again. You know how easily she takes a poor view of other people.

(211)   Sunday
                                   (Undated, 9th September 1917)
. . . Only a week since I was with you, and it seems like an eternity, although Göttel has quite taken me over, so that I really haven't had much time to think of my loneliness . . .

Yesterday, after he had absolutely insisted on my seeing *The Dancer* with La Konstantin,[4] we walked to the park and had tea, in

[1] Leo Tolstoy's (1828–1910) *The Living Corpse*, sometimes known as *Redemption*, was written in 1900 and first produced by the Moscow Arts Theatre in 1911. It was the third of Tolstoy's four plays and was published posthumously.
[2] Alexander Moissi (1880–1935), prominent German actor of Italian origin, Fedja in *The Living Corpse* was one of his greatest roles.
[3] Heinrich Jalowetz, pupil of Schoenberg's.
[4] Melchior Lengyel's drama *Die Tänzerin* (1916) offered the brilliant Viennese actress Leopoldine Konstantin a star part.

glorious sunshine, which actually made me quite miserable, because I couldn't stop thinking of Trahütten's open country. Seven o'clock to 'Ronacher's',[1] where there was a programme that seemed endless; it kept us till ten-thirty in a regular Turkish bath atmosphere. From there home and into bed after midnight. $1\frac{1}{2}$ minutes later I sank into a deep sleep . . .

(212)   Undated (10th September
                                         1917). Monday morning
                                         in the tram on the way
                                         to the office
Well, darling, here's the rest of my diary for yesterday. I worked in Jeanette's flat, then lay down for an hour and had a splendid nap, went to Mother Leska[2] and got a coffee, and afterwards to Schoenberg. Frau Pappenheim was there. We had a very interesting conversation on various things: on the new periodical supposed to be coming out, which will emphasize the futility of any critical 'judgment'. On the war—general opinion is that it won't last much longer. And finally on Schoenberg's personal prospects and plans. He thinks he may find a flat with three or four rooms, when he leaves the present one in October. Seems to me highly improbable. He worked out that with prices as they are he has to earn sixteen to eighteen thousand Crowns a year.

At seven I went to the Grünfelds,[3] where I was picking up the Leberts. An hour passed in lively discussion about politics and the war (here too they think it will soon be over). Antschi contemplated her magnificent future flat with all due delight.[4] By the way, Grünfeld advised me not to sell the Berghof, mainly because these days nobody knows what to do with the money. After eight, to dinner with the Leberts, to which I'd made my small contribution. It would have been very jolly if Auntie (who had had her dinner already at seven) hadn't yawned continuously and obtruded her tiredness from the time we arrived till a quarter past nine when I left . . .

On the way home I made a little detour across the square, where

[1] Famous Viennese music-hall.
[2] The mother of Berg's sister-in-law, Steffi Berg (wife of his brother, Charly).
[3] The Grünfelds were friends of Helene's step-sister, Carola.
[4] Arthur and Anna Lebert were moving to a new flat in Hietzing.

I met the Müllers[1]—and walked home with them. More excited talk about the war, and its end. They were hopeful because of the Russian defeats in Galicia. Such horrible endless bloodshed won't be supported any longer by the Russian 'Soldiers and Workers Council'. (A sort of 'government' which first exempted, for instance, all artists from military service, realizing that they are a country's only irreplaceable values. After all everything else grows again.) . . .

Pferschi, if I come, shouldn't I bring the 'chicory coffee' from the War Ministry, just for barter purposes? Mother Leska told me that in the country you get potatoes, eggs and fat for sugar, tobacco, cigars and spirits. Perhaps one shouldn't bother too much about such things but let them come as they will. Anyhow, I don't think we're going to 'starve' or 'freeze' to death, though falling ill is another matter.

(212a)   12th September 1917
Almschi has answered Stein saying, she can't be involved in the Schoenberg business in any way. And Grünwald has just told me on the 'phone that his prospective Maecenas is away and will only be in Vienna for two days next week. What *is* going to happen?

(213)   28th September 1917
Last night from 6.45 till 8.30 I was at the preliminary discussions on the 'Seminar for Composition' at the Schwarzwald School.[2] Quite a lot of people there, say ninety or a hundred, mainly women. Only about thirty signed forms were handed over, and disgracefully small amounts put down on them—about fifteen Crowns a month on average. This would mean that if Schoenberg gets 400 to 450 Crowns a week, he would have per year (nine months) about 4,000 Crowns.[3] And by the dresses and jewellery, etc., of the people present you might have expected them to promise at least 100 Crowns for twenty to fifty sessions. But not a single one of them did! The top were two forms with 40 Crowns a month. It's doubtful

[1] The Müllers were friends of the Bergs and lived in the same house.
[2] After being finally discharged from the army in October 1917 as physically unfit, Schoenberg immediately took over the direction of this 'Seminar'. His pupils included Karl Rankl, Josef Rufer and Hanns Eisler. In April 1918 he moved to Mödling near Vienna, and the seminar was disbanded. Out of it, however, grew Schoenberg's Society for Private Concerts. (See also Letter 222.)
[3] About £75.

if we can expect any more registrations. Schoenberg's inaugural address on the idea of the seminar was very fine, though. He got over the embarrassing subject of his salary brilliantly, partly with sardonic wit and partly with serious rebukes. Not that this makes any difference to the lamentable result.

Not much cheering news either. Schoenberg—three days before he moves out—has no flat. The one he was offered has fallen through, can only be used for offices. Plus the fact that he's still a soldier and at the moment on guard duty.

Late in the evening, after I had driven to Hietzing with Schoenberg, I went to see your people, who are going more and more into a decline with their hopeless grief.[1] Papa and Mama had been sitting alone for hours (they were waiting for the Leberts) round the huge table in the dining-room, just staring into space. I was so depressed by their unhappiness that, without staying till the Leberts came, I went home. For a long time I thought of my Pferscherl and how lovely it is for her now in her present environment, both people and nature. I was so happy that happiness has been granted to you, my All . . .

(214)   5th June 1918

Yesterday was nice. If only you'd been there![2] All very *gemütlich* indeed at Almschi's. Those present were Schoenberg and Trude[3] (not Frau Schoenberg), Werfel[4] and I. Schoenberg in brilliant form, and although there was plenty of arguing, everything went very smoothly with a lot of laughter. Dinner very simple, no meat, good black coffee. Main theme of discussion: the meanness of the rich. Almschi told some delicious stories about Panzer.[5] Then I got admonished again to go in for writing. Schoenberg had had another look at my *Guide to Gurrelieder*, and is apparently quite converted to it, for he suddenly found a mass of novel and interesting things in it. He talked very amiably with Werfel. That's to say, when they had

---

[1] Helene's brother, Frank, suffered from schizophrenia. He was in a sanatorium in Switzerland, and the family had no news about his condition as the frontiers between Switzerland and Austria were closed.

[2] Helene was at Trahütten.

[3] Schoenberg's daughter.

[4] Franz Werfel (1890–1945), novelist and dramatist, later married to Alma Mahler.

[5] Dr Panzer, nose and throat specialist, a friend of Alma Mahler's.

ALBAN BERG WIEN XIII/I
TRAUTTMANSDORFFGASSE 27
TELEPHON: AUTOMAT 84831

27. II. 1918

Mein liebes Pferscherl, gib recht acht
auf Dich und denk immer
lieb an

Deinen

'My dear Pferscherl, be very careful of your health and think always
lovingly of Your ...'

215

differences of opinion, S. was bound to prevail because of his terrific superiority.

All of them very sad that you have gone away. Write to Almschi often and nicely. She may sulk and not answer at first, but I don't think she's really angry. At half past three on Sunday we went to the rehearsal[1] at the *Musikverein*. Trude and Gucki walked in front. Almschi wanted the four of us to go by a cab she had ordered. I declined, and walked behind with Werfel. Rehearsal very well attended, but of course no critics there. Of the people we know, apart from some 'regulars', there was Ploderer and Göttel. I had met G. twice the day before, and was very reserved with him. First and second row: Frau Koller,[2] Itten,[3] Almschi, Werfel, young Koller, Trude, Frau Webern, Loos and the dancer girl, Wiener,[4] Kauder, Gucki, myself, Ratz,[5] etc.

The end and the beginning were rehearsed, then they played the whole work.

Everybody, including Almschi, very enthusiastic about several passages, Werfel sang the melody of the *Adagio*, which produced a delicious *intermezzo* from the disconcerted Schoenberg. Altogether there was a fine 'rapport' between Schoenberg and us. He asked me umpteen times 'do you like it now?', etc.

A lot of discussion after the rehearsal. (The Koller woman made me rather sick with her ecstasies, and she hadn't even got a ticket either, just went into the hall like Almschi as 'patroness'.)

Then we broke up. Almschi apparently returned home with her party. Frau Webern and Trude went to Mödling, Schoenberg, Bachrich,[6] Polnauer and myself to the Seminar . . .

(215)   8th June 1918
. . . Today I'm going to try to prepare Hofmann for my 'harvest leave' intentions. Seems he wants to go on a fortnight's leave

---

[1] Schoenberg directed ten public rehearsals of his *Chamber Symphony* op.9 (1906)—with no performance following them. The Viennese music critics had been excluded. Berg had written a thematic analysis of the work, which had been published by Universal Edition in May 1918.

[2] Whose son was the first husband of Anna ('Gucki') Mahler.

[3] Johannes Itten, the painter, was a friend of Alma Mahler's and Walter Gropius's.

[4] A friend of Alma Mahler's.

[5] Kauder and Erwin Ratz were young Viennese musicians.

[6] Dr Ernst Bachrich, pupil of Schoenberg's.

Hier, dazu das Gegenstück....
Zeigt den Schüler der Musik
Wie er redlich sich bemüht
Daß man ihn nur ja nicht sieht.

'And here the counterpart——
Shows the music-student
Taking great pains
Not to be seen.'

himself, which might mean my having to wait but it doesn't stop me applying at once, so that I'd have a definite day fixed for starting *my* leave. Perhaps I'll ask for July–August—and then hope to get agricultural exemption for autumn tillage!

Will I be happy to breathe the mountain air again! And everything connected with it.

Almschi seems to have gone already. I keep on telephoning, but there's no answer. Well, we shall find out tomorrow, Sunday morning at the rehearsal.

(216)   10th June 1918

... Spoke to Hofmann today about the leave. Highly successful. Except that he advises me to 'soften up' Steiner. So I am going to prepare my application this afternoon ...

While there's still time, Pferschi, lay in all the supplies we need, like lard (cheap for 40 Crowns); buy also one or two little pigs. Better start at once going over all the rest of our stores too. You have various things for barter, haven't you, and will let me know what to bring with me. Coffee, coffee-substitute, tea, tobacco (to be saved, as the ration stops just when I go on leave. So what I've got at the moment might well be my last tobacco, and part of that must be reserved for the coal man!).

To get flour for the Berghof is now almost impossible. But don't worry too much about it, we'll manage somehow.

For Gucki's birthday I wanted to buy a very nice one-volume edition of Büchner's works (*Wozzeck*, etc.). Might cost 12 to 15 Crowns, but I can't find it anywhere. I am thinking of buying her something wonderful: the letters of Bettina von Arnim to Goethe about Beethoven.[1] But I must find out first whether they're available. If I can't get them, I would like to send her a one-volume edition of Jacobsen's[2] works. But that would cost 20 Crowns. Perhaps something else will occur to me.

Der Friede (*Peace*) is a new periodical, and I could write for it. They pay 100 Crowns for three pages. Schoenberg also wants to write for it, Blei, Hegner,[3] Werfel, etc., etc. are other contributors.

Another rehearsal last night. Excellently attended, more people

[1] Bettina von Arnim (1785–1859), published in 1835 her *Goethe's Correspondence with a Child.*

[2] Jens Peter Jacobsen (1847–1885), the Danish poet, writer of poems which were the basis for Schoenberg's *Gurrelieder.*

[3] Jakob Hegner, German publisher.

than last time, although the Almschi set (Kollers, Kauder, Werfel) was missing. Schoenberg listened to Bachrich conducting the *Chamber Symphony*. He was very pleased with the sound (the clarity of chamber music!). After that he rehearsed various bits, then played it through. Everything going splendidly. Wednesday evening there's a 'dress rehearsal' in the small hall of the Concert House. Then on the Sunday a last performance, presumably in the morning. This will start with Loos reading his essay, 'Beethoven's Disease of the Ear'.[1] There is a terrific agitation against this whole ten-rehearsals idea: by Rosé and all his followers, and Korngold Junior.[2] None of them has attended a rehearsal so far. Nobody from *Anbruch*,[3] no Schreker pupils. No critics! Nor were they sent any tickets.

Remarks by Korngold Junior on his teacher Zemlinsky. Before the first night of Zemlinsky's opera *Clothes make the Man*: 'If this should again, prove to be no good, I'll throw him out altogether.' After the performance of Zemlinsky's string quartet, coming into the dressing room whistling a Strauss waltz: 'Sooner have that than the whole quartet.'

Lunch with Mama, then out to Mödling. Schoenberg by himself with Polnauer, Ratz and me. Thank heavens no excursion into the country, instead we sat on the veranda and had some stimulating talk. Schoenberg keeps coming back to his efforts to interest me in writing on music, among other things an extension of the Guide to his *Gurrelieder*—a self-contained book on musical theory, not to be used as programme notes; or an analysis of a Mahler Symphony. I think he's probably trying to make up for an injustice he did me when he made a lot of criticisms of my Guide, in fact hadn't a good word for it. But having read it again, he's quite enthusiastic about it. His first judgment was affected by the quarrels I got involved in, which ended by S. thinking less and less of me. This 'vindication' means a great deal and is very important to me, because I was very proud of my Guide, prouder than of all my own compositions. They are partly inspiration, after all, for which one is not fully responsible, whereas a theoretical analysis has to be wrestled out by hard brainwork alone. (Schoenberg himself is planning an analysis of Mahler's Ninth Symphony.)

[1] Adolf Loos was himself deaf.
[2] Erich Wolfgang Korngold (1897–1957), Austrian composer, son of the influential Viennese music critic, Julius Korngold (1860–1945).
[3] Progressive Viennese music magazine, founded by Universal Edition.

. . . Must give you a report on yesterday's concert (9th Rehearsal). It was wonderful. The hall very full. First a quarter of an hour rehearsing a few passages, then play-through. Then an interval, during which some people left, of course (like Charly, Göttel, etc.). But there was much more to come. Before the second play-through started, Loos went up on the platform and read a short essay, 'Beethoven's Disease of the Ear': the gist being that Beethoven's contemporaries found his music morbid and they believed this to be a result of his 'ear-disease'; therefore as his music has been heard for a whole century, the respectable people who are enthusiastic about it must be affected by Beethoven's ear disease.

This message, full of irony and passion, was greeted with hearty applause. Then came the second play-through. It went superbly. A storm of clapping and cheering at the end, the performers and Schoenberg were called on again and again, and it was a long time indeed before the hall emptied. I was absolutely 'shattered' by listening to the work twice—without following the score! I felt ten years younger, and as if, say, I'd been present at the first performance of Mahler's Third. Although I went to bed at 11.15, I couldn't get to sleep till two.

There were again heaps of people we know there, but also many new faces, and unfortunately a few music critics, who couldn't be prevented from coming. (They have passes, with which they can attend any concerts.) I sat in the seventh row, between Webern and Schmid, who of course were both in the heights of rapture. It really was so glorious. *You should have been there*. An irreparable loss for you, and for me as well, that you weren't.

Then we all accompanied Schoenberg to the Southern Station. Webern, who looks shockingly ill, is already living out at Mödling. Schmid came with me to Mama's flat, where I arrived at ten o'clock and found an excellent supper. But I found something else too, which proves my assertion that there are only three things for me: you, Nature and music (Schoenberg). I came into the room full of God and the beauty of this music, to find my family sitting round full of drink, unable to carry on a sensible conversation, and full of their conventional views. Can't tell you how disgusted I was, so that I could hardly refrain from making my disgust obvious. A great relief to get into bed and re-read your letter and *Goethe's Correspondence with a Child*.

Nothing else in the day worth telling you about. Oh yes, Schoenberg's Seminar is collecting a large 'food parcel' for him in honour of the *Chamber Symphony*'s performance. A few hundred Crowns already subscribed for it . . .

(218)   21st June 1918

. . . Was very annoyed with Papa yesterday. When he goes to see his daughter, he ought at least to have the courtesy to talk a few things over with her husband, who has been parted from her for some weeks, and at least to *pretend* some interest. I'm not at all for people putting on acts, but the opposite is an act too, the worst and most prejudiced pretence. I have long given up expecting truth and frankness, but surely a little benevolent dissembling! Or else what I have to expect from my enemies (artistic ones and those I have in the office at the moment): hostility but anyhow *respect*. But this sort of treatment, meted out to rude children or servants one wants to sack—disgusts me more and more the older I get, in fact I won't stand for it any longer. Do you see what I mean? Open hostility—well and good. But playing cards with him like boon companions and knowing he's inwardly despising me!

I've now relieved my anger, after having to swallow everything yesterday in silence. Outwardly nothing at all happened. I was intending to visit Papa again to say good-bye to him; but before I went, I'd been in our flat[1] and heard from the porter that he was going off today. Not having had any news from you for four days, I just wanted to talk to someone who would be with you the following day. But oh no! After the first words of greetings I was asked to join in a game of cards with the Leberts (who had also just arrived to say good-bye). The game dragged on so long that I hardly found time to add a few lines to Antschi's letter to you. I wasn't asked whether I was coming up to Trahütten at all, whether I had any messages for you, let alone what was happening about my leave. I felt very bruised by such insensitivity, plus the fact that my longing for you was growing more intense all the time, and my disgust at having to live away from you, with nobody to open my heart to.

Forgive me for doing it at least in a letter, and please don't be infected by my peevishness!

[1] While Helene was away, Berg stayed in his mother's flat (Linke Wienzeile, 118).

221

(219)   23rd June 1918

... Yesterday afternoon I went, as arranged, to the Leberts, where I had to fetch some food and ration card. Antschi had put the things together for me, and slipped a belated present for my name-day into my pocket (without Arthur seeing): a small bottle of excellent Amsterdam liqueur (Crême de Noyaux), bitter almonds and about a quarter of a pound each of butter and bacon! At the Food Distribution Centre I had bought a lot of salami, bread and butter; and with prunes for sweet and a half-pint of wine I had a fine cheap supper. This morning, after the second cup of tea, I had bread and bacon as well. And because it's Sunday I also smoked a cigarette in bed, where I am writing this food report. Hope you realize why I'm going into such detail: to put your mind completely at rest about my health at least—otherwise pages and pages about food would be revolting. And I'll do my utmost to continue, I mean taking great care of my health. Because I don't want a repetition of those boils or the attack I had at Trahütten this time last year.

Hietzing seemed beautifully secluded last night, as if in a fairy-tale. With all its quiet gardens and overgrown lanes where you hardly meet a soul, what a Paradise for someone who has been staying for weeks in a town, amidst grey houses and human ants scurrying to work. In our little garden in Trautmannsdorffgasse, lush and green with leaves swaying in the breeze, the little roses are in bloom in my rose-bushes. But I couldn't enjoy them properly: I was too depressed by the situation about the coming week (my leave), which is still unsettled, and by such a despondent letter in my pocket from Pferscherl. Yes indeed, what a filthy war.

(220)   24th June 1918

... At Steffi's for lunch yesterday: asparagus soup, roast loin with roast potatoes, roast pork with cucumber salad, cherry cake, black coffee. So life goes on! I rested a bit and then went out to Mödling by tram. Met the Webern family there, Steuermann and his sister,[1] and Frau Königer.

After tea the four of us—Schoenberg, Webern, Steuermann and I—pulled Trude's upright into the music-room, where we played Schoenberg's *Pieces for Orchestra* on two pianos. What a pity you

---

[1] Salka Steuermann later married the Austrian poet and theatrical producer Berthold Viertel, and became a producer in Hollywood.

don't know them yet. It was a great treat. And pushing the upright there and back produced a good deal of comedy and hilarity. Everybody except me left in the early evening, but Schoenberg had asked me to stay to supper with him, so I did. Very simple: sardines, polenta with salami and red currants. Washed down with two bottles of marvellous hock (from the Seminar's 'food parcel'). And while we were drinking it—the 23rd, naturally!—Schoenberg said we should call each other *Du*, not *Sie*.

The atmosphere was so easy and intimate, you could positively *feel* S.'s warmth and serenity. For the immediate future he is free of all worries. Besides the Mahler Stipend and the anonymous donation of 1,000 Crowns through Grünwald, something else happened: during the last rehearsal of the *Chamber Symphony* an unknown lady came up to him and asked him to accept an envelope from a patron who wished to remain anonymous. In it there was a sheet of paper with the following in disguised handwriting: 'To the great artist from an admirer, a Jew', and—10,000 Crowns (ten thousand) . . .

(221)   29th June 1918, afternoon
It is really sickening. Our applications went in to Steiner yesterday afternoon. Hofmann and I were both on tenterhooks, but instead of calling either of us, he left them lying there for quite a time, and then—but first I should have told you about one of our officers, a Czech first lieutenant called Schinko. Most of the others are quite efficient, but Schinko is useless for anything, so Steiner gave him the formal post of adjutant—and on this occasion handed him our applications. *He* put them in a drawer of his desk, and there they remained all day. Tomorrow, Friday, Steiner's off duty, the week-end's not likely to bring anything either, so Schinko won't be able to take the forms to him until Monday, and I shan't be able to get away till the middle of next week at earliest . . . I can't tell you how frustrating and annoying it's been.

If I'd been told that on such and such a day I could start my leave but not till then—I should have been sad but calm. But as it is, I've been all worked up and over-excited for weeks, with every hope followed by a disappointment . . . Staying here is becoming more and more distasteful to me.

For weeks no piano . . . and then the surroundings I'm living in. When I at last have the office and 'my mates' behind me. I should

like to get away into a physically and mentally clean atmosphere—
not to mention my spiritual needs!

Last year, when I lived in my flat and was either alone or had
your people for company, or two years ago, when I was always in
your lovely garden in the evening and had dinner there—then I was,
at least in my outside life, an aristocrat!

Also, what money it all costs today! One really has only the
alternatives of starving or spending madly. Nothing will induce me
to adopt the first course!—I want to come up to you perfectly
fit—so I have to opt for the second. Today, for instance, 29th June,
I have spent almost the whole of my July salary: I just mustn't let
my physical strength run down.

And all this just because of the filthy war. Sometimes I wonder
despairingly: what has all that got to do with me? And then I wonder
why the world doesn't wonder the same thing! Three years stolen
from the best years of my life, totally, irretrievably lost, and every
moment of freedom dearly paid for . . .

I fear, alas, that this letter may depress you too, my only one.
If it does, please remember that apart from you I have nobody,
that I talk to you as if it were to myself. So that in all my wretchedness I still possess the immeasurable happiness of your glorious
Trinity, body, mind and soul. In a week I shall be granted the
blessing of feeling only this and forgetting all the rest.

Your own

(222)   Monday, 1st July 1918
Well—my fate has been decided. Steiner has granted my
application and given me four weeks. 'Owing to service considerations a longer leave period cannot be allocated.' When he told me
this later, I looked very annoyed, and he tried to bargain. Then
he admitted that in certain circumstances an 'extension for a
further week' might be due to me. Of course I'll try to make two
weeks out of the one, so that if all goes well I might get six weeks . . .
It isn't much, but there's nothing to be done about that. And this
month of freedom has been dearly bought, with a month of tension,
disappointed hopes and anger.

I am already steeped in an intense longing to nestle up to you, my
silver pheasant, to come home at last out of my loneliness!—And
again a week more. Horrible, horrible.

Yesterday, Sunday morning, office; in the afternoon by train to Mödling . . . later a string quartet which Schoenberg arranged with two gentlemen from Mödling. A lot of music played, Beethoven and Schoenberg.[1]

Schoenberg has a marvellous idea, to start next season another society, setting out to perform musical works from the period 'Mahler to the present' once a week for its members; perhaps, should the work be a difficult one, to perform it more than once. Performers to be a string quartet specially selected, to rehearse very intensively, male and female singers, pianists, etc., not yet famous but good calibre. Hall, the one in the Schwarzwald School.[2]

(223)   2nd July 1918
Dismal days with their endless rain, and they pass just as dismally. My application returns to the War Ministry today, the so-called Home Command, from which I shall receive the order to report for leave. Perhaps this will even be tomorrow, so that I might actually travel on Friday. But don't count on it, there may well be new hazards among the various formalities I have to go through . . .

I try to cheer myself up about the weather by thinking it must be horribly cold up there, and however much I like rain, still if it goes on continuously for weeks, we should be confined in an overheated house, perhaps heated too by quarrelling with Papa!

There is a new moon on the 8th, and I like to imagine that the weather will change, and will continue fine for weeks, so that the long postponements will turn out to be an advantage for me. Had I come to Trahütten, for instance, at the beginning or middle of

---

[1] Quotation from Schoenberg's String Quartet No. 2 in F sharp minor, op.10 (1907–8).
[2] The first idea for the Society for Private Concerts, which later became famous. Schoenberg started it directly after the war, in November 1918 (See Letter 213). Berg was extremely active in preparing for its foundations, and was appointed *Vortragsmeister* of the Society together with Webern and Stein. That is, they had to direct the private and public rehearsals.

June, as planned at first, these five or six weeks would be over already in a few day's time. This is the sort of desperate comfort I give myself! . . .

A terrific amount to do here, as everybody's off sick. (This Spanish influenza apparently.) Hofmann away since yesterday, Hellin and Rittersbach both ill, Kollert on leave but also sick, likewise one of our clerks. I am *very* fit . . .

I'm eating enough, and mean to keep doing so this coming week. Although I don't know how to pay for it. The prices are crazy. For instance, last night: roast pork, cabbage and a glass of beer, plus tip—about 15 Crowns. Was still hungry after that, so I went into a delicatessen and bought a small piece of curd cheese, which I put on a little bit of bread: 4.20 Crowns, and a piece of salami, 6 Crowns, of which I ate half and kept the other half for today. Well, that's about 25 Crowns for one meal, if one really wants to feel reasonably full. This morning I was dreadfully hungry again. I miss the filling things: a dish of potatoes or beans or soup, such as you usually give me. Just work out how much all this costs per month. One meal for 20 Crowns, only one meal, comes to 600 Crowns in 30 days! How on earth shall I manage? . . .

(224)   5th July 1918
. . . Fate has spoken: Tuesday the 9th of July I shall be in Deutsch-Landsberg. So—auf Wiedersehen! Either Tuesday or Wednesday. The last paper kiss, my all! How happy I feel, how very happy!!!

(225)   Monday, 8th July 1918
My dearest,
Instead of my appearing in person—this letter comes. I finally fetched the signed pass from Home Command this morning, and went to Steiner with it to tell him I was leaving . . . but he simply made this Spanish 'flu a reason for cancelling my leave . . . and wrote on my pass: 'Commencement of leave postponed for eight days owing to service considerations.' So I have to repeat all today's performance of reporting for leave, to report back on duty; and in a week's time I can start from the beginning all over again. Nothing to be done about it, just obey. My feelings about the obeying are naturally beyond description. For hours it was really all I could do

not to burst into tears. For I had left Vienna already, was *with you*. I had it all in my mind's eye, was living through the vast store of delights. I had only one thought, *you*, YOU.

How sad you too must be: that makes my pain all the greater. But I can bring you a sort of comfort, which I experienced after this terrible disappointment. Once more, by pure chance, I escaped a great disaster: the explosion in Gumpendorfer Strasse—I expect you'll have read about it—took place perhaps half a minute after I had passed the spot. I was going to Charly's by tram, and jumped out near the Grabnergasse. Had just reached the house, when I heard the explosion. It was terrific, appalling. A shop nearby, which contained arms and ammunition, went up in the air. The window-panes were shattered all round, even the ground-floor windows in Grabnergasse. If the tram had passed at that moment, there wouldn't have been a particle of it left. What actually happened I don't know yet. In the middle of the road there was a woman's body lying among the debris of the adjoining houses. The explosions went on for hours. All the shops around were on fire, soon the whole house. Fire brigade, ambulances, huge hoses, ladders, shouts and groans—

After two hours the worst was over, the house of course in an indescribable state. I am sitting at Charly's and writing to you in haste so that you don't worry about me if you hear of the explosion, and won't perhaps connect my failure to arrive with the explosion. I am perfectly all right—only very sad . . .

(226)   9th July 1918
So it's once more writing letters, living on paper, putting off again my month of human existence and continuing only as a vegetable. I am immensely sad, disgusted, frustrated and madly impatient . . .

Went to my flat to look for mail, and found a note from Almschi: 'Dear Alban, I received a sweet letter from your Helenerl today. I am longing for her very much. When do you go to Trahütten? Could she not come here and meet you, and you both go home together from there? I really can't imagine a summer without you two dears. Your letter was sweet. Affectionately, Alma.'

What do you think? I could manage it, of course . . . but am really not all that keen. I am so much longing for *you*, for you alone, and just want to reach *you* and be alone with you . . .

(227)   12th July 1918
                                          On the 50th birthday of
                                          Stefan George
Another day nearer the goal. Perhaps it will at last work. We
have certainly earned it. Also the boil I've got seems to be coming
to a head, quicker than I feared yesterday ... At least the pain is
less than last night. Wonder if it will be still better today. I very
much hope so, of course, because it would mean my arriving at
Trahütten on Tuesday morning completely healed, whereas if it
gets worse, it might burst on my journey on Monday—which
wouldn't be very hygienic! I will of course take the Cerolin pills
again, should never have stopped them. It's quite clear to me why
I'm afflicted with these boils again. Not getting all the filling stuff
I need (noodles, vegetables, etc.) I'm eating too much bread. Not
only the army bread, but also the ordinary kind which last week was
an indescribably lump, probably containing turnip remains and
coffee mixture. So my predisposition is back again, and the smallest
heat-spot turns into an abscess ...

(228)   13th July 1918
   The last letter, written at Jeanette's. I'll leave on Monday
morning, shall be at Deutsch-Landsberg in the evening, and can be
called for early next day. Besides the few commissions you asked for,
I'll try to take my cigarette ration in advance. So in the end I might
finally get away at eight, and after ten be in your arms at last, at
last! If only I hadn't got this ugly boil. It still hasn't gone down, as
I hoped yesterday, in fact the swelling on the lower lip has increased.
The actual head either hasn't formed or is very low down so that
it can't open ... which means waiting ... in two days the thing is
sure to be ripe.
   Yesterday your express letter of the 11th came, the day you
waited for me in vain. How sweet the letter is, but how sad! That
was my greatest sorrow too, to cause you a new disappointment.
But now that day lies far behind us, and the day of our being at
last reunited is so close before us. If I *had* come then, four days of
my leave would have been gone by now.
   I shall probably drive over to see Schoenberg this afternoon and
say good-bye to him. Tomorrow, Sunday, I am still on duty. In the
afternoon I'll go to Hietzing to pack and say good-bye to the
Leberts. In the evening home to finish packing, and early Monday

morning to the station—Auf Wiedersehen, what a beautiful word!

Your own

I had a peculiar dream today. I was in a field, and a crow flew by with its tail-feathers on fire. It let me come near enough to help it, which I did, by smothering the fire with my cap. I wonder what this might mean!

(229)   Trahütten,[1] 7th August 1918
My darling,
    That was a sad walk home. I felt quite wretched leaving you alone in this weather. Luckily the whole plain, and particularly Deutsch-Landsberg looked rain-free for some time longer, so I could assume you got down safely. I myself went up the mountain very slowly, resting often, and eventually, as I was plodding on, without any intention of working, I found that the musical expression for one of Wozzeck's entrances, which I had been trying to get for ages, had suddenly come to me. There is a bit of me in his character, since I have been spending these war years just as dependent on people I hate, have been in chains, sick, captive, resigned, in fact humiliated. Without this military service I should be as healthy as before, and would never have let you make such a complicated trip as the one from Trahütten to Breitenstein—and back again—quite by yourself. Still, perhaps but for this that musical expression wouldn't have occurred to me. For since you went away, I have lost the proper will to work. Until I hear that you've arrived up there safely, I shan't be at peace.

(230)   (Undated,
                                                 1st September 1918)
    Back again in Vienna! I am constantly tormented by my longing for you and your dear special ways and habits. It is so wretched that we should be torn apart. Nobody can judge what a tremendous sacrifice I am making to the State. The train journey was splendid. Except that I couldn't get a wink of sleep, tired as I was, as I hadn't

[1] Helene was staying with Alma Mahler, running the household for her and taking care of her children Anna and Manon. A week earlier she had given birth to a son, whose father was Franz Werfel. The child, later christened Martin, died when only a few months old.

got a corner seat and my head couldn't rest properly in a loop I made (like a noose!) from my leather belt. So the weariness tormented me for the eight long hours, with some comfort in the black coffee you gave me. Around noon it even became quite hot. And I was refreshed in the best possible way by the apples! (Altogether, the most important sort of food on a journey is fruit. I would even say you need *only* fruit, it's a substitute for drink and all other food.)

I arrived home pretty battered, but found everything fine, thank heavens. Then I telephone Charly, who informed me that I had just received an official 'appreciation' for my work at the War Ministry: I had been recommended for the Silver Cross of Merit. But the State preferred to give me a paper diploma instead of silver. On that I could enthusiastically continue my service for another three years! But at the moment I am incapable of enthusiasm about anything . . .

(231)   6th September 1918

Nothing to report today. Extremely boring at the office. Have started orchestrating what I composed at Trahütten; after six days I had lost my inspiration so completely that I couldn't look at any music. Also I hadn't got the time for it or the opportunity. The stupid hours in the office drive one to despair. I could be so fresh for work in the morning, would feel so eager for it, and have to go to the office. Same in the afternoon after a short but sound half-hour's nap. To give up that and start work immediately after lunch wouldn't work either, because I'm always so sleepy after a meal that I'm not even fresh enough to read . . .

(232)   (Undated,
                                                          September 1918)

Yesterday morning I rang up Almschi, and she immediately asked after you. I told her you wouldn't be coming yet, at which she again pretended to be very disappointed. She asked me to lunch. There was another woman there, a Frau F., who didn't open her mouth. We talked a bit about painting, books and music. She had just received Pfitzner's Violin Sonata,[1] and was full of enthusiasm over it. Then Manon arrived, sweet as ever. Last night she was in

---

[1] Violin Sonata in E minor, op.27 (1918).

bed, refused to have any supper, and as usual had put the photographs of all her dear aunties round her. Someone tried to punish her by taking yours away, but she loves it so much she clasped it in her arms and wouldn't let go of it. Almschi decided little Manon should write a letter to you asking you to please come. Altogether I think Almschi feels a bit guilty, because she said to me, rather anxiously as ever: 'Now, what's up with Helene? Seems to me she wants to cut herself off from us. Tell her she really must come soon.' . . .

(233)   Vienna, 9th September 1918
  My Pferschi!
  Well, I was in Mödling yesterday afternoon. It was very nice, apart from my getting into some heavy rain going back in the evening. Schoenberg looks quite well, so does his wife—smooth skin, mind a blank! Trude has improved a bit, the boy is the same as ever. Frau Pappenheim was there, and a doctor called Frischauf,[1] just returned from the front—rather a pleasant fellow. Bachrich, Steuermann and Ratz turned up later. B. had brought with him a certain Fraülein Stampfer who wanted to have an audition with Schoenberg. Mathilde[2] 'didn't intend to meet new people' and so stayed away. We had some music; the girl sang Schoenberg songs— quite musically, though with vocal difficulties. It was better in the great Sieglinde aria.[3] I would so much like you some time to sing for Schoenberg. We would study it together very thoroughly beforehand, so that you'd be sure to come over successfully. You'd do it much better than the Stampfer girl.
  Steuermann looks very plain, but strangely enough, he's gradually turning into a distinctive 'face'. Bachrich and Ratz very nice as always. Afterwards Mahler's Seventh Symphony was played. Oh, that last movement. If you still have the Seventh out there, practise it, specially the last movement. At eight o'clock we all left, I took a tram to Hietzing.
  Pferscherl, the 13th is Schoenberg's birthday. Please send him a telegram.
  Yesterday we happened to be talking of Schreker when Schoenberg suddenly remarked, of course quite in jest: 'Yes, that's right,

---

[1] He later married Marie Pappenheim.
[2] Schoenberg and Mathilde Zemlinsky had been married since 1901.
[3] From Wagner's *Valkyrie*, Act One: 'Schläfst du, Gast?'

your friend.' I asked why he should think there was anything special with *me*, whereupon he turned to Frau Pappenheim and his wife and declared, still very lightly: 'Yes, our Berg has formed a friend-ship with Schreker behind my back, Schreker has made an advance into the enemy camp, he went to see the Bergs, etc.' Although it was said in such a jolly way, without any malicious sting to it, I found the whole thing embarrassing, and will go back to it some time when I am alone with Schoenberg.

Webern is still at Mürzzuschlag;[1] he seems once more to have rather lost favour with Schoenberg. I gathered this from remarks like 'Webern wants to go to Prague again', and when I looked puzzled and asked what he meant, Schoenberg wouldn't explain.

Steiner is in Steyer,[2] which means that I am off duty this after-noon. I am providing three pictures for the Leberts' empty wall. Have discovered three reproductions of the wonderful Segantini[3] triptych, 'Becoming, Being, Passing'.

Did you read about Villach? Big hunger demonstrations and an air-raid.

On an old house in Mödling I found a plaque saying: 'Beethoven lived in this house during the summer months of 1818, 1819 and 1820'—just a hundred years ago, in fact.

I am longing to smell the scent of the pale purple gentian violet. What times we live in! We used to write to each other about flowers, today all one talks about is lard.

My Schnudoa—if only we were together at last . . .

(234)   Vienna, 12th September 1918[4]
Yesterday afternoon Göttel rang me up at Jeanette's. He had tickets for the *Entführung aus dem Serail*. So at six I left the War Ministry, where he fetched me, and we spent two or three very enjoyable hours at the Opera (very fine corner seats, fourth row of the stalls). Kiurina was the best of all, I preferred her to Kurz. She really does make the part very striking, I don't like Piccaver at all, with his continual *portamento*, and sliding from one tone to

---

[1] Watering-place in Styria.
[2] Town in Upper Austria, some 60 miles west of Vienna.
[3] Giovanni Segantini (1858–1899), Italian painter of Alpine landscapes and subjects.
[4] Helene had gone from Trahütten to the Berghof.

another. Torture for me, though of course a feast for the audience.[1]

By tram to Göttel's flat in Hietzing, where we had an excellent dinner: Hungarian chicken with roast potatoes, stewed apricots, cakes from Gerstner's,[2] red wine. Was home at 11, found a postcard there from Webern, who had climbed the Hochschwab,[3] and will soon be in Vienna.

Back in the office today as usual . . .

I can't even think of how much I'm missing, with you being away all the time, and of how squalidly the days pass without you. It is all part of the trials and privations of this war service. But I won't go on moaning to you again. If I know you are well on the Berghof, and realize the usefulness of your trip there, I can endure these days too, with as much resignation as I endured the many lonely weeks of the summer.

Kisses, my darling

Your own

(235)   Vienna, Friday,
                                          13th September 1918
                                          (doubly unlucky date!)

Yesterday I received a letter from Jeanette, promising me a 200-Crown increase in my allowance (from 350 to 550). So I am at least rid of that worry, and we can take things a little easier—by 'things' I mean this filthy existence in this filthy war! Went to Hubertuskeller for lunch. On my way to the office in the afternoon I met Buschbeck,[4] looking in the Lanyi-window,[5] naturally. We were very pleased to see each other. He is a sort of literary director of the Burgtheater, and secretary to Bahr.[6] Suits me well, for it might give us the chance of going to dress rehearsals there.

Was on duty in the evening, tied up till quarter to nine, so that I had to have an expensive meal in town, 14 Crowns without drinks. Went home on the last tram, and at a quarter past ten proceeded to

[1] The soprano Berta Kiurina (1882–1933), the coloratura soprano Selma Kurz (1875–1933), and the lyric tenor Alfred Piccaver (1884–1958), were members of the Vienna Opera. In this performance of Mozart's *Seraglio* they sang Blondchen, Konstanze and Belmonte.

[2] Well-known Viennese sweet shop.

[3] Mountain in northern Styria, about 7,500 feet.

[4] Erhard Buschbeck, a poet from Salzburg, held the position of Literary Director (*Dramaturg*) to the Burgtheater for many years.

[5] Progressive Viennese bookshop.

[6] Hermann Bahr was then co-director of the Vienna Burgtheater.

bed, where I satisfied a sudden hunger with prunes. In the morning Antschi's excellent breakfast arrived: coffee and bread and butter. Yesterday at the Ministry's food distribution centre I received a pound of very good beef, which I gave to the Leberts. Enough of gorging! When I read through a letter like this, I'm horrified. But I know you only feel reassured when you know exactly what I've had for my meals and whether it was enough . . .

Keep on drinking plenty of milk at the Berghof. Don't be shy or wait till it's offered you. It's a matter of course that you should get yourself a glass of milk when you feel like it, even between meals. Remember that after this we shan't see any milk for months . . .

(236)   Friday, 13th September, 1918,
                                                        afternoon

At lunch-time today I went to Mödling to congratulate Schoenberg.[1] He was very pleased at my coming in person (unannounced). I brought him a box of fine cigarette tobacco which I had had in reserve for quite a time, and a copy of my String Quartet. Schoenberg was delighted with both presents. He told me at once that you had sent such a charming telegram. Then the three of us, he, Mathilde and I, had some very lively conversation. He is going to work very hard to get me out of the army at last; and three possibilities came up.

One is to have me exempted for the performance of the *Gurrelieder* in Switzerland (on 4th November). A letter arrived today from Volkmar Andreae,[2] who reports that the rehearsals are starting on 13th September, today in fact. Everything is going well there, and it will certainly be an event. An exemption for this would no doubt be possible, but that would be only for a month or two. How happy I would be to take you there with me, and what lovely days we should spend there: just to imagine it makes me feel melancholy—not to mention feeling furious to be living in chains as I am. Yes, it makes me furious and sad at the same time, to think of thousands of people sitting there with my 'Guide', hundreds with my score, and the music we know so well sounding forth in twelve rehearsals and one performance—and that we can't be there ourselves.

Schoenberg's second idea for my exemption was that Bahr

[1] On his 44th birthday.
[2] Volkmar Andreae (b. 1879), Swiss conductor and composer.

should apply for me as composer of incidental music for one of the plays he is to put on. Or finally, I should try to get to the Headquarters for War Correspondents.[1] If this should be no good either, I would put in for an officer-training course. Once I am an officer, it might be easier to find something for me in Vienna. (In extremities I am thinking of asking Almschi for help—she can get *anything* through!) Anyhow there's plenty of time, I can't do anything before October. Still, I must get back to my real work sooner or later, and to making some money. But I can only do this if I am free at least half the day.

What else? Oh yes, Webern really *has* fallen into complete disfavour now. This is how it happened. Some time ago he wrote to Schoenberg that he had more or less decided to go back to Prague to be conductor at the theatre—mainly for financial reasons: his capital would soon be exhausted, and he had come to the conclusion that the theatre was the right thing for him, etc. I must say that it's madness, to my mind, to change one's plans every six months, keep starting again from the beginning, and not take into account the immense expense of moving house. But as for his purely financial reasons, Schoenberg refuses to believe he has only got 16,000 Crowns left out of the seventy or eighty thousand he had a year or two ago. (I do believe it!) S. thinks he could easily earn that amount here.

But after all Webern moved in the spring to Mödling with rather vague prospects—he hoped to help in S.'s Seminar, in running the 'Society for Private Concerts', and to orchestrate operettas—so he might have made about 500 Crowns a month altogether. S. even criticized *that* move, although Webern made it only to be near *him*, which was surely rather flattering. Anyhow, instead of trying to realize those vague prospects, Webern is now setting out to do something else where there might be a better chance of the prospects materializing.

Schoenberg however, believes Webern has other reasons for leaving Mödling, chiefly disappointment at his life with S.—who also blames him for being secretive and deceitful. Webern, he says, had planned this change months ago, and had recently shown no interest in S.'s plans connected with his existence in Mödling, just letting him 'talk' to no purpose.

He (S.) was almost angry when I tried to put Webern's motives in a better light. (By the way, I am still convinced that Webern

[1] *Kriegspressequartier.*

was simply afraid of soon finding himself 'with no means of liveli-hood', and thought it would in that case be better if he had some sort of 'position'. Perhaps he hadn't the courage to tell S. this, and so kept quiet about it for a long time and then preferred to say it in writing.) Of course Webern has been a bit inconsistent on several points. For instance, when he and his wife came to Mödling, they couldn't get over the way one can still get everything one needs here, and that it isn't even as expensive as Prague. Whereas now he writes that one can live better and cheaper in Prague. So S. came to the conclusion: 'Well, perhaps no one can really live with *me*!' Now Schoenberg revealed to me the last chapter in the story: *Cherchez la femme*. Frau Webern's behaviour has been very strange. He believes that *she* is mainly responsible for Webern wanting to go. For instance, she didn't have the proper respect for S., had taken offence at some of his jokes and answered them with malicious comments, and altogether may have had an anti-Schoenberg influence on her husband.

He told me all this on the way to the station, and by the end my head was in a whirl, both because it was all so unexpected, and also because I couldn't help feeling very sorry for Webern. S. may be right on details, and no doubt all the points he brings up, and quotes, and proves by examples, are accurate in their way. But on the main issues I still think he's in the wrong. To condemn Webern completely I mean, and doubt his friendship, which is really quite beyond doubt. I can imagine how poor Webern felt on receiving S.'s answer, saying he couldn't and wouldn't be mixed up in the whole business any more.

On the way home in the train I was reading a rather dull biography of Mahler,[1] which has just been brought out in a cheap edition and came across this:

'It was an absolutely ideal marriage, between a man in the prime of life and at the peak of his creative powers, a man of quite fanatical chastity, springing from his deeply mystical philosophy—and a woman who gave him complete understanding and sympathy. Two children . . .'

After leaving the office went to the Hubertuskeller. Then to the café and met Kassowitz, who came to Hietzing with me by the last tram. To bed at 10.15.

Today, Saturday 14th, I am off duty, and still in bed, where I am

---

[1] Arthur Neisser's *Gustav Mahler*, Leipzig, 1918.

finishing this letter and sending you many, many kisses. Your cheeks have the lovely fragrance of the Carinthian air!

(237)   15th September 1918

My silver pheasant, you really must come soon! That's to say, I don't want to persuade you into leaving the Berghof sooner than you feel you should. If it's fine weather and you feel well mentally and physically, you certainly mustn't sacrifice a single day for my sake. And on the other hand (I'm sure you'll believe me!) I do wish you were here. Kind as the Leberts are to me, and however much the others—Schoenberg, Almschi, Göttel, Kassowitz—try to lighten my loneliness, it still doesn't work. This fortnight I have been away from you seems so dreadfully long—much longer, curiously enough, than the six weeks I was on my own before my leave. It feels like a completely lost time, or rather, a long empty interval which is exactly what it is.

Yesterday I went with Göttel to see *Fanny's First Play* by Bernard Shaw. I've been interested in Shaw for some time. I knew nothing of his work, but I didn't think much of him—and I found my opinion completely confirmed. He is no *poet*, although he is wrongly reputed to be one. Basically, he is no better than our Blumenthal[1] and the rest of them, who write more or less witty light entertainment. That's still the case even if he is full of sarcasms and is no doubt an admirable observer of the defects of his fellow-men, especially his fellow-countrymen. I am more interested in my fellow-men's 'qualities' than in their defects . . .[2]

(238)   Monday, 16th September 1918,
                                                                    morning

Well, the most incredible thing has happened!—I could sooner have imagined Lord George,[3] say, going to Berlin to embrace Kaiser Wilhelm. Webern has broken off his friendship with Schoenberg—simply broken it off with a few words.

You know Schoenberg wrote to Webern saying he couldn't be involved in Webern's decisions any longer, as they were always

---

[1] Oscar Blumenthal (1852–1917), Berlin theatrical manager, critic, and author of several well-known comedies, including *The White Horse Inn*.

[2] Berg's oblique judgment of Shaw is very much influenced by Karl Kraus.

[3] Should, of course, be Lloyd George.

being changed every six months. I read that shortish letter of his, and it was rather cool, no doubt, even severe and critical, but not insulting. After it Webern could either have stuck to his decision and tried to explain it in more less detail, or it might even have made him waver in the decision itself.

But instead he wrote something like this, on a half sheet of note-paper: 'Dear friend, I am not angry but sad. I would not have expected it from you, but I cannot change my decision. I shall prove to you that your efforts for me and advice to me over the years have not been wasted—if by that time you still wish to know me. The Prague project has fallen through.[1] I am going to Vienna. Good-bye—Anton Webern.' What do you say to that? Would you have thought Webern capable of it? I wouldn't.

Yesterday afternoon when I appeared at the Schoenbergs'—I was the first one there—he immediately showed me the letter, then dissected it word by word, with Tilde assisting: 'Besides being arrogant and uncouth, it's a very very feeble letter, of course, illogical, unintelligent and smug—which I never thought Webern was. Must have suddenly gone mad. I mean, I could have under-stood his sticking to his decision, but not his carrying rejection to the point of an actual rupture. Yes, I dare say it's largely due to a nervous breakdown'—and so on.

Later in the afternoon a young lieutenant appeared. He had been at the front for fourteen months, and a little while ago was severely wounded: bridge of the nose smashed in, also jaw, teeth, etc. He told us things about our higher command which are unbelievable.

Then Polnauer arrived, and we had tea together. General opinion that the war will be over in six or nine months. At least Austria would like to reach an armistice, which might then turn into a peace. I think this is a possibility anyhow. Because from what I know of our internal conditions, we can't go on much longer. Oh, how splendid that would be! With that prospect I could serve my time till then with no complaints! . . .

(239)   Thursday, 19th September 1918
I have been ill again. On Tuesday I was at Charly's for lunch, and we had fish (carp). Suddenly a bone stuck in my throat, and I just couldn't get it out. It choked me horribly, and I could feel the exact spot where it seemed to have stuck. It was in the left half

[1] See Letter 236 on Webern's Prague project.

of the throat near the gullet, in one of the deep folds and pits I have round my tonsils. I couldn't get rid of the pain, though, and so the afternoon went. It was awful! You know how bad I am at bearing pain. But I could hardly move my tongue, speak, yawn, without feeling that sharp stabbing pain which brought tears to my eyes. In the evening I was at the Lebert's and Anna examined me, but couldn't find her way round my mysterious throat—all she found was a scratch.

Next morning—that was yesterday—the pain was worse if anything. I 'phoned Dr Martin, and he saw me at eight o'clock, examined me thoroughly, saw the inflammation and the scratch, but couldn't see the foreign body—so he sent me to a specialist. In the afternoon I went to Dr Otto Mayer, behind the Votivkirche, who at once went about things very rationally. Having been unable to find anything on a preliminary examination, he pumped cocaine into my throat, and then began poking around in it as if it were an untidy drawer! He also found the spot. Right down in a tonsil he noticed a white patch, which was either a foreign body or the result of an injury caused by it.

Strangely enough, he couldn't do anything, painted it with some sharp tincture, and asked me to come and see him today. He also gave me a prescription for some gargle. Now, today, it's much better, and I keep wondering whether it's worth going to him again. The whole thing turned into a sort of throat catarrh, proving my theory that this type of catarrh has nothing to do with a cold, even less with a bacillus, but could be caused by some purely mechanical irritation. So if I don't have any more of the localized pain which made me afraid the foreign body was still there, I shan't go to the specialist again—or that carp might prove too expensive! Anyhow I am feeling much easier, and hope to be completely recovered by tomorrow.

But what do you think of these constant vexations to which my poor *corpus* is subjected? When I think of the last three months: boils, asthma, a seven-week cold, influenza, diarrhoea, and now the bone! What a splendid husband you have, what a sterling soldier for my Emperor and a healthy son for Mama! . . .

(240)   Sunday,
                                        22nd September 1918
. . . You are right in a lot you say about the Schoenberg–Webern case. Schoenberg certainly didn't 'kick Webern out'; rather the

other way round. He just refused to go on advising him, because, as the facts show, it isn't good giving him any advice. He couldn't go on talking responsibility for Webern's continual changes of mind. He never advised Webern to come to Mödling either, although it's obvious to everyone, of course, that he liked the idea of Webern moving near him. What he did, in fact, was simply to make clear to Webern what sort of existence might be possible for him, *even without the theatre*. And of course he declared himself ready to help Webern in that by word and deed. Well, Webern had ceased to react to this, even by the end of July, although he was then still living in Mödling: he simply 'let Schoenberg talk'.

So Schoenberg was justified in assuming that some time before his letter Webern was already planning to return to the theatre—that is, he dissembled. So far Schoenberg's charge that Webern was deceitful towards him is justified. But he didn't make the slightest reference to all that in his letter, or mention his well-founded suspicions that Frau Webern was behind the whole thing. As I've said, he only sent a very short answer to Webern's long letter, saying he didn't want to be involved in W.'s decision, as he had repeatedly gone into the greatest detail for weeks and weeks over the pros and cons of a change of profession in ten or twenty similar cases—and with some justification he could say: 'To no purpose.'

To that extent Webern's brusque answer 'breaking off communications' remains unfounded. In fact it's very unfair to Schoenberg, even admitting that W. has often rendered inestimable services to Schoenberg, who owes him a great deal psychologically and materially. Still, Webern would seem right to look for a secure position at the theatre; though come to that, he has already given up the theatre a dozen times. Anyhow, I wonder how he will fare now in Vienna, what he's likely to expect of *me*—and what Schoenberg's present views will be. (For I'm writing this in the tram, Sunday afternoon, on the way to Mödling.)

Only person at the Schoenberg's was an old uncle of Mathilde's, a dreadful Philistine. We played cards nearly all the time—delightful as you can imagine! With long discussions after every hand about what mistakes had been made. Even when playing cards Schoenberg is as precise and skilful as in everything else, solving all problems mathematically, reasoning everything out, and leaving the minimum to chance. Splendid refreshments, as it was Gorgel's[1] birthday: coffee and marvellous cake.

[1] Schoenberg's son, Georg.

Helene Berg in 1921

Berg c. 1920

Above, the cast for the Russian production of *Wozzeck* in Leningrad, 1927; *below*, the cast of *Wozzeck* in Oldenburg, 1929

When the uncle had gone, the talk turned to Webern. Schoenberg persists in his severe judgment of W.'s rebuff. Admits he was sometimes rather impatient with W. and Frau W., but says as older and wiser man he was bound to take a very firm line, etc. Anyhow, the differences have become more acute now after a clumsy letter Frau W. has written to Mathilde. Of course some new details have come to light which help to explain the breach. Among other things some latent anti-Semitism in the Weberns, their moodiness and readiness for a quarrel, etc.

Am now in the tram on my way home. Have an amateur tenor near me warbling away the song from *Rose of Stamboul*[1]—awful!

(241)   Monday,
                                                   23rd September,
                                                      in the office

At a quarter to nine last night when I came back from Mödling, I thought I would look in at the Leberts'. They both appeared at the door in their nighties, as they were just off to bed. So I went home to my flat, where I found a magnificent supper; bread and butter, salami, chopped meat steaks, lovely potato- and cabbage-salad, then some fine chocolate cream with fruit, and beer.

This morning I had some talks about coal. We and the Leberts will both definitely get something, even if it's only ten hundredweight. For I think it's practically certain we shan't officially get any coal in the winter. Who knows if the coal merchant will even be able to let us have the ration he still owes us. So it's essential to get in a small stock if we don't want to risk freezing to death this winter . . . Now we should be able to look forward to it fairly calmly, as far as food and fuel are concerned. Except for the potato shortage, and for that I suppose we shall have to find ways and means at the Berghof. Please see to that before you leave. Or do you think we can expect something from Trahütten? . . .

(242)   Vienna,
                                                24th September 1918

Yesterday Webern appeared. Difficult to tell you all we said, but the fact is, I now see the whole thing in a different light, and him as

[1] Operetta by Leo Fall, popular in Vienna during the First World War.

on the whole innocent. Even his letter, which had seemed so brusque to me, I can understand much better after he explained how very much Schoenberg's letter had hit him—'like a kick in the teeth'—and that his own merely meant that he was going into 'voluntary banishment', etc. The reasons for his returning to the theatre were always clear to me. They are purely financial and extremely pressing: he doesn't want to be faced in a year perhaps with complete bankruptcy. Moreover, life in Mödling is financially impossible, he considers, as all food there costs twice as much as in Vienna—one is dependent, after all, on a very few grocers. No chance of earning more money by lessons, etc. He had to take two or three thousand out of his bank every month. The flat has no amenities at all and costs 2,000 Crowns. He can't go on indefinitely like that (nor could we for that matter). And with some justice he called the prospects for other earnings rather vague.

The 'clumsy letter' from his wife to Mathilde which Schoenberg told me about, contained the following, according to Webern. He had promised S. some time ago that he would send him some food from Mürzusschlag, and when he got hold of this, he couldn't very well keep it for himself despite the rift. So he sent it to Frau S. with a letter from his wife saying: 'After your husband's letter it isn't possible for us to come to you any more' (or something like that), 'so I am sending herewith the food promised and due to you, which costs so-and-so much': and she gave a detailed account of all the provisions sent. The Schoenbergs returned all the food, *and* the money for food they had been sent earlier, without any covering letter, just the signature, Mathilde Schoenberg. 'Second kick in the teeth,' says Webern.

The funny thing is that Webern of course can't find a flat in Vienna (at the moment he is staying with his mother-in-law) and is today moving back to Mödling! And doesn't know how to avoid any of the Schoenbergs, who of course live very near. He can't imagine meeting S. socially in the foreseeable future. At the idea of it he became quite furious, just as he was when defending his position earlier. Sometimes he looked to me, even outwardly, much more, virile, resolute, unyielding. He doesn't want to stay in Mödling, but is still trying to get a theatrical engagement. If this doesn't work, he will look for a little cottage in the country, perhaps in Styria, where life will cost him next to nothing. Well—I very much wonder what the next developments will be.

While W. was there, Göttel 'phoned to say he had tickets for

Elektra with Gutheil.[1] I didn't feel much inclined to go, but the fine seats (second row in the stalls) and the casting of the title role tempted me. I'm quite glad I went, even though hardly any of the music moved me—I found most of it rather boring. Because I was thrilled beyond words by Gutheil's performance, which was perhaps even greater than when we saw her in the part not so long ago. The art of her singing has reached a peak, nobody else in the Opera sings like that. In her musical feeling and dramatic skill she outclasses them all, including the orchestra and the conductor. I have only heard the very greatest interpreters, like Mahler, Zemlinsky and Schoenberg, produce music like this . . .

(243)   25th September 1918
    Your letter arrived yesterday with the suggestion that I come and fetch you from the Berghof. Hey, my darling—it's not as simple as that. I should need three days' leave for the journey there and back, which I can't get out of Steiner quite that easily. Perhaps some time in the winter when he could hope I would bring him back some present again. To come half-way to meet you would be lovely, but there are other snags. In uniform I shouldn't get permission to use an express train for so short a distance; so I should have to travel in mufti. First, that costs a few Crowns more, though it might be worth it; but secondly, I run as much risk of being examined as you do. But don't worry, I'll try to meet you on the platform in the evening after the express train gets in. There's such a mêlée then, they don't bother to look at the small luggage.[2] If you bring some flour with you, put it in your hand-bag, with the dried vegetables, your toilet things, bottles etc., above it. Anyhow, I'll come with my rucksack, we can easily stick something in that to get it out of the station safely.
    I'm terribly sorry that you are travelling so soon after your illness. Should I against my deepest wishes advise you even now to postpone your journey till you are completely better? . . . No, I'm incapable of that degree of unselfishness, I'm afraid! I am counting the hours till you come, and the very thought that your coming might be put off again sends the blood shooting to my head . . .

    [1] Marie Gutheil-Schoder (1874–1937), dramatic soprano, famous for her performances in Strauss operas.
    [2] Control at the Vienna stations was very strict. The Government (because of the danger of black-market transactions) wanted to stop people buying food in the country and bringing it back into the city.

Otherwise I enjoyed your letter very much with all its details of your tranquil life. I can understand your cooling off with 'Tilde, but don't take it too seriously. As the Schoenbergs are leaving for Switzerland in the middle of October, that will anyhow prevent an association which might have become too intense. Yes, they may stay there for good, that seems to be their secret wish. Perhaps after the undoubted success of his *Gurrelieder* performances there, he'll find some opening for a secure livelihood.

I shall buy myself a monthly season ticket on the trams, with which I can ride on any line. It costs 50 Crowns a month. You may think me a bit extravagant, but listen how much I am spending a day on the tram: first ride to the War Ministry, second to the Hubertuskeller, third back to the Ministry, fourth to the Hubertuskeller again, fifth to Hietzing. That makes 1.60 a day, which, multiplied by 30, comes to 48 Crowns. And if I sometimes go from the Ministry to the theatre, or after lunch at the Hubertuskeller back to Hietzing to see you, or change, shave, etc.—that soon makes up the 2-Crowns difference! Even if I don't go to the office twice on Sunday, one always goes somewhere, to Jeanette, Almschi, etc. Then there's the pleasantness of being able to ride for even the smallest distances (a great saving of time), whereas now I can only ride on a certain line. Anyhow I'll try it for a month.

It's really disgusting that on top of everything else I have to spend 50 Crowns a month for this filthy military service—that means five or six hundred a year.

Good-bye, my darling. I had such a lovely dream about you last night. Love and kisses to your Mama.

Your own[1]

(244)   11th September 1919[2]

Motto: Everything safely home ... I felt very bad in Bruck, seeing you wander off alone into a strange town!

When I got to Vienna, there were two porters waiting for me, who were very officious and mysterious. They took all my luggage, and I walked out without anything to hide. The control man was very slack, and let everything pass. The porters then appeared

---

[1] Berg's last letter of the War years. Two months later he was demobilized.

[2] The Bergs had spent the summer of 1919 at the Berghof. On September 10th they left, Berg returning to Vienna, Helene going to her parents' villa at Trahütten.

somehow with my luggage in perfect order. They hadn't even needed the keys or the documents, but they again put on a very mysterious air, so that I had to give them 20 Crowns. The flat has been kept beautifully, there were flowers to greet me. By your letter it seems I was in fact expected yesterday, but not till the evening. Unpacked everything and put it away, then changed all my clothes and washed.

Went to lunch with the Leberts today, they were extremely glad to see me, especially Anna. She doesn't look at all well. The baby[1] is lovely, and so friendly—it couldn't stop looking at me. You will be quite delighted. And it's entirely Nahowski, except for having Lebert pouchy cheeks, which, however, suit him better than they do his father!

They took it for granted that I should have meals with them as often as I can, contributing partly with what I bring (vegetables, etc.), partly from my rations. Living conditions seem to be better actually. If one economizes and can do without meat, one can live on one's rations.

The Society is doing well. First programme includes Schmidt's symphony,[2] Mahler's *Lieder eines fahrenden Gesellen*.[3] Mihaczek will not work with us (apparently Strauss is behind it), but Fleischer is still loyal in spite of Weingartner.[4]

Schoenberg was very nice on the 'phone, invited me for lunch today . . . Steuermann isn't here yet. He had a terrific success in Dresden. On 10th January Schalk is doing the *Gurrelieder*. Good luck to him![5]

(245)   11th September 1919,
                                                                    evening

Went to Mödling for lunch, very warmly received by Schoenberg. They all asked affectionately after you and are looking forward to seeing you—one more reason for you to come to Vienna soon!

S. seems quite well off financially, has plenty of pupils who pay

[1] Hans, son of Arthur and Anna Lebert.
[2] Symphony No. 2 in E flat by the Austrian composer Franz Schmidt (1874-1939).
[3] 'Songs of a Wayfarer' (1883-84).
[4] Felicie Hüni-Mihaczek (soprano) and Arthur Fleischer (baritone) were at that time members of the State Opera and the Volksoper, respectively; Strauss and Weingartner were directors of these two opera-houses.
[5] Franz Schalk (1863-1931), Austrian conductor, Strauss' co-director at the Vienna Opera.

well, mostly foreigners. Shocking lunch, I found it, but then I'm spoilt: potato stew with tomatoes, noodles in milk, and everything cooked in American lard! But splendid coffee afterwards. Also saw Webern,[1] though only briefly. We talked solely about the Society, as I already have a rehearsal tomorrow: Reger's Beethoven Variations for two pianos.[2] Schoenberg, by the way, has quite gone off the Social Democrats, but doesn't really know what political line to take. His idea is, go back to the old régime as quickly as possible, but do things better—almost a monarchist position, in fact. He is very worried about the expulsion of foreigners, many of his pupils are involved, like Steuermann, Diesche,[3] etc. And even S. himself, as he was not a national of any country and only came to Austria at the beginning of the war,[4] is affected by the regulation. But of course it won't come to that . . .

The Schoenbergs don't look too bad—but they don't look too well either. Mathilde and Trude knit stockings. The boy wears one of Schoenberg's shirts, rather poorly taken in with tucks. Great poverty all round. But Richard Strauss has smuggled half a ton of wonderful food into Vienna. Pisk[5] has become second music critic of *Der Tag*, Wellesz[6] is their first critic, of course. Réti[7] is second critic of *Der Morgen*, under Graf[8] . . .

(246)   Vienna, Sunday,
                                          14th September 1919
. . . as I wanted to go off early to Mödling and not upset the Lebert's punctual mealtimes, I cooked myself a fine lunch: two sweet corns with a lot of butter, Berghof bread with a lot of bacon, radishes, a cup of tea with sugar. Then to Mödling, where we had very gay celebrations for Schoenberg's 45th birthday. His pupils and friends had all arranged to come, though some arrived unexpectedly

[1] The quarrel between Schoenberg and Webern (See Letters 236, *et seq.*) had been patched up.
[2] Variations and Fugue on a theme by Beethoven, op. 86, by Max Reger (1873–1916).
[3] A Polish woman pianist.
[4] See Letter 194.
[5] Paul Amadeus Pisk (b. 1838), Austrian musicologist and composer.
[6] Egon Wellesz (b. 1885), important Austrian composer and Oxford musicologist.
[7] Rudolph Réti (1885–1957), Austrian critic and composer, author of *The Thematic Process in Music* (Faber) and *Thematic Patterns in Sonatas by Beethoven* (Faber).
[8] Max Graf (1873–1958), Austrian music critic.

(Loos and his wife, the Pappenheims); all of them brought flowers as well as presents. There was a magnificent birthday table. Perhaps fifteen to twenty different kinds of flowers, masses of different food, an entire delicatessen shop of the finest sort: about five cakes, pastries, sweets, ten to fifteen choice savouries and preserves, marvellous fruit, wines, liquers, cigarettes, also books, ties, pens and pencils, condensed milk, etc., etc.—absolutely regal. I gave him a new book by Maeterlinck, the apples from the Berghof, which were much admired, and your bouquet: white phlox which Antschi secretly picked from your garden (not a word to Papa!).

During the afternoon congratulations and telegrams poured in. It was all very jolly. Loos particularly was in top form—honestly, his face becomes more and more superb. Of course he is aging visibly, but his features are taking on all the signs of special greatness and saintliness. He talked for hours—nearly a monologue—wonderful stuff: about politics and the history of civilization, all with the light, graceful raconteur's manner, almost anecdotal, yet somehow full of profundity. What a shame you weren't there to hear him.

There were about twenty-five to thirty there in the afternoon, and about 16 stayed on in the evening. We had a cold supper with Gumpoldkirchner 1917. Everyone went at ten except Webern and me. We stayed another half hour, then W. went too, and I spent the night at the Schoenbergs'.

Up early this morning. Excellent breakfast, and now, Sunday morning, on my way to a rehearsal . . .

p.s. Nobody must talk to me now for the next two or three days: the fourth and fifth act of *The Last Days of Mankind* has been published—a whole book, 450 pages. If it didn't cost 16½ Crowns, I would buy a second copy and send it you to read on the train.[1]

(247)   Vienna,
15th September 1919

Amazing what a person can do in one day! I started today's activities at 7 a.m. with a letter to you, then had a shower, then more letters, including a business one to Mama. Various telephone conversations in between whiles. Universal Edition is going to

---

[1] *Die letzten Tage der Menschheit*, the vast war tragedy by Karl Kraus, was published act by act through 1919. The epilogue, *The Last Night*, had been published before the rest, in November 1918.

handle the distribution of my *Pieces for Orchestra* and the band parts, which will save me a terrific amount of trouble.

Then the post came—with your letter.

After that the day proper! By tram to Mama's bank, then (on foot) through the districts of Mariahilf in Gumpendorferstrasse, (tax office), Lerchenfeld, Josefstadt, Alsergrund (to box office of Stadttheater to buy ticket for *Ghost Sonata*[1] production starring Gertrude Eysoldt[2]), and Während (to printers about new programme for Association Concert). Then to Berggasse for lunch in Communal Restaurant, quite good. Back to town, relax a little, five telephone calls, and start writing this letter.

During this time I have met: first, Frau Ploderer—she has become very charming to me and gave me a pressing invitation to dinner; second, Dr Réti (twice); third, Frau Stefan; fourth, Itten (arm in arm with quite a beautiful woman. He has been to Switzerland and is going to Weimar, hasn't any news of Almschi); fifth, Grünfeld, who thought I was looking extremely well, and sends you his regards—he knows we'll be coming to Trahütten. In the café I met Hugo Knepler,[3] who sat down with me and talked at me for a whole hour so that I got quite sick. A big quarrel has started between Heller[4] and Knepler about Mahler's Sixth and Seventh Symphonies. Almschi first preferred Heller (she gets 600 Crowns per performance) and is now all for Fried,[5] but Heller is for Bruno Walter as he has fallen out with Fried.

Continuing this later: in the afternoon I met Webern, who had just been at a rehearsal. Walked to the Southern Station with him, as we had various things about the Association to discuss . . .

It's now quarter to seven, I went out and bought an ice-cream! The air in Vienna is absolutely frightful, thick as manure!—in the heat you can smell it, taste it, inhale it. Indescribable, specially to you, breathing the heavenly air of Trahütten. Hope it will have rained by the time you come—it hasn't rained for a fortnight—and so spare you the worst . . .

(248)   19th–20th September 1919
Last night the rain I longed for came at last. It was quite unbear-

---

[1] *Gespenstersonate* by Strindberg, (1910).
[2] The great German actress Gertrude Eysoldt (1870–1955).
[3] Viennese impresario.
[4] Hugo Heller, another Viennese impresario.
[5] Oscar Fried (1871–1942), German conductor.

able, this hot, stinking, dusty period. My breathing organs were quite rebellious! Yesterday: wrote to you first thing, then rehearsal at Deutsch's,[1] lunch with Leberts. Had a rest at home, devoured hundred pages of *Fackel*, and shaved; then to the first concert. It went splendidly, quite a lot of new members. The Reger *Variations* which I had rehearsed would be just the thing for you. The *Violin Sonata* is even more beautiful and more difficult.[2] The Strauss *Lieder*—some very nice, some cheap stuff. I wasn't too thrilled by the singer Bruck-Zinner[3]—not at all an appealing voice, rather throaty, in fact. She is the daughter of a sort of caretaker at the Academy of Arts in Schillerplatz. Husband was an officer and a baron, is at the moment quite without means or job (his estate in Bohemia has been completely ransacked), so that they are forced to live on her singing; when they were married he was so jealous he wouldn't let her do it.

Made the acquaintance yesterday, or rather renewed it, of an extremely elegant and prepossessing young American. In the tram he looked at me several times, and later told me he had got on to it because he saw me. He apologized for staring, then introduced himself. He's a secretary in the Hungarian Legation in Vienna, name of Hajos. Now, of course, I knew who he was: years ago a smart young officer who wrote poetry and adored Smaragda. Today he is the famous Hajos who saved 450 million Crowns from the Hungarian Bolsheviks. The way he did it was almost like a fairy-tale, with hundreds of Red Guard soldiers, police and two companies of Home Guard after him. He came on with me for a bit, but I didn't do anything to continue connections, you would have liked him too much!

Sunday,
21st September 1919

. . . Lunch with the Leberts. Afternoon resting at home, reading the *Fackel*, sleeping, going through the orchestral parts. In the evening to Mahler's Ninth. Bad performance, as Fried exaggerates everything more and more. I stood through it for 4 Crowns, which left me very tired (Göttel was sitting in the fourth row, 25 Crowns). Went home, and Toni brought me supper at ten o'clock. To bed at eleven . . .

[1] Max Deutsch, a pupil of Schoenberg's and Steuermann's, later conductor in Paris.
[2] Max Reger wrote seven sonatas for violin and pianoforte.
[3] Bruck-Zinner, Viennese concert soprano.

(249)

Vienna,
28th December 1919[1]

Dear Mama,

I have just received your eight-page letter. I can't spend hours going into all the details, as I have a great deal of work of my own this Christmas week besides attending to your most urgent business, like checking telephone accounts, increase of rent for fifty tenants, etc. So only the most important things: please note and tell everyone else, as they still don't seem to realize it, the true reason for my going to the Berghof: I promised I would be at your disposal if ever family circumstances required it; so if I go now, it's only because, with Charly leaving the place, I'm *needed* there. To think, some people actually say Charly's leaving because I *want* to go there!! So there's no deep plan behind it, as you write (why not call it a 'plot' outright?); I'm just keeping my earlier promise.

This certainly does not mean that I am going because at the moment I have 'no proper occupation' in Vienna and can't get an allowance. Quite the reverse. I wish to emphasize, that:

(1) I have 'a proper occupation' in Vienna. To wit my position in the Association, three pupils, your affairs, which, as it is, cost me two or three half-days a week and sometimes more.

(2) I earn 850 Crowns a month therefrom, even without allowances.

(3) For various reasons Helene is not going to the Berghof . . .

I repeat: it's not because I 'planned' to take over from Charly or have ever wanted to; or because I think my being there is a wonderful piece of luck for my family and a salvation for me in my indigent state; or because I 'haven't anything really to do in Vienna'; or because I am a loafer who is not getting anything more from his mother and so lets himself be supported at the Berghof. No, I am going there solely because I declared I would be ready to do so if needed there, and because I consider it my duty towards you and the whole family.

Please make this known, dear Mama, to all my brothers, to Smaragda—and of course to May.[2] With lots of love and kisses, your grateful son

Alban

---

[1] This letter of Berg's to his mother is important for the understanding of the letters from the Berghof that follow. The estate was financially in a very bad way when Charly left it; and Berg took over at his mother's express wish.

[2] Girlfriend of Berg's sister, Smaragda.

(250)   Undated

                (10th January 1920)

  Well, here we are in Carinthia,[1] my Pferscherl. Beginning of the journey was a bit chilly, but the compartment got warmer after two or three hours. Passport control in Styria quite friendly, thank heaven no control in Carinthia ... A lovely day, but seemed incredibly dreary without you. At six o'clock in the morning I spilt the coffee from my flask all over myself. The flask was broken inside, don't know when and how it happened. How sad, specially as I was very tired. Then I cut my thumb with the glass—and no sticking-plaster! We'll be at Klagenfurt in a few minutes. A policeman has just taken my passport, I'm supposed to fetch it in Villach. Many sad kisses.

(251)   Berghof, 11th January 1920,

                      evening

  The first day has gone. I am completely blind to all the beauty which in happier circumstances would transport me into wild raptures. Incredible that looking at such a wonderful winter's day should have no effect on me at all, that I haven't an atom of interest for all the culinary pleasures even, but just think all the time with passionate longing of the two of us together.

  Hermann not being there meant that today was more of a gossip day. We didn't talk much about future plans for the Berghof, everyone tacitly assumes I am taking over, and there's very strong criticism of the former management. It's staggering how little idea anyone has of my normal existence and career. Even Hermann, who is really so touchingly concerned for my welfare, seems quite convinced that it can only be my greatest happiness to be steward of the Berghof. I believe he had quite forgotten that I have a profession and a vocation.

  Perhaps I'll find a chance to talk about it today. Of course it's hard for me to speak of my services to music and of how absolutely essential it is for me to be still able to compose and play. Anyhow, if you see Hermann, please seize any chance of giving him the facts—much easier for a third party: that after only a year's 'practice' following five years' interruption (war service, etc.), I am still getting

---

[1] Following his mother's repeated requests, Berg started his job as steward of the Berghof.

my works performed in many different German cities, have commissions, pupils, and get music published; which alone should warrant my not interrupting such a career for years. Not to speak of the purely artistic reasons—whether it isn't desirable, even essential, for me or for mankind that I go on writing music.

But why am I telling my Pferscherl all this? You know it better than I do. I just wanted to let you know that I've never been more aware of these reasons, sharpened by my feeling of unutterable loneliness, banishment and desolation.

I know that I have to accept it, because it is absolutely necessary for me to be here now . . .

(252)   Berghof, 12th January 1920
So dog-tired it's a terrific effort just to pick up a pencil and start writing . . .

My mood varies between deepest depression and resignation, fury and attempts to cheer myself up. I'd better say no more about it, just tell you briefly what I've been doing. In the kitchen, from seven in the morning preparing for the 'sausage-making', at nine to Villach, big 'shopping order', home at two, unpacking everything and putting it away. Inspect the stores, general discussion of work programme, then work in the house till eight. Dinner (oh, this roast pork, the excellent cabbage and the huge potatoes. If only my Pferscherl were having them, that's all I can think of when I eat all these good things; also the apples and cider!). And today they made mountains of sausages and brawn, and there's also a lamb still being prepared—and none of it going to Pferscherl . . .

(253)   13th January 1920
I want to write and tell you everything and pour out my heart, but my eye-lids are dropping from exhaustion . . . I've been on the go from 6.45 a.m. till 6 p.m. Was taking a look at the trees during the morning when I did have one beautiful moment. The whole valley, and everything above and below, was wrapped in a thin mist, so that there wasn't much visibility. Then at one point I happened to look up towards the top of the Görlitz, and it was like a miracle: above the sea of mist you could suddenly see that snow-covered ridge, which somehow seemed far higher than usual—

quite magical. But my delight soon waned with all the wretched cares of stewardship . . .

There's friction between May, myself and Schuh the bailiff, but I am not taking it too seriously. I am just collecting material for my plans. Today I talked to Mama about letting the Berghof. She seemed enthusiastic about it. I took the opportunity of speaking to her (for the very first time) about you. I said I wouldn't under any circumstances stay here for good, as that would mean the 'destruction of my marital happiness' and also my 'career', and I proved it . . .

So the dismal days pass. Only the hour from half past nine to half past ten at night belongs to me—and to you, my lovely . . .

(254)   Berghof, 14th January 1920
A letter from you came today, bringing a beam of sunlight into this shadowy existence of mine . . . I could have cried as I read your dear, kind, loyal words. The realization that I can be happy again, even if I *can't* be happy *here*, gives me hope once more for the future. I am so utterly exhausted I can't possibly put down the thousands of thoughts that keep going through my head while I'm working. After twelve or thirteen hours of work, and then an hour at dinner, I am quite unable to think straight. Today, for instance: wood-cutting and chopping from seven to half-past, breakfast, give orders and inspect things on the estate; drive to Villach, hundreds of commissions and running around. Everything tremendously expensive (1 lira—15.50 Crowns). Back home at a quarter past two, have a meal, then manual jobs in the house and yard till five. Then administrative work with Mama, business letters, dinner, and now to bed.

(225)   15th January
My letter continued. Seven o'clock, work in the house, then to the mill . . . home at a quarter past one for lunch, row over to Sattendorf directly afterwards to see the station-master and Mama's seamstress. From there walk to Annenheim station to the boat-builder to inspect the new fishing-boat—and walk back home, very slippery and terribly tiring. Tea. A farmer and his wife suddenly appear, wanting to take a lease on the Berghof for 8,000 Crowns. This led to a discussion on whether to let the place or sell it. Mama, May and Smaragda seemed to prefer the latter and thought it gave

better prospects. I would prefer it too, as I should be rid for good of the worry the Berghof is for me at the moment. (Don't say anything about *that* to Hermann.) At any rate the subject has somehow been broached, and also my attitude to it, that I do not regard the present position as at all a permanent one . . .

As far as health goes, I'm all right—quite amazed at how much physical work I can do . . .

News about our dogs: Lulu may have her litter in five or six days. Nero is as sweet as ever—my only friend here. All the others (except perhaps for Smaragda) 'love me not' . . .

(256)   16th January 1920, evening
. . . The day passed like other days, a bit more bearable or perhaps I felt more resigned. For some hours I was busy with sausage-making. Visited the Mendels.[1] One of their sons killed in the war, the son-in-law too. A younger son, aged twenty-two returned some time ago from a prisoner-of-war camp, suffering badly from malaria and a swollen spleen; short of breath, hollow-cheeked, bulging eyes and mouth, incapable of working: a man more dead than alive. All he got as settlement from the State was 53 Crowns.

Schoenberg wrote, asking me to write a long monograph about him. How lovely that would be! However I had to decline and also resign from the Association 'for an indefinite period'. It's horrible. But I've got to keep going here for a while. Perhaps it won't take all that long. We talk every day about a sale to the Italian, who bought the Annenheim. Today the lira is worth 17 Crowns! Weather around freezing point, or even colder, and it seems to be getting still worse . . .

(257)   17th January 1920
. . . Neither Mama nor Smaragda or May still believe that I am sacrificing everything for the Berghof. They know I wouldn't dream of staying here for good, but will be returning to my music, which I shall never give up . . .

Because this is my attitude, it has already become quite obvious after a week that some other way of saving the Berghof will have to be found. And now the idea of letting it has fallen through, alas, they have had this idea of selling it. I don't know at the moment,

[1] The Mendels were farmers, living near the Berghof.

254

of course, if and when anything will come of this, such things have to be thought over carefully. But sooner or later a solution will be found, which will restore my freedom and independence to me. By then we should also know whether the Association has any future or not, whether, in fact, it can pay reasonable salaries. If it can't, I'll have to have a serious talk with Schoenberg. That might lead to my either having nothing more to do with the Association, or to my taking over the literary side, confining myself on the whole to writing about music, arranging piano scores, etc. . . .

There are two reasons why I can't do any work here. One is that I just haven't any time, every day is too short as it is. Secondly, a combination of estate management and music is quite out of the question, there's far too much to do and think about here.

(258)   Sunday, 18th January 1920
. . . We won't have the Berghof much longer! The Italian from Annenheim is really after it. He was here again yesterday and talked directly about the purchase. He wants a farm, fishing stream, etc., which he can use for a hotel he is hoping to open in the summer. At the moment we are holding back, to get him to make an offer. Nor did we accept his invitation today to dine at the Annenheim, although the terrific amount of food supplies from Italy he talked about were decidedly tempting . . . It must have been very lovely at Almschi's. Delighted to hear of Ravel's interest.[1] At last a gleam of light on the music front. Look, if I now had my stuff published and could send it to Paris, I'm sure the people there would play the Quartet and the Clarinet Pieces. By the way, those Pieces were to have been performed at the Association on Friday. Now the concert has to be cancelled. Lord, how remote all that is, and all the music and the life I endured so gladly for all its anxieties. When I think of Vienna, the only light that shines for me there is you. Only you, my darlingest round-face!

Today the Italian was here again. He won't give in—something might be decided tomorrow. At least we are going to tell each other our prices. It all depends whether there's a lot of difference between them. Between you and me, May would like to buy the Berghof for the same amount. Because of her foreign currency she has three or four millions today, so she could easily afford it . . .

[1] Maurice Ravel came to Vienna several times during the 1920s, and showed great interest in the works of the new composers.

255

What a pauper I am in comparison, and yet so rich, having you, music, friends, belief in a thousand things and again you! Mine isn't the Italian currency, the Swiss nor the American, but the currency of the Infinite. In that I'm a multi-millionaire. Kisses

Your own

Have you sung for Anna-Gucki? Why not for Almschi? When I come to Vienna, you really must sing for *her* some time. She really should hear your fine musicianship.

(259)   22nd January 1920
I didn't write to you yesterday, my darling, it was too exciting a day. The 'business'—I'll call it that—has come off, and very favourably too. Nothing has been signed yet, but both sides are more or less morally committed. Unfortunately I can't tell you more about this most interesting occurrence, as I am even worried about this letter. The matter is at present completely confidential. If it came out here, it would endanger things irretrievably and perhaps stop any further developments. Accordingly, please don't say a word to anyone . . .

Otherwise I haven't much of interest to report. Weather and temperature bearable. I assume I shall be returning home during February, and then no devil shall part us any more . . .

(260)   Berghof, 23rd January 1920
My silver pheasant, I am at the moment in the Mill, where I am delivering the maize. As the miller isn't at home, I may have to wait for hours . . . They say here that a Soviet government has been proclaimed in Vienna.[1] Horrible to think of it: that you are there, and can't get away because the railways have been closed; that you may have managed to go to Trahütten, and I can't find out about it. Apparently all postal communications too will be suspended tomorrow, which means I'm *completely* cut off from you. Oh, if only you'd come here with me . . .

Back home I found your short letter, about being ill—but dated the 19th, so the uncertainty's terrible on that too. How are you *now*?

But just fancy: I had influenza too, the same day, the same hour as you, and with a high temperature. It started with a sore

[1] The rumours proved untrue.

Above left, view from Berg's study window at the Waldhaus; *above right*, at the Waldhaus; *below left*, Berg near the Berghof, 1930

Helene Berg in 1930

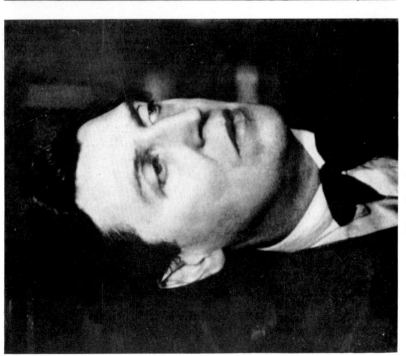

Alban Berg in 1930

throat, furry tongue, the shivers, and—just like you—the most frightful aches and migraine. You can imagine, knowing I'm not much good at bearing pain, what I went through! But what you can't imagine is how I missed you, my darling, with your way of nursing me, which turns every illness into something more like a quiet rest and holiday.

It's over now, I've been absolutely all right again for some time—so you needn't worry an atom! If I could only say the same of your state of health . . . But please, it hardly needs saying, *please* let me hear from you soon and often, and hear how you are. So, at least a thousand kisses, no, a million-and-a-half kisses,[1] my golden girl!

Your own

(261)   Sunday, 25th January 1920

I've been here only a fortnight, and it feels like months—one just grows stupid. Overtired all the time, no sort of intellectual inspiration, no intellectual activity possible—even reading; and of course no stimulating company here . . .

If I didn't know I was going to settle matters satisfactorily, I would leave everything and go straight back to my Pferscherl, and then nothing would ever get me away again. Tomorrow week the Italian returns from Trieste, then we shall put everything in writing which has so far only been agreed verbally. This means a week of suspense, and I wish it were over . . .

(262)   Monday, 26th January 1920

. . . It's getting colder still, the lake is frozen—it looks rather uncanny. I have been on my feet almost all day, upon the mountain, by the lake, in the house and cellar. Treated the cider, and prepared tremendous masses of meat to be smoked tomorrow. In between a visit from a couple, farmer-innkeepers; they want to take a lease on the Berghof, and offer 25,000 Crowns a year. They don't inspire too much confidence, but anyhow we'll make a note of them, in case the other thing falls through. All this activity was overlaid, as with a veil, by the constant anxiety for your well-being . . .

---

[1] A clue to the amount the Italian intended to pay for the Berghof.

AB–S   257

(263)   Berghof, 28th January 1920

Today was the first day when the ice broke. It was being smashed to large, thick pieces, and dragged to the shore: first to the bathing-hut, then by cart to the ice-hut, where they crushed it and stamped it down. A terrific job involving seven men, including myself (I worked pretty hard at it) and three horses. It might go on another two days. Horrible!

(264)   29th January 1920

Another day of ice-breaking. Funny how in the end you feel safe even far out, and even after cutting an opening quite near you which is as big as the whole Berghof house.

The slabs of ice are often as big as a billiard table, and are slung out by special instruments on to the ice we're standing on; then we slide them across the ice at a rattling pace. The cart with the horses stands on the ice, and they transport the slabs. There'll be about forty loads . . .

A day of incredibly hard work, in fact, and whatever you do, it isn't enough—you feel you're bound to have missed something important. In short it's really too much for me. Everyone recognizes that, and understands the necessity of selling. A lease wouldn't bring in enough for Mama and Smaragda to live on it . . . So there are only two alternatives: a sale which makes such an income possible, or keep it and work it ourselves. That means: me, and some capable woman in the family who would be prepared to do it! As I myself couldn't do it, and wouldn't, the second alternative is out of the question, and only the first remains—a sale ... The Italian promised to come somewhere around the first of February, and get our agreement to his offer, for payment in Crowns—in which case the whole thing would come to fruition.

You can imagine how nervy I am in these days of suspense; and on top of the work!

Plentiful food as ever: today goose with our own red cabbage, last night our own celery with *sauce Hollandaise*, and mashed potatoes. After that a sort of cheese-strudel ...

(265)   Berghof, 31st January 1920
... My uneasiness is growing. The Italian has still not returned nor have we heard from him. It would be dreadful if the whole thing came to nothing. On Friday I'll send some more butter. The cold still continues. The lake is completely frozen, people walk across it. One could go into raptures over the beauty of these days and nights—if it weren't for the *impossible* situation ...

(266)   Berghof, Sunday,
                                        1st February 1920
... About the book on Schoenberg! I would be so happy if I could write it. But he made out the whole thing and my agreement to be so urgent that I had to refuse at once—not to keep him and his publisher in the air. At that time I had no idea how long this 'drafting' to the Berghof was going to last or might last. As things stand now, we are expecting the Italian—understandably on edge— and he said he would come today or tomorrow. He'll telegraph before he comes. I am, in fact, waiting for this vital wire hour by hour, and can't think of anything else. It would be awful if it didn't come. There is no sign whatever that he might withdraw, but the urgency of the matter has brought me to an incredible pitch of nervous tension. I always meant to inform Schoenberg the day the sale went through, and ask him whether there's still time for me to take over the work. It would help a lot in my career and earn a nice sum ...

Webern's fate is dreadful. What a decision that must have been, to part from all his children—and I wonder what Schoenberg thinks

259

about his moving from Mödling! If only one could help W. His father used to own some antique Biedermeier furniture, one could easily get fifty or a hundred thousand for it. But perhaps he didn't inherit any of this?

And now the saddest thing: your illness, those headaches. I am terribly worried. And always having to wait three or four days for news. Please get a second opinion from another doctor. Are you eating properly, getting enough meat? Horse meat!!! Would you be really kind and take 1,000 Crowns from me? For that you can get about 30lbs. of horse meat, that's a pound every day all through February. That would be something—health-promoting. My Pferschi, I'd be so pleased if you'd accept it from me—if only to give me a chance at last of doing something good for you. You can't imagine how wretched I feel and have always felt, at not being able to support you . . .

Did the butter I sent—disguised as a book—arrive on Tuesday?

(267)   7th February 1920
Thirty-five years old! My dearest darling Pferscherl! The only comfort in these sad days is that my lovely one in spite of everything somehow enjoys life, now the nasty illness is at last disappearing. How wistfully I thought last night of the evening at the Association. Mahler songs, Schoenberg conducting, friends in the hall and the artists' room and on the rostrum. And in the front row perhaps my Pferscherl and Almschi. And I have to spend my days worrying about wood and flour, amidst cowpats and human dung, growing more and more dreary and dirty and dull-witted, as I wait for my release.

The Italian has not turned up, so we are still in suspense. Anyhow one has to go on running the farm regardless; it'll be very serious for the farm if this business does come adrift. Well, we'll give him a bit longer. Then I might fall back on the other sale and lease offers.

Life up here (except for the food) is generally ghastly . . . but it can't possibly interest you to hear how annoyed I get with everybody and everything . . .

(268)   8th February 1920
Today, Sunday, I had to go by car well beyond Villach and then

walk up a mountain—to see about a cow. Fruitless errand, but on such a magnificent winter day rewarding for a nature-lover—which I'm *not* really just now! Icy cold when I started, but almost like summer on a southern slope I climbed—reminded me of Trahütten. And then those colours, that view, the whole panorama across the Karawanken,[1] with the river Drau[2] down below and many peaceful villages. Oh, how I would have delighted in it if you had been at my side! . . .

(269)   13th February 1920

Yesterday the Italian was here, and of course began to haggle. He wants to pay only two-thirds of the amount I sent you in kisses,[3] although he had practically given his word for the whole amount: the forest, he said, was not up to his expectations. However, as we insisted on the amount which he himself had named last time, he asked for time to think it over till the day after tomorrow, Sunday. So we go on waiting—and have to reckon with the possibility of the whole deal falling through.

Before that I had been invited to a strange lunch party. Nearly all Italians, which means bon-vivants! Macaroni with tomato sauce, fried chicken with mashed potatoes and beetroot, apple strudel, figs and other fruit, Chianti, champagne, liqueurs and black coffee. A gramophone was playing—nothing but Mascagni: the whole of *Cavalleria* and *Isabeaux*,[4] with everyone joining in the well-known tunes . . .

We have lost Hexel, and now have only Nero. He is beautifully lean, noble, steadfast, and loyal to me. And so very clean.

'I knew a dog who was as big as a man, as guileless as a child, and as wise as an old sage. He seemed to have so much time, something you never get in human life. When he lay in the sun and looked at you, it was as if he wanted to say: "Why do you all hurry so?" And no doubt he *would* have said it, if one had only waited.'

                                            Kraus

I would like to put these words on Nero's grave when he dies.

---

[1] Part of the Eastern Alps, between Austria and Yugoslavia.

[2] The Drau or Drave, tributary of the Danube, flowing through Carinthia and Styria, forms part of the frontier between Hungary and Yugoslavia.

[3] See footnote to Letter 260.

[4] Mascagni's *Isabeaux* was first performed in Buenos Aires in 1911.

Today is Shrovetide Sunday. Everyone on the estate is 'celebrating', i.e. not working, and will go on doing so for the next two days. Yet there's an air of tragedy about. One of the farmhands is in bed with a bad 'flu, this whole side of the lake seems under a cloud of sickness. Yesterday we had to fetch and take home again a doctor from Villach. The farmer Plürz has his two little children dying; on top of that his only horse died some days ago. Whole farms are ill. Lucky we have all *had* 'flu here (apart from Mama) and got over it.

Atmosphere of gloom in other ways too. The time has expired when the Italian should have let us know. Significant that he hasn't done so. I could connect it also with the fall in the lira, which we've just read about in the paper. It means that the price for him would be very much higher, as Mama would hardly drop any more from the sum agreed on—so the whole thing is very much in doubt.

Funnily enough, there was an American here today, who is also interested. And would offer half a million to a million. There's more and more talk about it. And yet it's doubtful whether Mama would achieve the price, the one I 'gave' in kisses, which she considers the minimum. From this sum (plus interest) she could live, with Smaragda, just as well (eating as in peace-time, holiday in the country, etc.) as they both have in mind . . .

Both have their special 'conditions of life'. Mama can 'digest' only meat, eggs, fine vegetables, and all that in large quantities plus alcohol—i.e., no potatoes, no milk, etc. Smaragda 'digests' only the lightest (finest) food, must have white bread and butter, can't possibly eat things from darker flour or the like, or beans or cabbage. Also concerts and theatres only in the best seats, now and then little excursions, and so on. How do we paupers in Vienna live at all? And yet we have at least as fine nerves and senses and tastes and inclinations. I don't grudge them all that, but can't see why I should sacrifice *myself* for it.

Should the business with the Italian not come off, I'll take the next opportunity to din my point of view into them. They think I just don't like being here, whereas I have told them umpteen times that it would be a complete impossibility for me—even for the highest of salaries and in the best material living conditions, yes, even if you were here—to be steward of the Berghof, after being the Alban Berg I have been for thirty-five years. That Alban Berg would cease to exist directly he took on the farming of the Berghof as his actual life's work ... Please don't fall out with Schoenberg. Go to the Association's concerts. He will anyway be slightly hurt with me, first over the book, secondly that I have stayed out of things so long, thirdly because I haven't written to him for so long —but I will put *that* right very soon ...

(271)   Berghof, 18th February 1920

Although I worked almost without a break for twelve or thirteen hours the whole day passed more easily than ever before. I kept telling myself: 'Pferscherl is coming, Pferscherl is coming!' So I could put up with all the troubles the day brought like any other, put up with them quite easily and happily because, 'Pferscherl is coming.'

Funnily enough, Smaragda took me aside today, and (without having any idea of your intention) suggested it was really time to ask you up here. It would be such a good moment just now, as on 1st March they are going away for three weeks. I mean, it might be nicer for you to come into the house when it's not so full, etc., etc. I of course emphasized your general disinclination but let myself be persuaded to encourage you to come ...

So I await your communication!—as to when you intend to travel ... When we shall at last see each other again ...

p.s. Another bright spot today: the new issue of the *Fackel*. I have a glance at it every hour, without any time to read properly.

(272)   Villach, Café Parkhotel,
                                                        19th February 1920

A day in Villach—alone. Lying in wait for two farmhands, who are supposed to be coming for me from various labour exchanges. But I expect I'm waiting in vain. We do need at least one man so badly, though. Work keeps on piling up, the people we've got seem to work less and less. They get up late, stop work early in the afternoon, and in between just jog along ...

So you can imagine how pleasant it would be to run the place, even for someone who had come here very eager to do it, let alone me, hating everything as I do, humans and animals—yes, even animals, except for Nero ... As for the humans ... there's May with her constant know-all arrogance, Mama and Smaragda's sublime egotism—and outside the farm these business men, profiteers, scoundrels, thieves . . .

Enough of that, I don't want to talk about it, and can well imagine how it bores *you*. I've only gone on this much to show and explain my disgust. For it doesn't really give me any relief putting such things down on paper. Until I have a firm prospect of getting away from here, nothing in the world can lift the burden weighing on me all the time.

I did mean to write to Schoenberg as well, but really don't know what attitude to adopt. Am I supposed to know anything of his family affairs? Or of Trudi's attempted suicide? Could I or should I refer to this as if 'offering sympathy'? So in the end I don't write to him, but confine myself to reading the papers, since even this not very lofty occupation comforts me by bringing some connection with Vienna and my existence there . . .

(273)   20th February 1920
My silver pheasant,

Since the letter in which you said you might possibly come, I haven't had any news from you. So I am waiting for a definite announcement that you *are* coming! I need you so badly. Am often sad, and then again full of fury or sometimes resigned, but not for a single minute since I came here have I been *happy*. What a state of affairs. And it might go on like that, as once again we don't hear a word from the Italian, and the more the Austrian currency (I hate that word!) goes up, the less prospects we have.

So only your coming here can help things. To regain in your arms—do they really exist?—the courage to live, to live through the next bad weeks.

Today is another of the days when one is utterly bogged down in this filth. You won't want me to go into any more detail. And then hours of writing on Mama's complicated tax affairs. In complete and poignant contrast to all this I get a letter from Webern full of news that affects me deeply.

Schoenberg is leaving on 27th February: to Mannheim for *Pelleas*, to Prague on 3rd March. The four Association concerts, following the special concert at the Schwarzwald School: Schoenberg's Orchestral Pieces and Piano Pieces,[1] my Sonata, Webern's

[1] Six Little Pieces op. 19 (1911).

264

Orchestral Pieces,[1] Debussy concert by the Feist Quartet[2] (Zemlinsky, Ravel, Stravinsky), etc. From there Schoenberg is going on to Amsterdam, where he will perform *Verklärte Nacht*, *Pelleas* and the Orchestral Pieces.

Webern goes on: 'And now it's quite possible he may remain in Amsterdam and have his family join him there. Only a plan so far, so mum's the word. But how I hope it succeeds!' (So perhaps I shan't see Schoenberg any more.) 'The other day' (W. continues) 'I rehearsed your String Quartet with Feist, and all I can say is: Magnificent! But Lord, isn't it difficult! I'm so very anxious to put the whole thing across clearly and beautifully.'

You can imagine my feelings. With every fibre of my being I hope you will be coming soon—for if I didn't have that hope, I should despair completely, like that time in Bruck[3] . . .

(274)   Sunday
                                        (22nd February 1920)
My Pferscherl,

Your nice letter of the 19th has just come; I have at once sent a telegram to Almschi:

> A LETTER TO YOU DEAREST ALMSCHI STARTED WEEKS
> AGO AND NEVER FINISHED SHOULD HAVE LONG AGO
> TOLD YOU OF MY SAD AND WISTFUL FRAME OF MIND.
> TODAY WHEN IT COULD NOT REACH YOU ANY MORE
> BECAUSE YOU ARE LEAVING, THIS TELEGRAM AT
> LEAST SHALL REACH YOU TO TELL YOU THAT I
> THINK OF YOU WITH A CONSTANT AFFECTION
> SUCH AS YOU CAN SCARCELY CONCEIVE.
> YOURS. ALBAN.

Hope she gets it before she goes. That would be the last straw, for her to be angry with me. The same goes for Schoenberg, to whom I hadn't written since refusing to do the monograph (a month ago). So I quickly wrote him a short but sincere letter, which he also should get before he leaves on the 27th.

If they all only knew just how impossible it is for me here to write letters—when I have to steal hours from the day or the evening even to write to you, my darling.

[1] Five Pieces op. 10 (1913).
[2] A Viennese Quartet.
[3] See Letter 175.

The increasing expensiveness of life in Vienna is horrible. Makes it all the more necessary for you to come here. First, you save a lot of money, secondly you can eat once more the real food you need (tomorrow we are slaughtering two pigs). Not to mention the idealistic reasons . . .

(275)   24th February 1920, evening
So you're definitely coming.

Your darling letter made me very excited. My Sonata in the Association, and the Quartet now in Frankfurt too! But how is it possible? Feist is still studying it in Vienna, and I have only one copy of the parts, and a single copy of the score with that beastly publisher in Berlin.

Thank heaven the Schoenbergs aren't angry. I have just read of the Vienna Music Festival Week with the *Gurrelieder* . . . Today's post also brought a glowing letter from Almschi, which did me a lot of good. Also a nice letter from Ploderer, and one from the would-be tenant of the Berghof. His views about leases and sales are very pessimistic . . .

(276)   25th February 1920
Oh dear, there's only one night train from Vienna to Villach. Leaving Vienna at 9.45 p.m., arriving in Villach at 1.2 p.m. Pferscherl, be brave and travel even so! Some time there might be an express coming here again—but one can't wait for that, it might take two or three weeks! If you get to the station early, you'll get a good seat in a second-class compartment and can at least doze off. May and Smaragda are travelling by slow train (as there's no express) on Monday afternoon, and arrive in Vienna on Tuesday morning. So, Pferscherl, you know what to do, and you'll come, won't you! Be self-reliant, and brave, and a darling, as you always are.

                                                        Your own

(277)   Undated
                                              (26th February 1920)
I've been much calmer lately, although the sale has come to nothing and my situation hasn't changed at all: I'm calmer simply

because the Pferscherl is in sight. But if you *didn't* come, everything would collapse in ruins.

So come, Pferscherl! Spring is approaching, the wonderful moonlight nights, the frozen lake is blue like the paper I'm writing on, the mountains red at sunrise and sunset. You *must* see all this, or even that is lost for me too. See you soon!!

Monday March the 1st is Mama's birthday.

Your own

(278)   28th February 1920

I haven't heard from you for ages, my golden one. The last thing I heard was that you were intending to leave on Saturday, which is today. But then you probably didn't know that no expresses were running, so you would have to have left yesterday in order to arrive here at lunch-time today. Anyhow we'll drive to Villach at midday, so that we'd be there to meet you in case you really should arrive around 1 p.m. I spend the whole day with my heart thumping, we've been parted from each other nearly two months! . . .

During a conversation yesterday Smaragda—not from any malicious intent, just out of sheer stupidity—told me quite casually, expressing Mama's views, that 'if one weren't so modern and enlightened, one would be extremely surprised, not to say angry' that *you leave me on my own*. I gave her a piece of my mind: 'I'm amazed that you all refuse still to see the true position. It is not reckless or heartless of Helene to leave me on my own, but of *me* to let her down because of my family. She would have every right to blame me for jeopardizing my existence and thereby hers, just to safeguard my family's existence. She must have an abundance of kindness and patience to permit that.'

But the stupidity and selfish obstinacy of these people is so great they simply can't understand. They still believe I am interested in the Berghof business and in seeing that something is left after Mama's death. Whereas really *my* interest can only be to progress artistically and financially. I can't balance the prospect of perhaps inheriting a few thousand Crowns in ten years time—against the *certainty* of being unable to work and earn, and of having to spend those ten years as a peasant getting more and more like some benighted village idiot . . . [1]

---

[1] Some time afterwards the Berghof was sold. The Italian bought it, and built in its grounds a factory for making shoe-trees. In May, Berg returned to Vienna—eight years later he was back at the Berghof. (See Letter 386.)

PART THREE

1921-1935

CHRONOLOGY

1921   2nd June: Clarinet Pieces performed in Paris.
9th June: Helene Berg to Hof Gastein, to take the waters.
July: The Kolisch-Quartet founded.
September: The Association for Musical Private Performances finishes its activities
October: Composition of *Wozzeck* completed. Orchestration started.
December: Berg and Steuermann to Frankfurt and Darmstadt for *Wozzeck* auditions.

1922   April: Orchestration of *Wozzeck* completed.
May: Webern conducts Mahler's Third Symphony.
The Frankfurt Opera Houses refuses *Wozzeck*.
July: Piano score of *Wozzeck* goes to press.

1923   January: Berg announces subscription for *Wozzeck* score.
March: Helene Berg in Carlsbad.
April: Universal Edition decide to accept *Wozzeck*.
5th June: Webern conducts in Berlin the 'Präludium' and 'Reigen' from Berg's *Three Pieces for Orchestra* op. 6.
2nd August: First performance of Berg's string quartet in Salzburg (Havemann Quartet).
In Salzburg, Scherchen suggests to Berg *Wozzeck* suite for concert performances, and to offer it to the Allgemeine Deutsche Musik-Verein.
Autumn: Kleiber, newly appointed as General Musical Director of the Berlin State Opera House, sees *Wozzeck* score.
22nd October: Mathilde Schoenberg dies.
November: Helene Berg to Parsch, near Salzburg for medical treatment.

1924   January: First meeting between Kleiber and Berg.
Wozzeck audition.
15th June: First performance of the *Wozzeck* Fragments at the 54th Music Festival of the Allgemeine Deutsche Musik-Verein in Frankfurt (Scherchen).

1925   9th February: Berg finishes the Chamber Concerto.

May: At the 3rd Festival of the I.S.C.M. in Prague, Zemlinsky conducts the *Wozzeck* Fragments. *Wozzeck* definitely accepted by the Berlin State Opera House.

November: Berg arrives in Berlin to take part in *Wozzeck* rehearsals.

Crisis at the Berlin Opera, Max von Schilling resigns.

14th December: *Wozzeck* première.

1926   March: Fruitless discussions between Alban Berg and the publishers of Gerhart Hauptmann concerning 'And Pippa Dances'.

First Viennese performance of the *Wozzeck* Fragments (Jalowetz).

Summer: Berg suffers from severe stomach trouble and asthma.

October: 'Lyric Suite' completed.

11th November: *Wozzeck* at the Czech National Theatre in Prague; stormy first night.

19th December: Berg's mother (Jeanette) dies.

1927   8th January: 'Lyric Suite' performed for the first time (Kolisch Quartet, Vienna).

20th March: Chamber Concerto performed for the first time (Scherchen, Berlin).

May: Berg signs contract with U.E., who become the sole publishers of all his works.

June: Alban Berg travels to Leningrad for the first Russian performance of *Wozzeck*.

1928   March: Berg in Zürich as juror for the 6th Festival of the I.S.C.M.

June: Work on the libretto to *Lulu*.

October: *Wozzeck* revival at the Berlin State Opera.

6th November: First performance of the orchestral version of the 'Seven early songs' (Robert Heger, Claire Born, Vienna).

1929   31st January: Jascha Horenstein conducts for the first time three movements of the Lyric Suite in the version for String Orchestra.

Spring: The Prague soprano Ružena Herlinger commissions Berg to write for her *Der Wein*.

23rd August: Berg finishes score of *Der Wein*.

1930   30th January: Alban Berg elected Member of the Prussian Academy of Arts.

June: *Wozzeck* produced for the first time at the Vienna State Opera.

Summer: The Bergs acquire a Ford sports car.

1931   January: Berg as juror of the I.S.C.M. in Cambridge and London.

1932   February: Berg at Brussels (*Wozzeck*, Chamber Concerto). 9th May: Emil Hertzka dies.

November: The Bergs acquire the 'Waldhaus' near Velden.

1933   30th January: Hitler—German Chancellor.

February: Berg as juror for the Allgemeine Deutsche Musik-Verein in Munich.

30th April: Berg as guest of honour at the International Musical Congress in Florence.

17th May: Schoenberg leaves Germany.

25th October: Schoenberg sails for America.

1934   May: First draft of music of *Lulu* completed.

July: Political situation in Austria deteriorating.

30th November: First performance of the *Lulu* Symphony (Kleiber, Berlin).

1935   January: American violinist Louis Krasner commissions Violin Concerto.

9th February: Berg's 50th birthday.

22nd April: Manon Gropius dies.

August: Berg contracts fateful abscess.

11th August: The Violin Concerto completed.

13th October: Last letter to Helene Berg.

12th November: Berg returns from Waldhaus to Vienna.

11th December: First performance of *Lulu* Symphony in Vienna.

17th December: Berg brought to the Rudolf Hospital— operation.

19th December: Berg receives blood transfusion.

24th December: 1.15 a.m. Berg dies.

28th December: Funeral at Hietzing Cemetery.

1936   19th April: First performance of the Violin Concerto, Barcelona Festival of the I.S.C.M. (Krasna, Scherchen).

1937   2nd June: First performance of *Lulu* Symphony in Zürich.

1938   11th March: Nazis occupy Austria.

1945   15th September: Webern accidentally shot dead by U.S. army cook.

1951   13th July: Schoenberg dies.

(279)   Vienna, 9th June 1921[1]
My Pferscherl,
    Are you freezing? Last night and this morning it was really
quite nippy in the flat, and now it's the most glorious clear weather.
I am sitting on the veranda by the open window, while Toni in the
garden beats the carpets.
    Yesterday afternoon I went with Greissle[2] to the Architects'
Hall at 9, Eschenbachgasse, which we shall probably get next year.[3]
That's nice isn't it? Near Almschi, and near the No. 57 tram stop.
    Toni went to Papa's yesterday, and took him a letter from Mama.
As he left almost at once, she glanced through Mama's letter—you
know how discreet she is. In it Mama said Papa shouldn't stop us
coming up to Trahütten, where all we want is two rooms, a bit of
woodland air and cooking for ourselves, also that she (Mama)
doesn't have many pleasures these days and needs people to talk to,
distract her mind, cheer her up, etc. Well, when I go up to see Papa
tomorrow, I'll see how he behaves. If he refers to it, I'll have my
say too! I'd much rather clear things up so that we can be sure of a
peaceful stay at Trahütten.
    In the evening the Society's last meeting. As Gaudriot[4] did not
turn up, the Clarinet Pieces were dropped. Programme: Stravinsky,
Ragtime (Steuermann), something really very fine! Satie, all new
pieces (Steuermann); Webern, *Violin Pieces* (Kolisch[5] and Steuermann); Busoni, *Toccata* (Merinsky[6]).
    We again played in the back half of the hall (facing the platform).
Third item: Steuermann already seated at the piano, everyone
dead quiet, waiting for Kolisch. Suddenly he comes in by the central
door, in a dream, quite unconscious of what's happening, and

    [1] Helene Berg was taking the waters in Hof Gastein.
    [2] Felix Greissle, one of Berg's pupils, later son-in-law of Schoenberg.
    [3] The Society for Private Concerts used the hall of the Vienna Architects'
Society as concert hall.
    [4] A well-known Viennese clarinet-player and band leader.
    [5] Rudolf Kolisch (b.1896), Austrian violinist, founder of the Kolisch Quartet
(1922–38). His sister later became Schoenberg's second wife.
    [6] Hilde Merinsky, a Viennese pianist, who eventually became Mrs Eduard
Steuermann.

                              275

without a violin! Calls out in great surprise as he's walking through the hall: 'Am I on now?' Much laughter, of course. He has to go back to the artists' room and fetch his violin. He's hardly started Webern's *Pieces for Violin*[1] when suddenly there's the noise of a piano playing fortissimo somewhere. I hurry out and close the windows. Now it seems to have become quieter. Kolisch starts again, and so does the noise. In the end they found the disturber-of-the-peace on the third floor! Concert very well attended.

I don't know yet when I go to Küb.[2] Sometimes I feel it would be better to go quite soon, so as not to have to tear myself away later on when I'm in the mood for work. I keep on thinking of the music I've got to compose for the most difficult scene of the lot, the scene in the inn;[3] but it still won't quite come. Well, we shall see.

Society meeting this afternoon.

This is always the worst time, when I'm away from you and don't know what your new surroundings are like and how you are getting on there. Once your first letter comes, I'll be able to imagine it. But until then—! That's why the one who stays at home is always worse off than the one who's travelling. You should have sent me a telegram! Now do at least write a lot, and every day, and think lovingly of your

Pipiherz

(280)   9th June 1921
My dearest love,

I'm in bed, it's 9.30 p.m., and I want to write to you again today, as this afternoon, while I was out, your letter of the 7th and card of the 8th arrived. After reading your descriptions and seeing the card, I'm much closer to you. I can now imagine at any hour of the day what you are doing and thinking and feeling. I'm unhappy about the noisiness of your room, and happy about the good food you're getting. Eat as much as you can, Pferscherl, and don't think of the prices; I am also unhappy about that aggressive doctor, and all you may be missing. I would feel much easier if you were to come under Dr Wengraf's care. He should be there already. Consult him at least on the Gastein doctor's diagnosis and treatment; he's got more interest in you and in us than the Gastein chap has. On the other

[1] *Four Pieces for Violin and Piano* op. 7 (1910)
[2] Village in the Semmering district, where Berg's mother took a summer house.
[3] *Wozzeck*, act III, scene iii.

276

hand, that chap's diagnosis sounds quite plausible to me. When you write to Mathilde,[1] tell her of this diagnosis of nerves, so that she at least realizes one can't go tramping on your nerves, as she seems to think (*she's* quite a lot to blame, after all, for your bad nerves.) What does the man say about your rheumatism?

How nice it must be when you sit at the table all by yourself in the lovely dining-room! The thought makes me feel quite happy, and *at last* soothes my guilty conscience for having eaten better and more than you for such a long time (nine months).

Well then, Pferschi, I am expecting your 'phone call on Tuesday between 8 and 9 in the evening. You didn't write in your card how you slept the second night—I want a bulletin on that every day! I'm happy that Nature is so beautiful up there. How much I'd love to see and feel all that with you! But I must work:[2] slowly, very slowly, what I plan to write is taking shape. (Don't say anything about this to Mathilde, her husband thinks I'm working on the libretto.)

This afternoon, after a refreshing nap, I went to see my lawyer about our income-tax return. That was some job. This Dr Pilzer is a very nice chap. He worked with me from half past three to half past seven—four whole hours! Now I have to do a few hours more at home and then go back to him. What a job! Still, it has to be done. We are living in such a horrible age, everything so materialist. How dreamy and head-in-the-air I looked twelve years ago—and today like a man of facts and figures. Only you, my golden one, have preserved idealism in your face and ever youthful body; or rather acquired it in these last years—an idealism which is truly *angelic*.

On this thought I am going to sleep——

(281)   10th June 1921

Only a short note today. Incredible amount to do. Getting everything settled so that I can at last start composing. Was working on the tax declaration from seven in the morning, then to the Bank, then Papa. While I was out, Kolisch 'phoned. In the autumn he is getting a quartet together, and will start off by playing my quartet. So I have to prepare the parts and distribute to the four players

[1] Schoenberg's first wife.
[2] On the score of *Wozzeck*.

277

before the day is out! Two lessons to give in the afternoon, and then possibly to the lawyer. Dreadful!

Kisses, my darling

Your own

Do, please write a card to Frau Webern as well.

(282)   11th June 1921

My mind is all the time with *Wozzeck* (except when it's with you, as it is now after your two sad little letters). The inn scene is coming along very very slowly, but it *is* coming. If I succeed in getting it down as it's in my head, then the most difficult part is done and the rest will be child's play.

If only it were seven o'clock and I heard Pferscherl's voice calling me!

(283)   Sunday, 12th June 1921

Only a card, my Pferscherl, as I don't want to make any break in our correspondence. I'm off to Küb, then, this afternoon. If some important telegram arrives, they'll send it on to me. If it's not too much trouble, please ring me up, it would be so nice. Toni is staying in Vienna, she'll write to you fully today. As she will post (and presumably read!) this card, I must tell you that she is indeed a high-quality cook and a high-quality gem.

Thousands, or rather millions, of kisses.

(284)   12th June 1921, in the
                                                        train to Küb

Still feel rather in a whirl. Wrote you a card this morning in haste, as I knew the post is collected at ten. Then I did some successful composing, and packed for Küb, taking with me: *Wozzeck* libretto and sketches, 2 newspapers, 2 hankies, toothbrush (forgot comb!), aspirins, tobacco and paper for cigarettes, 'Indipohdi'[1] and writing paper. Afterwards went to the Leberts to say good-bye. The boy is really terribly sweet.

While packing, I found two things in the drawer of the bedside table which brought back vivid memories,: a little box of atrophine

---

[1] 'Indipohdi', a dramatic poem by Gerhart Hauptmann (1920).

and the calamus root. Memories of the happiest time (March 1920, Berghof, calamus root from Ossiacher Lake) and the unhappiest time (autumn 1920).[1] And yet I wouldn't have missed even that. How divine you were in nursing me, that's something you could never wipe out even if you turned into a devil! ...

After lunch I had a rest, and even slept. Then black coffee and a bit of work at the piano. Then to the station, where I found plenty of room in a third-class carriage, and went on working. By Mödling I had started to write, eating bread and butter and cheese the while. And now we're already in the pine forests. A cool, rather windy afternoon, but sunny. How I'm looking forward to Trahütten. But of course—the old man! An impossible character. Honestly, it's hard for me to write like this about Papa, and I can't do it to anyone but you. I only hope I'm wronging him, all I want is that the many warm feelings I have for him shouldn't keep being spoilt by that self-centredness of his which has become his normal attitude by now.

They did the *Gurrelieder* in Prague with Zemlinsky conducting. Terrific success. Magnificent performances. Many kisses——

Your own

p.s. Suddenly 100,000 country-folk have just got on the train.

(285)   Küb, 13th June 1921

Arrived here last night, Mama and Smaragda waiting for me and took me home. It's very beautiful here, the little house is delightful —we *must* have such a place one day. You will like it very much. When you get back, we must come out here for a few days. Weather cloudy but nice even so. I didn't sleep well—not till the second half of the night. Got up early and made a sketch of the house. In the morning a longish business talk with Mama, then a walk with her and Smaragda to Payerbach, a lovely way. Unfortunately, I felt a bit steamy (no asthma, though), not being used to going for walks in the morning. Took some aspirin, which did the trick. Good lunch (among other things marvellous cherries), then a splendid rest from 2 to 4. Now we all want to go for a little excursion, although it's overcast, to some afternoon coffee place—when I'll post this short letter. Tell you more tomorrow, Tuesday, on the way home.

---

[1] The previous autumn Berg had suffered very bad asthma attacks, and had to be taken to a sanatorium near Vienna.

279

Vienna, 15th June 1921,
                                              in bed at night
... After lunch, just as I was going to rest, who should appear
but Webern, wanting my advice—on whether he should accept
an engagement offered by the Schubertbund[1] as choir-master (for
12,000 Crowns[2] a year, evening rehearsals twice a week, and six
concerts). At 2.15 we drove to town. I went to the lawyer about the
tax return. Worked there again for nearly three hours. Now I am
finished with him, and have to do the rest by myself. A vast job of
copying. Then I bought Mama some Turkish delight for her
name-day, a football (2,300 Crowns) for Gert,[3] which will be sent
from the shop, and thirdly *Splendours and Miseries of the Courtesans*.[4]
The last week I've been searching for this in vain in about twenty
bookshops, and only now managed to find it: for my poor Pferscherl,
so that she has something to read. Then I went to a cinema in town,
and was back home at 8.30.

16th June 1921
    This morning Papa came to see me again. We're quite on his
beaten track all of a sudden, because he needs something from me.
Tax matters.
    In the afternoon by tram to the Neubau district to see an accor-
dion manufacturer. In *Wozzeck* we'll have a kind of *Heurigenmusik*,[5]
which should be very amusing.[6] It consists of a high-tuned fiddle,
a clarinet, accordion, guitar and bass tuba. To find out how far I
can go with a modern accordion, I have to get to know all the
possibilities. Unfortunately I didn't meet the man himself, but made
an appointment for next week. Then to Neurath,[7] where for
Jeanette's name-day on 24th June (don't forget it!) I bought six
teacups in country style, which she saw somewhere and liked so
much (350 Crowns). They haven't got anything of the kind in Küb.
Then to a coffee-house, where I drank a cup of tea and ate a cheese
sandwich. Now I'm sitting in a No. 60 tram on my way to Mödling,

---

[1] A well-known Viennese amateur choral society.
[2] About £25.
[3] Son of Smaragda's friend, May Keller.
[4] By Balzac.
[5] A small *ensemble* entertaining the guests at country inns.
[6] *Wozzeck*, act II, scene iv.
[7] A small china factory in Vienna.

being expected at the Weberns. It's another beautiful sunny afternoon.

In the evening, in bed
Nobly entertained at the Weberns': wonderful roast beef in butter with rice, fresh green peas, very good cherries (my second lot this year), cheese, butter and the Mödling rolls, beer—and as a climax, a superb wine, 1917 late vintage (180 Crowns the bottle).

At 9.15 Webern came along with me to the tram, we caught the last one, and sped back to Hietzing. It was a very jolly evening. Main topic of conversation: Schubertbund and Society, pupils' lack of respect, *The Dwarf*.[1]

I hoped to find some mail from you at home, as there was nothing in the morning. But still nothing. Just now, when I was expecting some news of your visit to the doctor and how you are generally . . .

(288)   Vienna, 17th June 1921,
                                                           evening

What a day! Even the afternoon post, when I'd been at the window for hours looking out for it, didn't bring anything. Finally I booked a 'phone call to Gastein. After an hour's delay the 'phone rings, connection with Gastein is closed. Just time to dash to the post office and send a telegram. Tomorrow morning I'm sure to have news, but how many hours away that is! The disappointment seeped through into the afternoon's work: giving lessons, and working on the lay-out of the *Wozzeck* scenes. I was so restless I couldn't bear it at home. Went to see Papa, who was already in bed. We chatted till ten o'clock.

18th June 1921
At last, at last! At 9 this morning, Saturday, your Wednesday's letter came—and what a lovely letter! From 7 to 8 I worked in great suspense, my heart thumping. From 9 on I hung out of the window, till at last the postman handed me a bunch of letters. First of all this wonderful one of yours. Then the return of my article on critics from Melos,[2] etc. I could have saved myself the telegram, for

[1] Zemlinsky's opera *Der Zwerg*, based on Oscar Wilde's story, *The Birthday of the Infanta*, produced for the first time in Cologne, March 1922.

[2] A year before Berg had written an article for the *Anbruch* called 'Two Feuilletons: a Contribution to the topic Schoenberg and Music Criticism'. It was not published there, so he apparently sent it to the German music magazine *Melos*.

Schmid, who witnessed my despair last night and has just rung me up, tells me that the postmen in Gastein are on strike, so presumably my telegram never got delivered. But it makes no difference now, I have the letter. I wonder when you'll ring me. Thursday morning I'm driving to Breitenstein, where I told Almschi I'd be with her between 2 and 4; then by train to Küb, where I want to arrive as a surprise on the eve of Mama's name-day. Friday afternoon back to Vienna. I only lost one morning's work, as I can get on with it splendidly in the train, perhaps even coming back as well. At the moment the relief from my agitation has left me—so much on edge, let's say, that I can't work at all, and that's why I'm writing to you at once. Then I want to get down to my accordion, which I have at home for a day, to make sure how to write for it.

Now to the letter. Did you get mine with the drawing of the Küb house? I was actually feeling a bit poorly, but not asthmatic. This poorliness has soon got better in Vienna, I woke up in the morning perfectly all right, as if it hadn't been anything at all. So it really wasn't too bad, and I may easily survive till I'm a hundred (hope so, if the Pferscherl can live till she's a hundred and one). I have already written to you about drink. Don't be worried, my darling, drink means something quite different to me from what it does to various other members of my family. I treat it as something sacred, like music! . . .

(289)   18th June 1921
Only a short note, my lovely one, so that it can go off tomorrow, Sunday, with the only morning post. The answer to my telegram hasn't arrived yet, perhaps it will tomorrow. I could almost claim my money back from the post office, as the delay was their fault, and it cost over 80 Crowns.[1] Think I'll make a complaint in Hietzing on Monday.

Sleep after lunch, then a lesson, then from 4 to 7.30 I worked without a break on my tax declaration. Now I'm finished with it, thank Heavens! In the evening I went to the cinema, sat in a very cheap seat, and saw two German films: *The Black Disgrace*, about German women raped and given V.D. by the Negro occupying troops, and a comedy. Both shed quite a light on the country's mentality. Significant enough that they should be shown together.

[1] About 3/-.

The telegram came today, Sunday, at 4 p.m. How nice: now I don't regret the 80 Crowns any more. And you're ringing up tomorrow! Wonderful.

This morning I worked, after sleeping till half past eight, no doubt a consequence of my agitation in the last few letterless days. Rested in the afternoon, then worked again, wrote letters, and now I'm going into town, meeting Steuermann at the Café Central.[1] Perhaps I'll have dinner somewhere cheap. Toni leaves now at five, and stays away all night. She has received a letter full of endearments—'sausage of my heart'—and is going through a new springtime of love. Altogether she's having an 'age of beauty', goes shopping in the morning in *dirndl* costume, and puts on a blue dress if she's going out for anything in the afternoons. Always standing in front of the mirror and flashing her new ivories (price 3,500 Crowns).

Kisses

Your own

p.s. Fame! In a photographer's window in the main street of Hietzing, there's a picture of the charming industrialist's wife from Penzing[2]—with child.

Yesterday, Sunday, continued thus. At six I met Steuermann, and we were joined an hour later by Merinsky. By half past eight afternoon coffee had turned into dinner. At home it is certainly much cheaper! In fact I'm rather worried about that with you, my golden one, that you're trying to economize because of the expense of eating out.

Later on Ratz came, and we talked 'shop', philosophized, discussed literature and philology, in fact conformed to our *milieu*. The café was crammed full. Polgar,[3] and Dörmann[4] appeared, among others, also 'my' Dr Alfred Adler[5] who asked after you and afterwards gave a bit of a lecture to a table of 'Maenads'—I badly missed

---

[1] Famous meeting-place of Vienna's literary and artistic world, scene of Karl Kraus's skit, '*Literature* or *We'll See*'.

[2] Helene's sister, Anna.

[3] Alfred Polgar (1875–1955), Austrian essayist and writer.

[4] Felix Dörmann, Viennese poet, dramatist and librettist (*A Waltz Dream*).

[5] Alfred Adler (1870–1931), the great psychologist, who broke away from Freud to found his Individual Psychology school.

Chloe Goldenberg![1] Altogether the artistic set at the 'Central' seem to have been pushed into the background, in favour of the chess masters at many tables.

Got home rather late, about 11. This morning at half past seven I was at work, till midday. Again the disappointment that no letter came. Judging by yesterday's telegram the post is functioning again. Perhaps there will still be a letter today, even at three. The last one was from Wednesday, and it's Monday today. And will you really phone me? Anyhow I'll be at home from 7 p.m. Before that I have to go into town to hand in my declaration at the tax office, and to Schwarzwald on Society business, perhaps to Lienau[2]— and to buy the new *Fackel*. The whole issue is called 'About Grammar'. What a feast for me.

Tomorrow I'll send Almschi a telegram, to say I'll be there for a few hours at noon on Thursday—so that I can go on to Küb in the early evening, to celebrate the name-day, and return home next day. Should the post strike still be on, ring me for sure on Saturday evening. If I can only hear your dear voice today, I'll feel happier at once—so I'm not asking much, am I? Things mustn't go on like this!

(292)   Vienna, 20th June 1921,
                                                     evening
... Your lovely letter has made me so very happy. As if you'd been trying to save up all your feelings of happiness for my name-day tomorrow, by our having been tortured the week before (with the post strike). So I couldn't have had a greater 'treat' today than your letter. First to know that you are feeling better and more hopeful, are sleeping better, and as a result the letter is so sparkling and finely written, giving me joy of the mind as well as the heart. Second, that the doctor seems to know his stuff, and that you are in good hands even if they're a bit aggressive ones (the thought makes me tremble all over!). Third, that you are looking forward to a nice happy July in Vienna. Fourth, that your room is a quiet one. Fifth, that in the Schnabels you've found nice people—I know him[3] quite well myself—from the old days at Bösendorfer.

Have you already told him about the Society? Shall I send you its

[1] The 'Maenads' and Chloe Goldenberg appear in Kraus's skit.
[2] A Viennese music publisher.
[3] Thomas Schnabel, Bechsteins' representative in Vienna.

programme, so that he can see that other firms as well put at our disposal the most wonderful pianos, because of the publicity value (in Schnabel's case it would be Bechstein)? We are thinking of another make, though, as we don't like the Steinway. It would be of great interest for Bechsteins' to try out modern music on their pianos—specially when such fine pianists as Steuermann use them for two-piano arrangements for four, six and eight hands, and for chamber orchestra with solo piano.

I'll soon be sending you a most enthusiastic article by Dr J. Bach[1] about the Association in the *Merker*[2] (where my Guide also gets a favourable mention). Anyhow, although Thomas is his Christian name, Schnabel surely won't be a Doubting one. And you needn't be shy of talking business; after all, it's not for yourself but for Schoenberg and great art in general. Or shall I write to him from here? He will certainly help us if he is really such an admirer of Schoenberg, and you can tell him everything.

Sixth in my reasons: I'm glad you are eating well. But you aren't eating enough! You shouldn't be 'slim', because I'm sure what you call slim is really 'emaciated'.

Anyhow, your letter made me terrifically happy, this evening you're ringing up, 'my' roses are blooming in the garden, work has gone well, a *Fackel* is appearing, I'm in good health—and the first half of Pferscherl's absence is over. What a splendid name-day.

(293)   21st June 1921
In answer to my telegram to Almschi 'May I visit you Thursday midday for a few hours?', Werfel telegraphed from Semmering that Almschi is in Vienna until Thursday afternoon. I 'phoned her at once, she was extremely surprised I knew she was there. When I'd explained, she asked solicitously after you. Then we arranged to travel together to the Semmering tomorrow afternoon, and I'll go on to Küb, while she goes on to Breitenstein. That suits me nicely. The sudden drop in temperature was worrying me a bit, in spite of the vest which I've put on as from today; and I'll have enough chance to talk to her in those three hours. Of course I'll be missing the Rax and the Mutzi,[3] those two delightful contrasts in mountains . . .

[1] Dr Joseph Bach (1874–1947), musicologist and critic.
[2] *Der Merker*, Viennese music magazine, edited by the composer Julius Bittner.
[3] Manon Gropius.

285

Almschi seems to like the idea, as she would otherwise have to travel alone, whereas now she has company. Of course she invited me to come on with her to Breitenstein or else go there on Friday, but I declined. She hopes to have us up there in the summer. It seems she's written to you about it. By the way, she feels 'marvellous'.

Yesterday: lessons in the afternoon. That's to say, Reich again (the second time) failed to turn up, without warning me he wasn't coming. Then Schmid arrived, I gave him his lesson, then played the opera to him. After that he accompanied me to P. Honestly, I had the most boring two or three hours there since I've been on my own, no, in my whole life. This 'set', these metaphysical ramblings, unity, universality, versa-unality—no, I can't repeat it, it makes me sick. In comparison W. is a Schopenhauer, Frau W. a Wesendonck. They had already had their dinner at half past seven, although they had asked me to come along for a meal and bring something with me; so that I had to eat my chopped steak and bean salad by myself. Then there was tea and cakes, and in the end Frau P. read to us a quite idiotic short story by Meyrinck,[1] while he kept striding frantically across the room saying 'What a scream!' over and over again.

Never, never again!

This morning I worked hard till twelve, then the telegram arrived —and the rest you know, my darling.

(294)   22nd June 1921

Your express-letter came this afternoon (the dearest and tenderest of them all so far). You have shed light into my loneliness, so that I can see for the first time just how poor I am when you are not with me.

This morning a French music magazine arrived, sent to me by Haslinger's.[2] It contains a brief comment on my *Clarinet Pieces*. They were performed in Paris on 2nd June, together with music by Stravinsky, Szymanowski,[3] etc. The performance was good according to the critic, who speaks of the Pieces very respectfully, but doesn't seem to have understood them properly.

How is your present room? Tell me, are you eating enough?

[1] Gustav Meyrinck (1868–1932), German novelist and satirist.
[2] Old-established Viennese music-publishing firm.
[3] Karol Szymanowski (1883–1937), Polish composer.

The menus don't strike me as too staggering. Please buy yourself some ham, but not the remnants off the bone—you're not a dog! Oh, if I could only be with you! I often think of turning up suddenly and unexpectedly. But besides all the reasons you know, which would make it pretty silly, there's also the fear that I might get another asthma attack in Gastein. I got so used to the terrific heat in May that the sharp air is unpleasant to me. That and even the short train journey to Küb, the long grass, the strange room, etc., made me feel unwell there, without actually having asthma, and I only recovered in Vienna. So I'm afraid of a long journey, hotel room, climate, being too much outside, and getting too excited at seeing you again!

By the time we go to Trahütten, I shall have become acclimatized —I haven't the slightest doubt of that. Even if I should have some difficulties with breathing, it would be a trifle with my health as good as it is at present.

In the morning I was composing again, but then I couldn't concentrate, I just had to write to you—and now it will soon be lunch-time.

News from Greissle: Schoenberg is in fine form. He's working at his book on harmony,[1] and means to stay at Mattsee[2] till *Jacob's Ladder* is finished. Scherchen[3] wrote like a man who had suffered the gravest injustice. He wants to give a performance of my Quartet, on which he is lecturing in the Berlin Hochschule. We're both invited!

(295)   23rd June 1921

Was at home from four o'clock on, and again wrote something for the Society. I got a bit stuck with my work, alas, which always depresses me dreadfully, so then I escape to my Swipol for a chat.

Yes, I *was* feeling rather sad on the 'phone the other day. For one thing, it took such a long time for you to come through, and I was afraid nothing might come of it in the end. (I know you'd said in your telegram that you were ringing, but there wasn't a word about it in your letter.) Secondly because of the doctor, and thirdly that

---

[1] Revising the first edition of *Theory of Harmony* published in 1911.
[2] Small town in the province of Salzburg.
[3] Hermann Scherchen (1891–1965), German conductor.

because of the telephone call you didn't write. But now all that is forgotten, and especially as today is the

23rd.[1] June

I have reason to be in a better mood, because I can give Pferscherl joyful news. The American Relief Administration (they sent me a form to fill in the other day[2]) have today sent me a kind invitation to come to No. 9 Elisabethstrasse on Monday and collect two food parcels containing the following: 44 lbs. flour, 18 lb. rice, 20 lb. bacon, 2 tins of corned beef (13 lb.), 42 lb. lard, 12 tins milk, 12 lb. of sugar, 21 lb. of cocoa, $7\frac{1}{2}$ lb. of oil and 10 tins of salmon.

What do you say to that?!

Altogether about 160 lb. of food. I can't begin to work out how much it would cost! Perhaps ten to twenty thousand Crowns (or more?). And all I've got to pay is a statutory sum of 400 Crowns[3]——and the carriage fare from Elisabethstrasse to Hietzing.

What do you say? What do you say? I bet you're laughing incredulously. I'd like to see your eyes shining with joy, hear your voice go all shrill with excitement.

So on Monday afternoon I'll go and fetch it, then home to unpack it. If only you could be here!

Yes, the 23rd has got something all right!

Of course because of the terrific joy my work, which started at seven in the morning quite successfully, is interrupted and has suffered accordingly. I just have to recover first from the 'intoxication'.

This afternoon I'll be travelling with Almschi to the Semmering. So if there is a break in my letters, don't worry. It could happen because I'm not in Vienna, though I'll still write every day, of course, from Küb. But a letter posted there may take days. In fact I'd better come back to Vienna with it tomorrow evening and post it here. As for this one, I'll send it express, so that you're sure to get it on Saturday . . .

---

[1] See footnote, Letter 139.
[2] As they had done to many Austrian artists and intellectuals.
[3] About £1. 8s. od.
The Austrian inflation had begun. Before the First World War the U.S. dollar had been worth 5 Crowns. It rose in July 1917 to 12 Crowns, in January 1921 to 683 Crowns, in January 1922 to 7,600 Crowns, in January 1923 to 70,800 Crowns. 20th December 1924 saw the end of the Austrian Crown. 10,000 Crowns were exchanged for one Schilling, the new monetary unit.

288

That was a hot, strenuous day. Indeed, with its climax transporting the foodstuffs. I took them item by item in a one-horse carriage (450 Crowns, including tip for loading and unloading) travelling at a snail's pace, between three and four, with the sun in our faces all the way from the Park to us. We stopped outside our kitchen window, where the whole consignment was handed to me, again piece by piece . . . I'd only just finished when Arthur arrived, wanting to take me to Papa. I sent him ahead, made myself some afternoon coffee, and went on working at the long letter for the Society. At 6.30 I went to Papa, where we drank a bottle of hock, one of his so-called 'last bottles', of which, incredibly enough, he still has a stock—what a hoarder! . . . He was staggered at the gift parcel, when I showed him the list and the extremely polite tone of the letter asking if I would be kind enough to fetch it! He called the parcel 'princely'.

When you're here (how good that sounds, 'when you're here'), we'll think everything quietly over. Perhaps we'll stay at Trahütten all through September. And now to amuse Pferscherl, a story about Papa and the Marcel funeral.[1] There was a terrific crush, he says, and he had 'taken up a position' in Maxinggasse. Suddenly a very high police official appears, sees him among the crowd—'Oh, Herr *von* Nahowski, you can't stay here among all those people, *please* come with me'—and leads Papa to the reserved part of the old cemetery, where three men stand guard. Pointing to Papa, he announces to them: 'Member of the Philharmonic Orchestra!'; whereupon the men introduce themselves respectfully and lead Papa to the open grave. For this occasion (with his Philharmonic status) he was wearing grey trousers, green jacket and brown hat!

(297)   28th June 1921
This is how today went. Morning, extensive work on *Wozzeck*, then shopping (food), then work on the Society letter for Schoenberg. I want to enclose it for him with my letter telling him I can't come to Mattsee. After lunch a good rest, although it was thundery all day and never cooled off . . .

I haven't got the accordion at home any more, I now know all I want to about it. At four Schmid arrived. He comes about twice a week, but it's more gossip than instruction. I showed him my

[1] Lucille Marcel (1887–1921), dramatic soprano, member of the Viennese Opera, married to Felix von Weingartner.

opera. Then we went to the Café Herrenhof. As we were leaving it, I saw Webern, Steuermann, Steuermann's brother-in-law, Berthold Viertel the poet, and producer at the Theatre in Dresden. I drove with him to the Park Hotel at Hietzing, where he's staying. He's a very clever chap, and I at once proceeded to pick his brains about the play of *Wozzeck*, which he is directing at the moment.

Lebert was waiting for me at the hotel. But I was feeling upset—because of something Webern had briefly told me, which made me turn quite pale. Rufer had received a letter from Tilde, saying they were all coming back to Vienna. There had been some anti-Semitic propaganda, and the Schoenbergs had decided to leave; they will be staying a few days in Salzburg and then coming home. You'll be stunned, I'm sure. Perhaps it won't turn out quite as bad as that, I still hope not. But don't say or write anything to anyone—highly confidential. The business about the 'anti-Semites' is something nobody should know.

As to Schoenberg's return, in case it should really come to that, the cause is never to be given as attacks against Jews, but they're going to say, I believe, that the climate was bad for him. I still hope everything will be put right there, after all the wife of Schoenberg's brother[1] is the daughter of the Mayor of Mattsee. The Austrian summer resorts are all full of Jews, and the whole population is anti-Semitic, but it would never occur to them to do any actual harm to the Jews. Anyhow, whatever happens, we two must arrange things for ourselves so that we keep our freedom.[2] Don't do anything hasty, wait for my news.

(298)   29th June 1921

I am rather put out by uncertainty about Schoenberg's coming. At the moment I haven't heard anything new, except that Rufer sent a telegram two days ago (the morning of the 27th) saying he would be arriving in Mattsee on Sunday 3rd July, and so far hasn't received a telegram back telling him not to come. I've been thinking a lot about a strange ten-year old parallel, which I'll set out here:

[1] The bass singer, Heinrich Schoenberg, was for many years a member of Zemlinsky's opera *ensemble* in Prague.

[2] Berg wanted to compose *Wozzeck* without Schoenberg's personal influence, and was afraid that if Schoenberg returned to Vienna, he would expect to be continually shown the score as it progressed—which Berg would find it impossible to refuse.

Summer 1911	Summer 1921
Schoenberg in Ober-St. Veit.	Intensive work on the *Harmony*
Intensive work on his book	book, second edition
on 'Harmony'	(after a fortnight's violent
Started when he had violent	tooth-ache, he had a tooth
tooth-ache	taken out in Salzburg)
Threatened by some mad	Threatened by the National
engineer	Socialists
Polnauer lives at	They say Polnauer has gone to
Schoenberg's	Mattsee just lately
Flight (to Bavaria).	Flight to Mödling?

It can't be sheer chance, can it? I still hope and trust it won't come to the last bit of parallelism. In any case I'll hear from Rufer should he hear anything (in answer to his telegram). And I'll send you a telegram as soon as I know something definite; for I'm sure you will be agitated about it too. Also I'm expecting your call on Saturday evening between 7 and 9. Perhaps this time we'll have six minutes' talk.

Worked on *Wozzeck* this morning, but wasn't at all in the mood. At lunch-time I had a date with Lebert at the 'Stöckl' Restaurant— but oh the disappointment, they don't serve the set menu for 130 Crowns any more. Had a magnificent soup, boiled beef with hot vegetables, chocolate cake, a glass of beer—I won't tell you the price! The place was terribly empty, only five tables occupied in those vast halls, and about twenty waiters, who *kept on* interrupting our conversation. And then our waiter tried to cheat me of 20 Crowns.[1] I insisted on comparing the bill with the menu and making him return the money. Lebert was even more disappointed than I about the *table-d'hôte*. He wasn't at all interested in the most beautiful surroundings (we sat on a balcony overlooking the garden of the palace of Schönbrunn) or the elegant service.

And now it's evening, Pferschi. You really must come soon, my longing is just too great for me to bear. That's how lonely I am: but all the same you must finish your cure properly first!

(299)   30th June, morning
Latest news:
I've just read the following in the News in Brief column of the *Neue Freie Presse*, headed 'Composer's Certificate of Baptism.':

[1] About 8d.

'A significant summer experience of the well-known composer, Arnold Schoenberg, is reported by our correspondent in Graz. He had chosen Mattsee as a place to spend the summer and had recently been asked by the local town council to give documentary proof that he is not a Jew. Should he be one, he would have to leave the place at once, as by a decision of the Council, Jews are not permitted to stay there. Although Schoenberg could provide proof that he is a Protestant, he has decided to leave Mattsee. It is not at all surprising that the composer has preferred to avoid further arguments with the local authorities; but it remains highly questionable whether the laws of the country can be so casually set aside in Mattsee'.

My last hope is that they may find something in Salzburg itself or that area.

30th June 1921, noon

Late final edition:

Polnauer has just 'phoned me; he has been in Mattsee from Sunday till yesterday, Wednesday, and has been in the middle of all the hubbub. Neither Trude's letter nor what the *Presse* reported is right. Schoenberg is still in Mattsee, and as matters stood last night, he wasn't thinking of leaving. At first things were rather upsetting, but now it's calm again. I hope the *Presse*'s indiscretion doesn't make him change his mind. This afternoon, when I'm expecting Webern, Polnauer will also be coming, and will tell us everything, probably a lot that he couldn't say on the 'phone.

(300)   Vienna, 1st July 1921

In the morning I worked a bit, then I had at last to write the big letter to Schoenberg, warning him that I mightn't be able to come. Rested after lunch, then worked again till Schmid came for his lesson. Half an hour later the bell rang, and who should it be but W.! He wanted to ring up Universal Edition and ask whether he could come and fetch something. Of course he sat down and talked and talked, till in the end I too had to go into town. I am getting fed up with these surprise visits, I can't understand such lack of tact— I would never go and visit anyone myself when I wasn't expected. But if I ever do have to, I'm away again in a minute and don't let myself stay on, even if the person I've surprised really presses me to stay. You never know whether this pressing-you-to-stay is dictated

292

by a feeling of duty, just to be hospitable. In fact, so as to make things easy for my enforced host to let me go (which secretly he may *want*), I even invent urgent appointments or business which makes it impossible for me to stay. So that the host hasn't the slightest pangs of conscience, and says to himself: 'I should have pressed him to stay, but no, it wouldn't have made any difference, he couldn't stay.'

That's how far *I* go. But W. doesn't only make surprise visits, he remarks that he's 'disturbing you', and you feel you're obliged to say, 'oh no, not at all.' Then he stays, talks solely about himself, and a third party, and Schmid, who actually came for a lesson, is left right out of things and in the end feels so superfluous that he just goes. In fact W. came with me and Schmid to the piano firm of Förstels, where I bought a lovely black upright (92,000 Crowns). Then W. had us escort him to Universal Edition, and took it as a matter of course that I should then say good-bye to Schmid, whom I had after all promised part of the afternoon, and get on a No. 58 to go back with him. That's to say, I got out at Hietzing, while he went on. Oh yes, the most incredible thing of all: he heard that Schmid was coming for another lesson Tuesday afternoon, where-upon he more or less said he would come too. He said he had to make a 'phone call, so I said, 'please use the phone any time you want to,' at which he remarked, 'Yes, and then we might have a bit of a chat.' Me: 'Schmid comes at three for a lesson, but you can still 'phone.' Him: 'Well, I'll see, anyhow you'll be at home.'

Anyhow I shall *not* be at home. That is, not from one o'clock on. Not for the whole afternoon. Even if I'm going back on what I said— and *I'll see* if I can't teach him some manners.

(301)   2nd July 1921
... About Schoenberg: In principle, of course, I'd be very glad if you went there. But (1) it puts off our meeting, (2) it's a strain for you, (3) the one day wouldn't make much difference as far as their being hurt is concerned, (4) I wouldn't know then how to avoid going there myself; which I have no wish to do and above all no time. Every one of these summer days is an irretrievable loss for me if I throw it away and don't work. Think of it, today's already 2nd July. I don't go to Küb, either, without a guarantee that I can use the upright, say, between 8 and 11. (5) I'm not too well—that's mainly an excuse for the Schoenbergs, I'm really quite well! But I was never so keen on travelling that I'd want to do a tiring journey

like the one to Salzburg twice. (6) And when I see you again at last, I want to have you completely to myself! So I won't go, and you needn't go either. They will be all right again in the autumn.

I'm glad to hear of the preparations in Trahütten. Good old Mama! But Lebert keeps supporting Papa against her.

(302)   Sunday night, 3rd July 1921
Just an account of today in brief. At work by 8, before that a bit of a letter to you finished and posted. Then work till 1. Lunch. Work again till 7.45. Then dress quickly (till then I was in my underwear with the brown smock) and off! Passed the Hotel Hietzinger Hof, the Park Hotel, the Stöckl Restaurant, the Park Hotel Bar—and everywhere they were playing the Blue Danube:

Then to Klein,[1] where Arthur was waiting for me. Home at 9.45 and to bed. Papa is going to Trahütten soon, wonder if he'll manage to come round to say good-bye to me. Yesterday he made me 'phone every quarter of an hour about his coal delivery. He can see how busy I am, knows how I have to steal the little free time I get. On the other hand, he can see that Arthur has nothing whatever to do, and we are both on the 'phone. But he wouldn't dream of asking that lazybones to do him a good turn. If he *doesn't* come to say good-bye, after coming here every day because he needed something—I'll really have to take action! But first I'd better go to sleep, it's half past ten.

(303)   Frankfurt, 15th December 1921,
                                    12 noon, in a café[2]
... The journey yesterday went very well. A bit cold and slightly

[1] Fritz Heinrich Klein, a pupil of Berg's who made the piano-score of *Wozzeck*.
[2] Berg and Steuermann went to Frankfurt for a double purpose. Steuermann was playing Berg's Piano Sonata in two recitals, and at the *Wozzeck* auditions he played the complicated score to the heads of the Frankfurt and Darmstadt opera-house.

bizarre, listening to a conversation between a furious Teuton and two Hungarian Jews, who for instance said 'the Kordian point' instead of 'the Gordian knot'. It became a bit wearing eventually. We at last got in to Frankfurt at 12.30.

Nobody at the station—we missed each other. I rang up and found out from Frau Seligmann[1] that she was expecting us. In the mean-time all the taxis had gone. So we walked with bags and umbrellas, they said it was only a quarter of an hour's walk. I asked for Schiller-Strasse. In the end, after wandering around for a quarter of an hour in the icy night, we got a carriage, and a few minutes later we were at 12 Schiller-Strasse—only there weren't any Seligmanns living in the house. It turned out that I'd made a mistake. The concert agency is in Schiller-Strasse, and it was their address Seligmann had telegraphed me the day before. So back into the carriage, and to the other end of the town. We finally arrived after one o'clock (38 marks). But before that, half-way there, the horse collapsed and had to be unharnessed, and we had to push the carriage backwards, etc.

Anyhow we arrived at last. Tremendous number of servants. A little palace, very distinguished. Frau Seligmann is a very smart-looking, warm, attractive person—rather like her son and also Rosa Steuermann.[2] Cold supper, a glass of Hock, then we all went to our rooms. Incredibly smart. Marble basin, hot water. Even so I had a rather restless night. Up at 8.30, washed and shaved, breakfast at 9.30 with Frau Seligmann: ham and eggs, very good coffee, butter and jam. Then I 'phoned Lert,[3] and went to the theatre, leaving Steuermann practising. During a rehearsal of *Tote Stadt*[4] (indescribable music) I had a quarter of an hour's talk with Lert and Rottenberg.[5] Both very nice, though I was struck by how completely unartistic Lert looks. We fixed the audition for Saturday 3.30. Now I've hurried off to a café, where I'm writing this. At 1.30 I must go to lunch, at three we're off to Darmstadt, where an audience of 1,500 awaits us, hall completely sold out. How I would like to have a long, full chat with you, my darling, giving you my impressions of

[1] The Seligmanns were their hosts in Frankfurt. Frau Seligmann's son, Walter Herbert, was a pupil of Schoenberg's.

[2] Eduard Steuermann's sister married Josef Gielen, theatrical producer, later director of the Burgtheatre, Vienna.

[3] Dr Ernst Lert (1883–1955), general manager of the Frankfurt Opera from 1920–1923.

[4] *Die Tote Stadt* (*The Dead City*), opera by Eric Wolfgang Korngold (1920).

[5] Ludwig Rottenberg, principal conductor of the Frankfurt opera.

the town (very attractive), prices (expensive in small, rather cheaper in the big things), etc., etc. Perhaps I'll go on with this tonight. My golden girl, how you would enjoy it if you were here!

(304)   Frankfurt, 17th December 1921
... In the afternoon Steuermann and I went to the concert hall, where he wanted to practise so as to get used to it. You can't imagine how nervous he was, he spent the whole day wondering whether he could go through with it. A minute before the performance he was still sitting in the artists' room in a state of complete collapse, wanting to call everything off. My talent for sympathetic and soothing communication came into play and proved successful—although I was so agitated myself that I didn't want to go into the hall and just pretended to be calm. Anyhow, what with seeing me so 'composed' and also some favourable conditions (hall like the Bösendorfer-Hall in Vienna, excellent acoustics, good Blüthner piano, though unlike the Darmstadt rather a small audience), he calmed down directly he'd finished his first items, and everything went marvellously—including my Sonata, which produced the first vigorous applause.
   At the end the applause grew louder and louder, and the brilliant encores (Chopin, Debussy, Ravel) had the audience in rapturous enthusiasm. Feeling very pleased with life, we went by car to the Seligmann's for a magnificent dinner—with a superb Johannes-berger Hock 1904. Slept well, and now I'm sitting in Steuermann's room. He's practising *Wozzeck* for the afternoon, and I throw in a comment now and then. That's why this letter is a bit distrait. But I so badly need to get in touch with my good spirit! I can picture her going round the flat in that white woollen dress—you darling. If only you were here with me in my crucial hour—today at 3.30 with Lert! Tomorrow morning at 9.30 we shall be at Darmstadt with Hartung.[1] When I next write to you, everything will have been settled.[2]

(305)   23rd May 1922, 2 p.m.
   By now you will already be deep in the mountains. I'm so glad you are having such wonderful weather for your journey,[3] what a joy for

---

[1] Gustav Hartung (1887–1946), general manager of the Darmstadt Theatre.
[2] In fact nothing was settled, and five months later Berg received from Lert the usual rejection letter.(See Letter 312).
[3] Helene Berg was on her way to Gastein.

your heart—that poor little heart which has been so restless lately. When shall I feel again its dear familiar beat? I'm only writing a quick note today so that you'll soon have word from me, even though nothing special has happened.

From the station (which filled me with a wild desire for travel) I returned to Hietzing. Met Dr Müller, and suddenly felt much closer to him because I know his wife is near *you*. At home I started on the income tax—revolting! Then a lady called, Frau Swarowsky who needs 4,000 Crowns advance for the six volumes of *Wozzeck*.[1] She hopes to have the first three volumes finished by Monday morning, and then, after correcting them with Klein, I'll be sending them to Frankfurt. By the way, it wasn't the first call from a lady. Before I got back, someone else had 'phoned without giving her name. Marie said I would be home around midday, and the woman said she would ring later. Perhaps it was Almschi, but up till now— 2 o'clock—she hasn't called back. I have to give five lessons in the afternoon, so this is in haste: the first pupil is waiting already. Just now my lady friend rang again. It was Frau Klarfeld[2] asking when the rehearsal for Mahler's Third begins. I couldn't tell her anything.

I'm enclosing a review by Korngold. He's beginning to take his revenge on Strauss, and also on Oestvig,[3] who's always had good notices from him till now—until O. cancelled his appearance in *The Dead City*.

And now to the pupils.

(306)   Vienna, Wednesday
                                          24th May 1922
... Last night I said good-bye to Schoenberg on the 'phone; he's off to Prague tomorrow. Suddenly, it was past eight, the 'phone rings. 'Alban, are you at home? We've been waiting a whole hour for you with a marvellous dinner.' It was Almschi. 'You must take a taxi at once, charge it to me, and come.' At 8.45 Almschi, Werfel and I were sitting down to huge feast: asparagus, meat-balls, then strawberries, cakes and champagne. Afterwards we played *Manon* and *Traviata*, Almschi at the piano. I stayed till midnight, then back home to Hietzing.

[1] A book-binder who had taken over the job of binding two copies of *Wozzeck* three acts, six volumes altogether.
[2] A pupil of Schoenberg's.
[3] Karl Aagard Oestvig, tenor, a member of the Vienna Opera.

At nine this morning I had to go to the Borgfeld shop to collect the two dollars, for which I got 9,220 Crowns. From there to the Music Society Hall for the rehearsal of Mahler's Third. Oh, if only you'd been there! Just imagine: Webern and I at the piano—four hands—but the piano part composed into the huge orchestra. First and fourth movement went almost without our being stopped. Webern was like a king. I've never seen anyone happier. At the end he kept stammering with joy, chiefly to Stein: 'Don't be jealous of me, Stein, don't grudge it me!' And that music! Pferschi, Pferschi, we can all give up. During the first movement, that unique continuous climax, I felt just like I did twenty years ago when Mahler was conducting. It's almost too beautiful, I could hardly bear to stay in the hall. And it's simply because here, for the first time since Mahler, we've had the right tempo and that's meant producing the right sound.

One comfort about your not being here for rehearsals is that apart from Stein and myself nobody's being allowed in. Do you remember the four kettle-drums in the Third, and on each one, played with two sticks:

That's exactly as it is in *Wozzeck*—and I was quite unaware of it.

(307)   Thursday, 25th May 1922
Worked all morning on the score (revising the words, scenic notes, etc.). Lunch with Almschi and Werfel. She's off tomorrow to Berlin and Weimar, may be away for a week or a fortnight. Your first card has arrived. I was so happy to have good news. Here I am longing for you. How beautiful it must be *there*. In a day or two I'll be able to tell you when I can come, at last.

(308)   25th May 1922
I wrote only a note to you in the tram at lunch-time, so now you deserve something longer. It was very nice at lunch at Almschi's, except that I felt a bit annoyed talking to Werfel about music, although he hadn't meant to annoy me. Anyhow I shall avoid any

musical discussion from now on, unless it takes place with music itself—at the piano, not the table.

At three I went to see Smaragda and May, who for a change were both quite bearable. Hardly a word said about *Wozzeck*. Strange people!

Now I'm sitting in the Ottakring[1] beer cellar. It's called that because only the 'locals' go there. Over there, for instance, I've been watching a very nice-looking young man who eats everything with his knife. Cuts up his meat with knife and fork, then laboriously puts the pieces of meat into his mouth with the knife. The potato salad too, of course. I'm not exaggerating: he never once put his fork near his mouth. I was fascinated—and all the time he was as quiet and dignified as an English lord.

When I saw your lovely portrait at Almschi's, my golden one, my longing for you mounted till it was past bearing. When, oh when, shall I be able to come—or even know for sure that I am coming! I still have no news from Frankfurt . . . I shudder to think of locking the flat, packing, arranging everything. But then with what joy and relief I'll breathe again in your arms. Almschi was full of nice things to say about you.

(309)   26th May 1922

Had a few words with the Leberts this morning before they left in the car. The little boy has a swollen eye, but it doesn't hurt, luckily. Almschi invited me for lunch—a fine good-bye lunch with champagne. She told me she had written to Lert today. Then she made me take her milk ration. I'll have it while I'm still here, then I'll let Papa have it . . .

(310)   Vienna, 27th May 1922

Two of your letters to answer, but first—I shall be travelling on Thursday 1st June. I shan't get the *Wozzeck* volumes till Tuesday morning, and shall then have to work on them with Klein and Mahler,[2] perhaps on Wednesday as well. Then heaps of small jobs, films, sweets for Dr Pilzer (who wouldn't take any money from me at all), going to the bank. I'm travelling on Thursday so as to avoid the Whitsun crowds, otherwise I would give myself more

---

[1] Ottakring: a popular suburban district of Vienna.

[2] Fritz Mahler, the composer's nephew was a pupil of Berg's and helped him and Klein with the vocal score of *Wozzeck*.

299

time, and wouldn't be in such a rush—despite my tremendous longing for you, for the mountains, and for rest, to be able to relax just for once.

It has nothing to do with the piano score. Klein will have finished that by the time I get back, and we can work over it together. As I haven't a publisher, we are in no hurry anyway. Lert has still not answered. If I don't have anything by Thursday, I'll leave the score with Klein. Then he can send it to Frankfurt in case a letter from Lert arrives later. As I wrote express and registered on Monday, I should have an answer by Thursday week. That will be ten days.

Yesterday's final rehearsal[1] went most promisingly. The Bittners were there too—she's singing the contralto solo, and quite nicely too. Tonight is the first performance, and how I'm looking forward to it . . . Do you know the most glorious part? It's in the movement with the female choir, that short bit like a funeral march, where the whole orchestra is slowly and continuously soaring, then dropping again, and with it all the time that tragic Bim—Bam. Remember?

Worked all morning today, then to the bank, the tailor, and got my hair cut. Then a lesson with Apostel,[2] his last (he's going away). A letter from Jeanette came, sending me warmest congratulations on completing the opera. She's said a prayer for its success at the little chapel in the forest. 'It would be my last wish,' she writes, 'that you achieve your aim while I am still alive.'[3]

Now to your last dear letters. I'm happy about the good food you're eating—and looking forward to it myself. Unhappy about your insomnia. Yes, I'll be getting off the train at Hof Gastein station, so mind you're there waiting for me! After the journey I might be too tired to walk—and suppose it's raining!

You know Frau Hertzka, don't you? Talk to her—it might be useful, who knows? Pferschi, who do I owe *Wozzeck* to but you? Without you, and the peace you've given me through five years—peace for my soul and my body—I couldn't have composed a

---

[1] For Mahler's Third Symphony, under Webern's direction.

[2] Hans Erich Apostel (b. 1901), composer and pupil of Berg's and Schoenberg's.

[3] Berg's mother died on 19th December 1926, a year after the first performance of *Wozzeck*.

single bar. The peace no one in the world except you could give me or have taken away from me. I mean to write this to Jeanette, too, and tell her that besides the Almighty I owe *Wozzeck* to three people: to her, for making it possible for me to work on it this last year and a half without any financial worries; to Schoenberg as teacher (even though he wanted to take away my joy in it); and to my golden one for the reasons given above. The Interlude at the end I owe to you and you alone. You really *composed* it, I just wrote it down.[1] That's a fact!

(311)   (Undated,
                                                    28th May 1922)

I'm not writing much today, as I have to go to Klein this morning, and then at 12.30 meet Stein, with whom I'll be going out to Mödling. Schoenberg is back from Prague, the concerts were terrific apparently.

Last night we had Mahler's Third, and you just can't imagine it. Without exaggeration: Webern is the greatest conductor since Mahler himself, in every respect. After the first and last movement I felt just as I feel after an Adrenalin injection, I simply couldn't stand on my feet. In the evening I nearly forgot to eat, only re-membered in bed, so I got some bread and a tin of sardines. I'm almost frightened to hear the performance again tomorrow, that's how shattering it was. I was sitting with Stein, and was glad that this assorted audience should be seeing and hearing what our music-making is like. They were all bowled over. If only you'd been here, how thrilled you'd have been. But I'm almost glad you were spared this overpowering excitement.

(312)   (Undated,
                                                    29th May 1922)

That was a sad post today. I had been so happy that everything was so lovely for you up in Gastein, weather, scenery, people— and now everything has gone wrong. The noise, your sleepless nights, and also that you're expecting me on Monday or Tuesday, and I can't come till Thursday. I would have come to you at once, of course, if I had known what today's post would bring. Rejection from Frankfurt, though in a very nice and plausible way.[2]

[1] See footnote Letter 150.
[2] See Letter 304.

'Dear Herr Berg,

Many thanks for letting me know that *Wozzeck* is finished. Unfortunately I am at present not in a position to bind myself in any way, as we are rather snowed under with commitments. Nor do I know how in the present state of our finances I can take on the responsibility of producing such demanding modern works, which require an enormous amount of rehearsing. I must confess that despite the great artistic success which Bartók's works had here, the financial result, alas, was such as to make one very wary of any new experiments. So we have no alternative but to await better times. As soon as these arrive, I would assure you that I shall be glad to bear *Wozzeck* in mind. I hope it will meanwhile have a great success on another stage, giving us the right for once not to be the theatre for all premières.

With kind regards,

Yours sincerely,

Lert

So we wait! Are you sad, my Pferscherl? So am I. But with one bold sweep I want to thrust everything away from me, and only look forward to our meeting again in your present Paradise. I told you what I was going to write to Mama yesterday, about how much I owe *Wozzeck* to you (to Schoenberg for inspiration, to her for material help, and to you psychologically). Among other lovely things I said about you was that you, who once accompanied me through the hell of military service as if it were a quiet walk, cleared the paths for me towards the heaven of creation. And now I'll say this too, that *all paths with you are paths of heaven*, even the present one so full of disappointments.

Anyhow, who knows how it will all turn out? I wonder what Lert will write Almschi. Got home at midday, and am going on with this letter. Happened to meet Werfel in town, and told him everything. He said something would have to be done, he would think it over and discuss it with Almschi. Hope he doesn't do something tactless off his own bat. Tonight at Mahler's Third I'll talk to Schoenberg about it.

I'm rather tired. Had some things to do in town: bank (new safe deposit for the score of Mahler's Ninth), and tailor. Now I still have two days work at home: revisions of *Wozzeck*, packing, 'shutting up shop'. Then I leave all the unpleasant things behind me—with only the happiness ahead of me.

302

(313)   Vienna, 30th May 1922
My Pferscherl, this may be the last card. The next item of mail
you'll receive is outsize printed matter: me. I'm arriving on Thursday
evening.

Mahler's Third last night. In some ways even more superb this
time, particularly the second half. I sat with Schoenberg. He
wouldn't have believed it possible. Webern's conducting is such
that it can only be compared with Mahler's himself, and all the
misgivings, even Mathilde's, were swept away, to be replaced by
unqualified admiration.

This morning I'm expecting Klein and [Fritz] Mahler[1] for an all-
day working session. That's why I'm writing only this brief card. A
thousand kisses, the last ones on paper.

(314)   21st September 1922
My Pferscherl,
I'm on my way to Waldheim[2] and to Kolisch, where my Quartet[3]
is being rehearsed. A card arrived from Scherchen today, saying that
he likes my Pieces for Orchestra very much, and wants to perform
them in Berlin with Webern's *Passacaglia* and Schoenberg's
Pelleas.

What dreadful weather you're having my darling.[4] It's raining all
the time in Vienna, and very cold. I feel lonelier than I've felt for
ages.

(315)   Friday, 22nd September 1922
Fine weather, thank heavens. Sunshine streaming on to my
veranda this morning. How Pferscherl's eyes will shine when she
looks out of the window. Stay there as long as it's beautiful! I'm
terribly worried about your nerves. All other troubles seem small
compared to the thought of your continual agitation, restlessness,
pallor, etc. Look how well I am. I even feel I can live without
alcohol, in fact I've made up my mind to renounce it completely.

Yesterday morning at eleven I went to Waldheim's, and got the
main thing I wanted,[5] though they wouldn't promise to go any faster

[1] See footnote Letter 310.
[2] A firm of music engravers.
[3] Op. 2.
[4] Helene Berg was on a visit to Berg's mother in Küb.
[5] With Alma Mahler's financial assistance, Berg had the piano score of
Wozzeck printed at his own expense.

in printing the piano score, which worries me slightly. The second thing that worries me is that I haven't had any response to my advertisements for pupils. I still haven't any except for [Fritz] Mahler, Watza and Apostel. There haven't even been any foreigners turning up. This is evidently a bad year for music teachers. Steuermann hasn't got any pupils either, nor has anyone else.

At twelve I met Schoenberg in town, and went with him for lunch. Excellent—included fried ham with spinach. Then Schoenberg and I set off to buy a French horn for Görgi,[1] it's his birthday today and he wants to learn this instrument, so that he can play it in an orchestra (a very good idea). After we'd been to all the instrument-makers in Vienna, Schoenberg finally decided on a horn costing 1,800,000 Crowns. He is quite well off financially, and has good prospects for next season (Holland, Switzerland, London, Prague).

He was very nice to me, by the way, less so with Stein, who is now running the Society in Vienna (as a sort of public company), and least of all with Steuermann (we met him at five at Kolisch, where we eventually landed up, completely exhausted). Steuermann had dared, without getting Schoenberg's permission first, to ask Busoni[2] for a job (no luck, though) and to start classes in Prague; he travels there one day a fortnight and earns about two million Crowns a month. Schoenberg was meeting him for the first time after the holidays, and started crushing him in front of all of us, although Steuermann put up a strenuous resistance.

(316)   23rd September 1922
... A great joy for me today: I rehearsed my Quartet, and can confidently say, after hearing it again, that it's worthy to be dedicated to you. Once it's well rehearsed, you'll be able to hear it, you'll be very happy with it, and I'll be twice as happy enjoying it with you.

(317)   25th September 1922
... Schoenberg rang up asking if you were already in Vienna, and whether I wanted to come to lunch, then go with him to the Webern concert. He was in a critical mood again. At three the nine of us went to Vienna. The concert was magnificent. Webern is the greatest living conductor: the greatest altogether since Mahler. It's

[1] Schoenberg's son, Georg.
[2] Busoni was at the time director of the Musik-Hochschule in Berlin.

indescribable what he has managed to do in just one rehearsal. The *Meistersinger* prelude! It was as exciting as a first or last movement of a Mahler symphony. And Beethoven's Fifth! Terrific success, completely sold out. Perhaps he'll be conducting for the whole season. Anyhow on Sunday you can look forward to the *Jupiter Symphony*, *Siegfried Idyll* and Bruckner's Fourth . . .

(318)   Vienna, 27th March 1923
I sit out on my beloved but rather cold veranda, and feel such an ache as I haven't felt for years. It was horrible this morning when the train left,[1] and I saw you gradually disappearing! That was when my travel fever let up, and I felt the pain of parting so violently that my heart thumped right up to my throat. To distract me when I got home, I plunged into the income tax declaration, which I managed to finish in the course of the morning.

(319)   Wednesday, 28th March 1923
Oh, how I miss you. I really don't know what to do to banish the horror of this time of day which I would usually be spending with you: the late afternoon and evening particularly, and the first hours of the night. At half past five today I went with Strutz[2] for a walk in Schönbrunn Park. Kassowitz had cancelled the lesson, that is, he could have only come for half an hour before his orchestral rehearsal in Hietzing. We went to the Café Gröpl. I was afraid to go home. How should I spend the next two or three hours without Pferscherl, without my unique one?

So—to the cinema in Schönbrunn: 'Marie Antoinette.' What a horrible fate, and to watch it so graphically! Came home rather shattered, cooked my supper, hot sausage with horseradish; and am now in bed, with cheese and schnapps. Just by me, on your bed, I have some cold coffee waiting for me tomorrow morning, and a cake I bought in Gumpendorf: 6,000 Crowns, but it should last for three days' breakfast and afternoon coffee. [My] Mama promised she would quite often be giving me some cold meat for supper. So as far as my bodily welfare goes, you don't need to worry. For the mind—well, we'll see when I start composing. For the soul, though —I'm quite lost since you left me, my darling.

[1] Helene Berg was on her way to Carlsbad.
[2] Herbert Strutz, pupil of Berg's.

29th March 1923

Woke at seven, had breakfast and worked in my head on the Chamber Concerto.[1] And to my joy I've solved a most important bit, on which I've been racking my brain for weeks ...

(320)   29th March 1923

Went to the hospital today to visit Toni. I liked it there tremendously. It's really marvellous how a place of horror where there's someone dying every night and all are ill, is turned into a friendly, wholesome retreat. Toni is much better. From there I went on to Mödling.

The Schoenbergs were in good spirits. But it wasn't too pleasant an atmosphere, because he kept on finding fault with my Chamber Concerto. He doesn't like the piano in this combination. Only he doesn't know, of course, that it is a *concerto*, not an ordinary octet.[2] And yet he wants me to tell him how the piece is shaping, what sort of thing it will be, and all the time with advice, admonitions, warnings, in fact generally pouring cold water. I am rather scared of Easter Sunday, when I'm invited for lunch and the afternoon.

At first there was an Italian there, and Eisler, who later on played his piano sonata. A very pretty piece, which Schoenberg will at once get played in Prague (through Steuermann). Then Webern arrived. His Quartet will be performed in Berlin ...

Altogether Schoenberg is now in his 'punter's' mood again. Witness his backing Eisler's sonata for Prague almost without reflection, and recommending it to Hertzka, although the third movement hasn't even been finished yet. He has already recommended my concerto to several *ensembles*, and had even asked a fee for me. He has also sent out some *Wozzeck* cards,[3] and has asked for new ones. This is all very kind and may do me some good (though I doubt it, as the people he's going to are mostly without any influence); but it all goes on with such an air of tutor to apprentice. even orders from higher authority, that I feel more annoyed than pleased. And he also has an air of doing something rather special

[1] Chamber Concerto for piano, violin and 13 wind instruments.
[2] Berg originally conceived 'the Chamber Concerto for Piano, Violin and 13 wind instruments' for piano, violin and six wind instruments. This first conception was only gradually expanded to the final ensemble, as is proved by a letter of his to Webern, dated 18th July 1923, in which he writes of a 'Concerto for Piano and Violin with the accompaniment of ten wind instruments.'
[3] Invitation for the subscription edition of the vocal score to *Wozzeck*.

instead of the most natural and effective thing. For instance, he recommends my concerto, which doesn't even exist yet, to an *ensemble* in Copenhagen, in fact he is already asking for an advance on it; instead of recommending the Pieces for Orchestra, which have been finished quite a while, to some important German or Austrian conductor. With the name he has today, that would be enough to get them performed. Or he could recommend my Quartet to one of the many German Quartet Societies which perform his and Webern's Quartets, or to one of the big German publishers who are very keen to have Schoenberg's works. Nor is he particularly interested in my *Wozzeck* negotiations with Hertzka[1]—because *Wozzeck* isn't his. According to him I should tell Hertzka: 'Yes, you can look after *Wozzeck*, but if Schirmer takes it, you'll have to release me.' Now, is Hertzka likely to agree to that? And if he doesn't, what then? ...

(321)   30th March 1923
Oh, I'm so desperate. Just at midday, before I left, your first letter came. You're ill again and I'm not with you. Compared with my realization of that, it's only a small worry that you may not be able to start on your cure. Which is annoying at most, whereas your being ill and me not there is dreadfully sad. And you didn't take your thermometer with you, and I'm sure you won't buy yourself one. So now I'll have to wait anxiously every day for the post, and won't get any news at all throughout Easter. It's horrible, and I can't see any way of helping you. No, never again will I let you go away on your own. We poor people[2]—

(322)   31st March 1923
So Hertzka accepts me for Universal Edition (it's now been agreed). He's doing everything to achieve this, and of course (the dangerous thing!) as cheaply as he can. He made me certain proposals which might be called more favourable for the author, in consideration of my having the vocal score engraved myself. But it'll take me several years to get all my money back—unless it should turn out a colossal success, in which case, of course, I might get it

---

[1] Berg was simultaneously negotiating the publication of *Wozzeck* with the American music-publishing firm of G. Schirmer and with Universal Edition, Vienna.

[2] *Wir arme Leut*—quotation from *Wozzeck*, act I scene i.

all back, and more, within a year. He offers me a share in the music material necessary for performances, and royalties on the libretto and score. I'll go through all his suggestions, comparing them with my former rough contract, a good deal less favourable, which came to nothing.

I'll also go through them with Schoenberg tomorrow, then make my counter-proposals. Of course nobody can guarantee that we'll find a theatre. But Hertzka has very good connections, and as he has to put in six million Crowns for printing the material, he too has the very greatest interest in recovering his expenses by finding a theatre for the production. Munich would be first choice, which would naturally be very fine. He also undertakes to start on the printing at once, directly I hand him the work (that's very important!), *and* to print my *Pieces for Orchestra*.

As he's not leaving Vienna yet, I've got a week or so to play with. Perhaps I can arrange things cleverly so as to wait for the Americans. Oh my golden one, this is quite a tricky business!

(323)   Easter Saturday,
                                              31st March 1923[1]
In the morning Annerl came to clean the flat, and I went into town to see Almschi, but found Jolly[2] there all by herself. She will put the candelabra[3] in the right place, light it, and then call Almschi. At Haslinger's I fetched the Bach Cantata in a beautiful facsimile edition: Easter present for Schoenberg. Then I drove back to Jeanette for lunch; gave her your letter.

Now I'm off home. Hope to work with Klein all afternoon going through the score, collating.

                                              Easter Sunday, 1st April 1923,
                                                        morning, in bed
Collating done. Turns out this is a most important job. Important for getting rid of all the mistakes in the music material. Printing of it to start very soon, we hope.

At half past eight last night I went round to Ploderer. He had a huge flower basket in his room with about twenty or thirty most glorious hyacinths, a real treat for sore eyes. You can't imagine the

---

[1] The letter was started on Easter Saturday and apparently continued in stages till Monday.
[2] The governess of Manon Gropius.
[3] The Bergs' Easter present to Alma Mahler.

fragrance in the room. I do love these flowers so much. Perhaps because they are the first real flowers of spring. All the rest may be very pretty and quite appealing, but they're mostly without smell. And then suddenly you have a real flower which stirs you in every way, form, colour, smell—like the flowers you get in summer when you're already a bit used to it.

So—I love hyacinths very much, and kept thinking 'we poor people'. We couldn't afford a single one this year or last. Several times I've been tempted, but thought how extravagant it would be and that buying food was more important, and that stopped me buying you one.

Had a nice time with Ploderer. We talked about very deep and scientific subjects. I came home at a quarter to eleven, went to bed, ate oranges (not making any juice marks!) and read the paper.

At half past eleven the 'phone rang, it was Almschi. 'Aaalban, how terribly naughty of you both, I'm so very touched,' etc., all shouted down the 'phone. She came home from the Schnitzlers,[1] entered the room, to find it dark except for the candelabra on the desk, fully lit. '*What* a lot you must have spent!' she went on. (Perhaps I should tell her the candelabra wasn't all that expensive! I await your orders.) Otherwise we didn't say very much on the 'phone.

Now, Sunday morning, I'm getting up. It's dull outside and starting to rain—Easter weather. Haven't heard anything from Maxingstrasse[2] these last few days, except for Annerl letting me know that there is no news of Franzl. It's quite simple: at the moment no one there needs anything from me.

Ten o'clock

See how easily one can be unfair. Annerl has just been, bringing me Easter greetings from Mama and a small Easter cake. I'm *very* pleased. By the way, what I said just now about none of them showing any interest in me unless they want something, certainly didn't include Mama.

Now it's eleven, and I'm off to Mödling.

Evening, in the tram,
coming home from Mödling

Got to the Schoenbergs at twelve; Mathilde's uncle was already

---

[1] Arthur Schnitzler (1862–1931), the great Viennese dramatist and novelist.
[2] Where Helene Berg's parents lived.

there. Schoenberg was very nice and once more very friendly to me. But alas at the expense of other friends who (according to him) whenever he talked about his achievements in musical theory would always say: 'Yes, I've done that too.' As he doesn't expect this sort of thing from me, he wants to show me all his secrets in his new works.[1]

Then we talked about Hertzka's proposals, which he said were unacceptable. This means in practice that if I write on those lines to Hertzka, he'll say 'one can't do business with Berg' and break off relations. So I've got to find a way of winning my rights without that. Or even better, I'll wait another two or three weeks, until the answer from New York arrives. Oh, isn't it difficult! And to have no one who can really advise me. Schoenberg didn't give much time to the matter, anyhow. What about a lawyer—one well up in copyright matters? Alas, I haven't got one. Perhaps I can talk to Almschi again, although on the 'phone yesterday she didn't suggest anything like this—I mean that I should visit her and have a general chat, saying I hadn't been in touch with her for such a long time. Then if I have the chance to go into things properly, I'll ask her again whether she won't have another talk with Weinberger,[2] or even whether I should talk to him myself.

Back to the Schoenbergs! We had a superb lunch: soup with dumplings, steak with rice and potato salad, and a cake (imagine: a huge round cream-cake, about eighteen inches in diameter—no exaggeration—tasting gorgeous), and black coffee. Didn't drink enough of the coffee, so that till four I was plagued by monstrous tiredness—and not allowed to smoke!

The rest of the afternoon he showed me new compositions.

By the way, they all send you kindest regards and were very worried about you. 'Hope Helene will write to us one of these days,' said Mathilde—so please do write, and quite soon.

Came back home, had dinner, and as I saw light at Göttel's, I went across, where I found the whole family. Was given a fine welcome, offered lots of sweets and cigarettes. Conversation pleasantly superficial, and we stayed together till half past ten. Came home by moonlight, wintry cold has set in again. It's rather cold in the flat, in fact. Thank heaven I've got my little gas stove on the veranda, where I'm writing to my darling. For all the people I've

[1] The principles of twelve-note composition.
[2] Joseph Weinberger, prominent Viennese music publisher, the founder of Universal Edition.

seen, I've never felt so dreadfully lonely at this time. Never again! But soon a week will be gone, and tomorrow I hope to have many little letters.

Easter Monday, 2nd April 1923,
in the evening and at night

A day in the family circle—lunch with Jeanette. As I eat with her, and generally have to be back home by three to work, I never get an afternoon nap. But funnily enough, I feel quite well on this, and sleep soundly and well at night, quite relaxed. Today's nap was most refreshing, though. At three I went to Hietzing with Jeanette. Took a taxi from the Square to Maxingstrasse—10,000 Crowns. We had marvellous afternoon coffee, a particularly good cake: vanilla, coffee and cream. Papa joined us too, and it was a real family circle. Parents, Antschi, auntie and me—only boring for me! I kept on thinking of my Pferscherl, wondering what she would be doing at each moment. Pictured your face, your walk, your movements—and felt unutterably sad. Hansi was shockingly naughty. He liked Mama's toys (the animals) very much, and Lebert senior's even more.

At seven I walked to Hietzing with Jeanette, and just managed to cram her into an over-full tram. I hope she got a seat. I'm a bit worried whether she got home all right. I had to go back to Maxingstrasse, where they were expecting me for dinner.

At half past eight the Leberts fetched me: I was to sample their Slivovitz. In a burst of high spirits Mama came with us, and the four of us sat in their drawing-room (Leberts, Mama and I; Papa had gone to bed). We stayed together till a quarter to ten, having a very lively, cheerful conversation.

But now I'm home again and alone—no, with *you*. You will be lying with your dear head on the pillows and—I do so much hope —sleeping soundly. Oh, if I could just caress you. Now of all times when you're far from the world, so touchingly helpless and needing to be protected.

Instead of which I'm lying in this bleak bed, tormenting myself with a few hundred words to express my billion thoughts of longing for you . . .

(324)   3rd April 1923, evening
A sad day if nothing from Pferscherl arrives. For all the work and

its variety, a day that has seemed endless. For without Pferscherl it lacks all aim and purpose.

At three I met Klein again. This job is turning out more tedious than I expected. It's a sort of 'spring-cleaning' of the orchestral score, dealing with the things one has missed in the fury of composition or put off till later. For instance, directions, like 'flute takes piccolo', 'oboe takes *cor anglais*', 'trombone takes mute', etc. Or when the violins have been playing pizzicato, putting 'arco' there, to show you want them to stop the pizzicato. Going through all the 35 to 40 parts for all three acts. It's important, in case the band parts are copied from the orchestral score, to have *all* the different directions taken into account—they matter so much—and not wait for the rehearsals to pick up the mistakes and correct them. We've been working on it now for four afternoons, five hours each, and still have another three or four hours work to go. Klein didn't leave till half past eight. I had dinner and went to bed. Am reading a bit, and thinking sadly of my golden one.

(325)   Thursday, 5th April 1923,
                                                    morning in bed

Drafted the contract with Hertzka, just as I had it worked out. 11.30 to Jeanette, an hour or so with her, and home again at 2.30 for Mahler's lesson. At 3.30 Klein appeared, and he and Mahler worked on the score (on the veranda) under my supervision, while in the music-room I gave three lessons: Seidlhofer,[1] Strutz and Kassowitz. Taking a look at the veranda now and then to see if the other chaps were working properly! At seven the four of us left, Klein, Mahler, Kassowitz and I. In the tram we talked about the libretto, which Mahler is collating at home. I was invited to the Steuermanns for dinner. It was quite nice, though not very exciting —chiefly because I was so tired . . .

                                                         Afternoon

Well, you are so beautiful and attractive that the blond idiot in the restaurant had the cheek to sit down next to you. Tell me, is he always going to have his meals with you now? Please don't let him, if there's even a hint of his making advances, let alone anything more. Go to a different restaurant. Oh, if only I could be with you. All my other worries fade out beside this one, even my indecisions

[1] Bruno Seidlhofer, a pupil of Berg's.

about *Wozzeck*. Really nobody can help me there. Pilzer and Ploderer are even less well up in these things than I am. And I can't afford a lawyer who specializes in it. I can't approach Weinberger, who might advise me; especially as Almschi isn't taking any action. In about a week's time I'll 'phone her. If she really feels like seeing me or talking to me about it again, she would find ways and means, I'm sure.

What she and Schoenberg have advised so far is all very fine, but no help if Hertzka won't play. It'll be a case of either breaking off negotiations or giving in. I can't wait for the Americans . . . Besides their answer won't be: 'Yes, we accept the score and will pay you 500 to 1,000 dollars.' At best it'll be: 'We are very much interested, and would like to acquire the work, how much are you asking, and what are the conditions?' Whereupon I would write back and in six weeks receive another draft contract, which if it's satisfactory I would sign. So if everything worked out for the best, they would start preparing the music material in the summer, which is too late, if there's to be any question of a production at all. Whereas with Hertzka some sort of first production is almost certain. Even if it's not Munich, it'll be some other town. Of course he can't and won't guarantee it. And until he has my signed contract, he won't lift a finger for my work. Perhaps I can manage to tack about for one or two weeks longer, keeping his interest alive without actually signing . . .

(326)   7th April 1923
Was at Almschi's this morning from eleven till half past twelve. I'm glad I went, she's a darling really, and I'm sure she was very pleased. But I told her I had deliberately let twelve days go by because she hadn't done anything in the matter. Werfel had come last night, but I don't think my being there worried them—as I fancy they aren't very happy together. He is very depressed, in fact (as she told me confidentially), over her cool and critical attitude towards him. So they were glad to have me there with my 'mediating talent'.

Almschi is now all for Hertzka, at least she isn't talking about America any more. All she wants is that I should get out of Hertzka what I could expect from my successive shares in the vocal scores: ten to twenty millions,[1] she says. The remaining twenty million she

[1] £100 to £200.

313

would secure for me in no time. Now, I don't believe I'll get amounts in that range, first because Hertzka won't pay, second because even Almschi can't secure twenty million that easily; but still I think I can expect quite a large sum. Almschi says in her categorical way, in front of Werfel: 'I promise you that with the help of Frau Bloch-Bauer[1] I'll raise the money!' So with that in mind I'll go to Hertzka on Monday.

She also told me that she is slowly beginning to make out the vocal score, and already understands it a bit. She said I should come more often, and invited me to dinner on Monday evening, when the Bittners will be there. She talked to Werfel about our wonderful marriage and waxed very enthusiastic over our candelabra, which stands just above the sofa and I suppose provides fairy lights for their love games.

She has just received your letter, and sweet Mutzi had hers from you. Almschi said the thing that's wrong about your cure is that you've gone too early in the year.

Went from her to Lanyi, to buy the *Fackel*. Terrific issue, 184 pages! Shall I send it to you? Since June Kraus has given away about 80 millions to charities. Then I went to Jeanette, who was overjoyed to hear Almschi's intentions, and was full of praise for her. At three I had lessons, also Klein and [Fritz] Mahler working on my score. All left at seven. At nine I went to bed.

---

[1] Friend of Alma Mahler's, the wife of a rich industrialist. Berg dedicated *Wozzeck* to Alma Mahler in gratitude for her help.

Sunday, 8th April 1923

Went to Mama at twelve and had an excellent lunch: cauliflower with butter, bread-crumbs and ham, stewed beef with potato croquets, black coffee. (You never write about what you're eating. I'd like to hear, just as you want to know what I'm eating—or are you bored with my menus?)

Then by train to Mödling. Schoenberg was again criticizing everything about me: that I'm still working on *Wozzeck* ('very Karl-Krausish, this eternal correcting'), that I smoke, that I 'shouldn't imagine *Wozzeck* will have any success, it's too difficult', and worst of all that I've still not started on the Chamber Concerto.

Now it's ten, and I'm on the train home, having waded through deep snow to get to it.

Monday, 9th April 1923,
morning

The post brought a letter from Copenhagen with 20 Swiss francs, (230,000 Crowns) for a *Wozzeck* score,[1] and at last your dearest, sweetest letter of the 7th. Praise be that you are better, can eat again, have a new doctor, and can get your meals at the 'Europa' house.

The flute-player from Copenhagen, the rich man who bought the score and has a wind quintet (he wants to commission my Chamber Quintet[2] for them), wrote charmingly, quite a long letter. He wanted me to let him know candidly how much I would ask for it, if I intend (as Schoenberg suggested) to dedicate it to his *ensemble* and sell them exclusive performing rights.

Well—first I've got to have it composed!

When you come back, you should lead a free life, not a maid's life. It's quite enough if you have to attend to the food in the early days, until Mitzi has got the hang of things. On the other hand, I want to work regularly the whole morning from now on, which is impossible when I see the way you toil and moil. After lunch we'll both have an hour's rest, then I have to give lessons two or three afternoons a week, seven in all. Then we'll have a walk for an hour or two every day. You need it for your health, and I need it for my work. Just imagine, in the countryside every day!

From this point of view I think it's impractical and not a very good idea for you to come home earlier, particularly as we haven't

---

[1] Berg sold the *Wozzeck* scores direct, on a subscription basis.
[2] See footnote Letter 320.

315

got a maid, which would also mean shortening your cure. Pferschi we both know only too well that I'd love to have you here already, that (like you) I'm rootless if we aren't together, in fact that this is no existence at all. And we realize it all the more every time it happens. You can see that I write you eight or ten pages a day, to keep my head even half 'above water'. I do that wherever I am and at all times of day and night. But the thought that you might not have made the most of your cure, by finishing it too early ... at once silences all my selfish longings. I should feel really mean if I didn't try my hardest to dissuade you. Don't you think I'm right? ...

(328)   Vienna, 10th April 1923
    Only a short letter today, as the discussions with Hertzka have begun. They started in the evening at Almschi's, a sort of social prelude. The Bittners were invited, as he wanted to play his new symphony to Hertzka. They talked a lot about *Wozzeck*, the chances in Mannheim, the very favourable article which has just appeared in *Musik*[1] (haven't seen it yet, but will send it you directly I get it), etc., etc. In short Almschi did everything to charm Hertzka, after they'd been nearly enemies for years. Hertzka became very keen, so tomorrow I start the difficult mission proper. I say tomorrow, but it's already today, 2.45 a.m. I came home from Almschi's a quarter of an hour ago, and tired as I am, I had to have a chat with you, as during the day I shan't have much chance tomorrow (I mean today). Anyhow I believe everything possible has been done to 'soften Hertzka up'. Now the business part begins, and that won't be finished in our first talk!
    The evening was peculiar. At first very pleasant and jolly. Food simple, but what drinks! (Bittner is a diabetic and pretty old.) The symphony is not at all bad and most attractive. But he wanted to play more than that, and started on a new song-cycle, all about his happy marriage. Some very nice bits in that too, interesting for me particularly, as I sat at the piano and could look at the score. But Almschi and Hertzka were in a jovial mood, and understandably, after a whole forty-minute symphony, didn't feel up to listening to sixteen love songs. At half past twelve, when we'd reached Song

---

[1] The article was written by Ernst Viebig (b. 1897), the music critic and opera composer, and published in the April issue, 1923, of *Die Musik*, an important music magazine.

No. 12, Bittner suddenly noticed they were laughing and chatting, and thought it was about him or his songs. He got up with his face red as a lobster, and dashed out with his wife in a rage. He just couldn't be restrained, though right to the hall I worked my hardest to mollify him. The whole thing was over in two minutes. Afterwards a whole hour of deliberation on what to do: telephone call and general consternation, sweetened by seeing the funny side and not really feeling too guilty!

(329)   11th April 1923, on the
                                                way to Mödling

I have come to an agreement with Hertzka. On the whole it has turned out more favourable than I expected a week or two ago. Of course I shan't see any money all that soon, although he is paying me something in advance; but I'll only get the big amount if it's a success. From what I read in *Musik*, what Bittner said and Hertzka's attitude (even if put on), I am very confident now that there will be a worthy first production next season. And the *Three Orchestral Pieces*, too, will definitely be published in the autumn, there will be a big publicity campaign for *Wozzeck*, and I've reserved 30 copies for myself which I can sell privately.

So I believe we can look at the business optimistically. Especially as the article in *Musik* is quite marvellous. Three pages of intelligent praise, then at the end, of course, the usual croaking about the difficulties of an actual production, so that the tremendous impression of the article gets slightly blurred—which is made up for, I hope, by a photographic reproduction of the *Cradle Song*[1] going with it. The writer of the article says about this: 'It is one of the most powerful lyrical inspirations known to recent operatic literature.'

I have only got one copy of the magazine and don't want to give this away. I want to show it to your people and Almschi, etc., and more important than anything, I might need it badly for publicity material! But Klein is dashing around all over the place today, to find another copy for you.

(330)   12th April 1923, in the
                                                evening, in bed

When I'm alone, I know only one way of feeling able to live, and

[1] *Wozzeck*, act I, scene iii.

317

that's by writing to you. So it happens that even in a state of complete exhaustion I prefer to write to you rather than close my eyes, which are so tired that they smart. Only a short note tonight. It's ten at night, I've just stopped working. Have been at the desk with Klein since three.

Friday, 13th April, morning

Shall be off to town at 8, meet Mahler at 9, at 10.30 to Hertzka, where I sign. As it is the Thirteenth *and* a Friday, it should bring luck. Then to Jeanette. At two Klein comes to ask about the orchestral score of the *Three Pieces for Orchestra*. Then at last, released from hateful work, I'll come home, where I hope to find a letter from my golden one and will write you a proper letter.

(331)   (Undated,
                                                             14th April 1923)

Concluded the contract with Hertzka about *Wozzeck* and the *Orchestral Pieces*. I told you about the first already; the second is favourable beyond all expectations. (More favourable, anyhow, than he usually agrees to with orchestral pieces, and in consideration of his getting *Wozzeck* so cheaply.) I have a good feeling, even though I haven't seen much money yet (he gave me a small advance, 3,000,000 Crowns[1]). In any case my career, which has stood still for fifteen years, will now advance with great strides. First, the libretto is being published presently in a very pretty format. Second, the music material will appear at latest for the beginning of the 1923 season. Third, the *Pieces for Orchestra* appear in a facsimile edition, a photograph of the beautifully written dedication copy for Schoenberg; that means a sort of collector's edition, and most important, without any mistakes. Fourth, he wants to take the *Quartet* soon, and the *Pieces for Clarinet*. But on that I mean to wait till I hear from New York. Perhaps I can sell it there better. Fifth, Hertzka is going to Germany tomorrow to start publicity. Sixth, during the Austrian Music Week in Berlin they'll almost certainly perform Webern's *Passacaglia* and my *Pieces for Orchestra*. At least I was told this as a fact, agreed on yesterday at Mödling between Schoenberg and Pella.[2]

---

[1] About £35.
[2] Paul Pella, conductor, pupil of Schoenberg's.

This morning, after quickly answering you, I went to town, heavily loaded—six scores and the case. First Universal Edition. Then to the Hotel Bristol, where I left the one score for 20 Swiss francs. Then the Bank, then the Finance Ministry because of the capital levy. I've already paid a good deal in advance, and now we have to pay the balance of half a million[1] at once—a lot of money! Then to Haslinger, to Jeanette, lunch, an hour's rest, home, two lessons, and now on the way to the concert of the Kolisch Quartet. But just before I left in the morning, the telephone rang. It was Almschi, asking me for dinner tonight. 'Just today I can't,' I said: 'Kolisch concert.' 'Well, then come after it. I'll keep a good dinner for you. I have to talk to you, we'll be alone.' (She meant, without any guests, not like last time.) Perhaps she has taken some action. I wonder what's up.

Evening

A great disappointment. When I got to Almschi's at a quarter to nine, I found her with Werfel, the Spechts[2] and Csokor[3], still at the dinner table (though they'd finished the meal); and she herself was in that mood of rather artificial merriness produced by too much drink. I would like to have gone away again, but in the end made the best of it, ate my dinner (Vienna sausages, red cabbage, potatoes, bread-crumb cake and tea), and listened to the literary and theatrical discussions, which were often quite amusing. I departed at eleven (last tram), leaving the party in a state of increasing alcoholization, especially Almschi, who (to Werfel's genuine despair) had already reached her fifth glass of brandy.

Why she asked me to come is a bit of a mystery. Possibly the other guests more or less invited themselves during the day after I'd been asked. On the other hand she and Specht seemed to have had something in mind, as became pretty clear to me from a lot of cryptic hints, but it failed to materialize, presumably owing to the drunkenness. I imagine the two of them wanted to play me something on the piano together, perhaps the Epilogue from *Wozzeck!* Anyhow Almschi had a bad conscience when I left, and asked me to come again soon: early Monday morning, so that we could be *alone*.

On 1st May she's going to Venice with Mutzi and Jolly at Moll's

[1] About £5.
[2] Dr Richard Specht (1870–1932), Austrian writer on music.
[3] Franz Theodor Csokor, Viennese poet and dramatist.

319

invitation. She achieved this by letting him know of her great impecuniousness (which she really does seem to be suffering from at the moment). What a good thing that I've come to an agreement with Hertzka. If there's an answer from America now, Almschi won't even be here.

Before this doubtful pleasure at Almschi's I had been to the Kolisch concert. It was rather nice. Webern got very fine music from the small *ensemble*, and in the artists' room afterwards told me about his present life. He *is* a nice chap, people are unfair about him. In the concert I sat with Karpath.[1] After the first piece (a newly discovered Haydn, distinguished 'shut-eye-music') he went to another concert.

15th April 1923

Started this letter in bed, and am finishing it now, Sunday morning, on the veranda. The garden is suddenly getting green—and I've bought grass-seed for the lawn. The chestnuts are stretching out their lovely arms, and when you return, everything will be prepared for your reception.

Last night I was suddenly overcome by the feeling of expectancy for you and anticipation. Till then I had stayed resignedly in the saddest feeling of aloneness, separation from you. But now I know that next week, whether at the beginning or the end, Pferschi will come. Then there will be only feelings of sheer joy. Now you are no longer all that far away, not as far as you were yesterday. I can already touch you, see you walking round the rooms, hear you singing in the bath—my dearest darling.

This afternoon, what a sacrifice, I'm going off to Mödling. Stefan will be there too. By the way, he was attacked by Kraus in the last issue of the *Fackel*. If I find out in time that you're not arriving in Vienna till the middle of next week. I'll send you the issue, best possible reading matter on the train.

(333)   Sunday, 15th April 1923
In the morning I wrote to you and several other letters, then to Jeanette for lunch. Rested half an hour, drank some black coffee, and went to the Southern Station, where I met the Stefans and we travelled to Mödling together. To Trude's, where all the Schoen-

[1]See footnote Letter 81.

bergs were assembled.[1] Just imagine: a flat the size of my piano room with the veranda, and in it two Schoenbergs, two Greissles, a baby, Novakovic, two Stefans, two Pappenheims, Polnauer and I —a round dozen (the whole dozen send you all their greetings). Still, it was friendlier today, Schoenberg much more agreeable, extremely witty and sparkling. Also he was quite mild about my signing the contract. He didn't mention the article in *Musik*, nor did he pester me about the wind piece.

Evening in bed.

Outside it's stormy and icy cold. I wonder how you are, my poor darling, in 'bleakest Carlsbad'. What a crazy idea to take the cure in March and April. What a lot of trouble and unpleasantness you would have saved yourself and (indirectly) me, if we hadn't tried so hard to save money. Now when it's too late I reproach myself terribly.

(334)   16th April, morning

This morning a letter arrived from a Berlin piano virtuoso, who wants new piano works from me, as he considers my *Piano Sonata* the most important work in modern piano music!

Evening

I hoped there would be some post from you, but nothing came. While I was waiting, I looked through my *Pieces for Orchestra*, which I have to clean up a bit for the photographic reproduction. But I couldn't even find enough concentration for that, so I had an hour's piano playing, which doesn't often happen, does it! I played the most glorious thing there is, Schubert's *Mass in E flat major*,[2] which Webern is going to conduct in the church at Mödling at the beginning of May. Then, what a wretched substitute for a letter, the paper arrived. Finally, when dusk fell on this horrible 'late-autumn' day in April, I realized hopelessly that no letter will arrive from you, and so I am still in doubt how soon you will be coming. When I look at this weather and imagine you exposed to it so far away from me, perhaps going sadly for a walk, or even lying alone

---

[1] Schoenberg's daughter, Trude (Mrs Felix Greissle), had just given birth to a son.
[2] Composed in 1828.

in bed, I feel so miserable I could almost hang myself. I have to think with all my powers of the moment when I'll have you with me once again. But even when I think of *that*, and think what a wretched little Easter present I can give you this year, when it ought to be so big and splendid—the sadness still won't leave me.

Just round the corner, a few houses away, there's a little Polish Jew, living in the most superb villa in Gloriettegasse. He became a soldier in 1917, served in the Reserve with Polnauer's father, started a rag business, sold food illicitly at the end of the war, then made some lucky investments, and today owns ten trillions, which are ten thousand billions, which are ten million millions— 10,000,000,000,000 Crowns.[1] His name is *****,[2] the richest man in Austria. And here am I—no, I won't make the comparison. But it would be lovely if I could present you with a few trifles for, let's say, ten million Crowns.

(335)   Tuesday, 31st July 1923
             Hallein, near Salzburg, with the Janskis,[3] morning.

Arrived safely at Hallein at 5 yesterday evening. Frau Schmid fetched me and took me to the house, which is three minutes from the station. I was quite surprised: a large, very pleasant and prosperous house, with a pretty garden (fruit, vegetable, chickens, etc.). Obviously an extremely well run household, though you notice some post-war defects which can't be done up. I have a lovely room here, and slept marvellously on a brass bedstead.

The Janskis are simple but well-bred people, proper Alpine provincial worthies. After our arrival we got tea with cheese sandwiches, then we went into the town. The Janskis' villa is with some others on the outskirts, and you get into the centre by crossing the bridge over the river Salzach. The town itself is quite large, much bigger than Deutsch-Landsberg—and very old. Something for you, in fact, with all those old houses. How attractive and interesting you would find it, seeing how taken you were by the few wretched

---

[1] About a hundred million pounds.

[2] A prominent industrialist and banker in the 1920s.

[3] Berg was taking part in the International Festival for Chamber Music (in Salzburg), from which developed the 'International Society for Contemporary Music' (I.S.C.M.). In the first concert his String Quartet op. 3, written in 1910, which had had one private performance, was publicly performed for the first time. (See Letter 102.) During his stay he was living with the Janskis, parents-in-law of his pupil Josef Schmid. Helene Berg was at Trahütten.

houses in Gastein. Unfortunately there aren't any good picture postcards.

The position of the place is marvellous, and although it looks as if this will be a brilliant cloudless day, it's not oppressive at all.

Last night there was a good dinner in the family circle, and I went to bed at nine, dog-tired. Up at 6.30 and 'got myself up' as well as possible with my only suit, now very sweaty. At 8.30 went by train to Salzburg with Schmid.

At the Mozarteum I found out that Havemann[1] was expected yesterday but hadn't yet arrived. Perhaps he'll be arriving this morning. I'm in a café at the moment. In the distance I can see Casella[2] and Nilius.[3] Many foreigners are expected. One well-known composer—Bartók. Weissmann[4] is just coming into the café. He's sitting down next to me and telling me that he has just come from Reichenhall,[5] where he was often in Havemann's company. That he had often listened to my very well played _Quartet_, that Havemann is expecting me in Reichenhall, and has written to me about it. Too silly. As I have my passport in Hallein, I shan't be able to travel across the border into Bavaria. So I'm now going to telegraph to say I'm here. He doesn't know that so far, because I wrote to him at the Mozarteum, and my card is still lying there unread. Meanwhile it has become terrifically hot. Radiant summer day!

In the music shops I have already seen all my music published by Haslinger in large quantities. But not the works published by U.E.

1st August 1923

Now I can at last go on with this. I telegraphed Havemann yesterday, and asked if the rehearsals are in Salzburg or Reichenhall. Because my _Quartet_ is all he's performing in this Music Week. I should certainly have the reply this morning. If he is staying in R. till the actual performance, we'll quickly get a visa (6,000 Crowns) and go by train there at eleven. But I hope he will come to Salzburg.

Owing to yesterday's terrific heat (not doing me any harm, by the way) we stayed lethargically for the first part of the afternoon in the

---

[1] Gustav Havemann, leader of the Havemann Quartet.
[2] Alfredo Casella (1883–1947), the Italian composer and pianist.
[3] Viennese conductor.
[4] Adolph Weissmann (1874–1929), German critic and author.
[5] Watering-place ten miles from Salzburg, across the German frontier.

unique Café Bazar, where we were joined by Frau Schmid and then Buschbeck, and Schmid's father, a very funny old man, like one of Thimig's[1] characters.

I can't write much today, I'm afraid, as directly after breakfast the train leaves for Salzburg. While walking yesterday in my new shoes, I got such a painful blister on the heel that today I had to wear old Janski's shoes, or I couldn't have walked a step.

After a magnificent thunderstorm over Salzburg's legendary 26 churches—today we have the famous Salzburg rain.

Directly I know if I'm going into Bavaria at lunch-time, I'll write you a card, which you might still get on Friday. Of course I shan't know yet how long I have to stay here. If I decide I only want to listen to 'my' concert, I might travel on Friday to Traunkirchen,[2] and then on Tuesday to Graz. Perhaps I'll stay here longer, though. Depends how I find the situation at the first concert, on Thursday, also who will be here, etc. If I send a telegram on Friday, you'll know by Saturday or Sunday. And when shall I hear from *you*? All the time I keep thinking: *that* would be something for her. You're much more observant than I am. If only—if only you were here.

(336)   Villa Janski, 2nd August 1923

A few hours to relax at last. Today we are not going to Salzburg till after lunch. I have another rehearsal in the afternoon and the concert in the evening. Yesterday was rather strenuous. Mainly because one is on the go from eight in the morning till midnight, and there is nowhere you can retire for an hour. Still, I feel fit as a fiddle, though I can't understand it! I'm bearing this heat very well, not a trace of asthma, the mucous membranes quite unaffected.

Your card came yesterday, kindly telling me all about the mail in such detail. Thank you, my golden one.

So, back to yesterday. Was in Salzburg at 9 a.m. and after looking for them for almost two hours, I at last found the Havemann four. Delightful people, really. Four fair-haired, cheerful, enthusiastic and hard-working musicians. In ten minutes we were firm friends. When I saw they knew my *Quartet* nearly by heart, felt it themselves as genuine music, and performed it with all that feeling—my heart

---

[1] Hugo Thimig (1854–1945), head of a famous German theatrical family, and character comedian of the Vienna Burgtheater.

[2] The Schoenbergs were having their holiday at the village of Traunkirchen, on Lake Traun, in the Salzkammergut, 35 miles from Salzburg.

opened to them. It's quite different from the amateur quartet-playing in the Society. How well the four of them played together, how perfectly it all works, how happy they are with the printed music! How each of them knows all four parts, in fact keeps a check on the others. Only hope it'll be as good tonight, as it could be if nothing goes wrong!

After the first rehearsal I had lunch—with Weissmann, who is always with us and behaves as a close friend—and then went to the café. (They serve you a lot of whipped cream, which I am quite ready to use.) Then by funicular to Fort Hohensalzburg. Very beautiful, but I'll *tell* you about that later. It would take too long writing about it as there is a lot to tell. I suffer all the time from you not being here.

From the top of the Fort down to the Mozarteum: second rehearsal. And from there to a restaurant, where the official reception took place. A vast party, Austrians and foreigners but no interesting people. I was a good deal with Loos, who is charming as ever. As the first concert is not till tonight, there were a lot of people missing who will be arriving today. As I see things at present, I shall have to be here for the whole Music Festival. I should do myself harm artistically and socially if I left. The question is, do I visit Schoenberg during the five concert days (skipping one or two) at or the end? As Traunkirchen is more or less on the way to Graz, and I should be doing something rather silly if I stayed away—I *could* cut the fourth and fifth concerts, but the most important foreign quartets and wind *ensembles* are playing—it would be wisest if I decide to go to Traunkirchen on the 8th and come home on the 9th. So I'll be in Graz either on the evening of Wednesday the 8th or on the 9th.

I must finish quickly. I know so little of your doings, my darling. Tonight is *your Quartet*. Oh, if only you were here!

(337)   Friday, 3rd August 1923,
                                                              morning

I have just sent the telegram. But it couldn't tell you *how* beautiful it was. It was, artistically, the most wonderful evening of my life, and I am full of sorrow that you couldn't experience it, you who have spent at my side so many sad decades artistically, you who are just as concerned in the *Quartet* as I am myself, you to whom it completely belongs.

I just want to tell you everything quickly.

325

There was a short but very well-turned speech by Mr Dent,[1] in which he inveighed against journalistic clichés like 'Futurists' and 'Bolsheviks'. Then, amidst general expectancy, my *Quartet* started. They played with indescribable beauty, and I can tell you, though only you, that despite my great excitement (I was sitting in the second row, next to Rufer, rather hidden, unrecognized by the audience) I revelled in the lovely sounds, the solemn sweetness and ecstasy of the music. You can't imagine it by what you've heard so far. The 'wildest' and 'most daring' passages were sheer harmony in the classical sense.

The first movement ended in an elevated atmosphere; complete stillness in the audience, a short breath for the players, and it went on.

At the end there was almost frantic general applause. The quartet themselves came back twice, and kept looking for me in the audience. The third time I was called for, stepped on to the platform quite by myself, and was received with terrific enthusiasm by the *whole* audience—not one sound of booing. The applause continued, and once more the five of us went up on to the platform. Quite an important success for Salzburg and for such a small work of chamber music. The rest of the programme, surprisingly, rather fell off in comparison. General opinion was that I carried off the prize that night. The concert was very well attended. A great many critics I knew or met: Paul Bekker,[2] Weissmann, Stefan, old Korngold (!), Max Graf, and apparently twenty to forty foreign critics.

Other people I knew who were present: Polnauer appeared for this one evening; for the whole Festival or a part of it, Zemlinsky, Jalowetz, the two Rufers, Hertzka. Hertzka is beaming! Of course he wants the *Quartet* and the *Clarinet Pieces* for the U.E. The *Wozzeck* libretto has already been published. Material nearly ready. Complete confidence in the future. All available scores of my *Quartet* are already sold out in Salzburg, and I need copies for the musicians. The Pro Arte Quartet from Brussels and the Hindemith Quartet will study my *Quartet* and play it. Havemann has immediately been engaged for Copenhagen and Stockholm to play it. During the next season they'll be playing it all over Germany repeatedly—that's how much they enjoy it. Wonderful men, really —a pity they've already left. A clarinet player introduced himself

[1] Edward J. Dent (1876–1959), English musicologist and critic, first president of the I.S.C.M.
[2] Paul Bekker (1883–1937), German music critic.

326

to me enthusiastically. He had played the *Clarinet Pieces* (which he said were beautifully written for the instrument) in Heidelberg and Mannheim; and he would be doing them next in other German cities. (We are going to rehearse here.)

Casella said (in French) the most wonderful things to me about my works. Everybody is staggered that the *Quartet* is 13½ years old. Also: Scherchen wants to play fragments from *Wozzeck* in a Berlin concert; he has some dramatic soprano available. I must discuss this with Hertzka.

Altogether I still have a lot of things here to settle on the business and music sides. So it's very useful my staying here. Schoenberg wants Rufer, Schmid and me to visit him after the concerts, that would be on the 8th, so that I shan't be in Graz till the 9th. Arrange everything accordingly, my golden one. Oh, God—I shall never forgive myself for not having brought you with me. Wouldn't you still like to come even now? Two, three concerts, nice people, and the most superb city and scenery. People should see what you look like, you to whom the *Quartet* belongs, you, who gave it birth. I'm putting down train times on a separate sheet—at 4.45 you would be in Hallein. Every evening in the artists' room at the Mozarteum! Oh, what lovely fantasies.

Anni and Křenek aren't here so far[1]—tonight is his Quartet.

I'm definitely expecting a letter from you today, my golden one! In great haste again, must stop. Train to Salzburg evening concert.

Many many many kisses

Your own

(338)   Saturday, 4th August 1923

Next year we'll have to do things quite differently. I tell you, I've never felt so fit as I do here. Although I am up till one every night, and although it's often very strenuous (for instance, an outing yesterday to Hallwang; extremely hot there, and back in a thunderstorm) I am sleeping better than I've ever done in my life. Seven or eight hours continuous sleep, and all this without any rest after lunch, daily train rides, never alone except for the two hours in the morning when I write to you.

Brief report on yesterday. Lunch at the Schmids', then an hour and a half by train to the home of Schmid's parents at Hallwang.

---

[1] Ernst Křenek was married at this time to Anna Mahler, the daughter of Gustav and Alma Mahler.

In the evening to Salzburg, first to a café, where I read newspaper notices. The Salzburg papers are against modern music, yet my *Quartet* came out well. Notice in the biggest Salzburg paper enclosed.

At the café, of course, always in the company of many festival participants: Zemlinsky, Loos, Szell,[1] etc. In the evening the first four pieces were indescribable muck. You could feel the boredom in the hall, which was anyhow not so full as yesterday. Only the *Quartet* by Křenek woke people up, and I must say—there's a splendid chap. From the first to last note, thrilling, full of ideas; a great pleasure to listen to it. All the others, e.g. Zemlinsky, were enthusiastic. Hindemith, whom I congratulated on his magnificent playing,[2] was 'bitter-sweet'. After the concert I asked Hertzka to introduce me to a lady: Dutch, singing at the Paris opera (compliments about my *Quartet*). She would like to sing my songs, is rather nice, and as for her husband, also a Dutchman, he'd be quite a bite for you! I had been struck by him before the introductions.

Now I am longingly expecting news from you, and to hear when you are coming to Graz. Take some time for the road down to Deutsch-Landsberg. It's terribly strenuous, and not as short as they say. One can be at the brewery in an hour, but you have to trot all the time, and that made my muscles ache for five days. So better allow three hours for getting down to the station, then you needn't hurry.

(339)   Monday, 6th August 1923
In very great haste, my golden one, so that the letter reaches you before you go to Graz. I have just sent you a telegram that I'll be arriving there at 7.45 Thursday evening. That still applies. If all goes well, I'm off by car on Wednesday morning to Traunkirchen...
I'm staying there till ten on Thursday with Schoenberg, and will then travel direct to Graz. On the way I'm meeting Schmid. I'll arrive with him, and stay the night with him, unless you have made other arrangements. How tremendously I'm looking forward to seeing you, my angel.

Read your two letters with greatest joy. I think only of our reunion, my rose-leaf. Enclosed a good notice. And I kept giving that critic the most scornful looks whenever we met, which was about thirty times a day—so you never can tell!

[1] George Szell (1897–1970), Austrian conductor.
[2] Paul Hindemith was at that time the viola player of the Amar String Quartet.

328

(340)   Vienna, 21st November 1923

My golden one, I am sitting, feeling unutterably sad, in my room (my piano-, work-, sleep-, dining-, reception- and digestion-room). Am only glad I'm so tired. It means I can sleep and forget that you are not lying at my side, my darling. And that you can't give me your dearest, toil-worn little hand, that a dear cold little nose is not bending over me. How alone I am, and shall be all night and all these weeks![1]

22nd November, morning

Didn't sleep too well. Woke up often, wondering how you were this first night. Whether you felt well or unhappy, whether it was quiet. When shall I hear all this? This morning I look out on a snow scene. At least no damp and dirty autumn weather any more.

Afternoon

Well, my golden one, this morning we had the dress rehearsal.[2] The opera won't have any big success. There is a lot in it that's undramatic, and the dramatic part itself is so harrowingly tragic (like the first entrance of the dwarf) that it is hardly bearable. What a pity considering the wonderful music. Of course the production too is second-rate. Even Oestvig, who's best of all, hasn't grown into his part yet. The minor parts are third-rate. The female chorus thin, rather inaudible; so the whole of the first part is almost boring. Staging, direction, decor (Roller), all bad to my mind. But despite all that and the stiff conducting (Alwin[3]) one can still get great pleasure from large parts of it, thanks to the wonderful flow of glorious melody. Incidentally, the music isn't too easy to understand (because there's so much polyphony). I am looking forward to Saturday, sitting in a seat behind a column, and just following the score.[4]

Didn't have much talk with Almschi, who was with Werfel and Rosé. Tonight I'll go across to see her. Klenau was also there. Very nice again.

In Zemlinsky's box there were Schoenberg, Webern and the

[1] Helene Berg had gone for medical treatment to Parsch, near Salzburg.
[2] Of Zemlinsky's opera *The Dwarf*.
[3] Karl Alwin (1891–1946), conductor at the Vienna Opera, husband of Elisabeth Schumann.
[4] At the first night Berg sat with Webern in two *Säulensitze*. These were the well-known seats behind the pillars of the Opera House and were generally used by students. Although little of the stage could be seen, small lamps were attached making it possible to follow a score (See Letter 342).

Greissles. After the performance I went with all of them and the Pappenheims to the Opera Restaurant. (Had a set meal, superb.) Schoenberg was in such an appallingly cantankerous mood, he was like a dead weight on the whole company. He complained about not seeing you any more, suggested that I moved to Mödling for a few days, and when I made Jeanette an excuse, said: 'Don't, then.'

Zemlinsky was hoping to take him to Prague, but all of a sudden he definitely turned this down. In the restaurant Zemlinsky burned the table-cloth (100,000 Crowns). He was very charming, and made lots of enquiries about you.

At five o'clock Almschi suddenly 'phoned, saying why had I been so 'cool' towards her at the Opera. That's quite right, because, as I explained, she was first rather cool with me. 'How is Helene?' 'Well, I hope.' 'What do you mean by "hope"?' 'Helene's away.' Amazement and dismay. When you said 'See you at Christmas', she took it as a joke. You must write to her straight away. She was also in despair over the opera production, finds it very poor, and so boring, and predicts a failure.

I then went to the Erdmann concert. You would not have disliked the symphony.[1] It's effective, lively, well orchestrated, Straussian, a bit of Mahler, some modern trimmings. Very little inner content, though. Ditto musical workmanship. But just to listen to once, quite pleasant. Audience rather enthusiastic. Afterwards I met Reichwein[2] in the artists' room, then went across to see Kolisch (also artists' room). Met Webern and his wife there, although he had told me rather grandly in the morning that after his experience the other day he would never again go to a concert where his own work was being played.

Kolisch, by the way, has improved *a lot* and also played Webern's *Four Pieces*[3] quite admirably. It was definitely a success for him, Webern and Fräulein Gál.[4] I had a long chat with Webern in the artists' room, partly about Kleiber[5] whom he has known for years,

[1] Symphony No. 1, op. 10, by Eduard Erdmann (1896–1958), Latvian-German pianist and composer.
[2] Leopold Reichwein (1876–1945), Viennese conductor.
[3] Webern's *Four Pieces for Violin and Piano*, op. 7.
[4] Pianist, sister of the Viennese composer Hans Gál.
[5] Erich Kleiber (1890–1956), Austrian conductor, General Musical Director of the Berlin State Opera from 1923 to 1935. He was already familiar with *Wozzeck* in the autumn of 1923 when he had just taken up his appointment in Berlin, but did not meet Berg personally until January 1924, when Berg played his work to Kleiber at an audition in Vienna. It was Kleiber, of course, who was to direct the première of *Wozzeck*.

Prague 1911, last year Düsseldorf. I remember now that Webern told me at the time how annoyed he was about Kleiber, who treated him in a very offhand way—which was why Webern just left him standing. Bachrich has been talking to Kleiber, who apparently said *how much he liked my opera* and that he would certainly do it.

(341)   23rd November 1923,
                                                                  afternoon

Went to lunch with Mama where I met the two girls,[1] both very friendly. I didn't tell them about Kleiber till some time after lunch —it made quite an impression.

Just now, 5 o'clock, your first letter arrived. What a horrible business, what's to be done about it?[2] Obvious thing would be to leave straight away, because *this* can't do you any good. On the other hand, you're probably right to think of waiting a week at least. And you know, darling, some things there might not be too bad—the mud-baths, massage, etc. Even if the clients and atmosphere aren't calculated to quieten your nerves, still, if you make up your mind just to ignore it and not get annoyed or feel involved, this sort of detached attitude might even help you. This is just what you have been missing all the time. Here everything affects you, affects you too much, because of your sensitive nerves. There nothing will affect you if you can manage to remedy particular defects (cold, noise, etc.). But if you find after a week that discomfort *doesn't* turn into detachment, then just finish with it.

(342)   25th November 1923

On my way to the opera première, I stopped off at Almschi's. It was again rather dull and disjointed. Křenek was there (on his way from Berlin to Breitenstein), and played the Tenth[3] to the Stefans, which I could have done without in this setting. Still, I don't regret my brief visit, as Almschi informed me, when we were

---

[1] Smaragda and May.

[2] The owners of the Parsch Sanatorium, where Helene was staying, could not afford to run it any longer and began to give the patients some sort of psychoanalytic treatment (Helene's physician is referred to later as 'Dr Sch'). See Letter 344.

[3] Ernst Křenek helped to prepare a performing edition of the first (Adagio) and *Purgatorio* movements of Mahler's unfinished Tenth Symphony, from Mahler's sketches.

alone together for five minutes, that Frau Hertzka had told her she hadn't forgotten my *Wozzeck* business. The debt will definitely be paid, whether from her private account (she always puts a bit of money aside for such purposes) or from the U.E.

The opera was a good deal better than at the dress rehearsal, and accordingly proved highly successful as well. I sat with Webern in the two pillar seats and followed the score, so that I got much more out of it than I would have done in the stalls. The thought that I shall soon be hearing it at your side, and can point out all the beauties and subtleties, made me—in my chronic sadness—happier than usual at least for these ninety minutes; even if deep depression hung over me in the next five hours.

It was quite a gathering, with dinner at Meissl and Schadn,[1] as you can see from the card. Everyone very sorry you weren't with us, especially Zemlinsky. Besides those you know, the card was signed by Elisabeth Schumann[2] from the Opera, wife of the conductor Karl Alwin, who by the way is not at all bad. Turnau[3] is the producer of *The Dwarf*. Oestvig arrived later, rather drunk (he's a terrible soak), and Loos happened to be there too. A bit later the poet Klaren,[4] librettist of *The Dwarf*, appeared in an absurd get-up, hair-style and beard (see drawing):

At first it was very tedious, just as it was in Prague, and we—Schoenberg, Webern and I—were planning to leave at a quarter to eleven. Suddenly Schoenberg became very full of energy, and it was decided to stay overnight. When I tried to leave with Webern, Schoenberg said his usual 'don't be a bore'—so I reluctantly remained, and did not manage to leave till half past one. The whole merry company went on to a café or a bar, and I got home by bus at 2.15. Feeling a bit in need of sleep, I am now sitting in the warm

---

[1] Well-known Viennese luxury restaurant.
[2] Elisabeth Schumann (1885–1952), the famous soprano.
[3] Josef Turnau, chief producer at the Vienna Opera from 1923 to 1925.
[4] Georg C. Klaren, Austrian writer.

room and writing to you. (It's my only happy time during the day.) Lunch with Jeanette, afternoon Mödling. Kisses from your lonely

Alban

(343)   26th November 1923

My daily report will be rather brief today. After lunch yesterday with Jeanette and the girls, I went out to Schoenberg's. Zemlinsky and Webern were there. Not very happy atmosphere, as always these last weeks. In fact the whole afternoon and evening was one long argument. Zemlinsky left at seven, Polnauer and Rankl came. Quite worn out (I should have slept out there!), I came home and went sadly to bed.

Your express letter has just arrived. First proviso: you mustn't get upset any more, whether you stay on or come straight home. Just pretend to obey the will of this Marquis de Sade. Accept the treatments you feel helpful, go to bed if you feel cold, and altogether give the impression that you have changed your mind about resisting. He will imagine he has tamed you. Your revenge will come, believe me. You will 'get satisfaction'. But whatever happens now, don't provoke him. As a born sadist with plenty of experience, he will always have ways of defeating you, and you can't do much against him on your own. Thank God you are an angel.

(344)   27th November 1923

Well, Jeanette arrived at 6 last night, found everything wonderful. and feels very much at home in her nice room.

Went to town to see Haslinger. Met Hauer[1] there, a poor fool in the fullest sense. Extremely poor and extremely foolish. As I still had some time, I went up to Almschi's, and she happened to be alone, so we had an interesting hour's chat: about Schoenberg, Zemlinsky, Křenek, Werfel, and her own affairs (Tenth Symphony, publishers, etc.). All this with none of the usual distractedness and rushed feeling. I learnt something rather interesting, too. Werfel's book is a 'Verdi Novel',[2] and in fact that's it's title. It's all about Verdi (his whole life) and his music. I fear that our 'quasi-friendship' will be shipwrecked on this book.

Afternoon coffee today at our flat with both mothers. Then your

[1] Josef Matthias Hauer (b. 1883), Austrian composer and music theorist, originator of system of composition based on twelve-note series, which he developed independently of Schoenberg.
[2] The final title was *Verdi, Novel of the Opera* (1924).

letter came at last, which I swallowed greedily! So Dr Sch. is in Vienna—better news, thank heaven.

You want me to write about myself. For the first time I haven't felt very fit, a slight 'flu, which has completely gone, however. But psychologically I feel I'm one big wound. I'm terribly worried about you. What will the next 'sessions' bring? If only I'd known that fellow was in Vienna. Anyhow, I'm glad you like it so much in Salzburg, and can take in some of its beauty. Have you been inside the Franciscan church, the Gothic one on the right side of the Cathedral Square? And the Castle Mountain? You simply *must* drive up there, at least up to the Stiegl brewery, and look across Salzburg. Have you seen the four Evangelists in front of the Cathedral? The Collegiate Church is more beautiful still.

Your description of the 'social life' in the evening is delicious, just as this sort of social life itself is nauseating. But take care you look down on it with amusement, sleep well at nights and in the afternoon, go for walks and excursions round Salzburg, and don't let the 'Psyche' of that Dr Sch. affect you. Then you'll soon find you've survived the week. Meanwhile I'll be cautious about Dr Sch. But once you are here, we'll discuss our plan of revenge. You yourself ask whether all this is not 'criminal'. Of course it is, that's why I'm going to punish his crimes. I'm just waiting!

I'm quite fit, as I said. I eat plenty of meat, sausages, ham, and all sorts of other good stuff. So don't worry. Mama might go back on Saturday. Although everything is going smoothly and is very friendly, I'll be glad when I'm alone again, for it's all rather distracting and time-consuming. In my room I've made things pretty comfortable for myself. I've taken two shelves out of the book-case, it's all full of writing things, a proper study—and warm! Jeanette has already ordered two sacks of coal. We aren't out of pocket either; the opposite.

Last night we had the Hindemith Quartet. Křenek's work, which I know from Salzburg, has a good deal of nice stuff, but a lot of it is immature. It got plenty of applause, and Křenek came forward to take his bow. But then Schoenberg's D minor Quartet. Really the most sublime music. How it leaves behind absolutely everything now being composed! Even Zemlinsky, not to speak of 'the boys'—but also Webern, of course. And me! These fifty minutes of music were the only beautiful ones since you left. I phoned Schoenberg this morning, and talked to him for about six minutes, without properly understanding a single thing he said. At the concert hundreds of people asked after you, of course.

(345)   29th November 1923
My only-one-in-the-world,
    Your letter yesterday would have made me so happy, but for its last sentence saying you have another 'session' ahead of you, which gave me a presentiment of all sorts of fears and terrors. I shan't learn till this afternoon what it was like, and then I shall again be just as powerless to do anything about it . . .
    Leave on Saturday, would be my advice. You'll save a lot of money, for he can't charge you more than the four days full board, whereas otherwise the four days would cost over a million Crowns. Secondly, don't go to any more 'sessions'. Tell the doctor I've forbidden it, and say that if there had been any question of psycho-analytic treatment, we should have gone to Dr Freud[1] or Dr Adler, both of whom we have known very well for many years. But we had no desire to do that at all; we went to an internal specialist instead, to whom I shall give a serious talking-to. He will have to explain himself to me, and if he was misinformed about Dr Sch., Dr Sch. had better look out. If he knew about it, however, *he'd* better look out.
    So I'm waiting for your telegram saying whether you'll come on Saturday. And now, *please*, try not to be too upset. In a week's time we shall be laughing about the crazy confidence trick of this 'psycho-analysis', and all these explanations of unfulfilled desires, sexuality, etc. A single day in the snow and woods of the Semmering will wash away all the inner dirt which has been poured into your poor clean little soul. Don't get involved, just don't answer him.
    As he can use all the filthy aids of this beastly science, psycho-analysis, and you are alone and defenceless, you are bound to submit to the butcher. But it takes two to make a marriage unhappy. For me it's a happy one, the happiest I've ever seen . . .

(346)   30th November 1923
    Why don't I simply take the train to Parsch, appear there all of a sudden, and wrest you from the claws of this vampire? I simply

[1] Berg consulted Sigmund Freud in 1908, in connection with his asthma.

335

can't bear it any more at home. My only comfort is writing to you, studying the train time-table, and imagining myself arriving in Parsch and getting my hands on that gentleman. I believe *I* could outwit him. Of course I write better than I talk, and I can do this when we are both in Vienna. But I would like to have tried him out against the two of us together, to see whether his crazy ideas, which might apply well enough to stupid whores, don't collapse miserably against us two. I mean all these ideas of unfulfilled desires and obscenities about 'glands' and similar pseudo-science, invented by the 'prostate': the brain of a psycho-analyst. Well, I've not given this plan up yet, but for the moment I'll wait for the post. Perhaps you'll write that you are leaving on Saturday, then I shan't need to go out there. But how shall I live through the hours, constantly looking out for the postman, my heart thumping, full of sadness?

In this mood I went to the Leider-concert with Jeanette. Incredibly boring, even if I'd been in a better frame of mind. This antiquated Wagner music (*Rienzi, Dutchman, Faust* overture) in the concert-hall! And the singing. A very good voice, though not a big one (which wouldn't matter to me), very well trained, assured and controlled, everything you could ask of the *instrument*, female voice. But completely soulless, in a way I wouldn't have thought possible. Not a note which touches the heart. Also completely colourless, without any modulation or adaptability to such simple musical qualities as you can find in the music: e.g. tragic, heroic, frightening, grand, lyrical, etc. Everything quite monotonous. Her appearance matched that lack of expression—the face looked completely disengaged the whole evening. Thin applause, although it was well attended, and I dare say the critics will have thought much the same as I did.

I'll post this letter at once, and go on writing at lunch-time or in the evening.

With many kisses, my little angel, waiting anxiously for your letter,

Your own

(347)   14th May 1925
Here, my Pferscherl, is *The Castle* by Franz Kafka. Wish I could buy you a real one.[1]

[1] Berg bought his wife a copy of the first edition of Kafka's novel before his departure for the Third International Festival of the I.S.C.M. at Prague.

Above, Berg standing between Adrian Boult (left) and Edward J. Dent (right) at a meeting of the jury for the Ninth Festival of the I.S.C.M. at Cambridge, England, in 1931 [see Letter 398]; *right*, a photograph of (left to right) Werfel, Helene Berg, Alban Berg, Countess Gravina, Margarete Hauptmann and Gerhart Hauptmann in Rapallo; *below*, Alfredo Casella (left), Franz Werfel, Alban Berg and Francesco Malipiero in Alma Mahler-Werfel's garden, 1932 [see Letter 424]

Alban and Helene Berg

My golden one,

How am I to tell you all there is to tell? I am living here quite simply in the villa of the Fuchs family;[1] but the musical life of the whole world is surging round me,[2] so that my brain is on fire. Here are the most important things. Kleiber is here for one day, conducts tonight and leaves tomorrow. I had a long talk to him about *Wozzeck*, and the thing is now firm.[3] All the roles cast twice and three times over, we discussed everything. There's nothing to stop us now! I have already talked to a hundred people I know, talked in all languages (my *Quartet* is being played in Moscow!), and feel pretty respected and distinguished! You may have seen the music magazine *Auftakt*[4] with my picture in it. At 6.15 tomorrow evening there's a piano rehearsal with Zemlinsky and Garmo,[5] Monday and Tuesday short orchestral rehearsals.

I can't help enjoying the matter-of-course luxury of this life. Oh, if I could only offer it to you! Every step I take—I don't take myself! All done by car, and what a car! My hosts spoil me: room with hot water, glorious view, Roger Galet soap, Venetian blinds, so that you can sleep with the windows open at night. At seven a breakfast trolley is wheeled to my bed, and I can't eat enough of these rolls (they would be something for you!). At eight a knock on the door, and in burst the two children, who won't be satisfied unless they can at last see the 'famous' composer. A seven-year-old boy a girl of 3½. Very sweet, I found them most refreshing. Then I was taken to the theatre, where I spent some time with Zemlinsky, and from there to Frau Werfel.[6] Then to a rehearsal of Casella and Kleiber's, then back again to the theatre (on the way I met Frau Zemlinsky). Brought home by car, good lunch, and now an hour's rest. I'll give you full details in Vienna!

Everyone asks after you and regrets that I came alone. Can't people guess that I'm not at all alone, talking to them?

---

[1] Herbert Fuchs-Robettin, Prague industrialist and musical enthusiast, married to Franz Werfel's sister (Mopinka).

[2] The *Three Fragments from Wozzeck* were performed (under Zemlinsky) at the Festival. Their first performance had taken place on 11th June 1924 at the 54th Festival of the Allgemeine Deutsche Musik-Verein at Frankfurt under Scherchen.

[3] That the Berlin State Opera will undertake the première of *Wozzeck*.

[4] A progressive music monthly, published in Prague.

[5] Tilly de Garmo, coloratura soprano of the German Opera in Prague.

[6] Mother of Frau Fuchs and Franz Werfel.

(349)   Prague, 16th May 1925
    First orchestral concert last night: very mediocre to quite
worthless works. This morning, after very good night, motor drive
into the beautiful countryside. Midday, from twelve to four, at
Werfel's mother's. Now, after an hour's rest, I'm going to the
piano rehearsal with Zemlinsky and de Garmo. Oh yes, after 'my'
performance on Wednesday we are all invited by the banker
Freund, whose wife, née Gallos, knows you well through Frau
Brandt.
    I hoped in vain for a letter from you today. It seems such an age
since I left. I am longing for you so much, my Swipol. The Czech
Opera (Ostrčil[1]) wants to acquire *Wozzeck* for the 1925–6 season.
It's already on the programme for Brno (Neumann[2]).

(350)   Prague, 17th May 1925
My Pferscherl,
    Zemlinsky is a colossal chap. How he gets hold of the *Fragments*,
even at the piano. With such passion it makes it even more thrilling
—if that's possible. He had an orchestra rehearsal yesterday, but
didn't want me there, as the orchestra had forgotten everything
again. Tomorrow, Monday, there's an orchestra rehearsal with
de Garmo, who is rather good (specially on the purely vocal parts)
and me. I'll have the chance then to bring up all my wishes about
the orchestra. Tuesday morning there is a more or less public
dress rehearsal, as so many critics and musicians might not be
able to attend the actual performance on Wednesday (including
Korngold!).
    We had dinner last night at a small restaurant, then an amusing
visit to a bar, and at midnight home by car. Today, Sunday, it's
already terribly hot at nine o'clock. Thank heavens I'm in such a
comfortable house with special summer amenities. In the town I
would have died. When I hear from you, I'll write a nice long letter.
Now I'm three days without one. Tomorrow will be the fourth.

[1] Otokar Ostrčil (1879–1935), chief conductor of the Czech National Theatre
in Prague.
[2] František Neumann (1874–1929), chief conductor of the Czech National
Theatre in Brno.

338

Prague, Monday
18th May 1925

My golden one, your letter has only just arrived, and it would probably be too late anyhow for you to come. Of course I had hoped deep down that you would be here, but I would certainly never have advised you. Particularly as you suggest leaving on Wednesday morning; that would mean getting up at 4.30, train from 7 to 2.30 in the heat, a short rest in Bubeneč[1] (and even then we should be talking nineteen to the dozen), at 7 to the theatre, at 10 or 10.30 a big party staying up till at least 2 a.m. Then travelling back next day, could I really have *advised* you to do that? It would have been criminal. Anyway, I put the passport out, just in case! You can get a visa in two to four hours, and tickets in the station itself. Only full price, though; it would have been too late to try for a reduced rate. But as I said, you will already have decided one way or the other, perhaps with advice and help from Wiesengrund.[2] If you come, you can stay *here*, of course. I had only to mention the possibility of your carrying out such a daring exploit for the Fuchses' and also Frau Werfel to offer you hospitality. No, I would have no worries on that score, only about your health, your poor nerves.

Orchestra rehearsal this morning. Zemlinsky does it wonderfully, of course, as far as the music is concerned; the orchestra is technically faultless, and most of the time plays with deep feeling. But the acoustics of the house made me unhappy in some parts. And there were also critics there today. De Garmo vocally very fine, but not nearly so dramatically effective as Sutter.[3] Tomorrow morning dress rehearsal, Wednesday evening performance. I shall be taking the train at midday on Thursday, and shall be in Vienna that night. Please sleep all afternoon and from nine to twelve at night, so that my arrival doesn't upset you. I am at the main post office and want both express letters to get to Vienna tomorrow morning. Hence my haste and not putting anything more in the letter than this—and a thousand kisses.

---

[1] Suburb of Prague where the Fuchs family lived.

[2] Dr Theodor Wiesengrund-Adorno, musicologist and philosopher, a pupil of Berg's.

[3] The soprano Beatrice Sutter-Kottlar sang in the first performance of the *Fragments* in Frankfurt.

(352)   Prague, 19th May 1925

My golden one,

I'm very surprised indeed not to have heard from you today.
What can it mean? Are you perhaps on your way to Prague? But
you will let me know, I hope. The very thought makes my heart
thump madly. May I wish for it? It would be madness indeed,
though lovely madness.

In case you have stayed in Vienna, I just want to give you a
hasty report of anything important. Yesterday afternoon I spent
mainly in the post office, writing the express letter to you then to the
Café Arco (!),[1] where Dolbin[2] did a portrait of me while I wrote a
few cards. Kastner[3] of the *Vossische Zeitung*, Berlin commissioned a
sketch (not a caricature).

In the evening to the Czech National Theatre (without the
Fuchs family, as one of their relatives has had a serious operation,
so they're not going out much) to see *The Cunning Little Vixen* by
Janáček, the composer of *Jenufa*.[4] A very beautiful theatre, like a

[1] Regular meeting-place of the Prague literary circle.
[2] Berlin painter and cartoonist.
[3] Berlin critic.
[4] *Příhody Lišky Bistroušky* (1921–23), comic opera by Leoš Janáček (1854–
1928), whose opera *Jenufa* (*Její pastorkyna*) had become a world-wide success.

court theatre, marvellous orchestra, faultless production, mediocre singers.

10 p.m., dinner with the Fuchs family at home. He has got the most wonderful wine in the world. But I am very moderate in my drinking, so that I have up till now spent these days in Prague without feeling muzzy, short of sleep or headaches.

This morning at half past nine I was driven to the theatre. Dress rehearsal went very well. Zemlinsky obviously enthusiastic, the orchestra applauded, and the singer too very fine. Great array of critics there, headed by Korngold. Polnauer and Eisler from Vienna.

Returning home at midday, I found no letter from you, which disappointed me *very* badly. Since I've been here, I've had only two short pages from you, while I've written about thirty. That's sad for me . . .

(353)   Franz Joseph station, 7 a.m.[1]
                              (11th November 1925)
Still time, my darling, to send you a thousand kisses. They've just told me that I've got my hat on back to front!

All my love, and give me your loving thoughts.

                                              Your own

(354)   11th November 1925
The taxi-ride to the station consisted in my banging the door of the wretched cab shut about seventeen times, and holding it with my hand for the rest of the ride. I only just got to the station in time. I'm so sad that I didn't leave you a few chocolates behind which you wouldn't be able to resist. For I'm afraid you won't eat properly while I'm away. But I was so distraught yesterday that I forgot the most obvious things, and today it was too late. Promise you'll be a very good girl and eat plenty! Come to that, I promise I'll be a good boy!

It goes against the grain, really, to have to 'reassure' you about me and Mopinka. Perhaps I'll just say that faithfulness is one of my main qualities (I'm sure I must have been a dog in a previous incarnation, and perhaps shall be in a later one, but anyhow, to

[1] Setting off for Berlin (via Prague), for rehearsals of the first *Wozzeck* production.

341

start from the beginning, may I die of distemper if I ever sin against faithfulness!). Faithfulness towards you, and also towards myself, Music, Schoenberg (and *he* makes this really hard for one), even towards Trahütten. As for that, now the green and brown country-side flies past, I feel remorseful almost to be forgetting holy Trahütten—in these days of fighting for my art, of ambition, thirst for fame and the chase after money. (But when the hurly-burly is over, nothing shall stop me from staying at least three months up there!)

So: being of such a conservative disposition, how could I help, my darling, be anything but faithful to you and remain faithful for ever? Believe me, as I believe the same of you. I hope to post this letter at Schwarzenau, where the train stops for three minutes. The next letter will come from Prague, then a telegram from Berlin.

Now I want to thank you a thousand times for all the trouble and rush you had with me this morning. Everything is now perfectly all right. My nerves are quite calm now as I sit in the train, and everything will go according to plan. A thousand kisses, my dearest.

Your own

(355) Prague, 11th November 1925,
evening—in bed

My Pferscherl,

Just to report briefly: Herbert Fuchs came to the station. Terribly kind of him, and he at once invited me to stay with them on my way back from Berlin as well. We reached his house at half past two, I sent him off to have his usual snooze, went to my room and had a rest myself. At half past four we all met for coffee (he told me lunch had been prepared for me, but I declined as I was full up with the food you gave me for the journey). Mopinka also appeared then with the children. The boy is growing fast, the girl is sickly, though, and looks ill—not even pretty because of that. But still such a dear that you would certainly like her. Altogether, once you meet these people, you'll like them just as much as I do. It's really a friendliness and warmheartedness without any holding back. That's why, that's the only reason why I'm so fond of them. And you will feel the same.

You know, my darling, why I'm making so much of this. Not

342

because it's so terrific here (my thoughts are already in Berlin), but to stop you worrying about Mopinka's charms!

After coffee we played with the children almost the whole time. Then dinner: lobster eggs, grouse with potatoes and apple sauce, cheese, fruit—and a superb wine! Herbert and I drank a whole bottle. After that a magnificent brandy. Blame the wine and the brandy for the fact that I'm nearly asleep. It's half past ten. Good night! Tomorrow a few lines from Berlin.

(356)   12th November 1925,
                                        on the train to Berlin

We're now about an hour and a half from Berlin, and I've occupied myself so far with *Wozzeck* production problems. Tonight I may be too tired to write, and tomorrow I probably shan't have a minute free, so although there's little to say I'll write a few lines now, and perhaps finish the letter after my arrival.

I slept well and got up late (about 9). Before that I had a wonderful coffee in bed with Prague croissants and jam. Then Munzo, the little boy, came into my room. Spent most of the morning with the children, did some work and chatted, had an early lunch and went to the station soon afterwards. Bad journey to start with: several Czech peasants got in at each station, and were with us for one or two stops. Meanwhile, there was a wet, cold snow-storm outside. But after the German frontier things were excellent, pleasant fellow passengers.

And how's my Pferschi? Hope to find a letter or card from you when I get to Berlin! Schmid was waiting for me at the Anhalter Station in Berlin, also an assistant of Kleiber's. The three of us went into a café, drank a glass of beer, and they gave me all the news. The cast is splendid. Schützendorf, a top star in Berlin, Johanson a very young, brilliant singer instead of Strozzi, Koettrik as Margaret, Soot, a real *Heldentenor* as the Drum Major;[1] a wonderful Captain, two very good artisans; the Doctor not a very good character actor, apparently, but a very fine voice. So I can be well content. Tomorrow at ten there's a big rehearsal with the main parts. A delightful little girl as the Boy. Terrific anticipation in Berlin. Only Pfitzner, whose *Palestrina* is being newly produced, is very much

[1] Leo Schützendorf, Sigrid Johanson, Jessyka Koettrik and Fritz Soot were all members of the Berlin State Opera.

against us.[1] Wonderful sets, they say. And in the orchestra all I could wish for.

First night: 14th December.

It's 1 a.m., so good-night, my darling.

(357)   Berlin, Friday
                                                  13th November 1925
I spent my first rehearsal with Kleiber, Schützendorf and Witting (Andres), Marie and child, under the megalomaniac impression that *Wozzeck* is something really great, and that accordingly the performance too will be something really great. I never dreamed I could find such understanding as a musician and dramatist as I am finding with Kleiber; and of course this gets transmitted to the singers, who are almost all first-class. The sets (at least on paper) are magnificent, the direction (and what direction!) is really Kleiber's, and Hörth's[2] part in it has been reduced to a minimum. Everybody concerned is enthusiastic in the highest degree. I can confidently leave everything to Kleiber.

This morning Schmid fetched me from the hotel, and took me to the theatre. Then I was with Kleiber till 2. Had a marvellous lunch, followed by a bit of a rest in the hotel, and I'm now in a café writing this hasty note, then to a second rehearsal: doctor, artisans and again the Wozzeck-Marie scenes. Going to a big party with Kleiber tonight.

Tomorrow rehearsal with piano, visit to Schillings.[3] Leave on Sunday morning, Sunday afternoon till midday Monday in Prague, evening (or late at night, rather) in my Pferscherl's arms—some time between 12 and 12.30. I'm feeling very excited except that I'm much too tired.

Kisses from your 'great' husband—only by greatness can he be worthy of you.

---

[1] Hans Pfitzner had written a pamphlet *The New Aesthetics of Musical Impotence* to which Berg wrote a scathing retort: *The Musical Impotence of Hans Pfitzner's New Aesthetics*.

[2] Franz Ludwig Hörth, chief producer of the Berlin State Opera.

[3] Max von Schillings (1868–1933), General Musical Director of the Berlin State Opera, who resigned his post in November 1925 after a protracted crisis and thereby endangered Kleiber's position.

(358)   30th November 1925,
                                               in the train from Vienna
                                                        to Berlin[1]

My golden one, the journey is going according to plan. Half of
it is behind me. I read the paper first, then attended to 'duty
letters': Schoenberg—I tell him that you are informing me every
day about the state of his health (so please do so!); greetings to the
Fuchs family while passing through Prague (where I'll post everything, and thank Herbert Fuchs for his letter and the invitation
to you) . . .

(359)   Undated
                                               (30th November 1925)
                                               in the train to Berlin,
                                                      late afternoon

By now you will have received the first letter, which I posted in
Prague. I have become unbearably tired. For an hour or two
beyond Prague it was all right, but then I just could not sit there
any longer. On top of that the heat—for the last seven hours, in my
warm suit, I have been bathed in sweat. Eventually at four I went to
have some tea, which anyhow refreshed me enough to allow me to
write a little to you now (4.45). In a quarter of an hour we cross the
German border, tell you about it later. In the last light of the day
a glorious snowy landscape is gliding past outside: between Leitmeritz and Schreckenstein,[2] which seem completely German
places, even scenically. My eyes and senses weary, I thought of
Trahütten, to which I have become so disgracefully unfaithful—
but by God, or at least by St. Cecilia, I'll return there as a penitent.
We are now in Dresden.

In Bodenbach we had our baggage checked. Everything goes so
smoothly and slowly you really needn't worry, even if you travelled
by yourself. So have no fears on that score. Also there are very few
people travelling these days, the train is half empty. In Dresden I
bought the *B.Z. am Mittag*[3] and found my name on the front page.
I feel very calm, and shall resign myself quite peacefully to the
coming $3\frac{1}{2}$ hour's journey. (Equivalent to Vienna-Graz.) Oh dear,
there I am again with my thoughts on Trahütten.

[1] On the way to Berlin for the last rehearsals and opening night of *Wozzeck*.
[2] Leitmeritz, Schreckenstein and Bodenbach are towns in Northern Bohemia.
[3] *Berliner Zeitung am Mittag*, a popular afternoon paper.

345

If only the Theatre doesn't economize too much, that is, doesn't start its economies over the production of *Wozzeck*!

Once more, Pferscherl, please send a few lines every day saying how you are and how you slept . . .

(360)   Berlin, 1st December 1925

I believe it is a good sign that my stay here has not started well (compare Frankfurt 1923!). Schmid was at the station; I dashed off to another platform where the express to Vienna was standing, to post my second letter to you (which you'll therefore be getting today), then hurried to the hotel near the station, where I was oaving my luggage taken. There I learned that because of the Motor Show they hadn't got a room available (there isn't a hotel room in Berlin!) and that they had reserved me one in a *pension*. Meanwhile the porters brought the three bags—so I could have saved the money, as in any case I had to take a taxi now. Went with Schmid and the luggage to the Pension Steinplatz (very near to Schreker's place[1])—3-Mark fare. One of the biggest and best *pensions* in Berlin, where I took the cheapest and also the most primitive room. A big ball was taking place and it went on the whole night. There was a sort of bathroom next to me, dancers going home, music, etc. (That would have been something for you, wouldn't it!). Still, thanks to a glass of beer and some ear plugs, I slept quite well, from 1 to 7, and am really feeling quite fresh this morning after a good breakfast, which is included in the price of the room. Now I must start telephoning. Habsburgerhof Hotel, where they think I'm staying, Kleiber, Frau Herz,[2] perhaps Schreker. It's nine now. Who knows when I'll have another chance to write!

Half an hour later. I have done the 'phoning! Kleiber didn't know I'd arrived, and was surprised but very pleased; asked me to a rehearsal for orchestra and singers, second half of the second act, and third act. Imagine—in an hour's time I'll hear my score! If only you were with me! At lunch-time I'll be with Kleiber, who is charming as ever. Then I 'phoned Frau Herz, who sounds very nice on the 'phone, and will be delighted to see me at any time. So I'll go out there in the afternoon, when we aren't rehearsing, and how I'm

[1] Franz Schreker (1878–1934); Berg had made the vocal score of his opera *Der ferne Klang* (1912).
[2] An aunt of Schoenberg's pupil, Seligmann, from Frankfurt.

346

looking forward to being in a private house (a *pension* is the most horrible thing in the world; in comparison a hotel is pure gold). As Kleiber is going to the Czech Embassy in the evening, and Frau Herz to a party, I might go and see the *Ferne Klang*—but I'll ring Schreker before that.

Half past midnight

Be glad you weren't at the first rehearsal! True, I had the joy of at last hearing the thing played by the orchestra, but I also had the torment of all the points which are still wrong. If I didn't know that one can't judge after such a rehearsal, I should be very apprehensive, if not downright depressed. But from everybody's assurances, and above all from the terrific eagerness of all concerned, I'm sure everything will be all right and just as I imagined it. Quite a lot is wonderful for sound, almost the whole of Act I (one 'gem' after another). Several things in the second act were good too. The orchestra itself is really marvellous. But will Kleiber be able to follow my intentions, as he is not going to rehearse any more with the orchestra alone, but always with the singers on stage? There are not many more orchestral rehearsals. Now there is a three days break, because he has a contract with the orchestra (Mozart). The next orchestral rehearsal isn't till Saturday, and then every day from Monday on. Not excessive to my mind! Tomorrow, Wednesday, I'm having stage rehearsals with Hörth, also Thursday and Friday, when I hope to get the singers absolutely perfect. Especially the music in the Inn Scene, which is quite impossible so far and gives me real headaches. Please don't talk about my doubts too much, and also be careful on the telephone when you're reporting to Stein. Say it's going to be a tough nut to crack but that we'll manage it.

Two to three, lunch with Kleiber, who is standing above the crisis. At the *pension* from 3.15 till 4.15, and slept a bit. Then to Dahlem,[1] half an hour or three quarters by car; seemed hours and cost about 6 Marks—wished I'd stayed at the *pension*! Coffee with Frau Herz in Dahlem at five, then hastily got out my evening things; to the underground at six, and nearly late for the Opera (at seven). An hour from Dahlem to the Opera—that's hopeless. Frau Herz is around fifty and must have been very beautiful once, still has something very pretty about her face. Apparently there's no master of the house, and the children are abroad. She has a car,

---

[1] Elegant residential district in the south-western part of Berlin.

and I can spend 'millions' in car fares, unless I sacrifice three or four hours, say for changing.

Tomorrow morning she is driving to town with me. I rehearse till 1.30, find somewhere for lunch 2 to 3, at 3.30 rehearsal of the Inn Scene band, 6.30 to 8 rehearsal with the singers, in the evening invited to the Kleibers. So between 3.30 and 6.30, instead of having a rest, I've got to rush around for three hours, change in an hour, perhaps drink some rather nasty tea with her. The hospitality here can't be compared with Frankfurt or Prague!

She told me in the afternoon that after the theatre I should go and have my supper somewhere, and she will have me fetched from there in her car, so that I can then go back with her to Dahlem— as I wouldn't get home too easily from the underground station: a quarter of an hour's walk through the snow. This 'somewhere', however, was about as far as Hütteldorf,[1] and I could never have found it without a car—it was Dernburg's home.[2] Instead of my being taken there in her car, which really has nothing to do but drive her around, I again had to pay 5 Marks for a taxi. Of course I was presented to everyone (in grey trousers and dark jacket, all the other men were in tails). I got some ridiculous little sandwich and a glass of beer (all this in a sort of palace with hundreds of guests), and eventually got taken home. My rooms are marvellous, though, and I get service front and rear. For you and me together there are superb adjoining rooms, and a separate bathroom—only it's not at all home-like. If things go on being as tiring and expensive as today, I'll move to the hotel with you. You could manage these jaunts in the snow even less than I can.

Der ferne Klang had a good production, but the opera is awful. I spoke to Schreker on the 'phone, and he evidently felt he must be on his dignity. On the other hand, Hörth was tremendously charming and seems 'sold' on me and my work—he paid me heaps of compliments anyhow. After the theatre I had a cheap supper at a café, then to Dernburg, as I said. It's now 1.45 a.m., so good-night, Pferscherl.

2nd December 1925, 10 a.m.

Breakfast was marvellous: a complete lunch! Slept very well, a thousand kisses.

[1] Viennese suburb.
[2] Bernhard Dernburg, member of the Reichstag, later German Chancellor of the Exchequer.

p.s. In case of a mail strike: even if I don't hear from you any more, I'm expecting you on Wednesday 9th December at the Anhalter Station. Travel to Prague on Tuesday 8th, and you'll find post from me there. Stay at the Fuchses' from Tuesday midday till Wednesday, then come on to Berlin, where on Thursday I shall have such infinite happiness to lay my work at your feet.

(361)   Berlin, 2nd December 1925,
                                                            afternoon
    I hasten to report to you on this *Wozzeck* day. Stage rehearsals with piano, without sets, only the necessary props, walls and singers. A rehearsal pianist at the piano, regisseur, chief designer, prompter and stage manager (as a sort of audience), but all behind the closed curtain. Impression, despite breaks and going over things again, terrific, overwhelmingly powerful. All the singers marvellous. Schützendorf superb. The Captain—not an outstanding voice but characterization a delight. The Doctor—not a very intelligent singer, but a wonderful voice, and quite up to this 'unsingable' part. Johanson also very good. So if Kleiber succeeds, as he will, in getting the last bit out of the orchestra, we shall have a really remarkable production. Today I feel once more that it will be something absolutely fantastic. Hörth is tremendously nice to me, because—he keeps telling me—he is simply bowled over by my work.
    This afternoon there's a very important rehearsal with guitar and accordion players, and clarinettists, so I hope the stage band will be good too.
    All this in great haste, just to counteract my pessimistic letter of this morning. More tonight.

(362)   2nd December 1925,
                                                      half past midnight
    Summary of the day's proceedings: 10 a.m. Frau Herz took me in her car to the bus; I rode south for half an hour towards the town, but she had put me on the wrong bus (and she'd gone on, of course, in her luxurious car); to avoid being late for the stage rehearsal, I had to take a taxi from Potsdam Square to the Opera (1.50 Marks). I told you this afternoon about the rehearsal. Meanwhile I have got Kleiber to put on another orchestra rehearsal for clearing up odd

mistakes. He is all-powerful at the moment, so I can prevail on him to do almost anything.

Stage rehearsal till two, and directly after it a rehearsal for the Inn Scene band. Everything with the musicians: successful! After such a good breakfast I only had a couple of sausages for lunch, particularly as a huge dinner awaits me tonight. I had them during the rehearsal, as it lasted till four. After that, since I was passing his house, it seemed a good opportunity to make a call on Schreker. His wife was very nice, he rather patronizing, though cordial and very much the honest colleague. He quite agreed with my refusing the position for 550 Marks.[1] In a year, or two years at latest, they might offer me a professorial appointment at 800 Marks; perhaps even earlier. The chap who got my position teaches not very interesting minor subjects. I stayed with the Schrekers about three quarters of an hour, and might go there again one of these evenings.

To go out to Dahlem to change, drink a cup of tea and make conversation, all in three quarters of an hour, didn't seem worth the money. I preferred to have two hours' rest in the Museum Café, so had a good wash there, turned my cuffs, and went to my dinner party, though not in evening dress. At the café, I also wrote my short letter about today's rehearsals. Schmid arrived there, also Rufer, who is writing an article about me in the *Vossiche Zeitung*. At eight I was off to this dinner with some tremendously rich friends of Kleiber's, Frieda Leider and her husband (the leader of the orchestra, a friend of Kleiber's), Kleiber and myself. Very jolly and informal, magnificent food and drink.

Kleiber brought me your express letter. What joy to hear such dear, familiar, loving words. To give you latest news and stop you worrying about the Schillings crisis at the State Opera, I'll send you a telegram tomorrow—you may not get this letter—because of the postal strike. They take a much calmer view of the crisis here. The press is only printing things unfavourable to Kleiber. He is still conducting three times before the 14th, so we shall see if the audiences are against him. I don't notice any sort of friction in the company or the orchestra—far from it. They feel too strongly what a big personality he is. And it would be sheer lunacy to give up the chance of a production with Kleiber, Schützendorf and the orchestra (though that could still happen even at 6 p.m. on the 14th!). By the way,

---

[1] Berg was offered a minor teaching post at the Berlin Hochschule für Musik, whose director Schreker had been since 1920. He refused it because of the low salary.

there is a Wagner orchestra concert that night at the same time, with Frau Kemp;[1] so the enemies will go there!

Home at midnight. I took a taxi, paid for by the State Opera (Kleiber is getting a fortnight's expenses for me). It's now 1.30, I'll switch off the light and reach out with my right hand to where Pferscherl is sleeping. Good-night.

(363)   Thursday, 3rd December 1925,
                                                                at night

It's comparatively early today, 11.30. Physically I feel rather well, thanks to the quiet at night (have never felt such a peaceful atmosphere before) and the good air. I'm living in a winter fairyland, and when I notice it amidst all my worries and work, I can hardly believe my eyes.

The day was sad, as I had no letter from my Swaprunk. Hope there will be one tomorrow. Stage rehearsal pretty successful again. Particularly the cradle-song scene with the child, who is delightful. The last Inn Scene also very good, but the big Inn Scene isn't quite satisfactory yet, although the staging is all right and full of brilliant touches. But I am afraid the musical side gets a bit lost because of all the production and acting details. Besides which, the stage band is still bad, my biggest problem child, despite all the extra rehearsals. 'What is going to happen?' says Wozzeck. Oh yes—the guard-room scene is very good.[2]

I'll be glad when Kleiber has his concert behind him. It's tomorrow night. Saturday he is starting again with the orchestra. I wonder whether the audience tomorrow will show any feelings for or against him. He was very upset today about these impertinent reports in the *Stunde*[3]—although it is hardly read here. He'll get his lawyer to have an apology printed.

Was there anything about *Wozzeck* in the Vienna papers? The management is going to send out invitations for complimentary tickets, and wants me to suggest a few people—professionals in drama and music, of course—so I can make things easier for anybody who comes. This afternoon I was interviewed. For a special issue of the State Opera Magazine programme, which is being given away free to every member of the audience. The photograph, one

[1] Barbara Kemp, German soprano, wife of Max von Schillings.
[2] *Wozzeck*, act II, scene v.
[3] A Viennese lunch-time paper.

351

taken by a woman here about three weeks ago, shows me as a grumpy old thing (which I am, too!) but its quite good. I went to see the photographer tonight and got a print of it. There will also be three stage photos published in the magazine, with this article about me.

After that I was at the café with Schmid, Eisler, and Rufer. At 10 p.m. home by underground and then a walk through the snow. A funny life, but not very agreeable. You got my telegram, I hope. I was a bit worried because of the postal strike. Thank heaven that's over.—Now it's just midnight. I'll sleep till eight, at nine to town again, then rehearsals from ten to three.

(364)   Friday night 4–5th
                                        December, 1 a.m.
. . . Today I'm more optimistic again about *Wozzeck*. A magnificent accordion player, an American virtuoso. So the biggest danger is eliminated. Then rehearsal with the Doctor, very good vocally, *bel canto* as I wanted it. Everything singable. In the evening Kleiber concert with big ovations for Kleiber (Schillings is already beginning to retire). A Mozart programme, very fine. Dinner with Schmid afterwards, and home by underground and foot. A harsh, severe winter. But I feel very well, thanks to the vest you gave me!

(365)   Saturday night 5th–6th
                                        December 1925, 1.30 a.m.
A letter from Pferschi came, lovely to have, even though it's a sad one. My longing for you is so intense, and the only thing that makes our separation a little easier to bear is the knowledge that you aren't missing anything at the present stage of the *Wozzeck* rehearsals, in fact you're being spared a lot of anxiety and apprehensions. Otherwise I sometimes feel terribly lonely amidst the crowd. In Dahlem most of all. Tonight the lady of the house gave a dinner, mostly very dull people, although (or because?) they were very aristocratic and very rich. Anyhow these five or six hours were rather dismal. I wish I knew how to get away from here, it's quite senseless my staying. Most tiring for me, as I'm up for 16 to 18 hours without any time for rest. Now I'm alone it's not too bad, but when you come I shall probably take you to a nice hotel room. There we might stay very comfortably, probably near the Opera; we shan't

Right, one of the last photographs of Berg, taken in 1935; *below*, Anna Mahler's head of Alban Berg; *below right*, profile of Anna Mahler's sculpture

Berg's study at the Waldhaus, an arrangement by Helene Berg which commemorates her husband's death on December 24th, 1935; *below*, Berg's deathmask by Anna Mahler

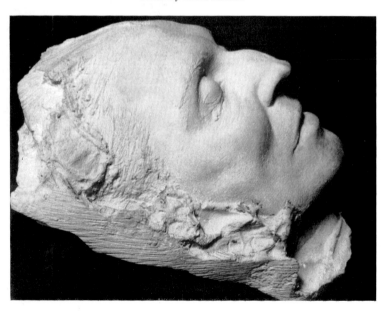

spend more money than here, and can sleep late in the mornings, as there is no stage rehearsal till 10.30. We can go home every afternoon and have time to change in comfort.

Today there was a rehearsal for the Inn Scene band, which went quite well; but the orchestral rehearsal with the complete stage 'effects' was really chaotic, I really don't know how everything's going to work in a week's time. My only comfort is that Kleiber himself is a perfectionist. Particularly in this case, where he stands or falls by the success of the first night, and therefore knows he must have his perfection *in time*. The sets are very beautiful.

I spent part of the afternoon with Schmid at the café. I'm glad I have somebody, a friend and a musician, to talk things over with. Towards evening I went out with him to Dahlem, where I changed into a dinner jacket and spent this dull evening.

At 10.30 tomorrow morning I go with Kleiber to a big musical discussion about *Wozzeck*; then to a lunch party at his house. Tomorrow night I'll write you my last letter to Vienna, the next will be to Prague. What balm to have you with me again at last!

Your lonely
Miffka

I am definitely moving away from here when you come. Shall we go to the Hotel Continental, where Almschi is staying?

p.s. My Pferscherl, be at the station soon after one, as otherwise you won't be among the first passengers let through the barrier. The train leaves at 1.40, a large coach going direct to Prague stops right by the barrier. Pferschi, give me your best and fondest thoughts. I have a single goal, a good *Wozzeck* production, and a single joyful expectation, to lay it at your feet act by act on Monday and Tuesday. Kisses!

Your own

(366)   Monday, 7th December 1925,
                                                        at night

Another strenuous day behind me. And this time a profitable one for *Wozzeck*. How fine my favourite scene sounds, the jewel scene![1] Today we had the whole of Act 2. The Inn Scene is still a bit of a problem—getting a thing like that really satisfactory. Well, you'll soon hear and see, my golden one. I do wonder what you'll say. Perhaps you'll be disappointed at first, expecting an absolutely

---

[1] *Wozzeck*, act II, scene i.

AB–Y   353

perfect performance. Through all the rehearsals my anxiety over your health has been like a slight nagging ache. It seems to me that you aren't as well as you say you are (more ill, in fact, catarrh and other things). I hope you are reading this letter in Prague, where you will certainly feel in good form—best greetings from me to all four members of the Fuchs family. Tell them the dress rehearsal is on Saturday morning at 11, and they should leave if possible not later than Friday night. To hear it only once is not enough, it's terribly hard to understand. I am expecting *you* on Wednesday night at the Anhalter station. We'll go to a hotel near the Opera, and stay there the rest of the time. Dahlem is out of the question for us. More about this when I see you. Kisses, my dearest, and at last, at last, auf Wiedersehen!

p.s. I am quite fit, despite working 16 hours a day, despite having irregular (but adequate) meals, walking through deep snow for two hours, and insufficient sleep. Today, for instance, I left before nine, was already working on the score in the underground; 10 to 11 stage music, 11 to 2 second Act, 2 to 3 production meeting, 3 to 5 lunch and talk 'shop' with Schmid, 5 to 8 with Kleiber, discussing all the tempi. Accompanied him to the Kroll Opera,[1] where we listened to a guest singer, 9.30 to 12.30 with Kleiber and Arravantinos (designer of the sets—a real artist too![2]), at the restaurant. Then home by underground and through the snow with 10 lbs. of score under my arm. I am now in bed at 1.30 a.m., finishing this last letter to Schnudoa, who by this time the day after tomorrow will be by my side. Tomorrow morning I'll 'give notice' here for the following day —a most awkward and embarrassing business.

(367)   8th June 1927,
                                         still in Austria[3]

Of course there has to be a dining-car in this train—and I have to discover it after eating the ham and the oranges! In our compartment for eight there are four of us, including a dear little girl. I couldn't deny myself afternoon coffee in the dining-car. Temperature reasonable; occupation, reading the papers. Any wrongs done to me seem to bring retribution some time. For instance, that man

[1] Berlin had at this time three opera houses: the State Opera, the Municipal Opera (Charlottenburg), and the Kroll Opera, which was under the direction of Otto Klemperer.
[2] Panos Arravantinos (1886–1930), chief stage designer of the Berlin Opera.
[3] On the way to the Leningrad première of *Wozzeck*.

354

Höllering,[1] who started as an orchestra attendant and has become a theatre manager, has gone bust. Bankruptcy, prosecution, etc. And as for la Kittel,[2] they are now spitting in her face. Real Strindbergian retributions!

Other newspaper items: Deutsch-Landsberg is flooded; half of all Austrian school-children suffer from goitrous conditions; at the first night of *Der ferne Klang* (night before last) a singer fell down a flight of steps and had to be carried off.

You'll be interested in the enclosed article on Stifter;[3] please keep it for me—rather like a selection from my own reading. Outside, the gently undulating countryside flies past. When shall we two enjoy it again together? . . .

(368)   8th June 1927,
                                                somewhere in Poland
                                                        (Petrovice)

The frontier between Czechoslovakia and Poland. It's 10 p.m., I had an excellent dinner and am now going to bed. At 8 tomorrow morning we reach Warsaw. So everything is all right—physically. Mentally, I can only say that everything I experience, I experience with you. I really think and react with two heads and two hearts, it's the only way to endure our separation, especially such a futile one as this—and make it not a separation at all. Please, please, be a good girl and take care of yourself.

Till 8 p.m. we'll be going through Poland; after that Russia. How? Nobody knows.

(369)   In the train, 9th June 1927,
                                                                7 a.m.

Never before have I made a journey feeling so uninvolved, so purposeless. As if brain and heart refused to hear about it, and only the body were obeying orders. The brain isn't functioning, except to worry about *your* worries over this journey of mine. So in the evening, when I found your letter in my pyjamas, the feeling of depression grew to the deepest heart-ache, and I could have burst into tears. Then I racked my brain for hours on how I could free

---

[1] Georg Höllering, Viennese theatrical manager.
[2] Hermine Kittel (1876–1948), contralto, member of the Vienna Opera.
[3] Adalbert Stifter (1805–1868), Austrian poet and novelist.

you from your madly exaggerated fears, these obsessions about the physical well-being of the few people who are near to you, above all myself. It's only these obsessions that force me to conceal things. If I tell you, for instance, that I took aspirin last night as a precaution (when travelling), you already picture me ending up as a morphine addict in Steinhof.[1] And if, to stop me coughing, I take some harmless drops of codeine, you're afraid I'll die of tuberculosis in Alland.[2] You have no real evidence that I'm iller, frailer, more nervy, thinner today than I was ten years or ten weeks ago. No ordinary doctor, specialist or psychiatrist finds anything which might be disturbing or not quite normal for my age. One can have a bit of bowel trouble even at eighteen. But you have these obsessions about my pegging out, and it's the same with all the other obsessions.

Just as well I was alone. As the sleeping car was empty (to talk now about the external things of this journey), I managed by a little tip to get an empty compartment, and so was alone from 11 to 6 with the marvellous travelling pillow (thank you *so* much, my darling) in a lower bunk, had a wash-basin quite to myself, of which I made best use, not knowing what the next nights may bring. Nobody knows when we arrive in St. Petersburg. As we are not arriving (my Russian fellow-passengers and I) at the Polish-Russian frontier till tonight (Thursday), nobody thinks I can be at St. Petersburg by tomorrow morning. By lunch-time, at very best, if there is a connection, and I don't need to travel via Moscow. At the moment I am with these fellow-passengers at the station restaurant in Warsaw. In an hour's time, at 10 a.m., we go on, and then I'll find out in the train from the guards how and when I'm arriving at St. Petersburg. Before this letter arrives, you'll get a telegram from me. In any case: don't worry about me, though I can't help worrying about you, my immortal beloved problem child. What sort of silly things will you do *now*? I implore you, be sensible—sensible in my sense! Don't get in a state. I kiss the tears away from your sad little eyes.

p.s. In Oderberg,[3] from where I wrote you a card, they served a very good dinner: half a huge chicken, potatoes, stewed fruit, beer. This morning when I got up, a small glass of black coffee (no more, I have to economize!), and now at the restaurant a breakfast of tea. Also, we've got a dining-car throughout the day. So don't worry

[1] Lunatic asylum for the province of Lower Austria.
[2] State Hospital in Lower Austria for the treatment of pulmonary diseases.
[3] Czech frontier town at the Polish border.

on that score. My cough has nearly gone, lumbago not so good yesterday afternoon, but this morning—just disappeared.

My heart aches, but no heart specialist would diagnose that. And I am smoking very little. Once more—kisses.

Your own

(370)
Friday, 10th June 1927,
morning

In the train—at a time when I imagined, and was told in Vienna, I should already be in Leningrad! At the moment I believe I shall be there at 9 a.m. tomorrow (Saturday). Yesterday morning in Warsaw I posted the first letter. There we got out from the Vienna sleeping-car and after half an hour into a very good Polish express coach. Meanwhile I had dashed into a travel office in the town (nobody knew anything on the station) and there learnt definitely that I have to travel via Moscow, and couldn't be in Leningrad till Sunday morning—*after* the opening night, brilliant prospect!

The whole afternoon there were four of us in the wonderful coach, and we ate excellently in the dining-car. But nobody on the train knew whether I should get a connection at the frontier. Eventually at the Polish frontier town I learned that on the other side, at the Russian frontier town, I would find a direct coach to Leningrad, but nobody knew when I would reach there. In the Russian frontier station all they could say was that I should get to Leningrad either Friday midday or evening or Saturday morning. So I sent a telegram to Leningrad, which was quite a feat in itself as the man in the post office couldn't read the Latin letters; then I bought a ticket to Leningrad direct, *not* via Moscow, went through the customs, and parted from my fellow-passengers, who got on a coach for Moscow. I was told I couldn't find out definitely when I'll reach Leningrad until my coach has been disconnected from this train. This will be at Orscha[1] at five in the morning.

I got on my coach, which was stinking, very old and lit only by candles, though it must once have been very comfortable. I got a compartment for myself, and I was the only passenger in the coach too. Apart from me there were just two conductors on it, looking like cut-throats; neither understood a word of German or the like, so I couldn't even ask them to wake me up at Orscha! But I slept very well, woke up at about five, big station long stop. Reluctantly left

[1] District capital on the river Dnieper, in the Ukrainian province of Mogilev.

357

my nice bed, got dressed, and went out into the cold morning. Was this Orscha? Like Hell it was, we shouldn't get to Orscha till twelve o'clock, and there I could send a telegram. Apparently we shan't arrive at Leningrad till nine on Saturday morning. A bridge collapsed in the flooding a few days ago; if it had been still there, we could have got in tonight. In any case this is the very worst route. The one via Germany was the only real alternative, though, and for that you need two more visas (or the one via Moscow, which got in too late). What a piece of luck anyhow that the whole railway line and the coach are as perfect as anywhere in Europe, so that I can quite well stand another 24 hours here, comfortable and on my own, sitting or lying down, as if I were in a little room of my own.

I hope I'll be able to send you a telegram from Orscha saying when I at last reach Leningrad, though heaven knows when you'll get the letter. As I am still feeling quite uninvolved in this journey, I am not too much affected by these trials (70 hours all by myself in a carriage, and 48 of them not knowing whether and when I'll be arriving). These are all only external facts, which I'm putting down in chronological order as if it were an official journey time-sheet. What really affects me is somewhere else, and doesn't belong to this bare report, so please read it only as that. I know this is not a letter in the sense you or I understand letters, but it's something you are expecting from me, although you can't even telegraph a single line to *me*. Of course I'm now at best only a *traveller*, not an ordinary person . . .

(371)   *Telegram*
                                              10th June 1927
NOT ARRIVING LENINGRAD TILL SATURDAY MORNING
JOURNEY VERY GOOD

(372)   Friday, 10th June 1927,
                                         afternoon, in the train
   Well, it seems I really shall arrive at Leningrad in the end! At Orscha (where I posted you a letter and a telegram) I kept getting different answers: arrival tomorrow morning or tomorrow lunch-time. But I have now just heard that the train does arrive at 9 a.m. There's only this one slow train from Orscha, but thank heavens I've met a few people on it from Leningrad who speak German, so I

358

am not quite so helpless any more. In Vitebsk,[1] for instance, where we stopped for two hours, I had a look at the town (about as big as Villach), the country and the people. That would have interested you! I say 'interested', for nobody could possibly *like* it. Nor the landscape either—since Poland, for days on end, it's been one vast plain, with very few trees, here and there a so-called town in the style of allotments near Mauer.[2] A lot of marshland, population the poorest and dirtiest in the world. Spent the afternoon partly sitting, partly lying down. In the evening I'll get a meal somewhere, go to bed, get up at seven and have a bit of a wash, finish this letter and post it first thing in Leningrad. In Vitebsk I've just read that I'm expected this morning at Leningrad. In Russia the Whitsun holiday starts earlier—the day after tomorrow (Sunday).

Saturday morning

Night went very well, slept eight hours, though bothered by all the daylight—for they have 'white nights' here: only dark for half an hour and then like dusk at home, after that full daylight again. In an hour's time (at 9.5) we'll really be at Leningrad. I can hardly believe it or imagine it, still less that in 66 hours I'll be travelling back! I've just been handed a newspaper. First night isn't till Monday, 13th June; dress rehearsal 12th June (Sunday, twelve noon), and tonight there is a closed performance for a workers' guild. (So here they do one or two public rehearsals, which is a very good thing.) Big articles in today's paper. Leningrad in ten minutes. Please send me a telegram! Oh, if only you were here!

(373) *Telegram*
Leningrad, 11th June 1927,
Hotel Europa
SUNDAY DRESS REHEARSAL MONDAY FIRST NIGHT

(374) *Telegram*
12th June 1927
TERRIFIC APPLAUSE AFTER PUBLIC DRESS REHEARSAL
VERY EFFECTIVE PRODUCTION

[1] District capital on the rivers Vitba and Duna.
[2] Viennese suburb, not far from Hietzing.

359

(375)   *Telegram*
                                                   14th June 1927
NO CAUSE WHATEVER FOR ANXIETY TUMULTUOUS
SUCCESS WILL TELEGRAPH ARRIVAL TOMORROW

(376)   *Telegram*
                                                   14th June 1927
DIRECT JOURNEY NOT POSSIBLE TILL THURSDAY MORNING
ARRIVING SATURDAY MORNING WOULD LIKE TRAHÜTTEN
TUESDAY KISSES

(377)   *Telegram*
                                                   16th June 1927
TOMORROW START FOR HOME AT LAST LOOKING FORWARD
TERRIFICALLY

(378)   *Telegram*
                                                   17th June 1927
ARRIVING 11.25 SATURDAY NORTHERN STATION AT LAST
DARLING

(379)   23rd March, on the way
                                                       to Zurich[1]
Standing on the Vienna tram.
My darling, by the time you receive this card, a third of our
separation will be over. And just as today I'm only preoccupied
with worry about you, so it will then be the joyful thought of seeing
you again, increasing every hour, to find at last—I hope so much—
its carefree climax in fond caresses! . . .
All my thanks for the breakfast, for getting the bath-water hot,
for the food, etc., etc.

(380)   23rd March 1928, second card
In ten minutes they'll let us on to the platform, so I got here at
just the right time. Before I get on to the train, one more hearty kiss.
[1] To a meeting of the I.S.C.M. jury for the Sixth Festival in Sienna.

(381)   Zurich, 24th March 1928,
                                          8 a.m.
My golden one,
  I've just had a big breakfast, now I'm going to my room, which is
very nice, to clean up, unpack, etc. At ten we have our first meeting.
Directly I know anything more, I'll wire when I'm arriving in
Vienna. A thousand kisses!

(382)   Zurich, 24th March 1928
  Praise be the day's over, my darling. The struggle I had with sleep
today!—though I've never before overcome it so successfully. I
was dead tired already on reaching the Hans-Huber-Gasse (marvellous villa of Volkmar Andreae), where first of all we read scores
for three or four hours. Then we had lunch. After that, first jury
discussion, in French, with bits of Italian from Casella, Swiss from
Volkmar Andreae, English from Dent, Czech from Jirák[1]—we went
on with the scores continuously till seven at night. When I got to the
hotel, I dozed off on the sofa till I was woken up by the maid coming
to make the bed. Now I have eaten a bit at the café, where I am
reading the papers and writing this report to Pferscherl, so that she
won't be without a letter in case I'm not back by Tuesday. It's quite
possible that even with strenuous work on Sunday and Monday we
shan't get through it all; which means I can't leave till Tuesday
evening or (at latest) Wednesday morning. Tomorrow evening, in a
concert lasting about five hours, we are to hear Bach's *Art of Fugue*
(orchestrated!) under Scherchen . . .

(383)   Zurich, 25th March 1928
  Sunday in Zurich: the dullest of the dull. This morning we again
worked very hard, 'judging'. Lunch at the hotel. Marvellous menu,
13 Swiss francs (the I.S.C.M. pays!). After lunch I slept for an hour,
had a shave, cup of tea in my room, and now to the Church to hear
the *Art of Fugue*. During the two-hour interval I'm dining with
Scherchen.

(384)   26th March 1928
  We leave here Wednesday, and I shall definitely be arriving
(have already got ticket for sleeping-car) Thursday morning 9.10
_____
[1] K. B. Jirák, Czech composer and writer on music.

at the Western Station, 9.45 on the lips of my golden one—longing for that as never before ...

The work here is nearing its end, session today from 10 to 6 (with short break for lunch). Final session tomorrow afternoon. I may have succeeded in pushing through Webern's *Trio* and Zemlinsky's last *Quartet*, otherwise there won't be much of interest in the three concerts in Sienna. Yesterday's *Art of Fugue* was wonderful! A work hitherto considered mere mathematics, orchestrated by a young German:[1] really profound music.

Afterwards at a Swiss party with Scherchen and his new wife. Didn't get to bed till very late. Lunching today with an incredibly rich Swiss family, where Dent is staying; they absolutely insist on seeing me. Tomorrow after the final session I'm going to Winterthur for a Casella concert, and then at last—home!

(385)   Trahütten, 17th June 1928[2]
... Weather indescribably horrible, and for your sake I'm almost glad you've been spared it. Apart from the day of the journey, which was really glorious, it's been getting more disgusting every day: fog, rain, hail, cold (5°C.), and the barometer keeps on going down. It's also due to the weather that despite the heated room I now and then feel a bit steamy. But it doesn't worry me much, as I have plenty of time to make up for minor disturbances through sleep! I am also careful how much coffee I drink, but I drink a lot of valerian tea. The work[3] is making rather slow progress to start with. When I think of you alone in Vienna, and in pain, my heart literally aches.

Not much to report from here, I'll save it till you come. For today just one piece of news: thanks to my patent sash-window, swallows are nesting on the kitchen veranda—one of them's broody.

Annerl is arranging as much as possible in the house, but there will still be more than enough work for you. I've had only the essentials done to let me stay here in comfort. Part of this comfort is my old trousers with all the bilberry stains. I'm very much

[1] Wolfgang Graeser (1906–1928), the Swiss (not German) composer and musicologist, made this transcription shortly before his early death.
[2] Berg was staying on his father-in-law's estate, waiting there for Helene to travel with her to the Berghof. (See footnote Letter 386.)
[3] He was working on the arrangement of Frank Wedekind's play *Erdgeist* and *Die Büchse der Pandora*, which was to serve, in condensed form, as the libretto for his second opera *Lulu*.

enjoying wearing them again! And even those trousers are much too good for the company in these parts!

In the afternoon I am having a big business discussion with Hansl;[1] the roof, the fence (which has turned out very nice), settlement, etc. I'll write to Mama separately about all this. Of the post so far I only want to tell you of a very nice letter from Kolisch, who writes: 'I don't know how often we have played the *"salon"* arrangement.'[2] Mainly as a result of Gershwin's publicity.[3] Gershwin has been fêted like a king in Paris, and he asked the Kolisch people to play my piece every day at the parties and receptions given in his honour. Next year America.

Pferschi, please bring with you: first, my hygienic corset,[4] which I forgot. I don't need it for the moment, but perhaps I may in the next four months. Second, the last issue of the *Fackel*, it's in its place in the veranda bookcase in a cardboard box, at the right-hand end of the row of *Fackels*; the box has '*Fackel 1928*' on it. (It's the last of the three or four issues—have a look at the number.) That's also good reading for you on the train. It contains the wonderful 'Poems of a Fool.'

The Private Life of Helen of Troy[5] is a delightful book: the only possible interpretation of Helen as Lulu.

I'm sending this letter express, so that you'll get it even if you leave for here on Thursday. But then we'll have a joyful reunion, such as has never been known in the annals of Styria. My heart beats faster already to think of it.

(386)   Berghof,[6] Monday afternoon
(Undated, summer 1928)

Just so that you hear something from me tomorrow, I'll write these few lines, my dearest. My heart was rather heavy when I left you: first, because you went away completely against your own wishes; second, because you are ill; third, because you're having

---

[1] The leaseholder of Frau Nahowski's estate 'Teiselgut'.

[2] The Kolisch Quartet played at its recitals movements 2, 3 and 4 of Berg's *Lyric Suite*, which of course was originally written in five movements.

[3] George Gershwin (1898–1937) was an ardent admirer of Berg's music.

[4] Owing to an old stomach prolapse Berg had to wear this 'hygienic corset'.

[5] By John Erskine (1879–1951).

[6] Berg had found a summer apartment in the former flat of the manager of the shoe-tree factory set up by the Italian who bought the Berghof (see Letter 278). After the forest had been cleared, the factory was closed, and the whole estate was bought by a Dr Löwe who put the rooms at Berg's disposal.

such wretched travelling conditions (third-class, and the heat); and fourth to a million-and-fourth, because you are in situations which cause me a million worries. (I can only put up with them because I cling to the million joys of seeing you again in a week's time.)

From the Berghof I went to some greengrocers, where I was told: 'There soon won't be any homegrown salad to buy.' Eventually Frau Müller in St Andrä promised me she'd get some salad for me in the afternoon.

Afterwards I had a bathe from our dear lonely jetty, had lunch (Chaliapin and Slezak[1] were singing on the radio), worked a bit but wasn't quite on form, so I started this letter which I am now finishing at 6.30 in Villach.

From the café to the cinema to see *Olympia*.[2] But on one's own it's so very boring. It will be very different in a week's time, when I 'speed' along the road at 18 miles an hour with my darling at my side![3]

BE SENSIBLE

I shout it at you in capitals. It's not important that you should save some money, only that in this week you should get as much done as possible. Then you won't have to leave me again.

(387)   Berghof Factory, Tuesday
                                                      afternoon
                                        (Undated, summer 1928)
You are hardly 24 hours away, and it already feels like an age to me. Still, in one way I'm glad you're not here. The neighbour (Frau Mendel) is very ill indeed—she's already received the last sacraments. This morning at six Resi came, asking for some brandy, which is supposed to 'cool the burning'. Later on I got up and have been at work, which has gone very satisfactorily, in both quantity and quality. From half past twelve to a quarter to one I had a quick bathe, lunch at one, reading the paper, slept for half an hour, then went on working. And now I am writing to my lovely one, while it's raining slightly

[1] Feodor Chaliapin (1873–1938), the famous Russian bass singer. Leo Slezak (1873–1946), the Austrian tenor.

[2] The American film based on the comedy of the same name by the Hungarian playwright Ferenc Molnar (1878–1952).

[3] Berg had become a keen motorist; from the royalties on *Wozzeck* he bought a Ford sports car.

outside, as the barometer yesterday indicated it might. The bad weather will continue, too. If only it's nice on Monday. At six o'clock I'm driving in to Villach with Dr Löwe, where I'll perhaps go to a cinema. Yesterday's *Olympia*, the famous Molnar play, was very good— pity you missed it. A lady sitting in the café looked at me several times, smiled, and eventually waved to me. I hadn't responded to any of this, not realizing it was meant for me. As she left and was passing my table, she introduced herself; then I at last recognized her as the singer who sang the *Seven Early Songs* on the Berlin radio with me at the piano. We talked a little without sitting down; she and her husband live near Lake Wörther.

I am so much looking forward to tomorrow morning, hearing Pferscherl's voice. If only I don't hear any bad news! Longing to know whether you're well, slept all right, had a pleasant and comfortable journey, and arrived safely at the flat—and whether you're looking forward to Monday with as much jolly joyful jubilation as your

Phöbus-Möbchen[1]

(388)   26th October 1928, in the
                                              sleeping-car[2]

Everything has gone all right so far, my golden one. Except that *you* should be here with me, then I should have all I could wish for. In this marvellous new Mitropa sleeping-car (all in brown) you would have slept just as well as I have; we should have arrived in Berlin well rested, and it would have been a pleasure for you, not a strain. But as things are, I jolt along towards Berlin on my own. In an hour's time we'll be there . . .

At the station I still had a bit of time left, so I went and bought an evening paper and a tiny bottle of brandy. My travelling companion seems very pleasant, though I have hardly seen him, as he has a friend in the next compartment and is there all the time. He came back here to sleep when I was already in bed, and vanished at seven, shaved outside, while I had breakfast and dressed.

I'd had my supper (and found your little note) just before we reached Linz. There I had got off the train quite serenely when I

[1] One of Berg's completely nonsensical pet-names.
[2] To Berlin for a revival of *Wozzeck*, then to Duisburg for the *Wozzeck* première there.

suddenly saw two German customs officials on the platform. I asked the guard: 'When do we have the customs control?' 'Now, on the train.' You can imagine my horror. I thought it would be at Passau at 11, not at Linz at 9. Dashed to my compartment, took out the bowl,[1] put it beneath the mattress, and sat down at the edge of the bunk. The customs man made a modest enquiry and then walked on. I didn't dare take it out again before Passau, so I lay down on the bowl-mattress, and slept beautifully on it! This morning I put it safely into my bag again! The coffee tasted splendid to me, I couldn't help thinking of your touchingly guilty conscience at having taken the old coffee by mistake. You darling! The pastry was very good too; but I couldn't find room for the cheese roll. Perhaps at Berlin . . .

(389)   Berlin, 26th October 1928,
                                                              afternoon
  Arrived safely. Frau Schmid was at the station she accompanied me to the hotel and took over the distribution of complimentary tickets for *Wozzeck*. As the tickets I ordered under the name of Sch. were three stalls, I bought a single ticket for myself in the second row of the top gallery. There, praise be, I'll sit quite on my own. In the hotel I washed, shaved, changed, and telephoned Frau Wedekind[2] to make an appointment for 12 o'clock. In between there were a couple of 'phone calls: Frau Sch. (I got rid of her), and the Academy of Arts[3] (Schoenberg's telephone is out of order; he doesn't seem to be there). By now it was twelve, so I called for Frau Wedekind and we went for a little walk. It's an incredibly fine 'summer day in autumn'.
  I liked Frau Wedekind for her completely natural manner, nothing histrionic about her. She's almost ladylike, in fact, as far as it's possible to be in these artistic circles!
  I learned a lot of important things. We only touched briefly on finance, but enough to let me presume I'll get the ludicrously low terms Ettinger had.[4] Everything will be settled in two letters between Hertzka and her two lawyers. We lunched in her hotel,

  [1] A gift for Erich Kleiber.
  [2] Tilly Wedekind, German actress, Frank Wedekind's widow.
  [3] Since 1925 Schoenberg had been directing a master class in composition at the Prussian Academy of Arts in Berlin.
  [4] Max Ettinger (1874–1951), German composer, who wrote an opera (1928) based on Wedekind's drama *Spring's Awakening*.

nice simple meal (no black coffee, no alcohol), and at two I was back in my hotel, where I had a splendid rest for two hours. Now I'm sitting in the hotel drinking a big black coffee to go with this letter.

I've phoned Rezniček:[1] we're travelling together at ten o'clock tomorrow: he's going third-class to suit me, which is very nice of the old gentleman.

Anything else? Well, Berlin is marvellous. The difference from Vienna seems bigger and bigger, you would be just as enthusiastic. At the hotel they all remembered me still. I have a very quiet room.

I've left the most important thing to the end: Wessela[2] is singing. Otherwise there are some new people in small parts (Margaret, the two artisans, etc.). It begins at 8, ends at 10.30. After the performance is over, I shall go and see the unsuspecting Kleiber.

By this time tomorrow I hope to have the first letter from you in Duisburg. How I am looking forward to it! And even more so to next Tuesday!

Meanwhile, even though far away, very near to you, my Schnudoa.

Your own

(390)   On the train from Berlin
                                                     to Duisburg, 27th
                                                     October 1928

Eight hours in a third-class compartment, and without seeing a single mountain! You'll have received my telegram and picture postcard, I expect. *Wozzeck* was put on without fuss, just like any other opera in the repertoire; which was very good. Pretty well attended, and the critics were again present. I didn't like Wessela very much, and what's more, nor did the audience; Hörth and Kleiber are for getting rid of her. Perhaps she will be better on Tuesday. Hörth says he's going to get another Marie—only when would she be ready, knowing her part, etc.? Meanwhile Johanson might sing again, a lot of people like *her* anyhow—Rezniček, for instance, who really is a great *Wozzeck* enthusiast.

From the gallery you can hear marvellously, every word of the singing; and also the orchestra, which sounds really beautiful—even with my present taste, which has rather moved away from that

---

[1] Ernst Nikolaus von Rezniček (1860–1945), Austrian composer who had been living in Berlin since 1902.

[2] Soprano at the National Theatre in Prague, who had joined the Berlin company as 'guest star' to sing the part of Marie.

style of composition. Henke and Soot[1] were a bit better, the child (same one as before) very good. Production has got a bit slack, and things didn't quite work in properly.

Unfortunately I was recognized in the gallery and stared at. In the interval I didn't know where to look.

Rather mild applause after the first act, the singers only came on twice. After the second act five curtain calls. Before Act Three special applause for Kleiber, and after it everybody very enthusiastic, many calls, also for Kleiber.

Then I appeared at the stage door, met Hörth, Henke and others, and went into Kleiber's dressing-room. He was nearly naked, having a wash, and had his wife with him. Terrific surprise to him, my coming—both of them highly delighted. Although he needs rest very badly and should have gone straight home, we went for an hour to the restaurant Töpfer, where we had the big dinner after the first night. The Kleibers and Frau Wedekind were very anxious to meet each other; and we also had the chance to talk over some of the financial details of *Lulu*, which was very useful. Because now I can ask Hertzka to do something to bring down the Wedekind share. Her lawyer advised her to ask for 40 per cent instead of 30 per cent. She could see from my face that I didn't like this, and I have the impression that she will let me have it for less. I estimate 33 per cent at the most, one third, that is, instead of half, as in *Pippa*.[2] On the other hand, my share in the sales of the libretto seems very favourable. I refused straight away the suggestion of parting with a share of the music royalties. An exchange of letters will now take place between Hertzka and the lawyer, which will settle things in a way satisfactory to all.

Kleiber is enthusiastic about the *Lulu* idea, specially as he has at the moment a magnificent Hungarian coloratura soprano for it. At dinner I handed him the bowl. Both were very moved and tremendously pleased. But they were very sad, too, that you weren't there. So was I! . . .

After a restful night I packed, and met Reznicek at the station. A funny chap, but really a good sort. He brought lunch for two and asked me to join him, so that I didn't need go into the dining-car.

[1] Waldemar Henke (Captain) and Fritz Soot (Drum Major) sang the same parts as three years before.
[2] In 1926 Berg had tried to acquire the rights of Gerhart Hauptmann's *Und Pippa Tanzt*. Discussions started between him and Hauptmann's publishers, but broke down when Berg was told he could not have the sole rights of setting the drama to music.

The journey is pretty tiring, as I have a middle seat with no arm-rest, third-class, for eight hours.

Now we are in Westphalia, quite pleasant undulating country, whereas Brandenburg is so horrible one would really rather not look out of the window.

In an hour or two we'll be at Duisburg, where I'll surely find a letter from you. Wonder how the kitchen looks now,[1] and how you're getting on with everything. I'm quite anxious about you doing such a lot.

I am feeling very fit. I have read lately that someone suffering from asthma cannot also be a diabetic. And as I can't get any uterine disease and one doesn't die of asthma, I shall probably live for centuries! Reznicek has just invited me to come to the dining-car with him and have some coffee. Good idea, and as this letter is finished anyway, I'm going coffeewards. I hope you get the letter on Monday. By that time you will also have my wire saying when I arrive in Vienna . . .

(391)   Berghof, Monday afternoon
                              (Undated, 22nd September 1930)
My Pferscherl,
    I am sitting at the Park Café, after seeing to everything: most important, the little red ball[2] for the car, which makes it look even smarter and has proved its worth tremendously (as I have noticed from the reactions of other car-drivers around). I hadn't realized properly till now what a splendid car I'm driving!

    Frau Löwe came to the café just now, she will be my witness that I ordered only a small black coffee and drank only half of it. She brought me the post. A very nice letter from Klenau.[3] He is on his own in Vienna and will certainly be extremely glad to meet you—ring him up. Then one of Schoenberg's nicest letters, terrifically enthusiastic about my canon and the poem.[4] Also quite a mass of notices about Aachen[5]—really fine. It was indeed an 'international

---

[1] Helene was going to repaint the kitchen furniture while Berg was away.
[2] A small decoration for the Ford.
[3] Paul von Klenau (1883–1946), Danish composer and conductor.
[4] For Schoenberg's 50th birthday Berg sent him a copy of a canon he had composed to his own words for the 50th anniversary of the Opera House, Frankfurt. It contains musical and verbal allusions to Schoenberg's opera *Von Heute auf Morgen* which had its première there in January 1930.
[5] *Wozzeck* had been produced there.

cultural event'. I am waiting for the papers (to see what happened in the German elections[1]), then I'll drive home.

Goodness, what a rush at the station, it quite put me out. And we couldn't say one loving word to each other—so I am doing it now in this letter. My love, my love, my love!

(392)   Tuesday, 23rd September 1930
My poor darling,

That was sad news this morning.[2] I really have to force myself to go on working. I can't wait for tomorrow when I'll be talking to you on the 'phone. Do hope there's better news then. But anyhow it means you can't possibly come before the end of the week and even then we shan't be alone. I feel rather despairing, but still I can only advise you—to arrange things with Franzl so that you can definitely have a month or two's peace. Don't worry about *me*, though, I'm feeling very fit and am if possible even fatter! Only a note today, as I've got a lot of mail to attend to. The Kanzel[3] looks right down into my room. But without Schnudoa it means nothing to me. A thousand kisses.

(393)   Wednesday, 24th September 1930
So now I have spoken to my dear heart. It was so lovely, and yet I was a bit dejected, first about the bad house *Wozzeck*[4] had, and second about the behaviour of A. One could write or talk about it for days, but it wouldn't help, he's got us all where he wants us . . .

What do you say about the horrible result of the German Election?

The 'blue bird'[5] is behaving all right, as ever . . .

(394)   Thursday,
                                             25th September 1930
I am so restless that I can't even find the calm to write letters,

---

[1] The General Election which made the Nazis the second largest party in Germany.

[2] The condition of Helene's brother, Franz, was deteriorating. (See footnote Letter 213.)

[3] A mountain in Carinthia.

[4] In June 1930 *Wozzeck* had been produced at last at the Vienna State Opera.

[5] Berg's pet name for his car.

you poor dear. I can't advise you—or help you. Though the time is getting nearer every hour when you will at last come home, the uncertainty about it is growing all the time. I simply can't wait for eight o'clock tomorrow morning to hear your voice once more. But *what* news will I hear? Did you decide anything about Franzl? If so, is it a solution? If not, can you still come on Saturday, and will you know that for certain tomorrow morning?—and get me out of my restlessness? Everything else seems to me superfluous now and unimportant. For instance, that I spent an evening with Löwe and listened to his philosophical discourses, or that I've written to Klein, Apostel, Reich, Heinsheimer,[1] Panzer—or even that now, with Vaugouin,[2] complete ruin is descending on Austria and on us. What interest is all that when I know you are in these agonizing situations and know that your 'lunch' consists of a pound of plums?

(395)   Thursday, 29th September
                                              1930, afternoon
What a lovely letter of yours. I'm so happy to have it at last, at last. I hope another will come soon, so that reading and re-reading these letters I shall have a small but undiluted Pferscherl-substitute until you come. Half the time is over, and tomorrow I'll talk to you again . . .

Did you read of Köppke's[3] suicide, and that she spent her last evening with her best friends, Lina Loos[4] and Csokor. Don't worry about me. All my 'complaints' are much better, and it's absurd really to talk of me as a 'patient'. Appetite, sleep, work, car-driving, everything is all right, and the only thing missing is you! Come soon. On Sunday at the latest, if you can't manage it on Saturday because you want to go and look after things at Steinhof. And tell me in good time, so that I can fetch you at the station in Klagenfurt . . .

Post: more magnificent notices from Aachen, from which I also learn that I have again become a member of a jury, this time in Oxford.

---

[1] Hans W. Heinsheimer, then head of the opera department of Universal Edition.
[2] Carl Vaugouin, Austrian right-wing politician.
[3] Margarethe Köppke, an extremely talented young Viennese actress.
[4] Lina Loos, Viennese actress, first wife of Adolf Loos.

(396)   Berghof Factory
                            (Undated, September 1930)

Wonder what you're doing at this moment? How disturbed your
days must be, whereas mine are flowing along so tranquilly. To
think you've been torn away from it when a restful life does you so
much good and a disturbed life is so specially bad for you. I am
really very sad about it and feel my loneliness twice as much! This
morning I worked very hard and successfully . . .

Weather awful, cold and rainy. The sunshine is missing, and by
that I don't mean the mere sun in the sky . . .

(397)   Berghof
                         (Undated, 29th September 1930)

I'm very upset. Now you have done everything in vain, my poor
darling. The whole paraphernalia over Steinhof has been to no
purpose. If they had left Franzl for one month more in Rekawinkel
you wouldn't have had to go to Vienna, and it wouldn't have been
too late in October for Tulln.[1] I can imagine you certainly won't be
able to get away now, for how would the others manage? And I have
to carry my unselfishness to extremes when I give you the advice
I'm going to: if it's a matter of a few days, and you know that then
Franzl will definitely be taken in at Tulln, then wait the few
extra days. At least you can be completely quiet once you're here
again; it's better for you, and I prefer it to having you come here
two days earlier and then worrying for weeks: 'how is he getting on,
how is he taking it, if only I'd spoken to this or that nurse, talked to
the doctor and superintendent about this point or that.'

I'll definitely ring up at eight on Wednesday morning. Should you
by then be already on your way—how marvellous that would be!
If nobody answers the 'phone on Wednesday, then even without a
telegram I'd assume you'd left, and will come to Klagenfurt.

This morning's post again brought a mass of stuff that's got to be
dealt with. The most important letter is from Jalowetz, who says
Cologne is sad that I am not coming,[2] and if I'm really not coming,
he'll read my lecture.[3] He needs the manuscript for that—can you
send it to him?

[1] In Rekawinkel and Tulln (Lower Austria) there were nursing homes for the
mentally sick.

[2] To the first night of *Wozzeck* there.

[3] For the opening night of *Wozzeck* in Oldenburg (1929), Berg had written
an introductory lecture which he later repeated at the opening night in several
other cities.

372

Clemens Krauss[1] writes a charming letter about the wonderful production and that all singers will stay for further performances; also asking about the *Pieces for Orchestra* (how long they are). He wants to meet us, etc. etc.

Further notices from Aachen—best ever.

Scherchen is going to do the *Lyric Suite* at Winterthur. But what good is all that when your letter is so sad, and you yourself 'tired and harassed', and found me 'reserved' on the 'phone. It's so terribly important for me to hear from you, and of course I'm always asking *you* questions. I am all right. I'm sensible and know how to look after myself. Unlike you, really driving yourself to distraction by trying to help everybody; not eating properly, I'm sure; working too hard in the house to avoid spending two or three Schillings in a restaurant; walking everywhere or using the tram—all to the detriment of your health, which you treat as unimportant . . . I beg of you not to *economize* these days. Leave the cooking, washing and shopping. Go to restaurants, take taxis, don't walk a single step if you can go in a car. Apart from everything else, you gain time that way, and can sleep in the afternoon as well as at night. Oh, I am so anxious about you, I would love to abandon everything here and come to Vienna. If only you would be sensible! I'll ring you tomorrow to see whether this letter has arrived. Thousands, no, billions of kisses—from your very sad

Mipel

(398)   10th January 1931,
                                    on the way to London[2]

Before Linz, where I can post a few lines. I feel surprisingly well. Rest comfortably, dozing a bit, in the well-heated compartment, have quite a nice neighbour, who doesn't disturb me, doesn't smoke (what marvellous luck) and has already spoken to the sleeping-car attendant to let him have one of the empty sleeping compartments for the night, so that I too shall be sleeping alone. So this whole journey is a continuation of my careful and sensible behaviour, in fact I'm behaving even more carefully and sensibly, as for twenty hours I shan't leave this well-heated room (compartment), and shan't

---

[1] Clemens Krauss (1893–1954), Austrian conductor, general manager of the Vienna Opera from 1929–1934.

[2] As a member of the international jury for the ninth Festival of the I.S.C.M. in Oxford and London.

do anything but take care of myself, mostly reading. So for heaven's sake don't worry, and you can be sure I'll know how to look after myself if it should be cold in England. After this you won't hear till Monday about my arrival in London or Cambridge, and then by telegram. It'll be quite a time, I'm afraid, before you get a letter— and that will be from Cambridge . . .

(399)   Saturday, 10th January
                                     1931, late afternoon

Must write to you again, darling, to tell you first, that I'm well, second, that for the first time in my life I myself have personally stopped a whole train, and a saloon train at that. This is how it happened.

I'd been told for hours that coffee wouldn't be served in the dining-car till the lunches were over. That meant after Linz, where we should be arriving at 3.30. So I waited, and then at Linz I wrapped my fur coat around me, posted the express letter to you, went back to my compartment, took off my coat and walked through the train to the dining-car, which I knew was right in front. I ordered tea, and after a while we went on. As they served the tea, the waiter asked me: 'You're going to Paris, I suppose?' The dining-car was going to Paris, you see, not to Ostend.

The thing was, that in Linz, after I'd walked through the train, they divided it. I was now in the front part, the waiter explained, and that goes via Salzburg to Paris, whereas my sleeping-car, which would be coming on soon, would go via Passau with a new dining-car. Can you imagine my horror? Without luggage, ticket or passport, hat or coat, speeding on to Salzburg. They told me this Paris train branched off at Wels but wouldn't stop there—but the other part that followed with my sleeping-car would. So the first part would have to be made to stop there for me to change trains. The guard refused, suggested I go to Salzburg, the luggage would be taken off at Passau, etc. You can imagine my helpless fury—but not helpless for long. There was nothing for it but to pull the communication cord. Forbidden, of course, but worth the 30 Schillings fine. The tension of that quarter of an hour before we got to Wels, you can't imagine. A little before Wels I pulled. A whistle that lasted for ages, the train braked and stopped even before the station, still whistling wildly. I got out proudly and hurried to the station, behind me the shocked train people, coming towards me

374

the excited station people. Explanations—the train went on to the left, I paid the fine, and soon *my* train turned up. I jumped in quickly (nobody had missed me), and soon *we* went on to the right.

Just fancy if the chap in the dining-car hadn't asked me. I would now be on the way to Salzburg *without anything*, I'd have to go back to Linz, from there to Passau, etc.—quite incredible. Don't let anyone tell me again that travelling is dead simple. Even now, when I'm travelling comfortably and enjoying my journey, it's just as full of unexpected adventures and agitations as when we were still travelling third-class on slow trains.

That's what comes of my always having to be right! But now it's over, I can laugh about it and don't even regret the 30 Schillings. The excitement, as a strong physical impulse, may even have done me good. In any case I feel almost better now at six in the evening than I did a few hours ago. If I could only hear from you as much and as quickly as you hear from me! That's the specially sad thing about a separation like this. Well, the thirtiest part of it is over.

Love me, as I love you.

p.s. I had a good dinner and now have no one else in the carriage.

(400)   11th January 1931

Sunday morning, short 'bulletin', in case I have the chance to post a letter. You'll have had my two letters of yesterday and seen that I had a good dinner (see menu), and went to bed at nine. Had a compartment quite to myself, which was very soothing. Slept quite well, though not so well as at home, woke up often, but didn't cough. At half past seven I drank some black coffee, after making a mess on bed and pyjamas (as the cup had a hole in it). Ate some biscuits, had a good wash, then went along to the dining-car for some good hot tea. There I met my former travelling companion, who is going to England for the umpteenth time, so I'm going to cling on to him! He thinks we'll have a smooth crossing. (To be continued.)

On the high seas.

My neighbour was right, it's a wonderful crossing despite the breakers. Reaching Ostend about 9.30, where you can get on the boat (quite a small one) without any formalities. Two hours hanging about before we at last sailed. Very smooth, I got hungry and had

375

lunch at twelve. Down in the dining-room it wasn't too pleasant . . .
Afterwards went up on deck, where I dozed off in the wonderful
fresh air. I was sitting in my coat on the open promenade deck, right
on the roaring sea.

Now I've woken up, the sun is shining, and in the distance
England's white chalk cliffs are gleaming. We land in half an hour.
I'll try to telegraph while we're still on board or from Dover. Hope
I can also post this letter immediately. At three we go on to London.
I'm fit. Only sad at being without Swipol!

Your own

(401)   Cambridge, 12th January 1931
Only a note to 'put you in the picture'. (In five minutes the
Reverend's car is taking me to the College.)

Got here safely at eight last night. Spent the hour-and-a-half in
London very pleasantly with Clark.[1] Although it was dark, and a
Sunday, I got some impression from riding right across London.

Dent met me at Cambridge,[2] also the Reverend's wife in her car
(a very ancient affair).

So far I've only the impression of a provincial place, but not a
German one. Sort of super-Deutsch-Landsberg.

They've come for me.

My health is quite satisfactory, the climate's splendid. A thousand
kisses.

(402)   Cambridge, 12th January
                                   1931, afternoon
To recapitulate: the Reverend's house is very nice, a genuine
old English country house. My room very small, thank heavens, so
that it gets warm quickly (gas fire) and I shan't freeze! At night a
special hot water bottle in bed. Food good and plentiful. *He* looks
very kind and distinguished, like a man of eighty though in fact he's
only sixty-five. Three daughters here too, but they aren't the three
Graces . . .

I'm mostly out of the house during the sessions. They started

---

[1] Edward Clark, a pupil of Schoenberg's, who was working for the B.B.C.
[2] The sessions of the jury for the London-Oxford I.S.C.M. festival took place
in Cambridge, where Professor Dent, President of the Society, occupied the
chair of music.

at ten this morning. Lunch at Dent's, where I was so tired I asked if I could lie down afterwards. Had a good rest and am now waiting for Dent, who is taking me to the next session. One joy is Fitelberg.[1] He is a member of the jury, a Pole—played my *Three Pieces for Orchestra* in Warsaw.

Continued (back home in my little room).

Dent called for me, and we went on working in the College. Altogether this is the oddest town I've ever seen. More about that when I get back.

Dent, who is like a kindly nanny to me, made a splendid tea in the afternoon. We worked till about seven; and now the car is fetching me and taking me home to dinner. We had a very fine lunch at Dent's, except that the food had no taste at all. In this country a pheasant tastes exactly like a turkey or a chicken.

At a quarter to nine we are going to the theatre, where they are performing a satirical melodrama, supposed to be incredibly funny.

Tuesday morning
(13th January 1931)

It was really very nice, the play, in some ways quite special and outstanding. We got home rather late, around midnight, drank a few glasses of whisky, and I again slept splendidly the whole night. It's now half past eight, and I'm getting up after having breakfast in bed. At ten I'll be at work again in the College. My health is so-so, but getting better every day. I believe this climate is very good for my catarrh. (We're living right out 'in the green', and you can call it that—even in January—because there are lovely meadows where sheep are grazing, and they really *are* green.) If all goes well, I'll return to Vienna without a cough . . .

(403)   Cambridge, Wednesday
                                           14th January 1931

Yesterday brought only one remarkable event: your telegram. Dent brought it at three. Well, how am I to take it? From my many letters you must have seen that I am feeling pretty well. Not so well at first in fact (just like in Vienna), and then better each day. Haven't you had the telegram from the boat on Sunday, then, and my five letters—from Linz, Nuremberg, Dover and two from Cambridge, dated 12th and 13th? This is my sixth letter. I'll write again

[1] Gregor Fitelberg (1879–1952), composer and conductor, pupil of Schreker's.

tomorrow so that you have a letter on Saturday, and I may telegraph from London—will be leaving there at noon.

Otherwise—I've been working hard all day, had a fine lunch (my 'favourite' roast lamb), home to dinner, played the gramophone afterwards, and went to bed early. It's become colder. But thanks to all sorts of drinks, good warm pants and woolly vests and galoshes, I'm managing quite well and never catch cold. We all get on well on the jury, talking French almost all day—although we're from six different countries: Italy, France, Belgium, Poland, Austria, England . . .

I'd better get up now. My gas fire has been on for three hours, and I've got hot water too, so don't worry.

(404)   15th January 1931, on the
                                        way from Cambridge to
                                        London
Thank the Lord, Cambridge is over. This evening I'll be in London, and shall meet various English musicians at Talich's[1] Philharmonic Concert. Tomorrow, Friday, I'll spend seeing London —Clark is going to show me around. On Saturday my train will be leaving. Cross the Channel in the afternoon, and Sunday at last, at last, with Pferscherl.

Now (another 'at last') I've had a letter from you. You were worrying unnecessarily about my health. I have got better every day, just as intended! Not only the catarrh, but general fitness. It took time, but I'm now feeling very fresh again, and the catarrh is almost all right. The climate in Cambridge is splendid. Yesterday it turned very cold, but by the afternoon it was above zero again. If I stayed here two or three days longer, I would almost certainly get rid of the cough. But not an hour more in that dull place. Hope I keep on getting better in London.

Still, I've experienced something else in Cambridge, something very interesting. I was taken to dinner at Trinity College hall, among dons and undergraduates, and that really made an unforgettable impression.

By the same post as your letter I had a very interesting one from Reich. He told me about the shock you got at my communication-cord pulling—you poor thing![2] I hope you get this letter before I

[1] Vaclav Talich (born 1883), Czech conductor.
[2] See Letter 399.

378

arrive. Good-bye till then, and be sensible—just for the last hours before I come anyhow! As regards health, I mean. I'm so afraid you may *not* have been sensible for the last six or seven days! I have, if only on selfish grounds, but also and always for the sake of my dear sweetheart.

(405)   Winterthur,
                                                    15th November 1931[1]

Well, here I am. After a very good night in the Reinharts' house,[2] we met at half past nine for a wonderful breakfast.

Almost the first thing Reinhart said yesterday was that I must definitely stay here till Ansermet's[3] concert on Wednesday, and that Ansermet had come a day earlier himself so as to see *Wozzeck* (his rehearsals aren't starting till tomorrow). I didn't agree to this at once, but I think I shall have to do it. In that case I shouldn't be back in Vienna till Thursday night.

Hans Reinhart is arriving at lunch-time today, and the Ansermets in the afternoon. We're all going to *Wozzeck* together. Afterwards a meeting with Kolisko[4] at the restaurant; then we all drive to Winterthur. You'll hear from me again before then.

Have just been talking to Kolisko on the 'phone, he wants me to come on stage at the end, etc. I declined. After the performance we all meet at the restaurant.

(406)   Monday, 16th November 1931,
                                                                  morning

It went well again. The house was chock full, the Zurich folk, who aren't usually very passionate, stormed the box-office so hard in the evening that the barrier in front of it was demolished! About 200 had to go away without getting tickets; there will be one or two extra performances coming up. This means I can make my journey home even more comfortable. Zurich (4 p.m.) to Innsbruck, third-class; Innsbruck to Vienna, second-class, sleeper. Arriving West station at 9.43. I have to stay for the Ansermet concert here, so can't leave till Thursday.

[1] Travelling to Zurich for the opening night there of *Wozzeck*.
[2] Berg stayed at the Winterthur house of the famous Swiss art patrons, the brothers Werner and Hans Reinhart.
[3] Ernst Ansermet (1883–1969), Swiss conductor.
[4] Dr Robert Kolisko, Austrian conductor.

379

The Ansermets came at five, we had a lively chat, then went by car to Zurich. Our party—Hans Reinhart, the Ansermets and I —sat at the back of the stalls, slightly raised seats, where you can see and hear well, but you're rather 'exposed' unfortunately. Atmosphere in the house splendid. After each act the manager came up to me and tried to persuade me to come on to the stage. In the end, after the third act, I just had to give in, whereupon the usual ovations followed—and further performances were guaranteed.

The production can definitely be called a good one. Some things specially good, some less so, like the first Inn Scene . . . Even where Kolisko doesn't have the full creative power, there's always an effort to fulfil my demands exactly, which really explains the powerful impact it makes on *this* stage and in *this* country despite various weaknesses in the production.

After the performance about a dozen of us met at the Café Odeon, where we stayed till midnight. It was very nice, particularly because of Ansermet, with whom I get on extremely well, I like him more and more. Altogether everyone was very kind to me and full of sincere and extreme admiration for *Wozzeck*. It kept making me feel even sorrier that you weren't there to join in the *Wozzeck* rejoicings. Werner Reinhart also keeps saying how sorry he is you're not here.

The five of us drove back to Winterthur. I always sit in front, of course, by the chauffeur and 'instruct' him. To bed at one. The peace here at night is indescribable. It's really *utter* quietness. Now I am walking through Winterthur to Rychenberg, and hope 'at home' to find a letter at last . . .

(407)   Winterthur,
                                                 18th November 1931
Further time-table for today: final rehearsal, go to some art exhibition; then Ansermet concert, then a meeting at the College of Music. Should be 'jolly', that. Wish I had it behind me, with that continual talking in French. A-propos French—I looked through the French text of the *Wein*[1] aria with Ansermet. Had composed it quite wrongly, and have now put it right. The negotiations with Geneva have begun. Perhaps they'll come to something—hope so . . .

[1] Berg's concert aria for soprano and orchestra, *Der Wein* is based on a poem by Baudelaire with German translation by Stefan George.

(408)   Hof Gastein,[1]

16th February 1932

My Pferscherl has gone, and with her the sun too: it's snowing. Still, it's warmer, praise be, and so will be even warmer in Vienna. I'll be talking to you tonight anyhow—and I'm nearly dying of impatience.

After an excellent dinner I went to see Marilaun.[2] We had a good chat together. He wants to publish an interview with me, which might be quite good publicity if it appears before the revival of *Wozzeck* in Vienna . . .

Slept well, had a nice bath, slept again; no walk, as it's snowing. Just now (afternoon) your card arrived. How glad I am that everything's going more or less all right, that it isn't too cold, and that you've been a dear and written. Thank you also for the New York notices[3] . . .

(409)   Wednesday

(17th February 1932)

Lovely to hear your voice yesterday, and to feel your atmospheric presence, just as if I were standing in the hall. Well in two days I'll be on my way to you already. How I'm looking forward to it. And I'm looking forward to getting away from here. In spite of the work (I'm working very hard) the days are long, no sunshine, no congenial company (even Marilaun is beginning to seem boring). So, before I forget (although I'm going to write to you again tomorrow), I'll be arriving at 8.40 Friday evening, West station. You can stay in the car, I'll find you. Just ask where private cars park, and I'll come there with the porter.

Last night I spent another hour with Marilaun—rather dull. I was in a bad mood about the cancellation of *Wozzeck*. Today I don't care a bit. Vienna is like that and always will be. Egon Pollak[4] is supposed to be conducting guest performances.

Worked intensively this morning, then went for a little walk. Your letter has just arrived. How sweet it is. I am very happy now, and shall find life more tolerable . . .

[1] Berg and Helene went to this well-known spa, and Helene returned earlier to Vienna.

[2] Carl Marilaun, Viennese journalist and author.

[3] Of a concert performance of *Wozzeck* under Leopold Stokowski.

[4] Egon Pollak (1879–1933), German-Czech conductor, head of the Hamburg Opera from 1917–31.

Hofgastein,
18th February 1932

It was strange last night. I went for quite a long walk in the afternoon, then in the evening Marilaun and his wife came, and we had supper in the dining-room: some mayonaisey hors-d'œuvre, goose with stewed fruit and rice, cheese plate. Down below, in the radio room, they served cakes, black coffee, and wine—but I hardly drank any. At ten o'clock Frau Marilaun reminded me to turn on the radio. It was tuned to Vienna, and we heard several dance numbers. I turned the knob, and got a Mahler symphony from Berlin. The atmospherics spoilt it, so I turned the knob further and landed right in the middle of a lecture. The third word I hear is Alban Berg. Turned out that this was a lecture from a book club: 'Cross-section of different countries.' Now it was Austria's turn, and I'd evidently switched on just when they were discussing music. Someone talked about Viennese music, very much along our lines: the Schreker school, the Academy and Korngold didn't come out well. He also said it was significant that Schoenberg, Berg and Webern had no official posts, etc. To illustrate the lecture, they read a scene by Billinger,[1] and—played the second movement of my first String Quartet. The Amar Quartet played it very beautifully. My golden one, that's really fine music. I can say it quite objectively. Oh, if only you'd been here!

Wasn't it a coincidence, though? Quite a chain of unconnected happenings needed for me to tune in to that station just then, in time to hear my name, and listen to a twenty-year old work which I haven't heard for ten years.

That's the most important news; everything else the same as usual . . . bath, work, walk, meals, sleep. But all this with a nice taste of going home in my mouth! Tomorrow, Friday evening, 8.40, West Station . . .

Vienna Station,
22nd February 1932[2]

My darling,

A few minutes left for a little kiss, and to implore you once more to be SENSIBLE. At the moment I am alone in the sleeping-car. Mayr

---

[1] Richard Billinger (b. 1893), Austrian poet and dramatist.
[2] Berg was travelling to Brussels for performances there of *Wozzeck* and the *Chamber Concerto*.

is on the train; I told him about Brussels. Be a darling and think of
your darling A.B.

(412)   On the journey
                                            (22nd February 1932)
Soon I'll be leaving Austria. The first part of the journey was
quite dull and peaceful. I went along to the dining-car soon after
we left Vienna, and sat down by Mayr, who is going to Salzburg.
I drank a cup of tea, while he had a goulash and a whole small
bottle of red wine (at ten in the morning!). We had a very pleasant
talk. Then he went to his compartment for a sleep, and I read the
midday papers. 12.30 dining-car. Now I'm going to lie down for a
bit. I'm still alone, praise be, and only not alone because I'm in my
thoughts with you, my silver pheasant, who hereby gets a genuine
Austrian kiss from
                                                       The Flea
p.s. A German and a Belgian one will follow shortly.

(413)   On the journey. Nuremberg
                                                       6.40 p.m.
                                            (Undated, 22nd February 1932)
Hope you've received my two cards. Had to hand the second
one to a guard, as Passau is in Germany and I have no German
stamps.
Slept a bit (I'm still alone!), then looked very carefully at the
score of the *Chamber Concerto*. 5.30 coffee and refreshments, and
now, before Nuremberg, this letter. Feeling a bit sad. 'Journeys
for art' mean nothing to me any more. I would like to travel with
you for pleasure as we're used to from our motoring. I always
gaze quite spell-bound at the lovely roads running along by the
railway. Well, that will come again, we must swallow these next two
or three months, till we can start *living* once more. What we do now
is only vegetating.
I've already had a minor mishap—my glasses broke. Perhaps it
means good luck. We'll see how things look in Brussels tomorrow
afternoon. Mayr gave me pessimistic warnings. I'll write to you the
same evening; but you won't get it till Thursday evening or Friday
morning. Perhaps if there's something interesting or important,
                                       383

I'll send a wire, in any case don't worry. I'll live only for the re-hearsals and my health, taking in only as much of the social side as fits in to that programme. The whole thing will be in French, more than enough of a strain for me as it is. And as it's a whole week, not just two or three days, for which one might manage to keep going, I'll be forced anyhow to take things fairly easy.

But you must be sensible too. Did you find my little note in the left drawer of the dressing-table? And did you do what it said?! Only nine hours! Still twice as much to go—another eighteen.

(414)   23rd February 1932
Funny—a different country and a new world. Everything is different, the scenery, the towns, the people, and certainly the air! It's dripping wet (without rain), foggy, pretty warm, and all a bit dirty. The countryside looks muddy and rather neglected, and in the towns everything's grey and shabby—in short, just the opposite of Germany. Even a town like Louvain, where we just stopped, doesn't show a single friendly or pleasant little house. Still, this is only the first impression of the first hour in Belgium.

I have been in the dining-car since 8.30 sitting over breakfast. They wanted to serve me a whole meal, but I only drank my coffee and ate some fine buttered rolls.

You had my letter from Nuremberg, I hope. Going back to my 'report': last night I had quite a pleasant conversation in the dining-car with sports journalists. Then to the sleeper, where I was alone, praise be. But I didn't sleep well, although there was nothing that actually disturbed me. I was silly enough to stay up after the frontier control (7 a.m.), when I could really have slept another hour or two. But as (a) I wanted to shave, (b) write to you, and (c) study technical musical terms in French, my mind was too active, and I got up, washed, shaved, breakfasted, am writing my letter to you, and now return to my compartment, which in the meantime will have been cleaned. I've packed already. In Brussels itself I have only two hours till the rehearsal starts (at one).

(415)   Brussels,
                                                      24th February 1932
What a hectic day! You can be glad you've been spared it, my Schnudoa. I was met at the station by Askenase and Madame
384

Collaer,[1] and they took me to a hotel which is modest but excellent; about a quarter of an hour from the theatre. I unpacked (they came with me to my room), so I had to talk all the time, partly in French. Then I sent you a telegram, and we went for lunch. This French hors-d'œuvre they have here is really something for me! For 35 Schillings you can eat ten different glorious items. After lunch to the theatre. At one time I would have been delighted at the high level of such a production. For the orchestra is first-class, the singers excellent, the theatre itself magnificent though old-fashioned. The staging quite reasonable, sets nice though without any touch of inspiration. But the final touch, or the last-but-one, is missing, and that's irreparable. The trouble is with the musical director. He's studied it down to the last detail, but in the execution he leaves a lot to be desired. He looks so superb you'd think he feels all the subtlety and warmth and bloom of the music, and could convey it. But it's mostly stiff semiquavers, and if the orchestra weren't so wonderful (the instrumentalists often playing with a beauty I've hardly ever heard), I should be rather in despair.

As things are, I hope it will be at least respectable, and make its impact. But I'll have to put a lot into it myself, and work like anything. Nobody talks German—but so far everything has gone quite well; I've managed to talk about the most difficult technical matters, and I understand everything. After three hours of rehearsing and several hours of discussion, one would like to close one's eyes—or write to one's sweetheart, and for that purpose spend half an hour in a nearby café with a good strong cup of black coffee. In the theatre they were all terribly kind to me, of course, though one trouble was that I could never get really warm. It's a very elegant (royal) institution with three directors, therefore conservative by its very nature. On Saturday they have the hundredth performance of *Marouf*.[2] The artistic opposite pole to that is the Pro Arte Society—but I've not met them yet.

Continuing this at night. After the café I went to the Collaers, with whom I had a very good dinner. Simple people with a lot of idealism, the flat belongs to the mother, as the Collaers themselves live in the country. Askenases were there too. Everything in Brussels reminds one of Paris: the indescribable mass of brasseries, cafés, cinemas, cabarets, the night-life, the speeding taxis, etc.

Two hours with the Collaers, then back to the theatre, where

---

[1] Wife of the pianist, Paul Collaer.
[2] Opera by Henri Rabaud (1873–1949), first produced in Paris in 1914.

all the singers were waiting for me, and the whole opera was done with piano. Quite a job to explain everything in French. I managed it, though, except for the insurmountable difficulty of getting Marie to 'speak', although I showed her how I wanted it in French !!! Rehearsal wasn't over till past eleven. I went into a nearby beer-cellar, and drank two glasses; you can't drink much, as there's half a drink ban in Belgium ...

(416)   Brussels, 24th February 1932,
                                              Wednesday night
Hasty report to tell you the more important things. In the morning I went to the U.E. representative to get money (I had a cheque from Hertzka). He's a nice Belgian who actually speaks German, praise be, showed me the town a bit, and we lunched together near the theatre, where I ate twelve different hors-d'œuvre items and nothing else. Marvellous, that's the best thing here! And of the two lunches I've had here so far, both were paid for by some-one else—rather embarrassing, though, this habit of calling for 'l'addition'.

One to five at the theatre. And now to the important point. I've been wondering all the time, of course, whether to try to persuade you to come here. After this rehearsal my desire to have you here at the first night has greatly increased. The whole thing will be on quite a high level, which will be valuable at least for comparison with other productions. You could also see Brussels, which is really *worth* seeing. Thirdly, everyone here would so much like to meet you (the Askenases, for instance, are mad about you and tell me to send a telegram), also Stephanie[1] and Thoren.[2] Fourthly, you would definitely cut an excellent figure here. Fifthly, sixthly, and 'all stations' to twenty-thirdly, *I would like to have you here.*

The few things against it are unimportant, I only mention them so that you shouldn't have any illusions. Socially it is not a 'top event'. The King goes only to see old stuff, e.g. *Marouf* on Saturday, to which I have also been invited, with dinner afterwards (white tie and tails.) For *Wozzeck* there are so far no plans for anything like those celebrations. That's to say, although I'm on the best of terms with Thoren and everyone else at the theatre, no one has even tried to invite me. So I am dependent socially on the people

[1] The daughter of Dr Müller. (See footnote Letter 212).
[2] De Thoren, conductor at the Brussels Opera.

I've met in Vienna, and am almost glad to have only them most of the time to talk to. Besides, it's possible we shan't even have the usual *Wozzeck* success. The audiences here are very conservative, rather like those at the Paris Opéra; one almost wishes there could be just a little booing after the acts—to set off the applause all the more.

But these two reservations are so small that the things in favour of your coming (Points 1 to 23!) are well worth a few hundred Schillings—it can't cost more than 500 to come here, and just think that it's also a *pleasure* trip, with seeing Brussels and two first-nights, etc., etc., for which one can really spend a bit of money. I can already see the difference in the theatre between yesterday and today. Everything is being done, and after the dress rehearsal, which is a private one, I shall still be given the chance to express my wishes and have them carried out.

You've got the clothes. Here, where they wear tails every night, you can well use your things. So all you have to do is make up your mind to come. If you leave the West Station Sunday morning at 9.20, for instance, you can rest in the train for 24 hours, I guarantee you will be alone day and night. At 10.30 on Monday you are in Brussels and can go on resting in my room; there's a second bed in it anyhow, for which I haven't paid anything so far, and it's absolutely quiet. Then in the evening you go to the first night. Next day rest, car drive through the city, in the evening *Chamber Concerto*. Next day rest, see the city, and at 7 p.m. to the sleeping-car, where we stay till Vienna, arriving 8.45 p.m.

So please, please, please, make up your mind to come, and quickly. You have Friday and Saturday to get ready for the journey, i.e., (1) Visa, passport (2) ticket for Vienna-Brussels express and return, also sleeper, leaving Vienna 28th February 9.20. That will all cost about 300 Schillings. For the journey take about 200 Schillings with you. No foreign currency. I hardly need any here, and can make do with what I have.

The best thing is, you telephone all this to Reich, who will arrange everything in a single morning. He can also advance the money for the ticket, and we'll owe it him till we get back. A memory like the Brussels production of *Wozzeck* we really must *share*. The city is terrific—so is the food! You'll love it. Tonight, for instance, I had dinner with the Askenases and the wife of the Polish ambassador. I had: a small lobster, then a wonderful fish dish (sole), then a magnificently made apple pancake with caramel, a speciality—

you have no idea!—and all this in a cramped little restaurant like dozens of others here. *Everyone* is a gourmet. So do come, please don't say no straight away. Think it over, then say yes, and start at once with the preparations . . .

(417)   Brussels, 25th February 1932,
                                                        Thursday evening
. . . What a strenuous day it's been. In the morning, after I'd written to you, Steuermann and Scherchen, I went to the main post office (at 9.30) to post you the express letter; then to the theatre, to look for mail. Found yours, and a very sweet one from Klenau, who is in Paris; then to the *Chamber Concerto*. Lord, what wonderful wind-players—pure harmony. I've only just remembered, that's another weighty reason why you should come. I'm very satisfied with the composition. The lady violinist isn't much to look at, but her tone is excellent and warm. The conductor is like the wind-players: military band, but in the very top class. Collaer at the piano is the weakest, alas. Full of musical sense, but not professional enough as a *pianist*.

We went out to the Collaers after the rehearsal, they live in Malieu (birthplace of Charles V,[1] by the way). We had to walk a bit, then take a tram, then half an hour by train, then ten minutes walk. There were five of us—Collaer, the Askenases, the lady violinist and me. Talking all the time, in French. Then lunch (good: jellied sea fish, asparagus with butter and bread-crumbs, calf's liver, stewed fruit, black coffee). Despite the coffee I was getting more and more tired. (Our host played the piano!—after we had *rehearsed* for an hour.) I 'sat it out' till 6.15, and refused an invitation to stay for dinner—politely but firmly. So the Askenases and I returned to Brussels. They are very accommodating people, and quite understood that I felt like a bit of rest, in the train and the hotel. Then we had dinner together,—rather letting ourselves go!—and at last, at ten o'clock, to bed. We sent you a card from the restaurant, and had only one thought: that you could enjoy this superb food with us. First place we'll go to on Monday, how I'm looking forward to it . . .

Today's evening paper, by the way, has a picture of me with de Thoren . . . Tomorrow dress rehearsal. After that I'll send you a wire. I'm thinking far more of you coming here than of my produc-

[1] Berg's mistake: Charles V (1500–1558), Holy Roman Emperor and King of Spain was born in Ghent.

tions, and can hardly wait for your telegram 'Arriving today'. There's still time, that's why I'm writing express. Even if on impulse you've said you couldn't come, you can still travel on Sunday. Just send a telegram that you're coming, so that I can arrange things with the rehearsals on Monday and Tuesday for the *Chamber Concerto*; also for theatre tickets.

I give you my guarantee you'll feel in your best form here. So: comecomecomecomecome.

p.s. 8 a.m. 26th

At last I've had enough sleep; am feeling *very* fit, and full of hope that you will come. The other day I dreamt we had another bird to keep Pibizi company: just a common sparrow. They got on very well together . . .

(418)   Telegram: 26th February 1932

DRESS REHEARSAL WENT WELL PLEASE DO COME FLOHDI

(419)   Friday night,
                                 26th February 1932

Am writing this in the hope it's wasted ink! That's to say, by the time it reaches Vienna I hope you'll be on your way here, perhaps getting quite near Brussels. The fact that no telegram has come today gives me *hope* that you at least didn't turn it down flat, that you're thinking it over, have perhaps taken the necessary steps, may even have already decided to come. Meanwhile you'll get my telegram tomorrow morning and will be able to wire me when you're arriving. How jumpy I'll be tomorrow.

I'm only writing today because I'm so used to talking to you, and because until I'm quite *sure* you're coming I simply have to tell you everything. But I'll keep it short, first because I still 90 per cent hope the letter won't reach you, second as a punishment for disappointing me so badly if it does reach you!

In the morning I wrote picture postcards at home, 11.30 to the main post office to post the express letter, at 12 to the Theatre Restaurant to meet the Askenases and the violinist and her husband. (They were coming with me to the dress rehearsal afterwards.) I had a light meal this time: sole (I've almost forgotten what meat tastes like!) and coffee. Dress rehearsal (closed, very few people there), rather a poor performance really, although lots of things have improved. De Thoren in low spirits, orchestra made mistakes

389

they've never made before, and quite a lot happened on the stage too. But as you know, that's the way with dress rehearsals—as it should be!

Short rest, coffee, and in the evening met the U.E. representative and the inevitable Askenases, whom I've got used to, quite a good thing, as otherwise I wouldn't know what to do in my free time except to wander around all by myself. (No one from the theatre would 'take me over', the Collaers live in the country, Stephanie is in Paris.) We dined at a place where the speciality is *moules* (mussels) in a wonderful wine soup. The goulash of Brussels: really marvellous. After that a fine turbot! Afterwards to the cinema, a wonderful French film based on the play *Marius*. Home at 11, where I'm writing to you in bed. More tomorrow.

Saturday morning.

So far—10.30—no telegram. I'm indescribably on edge to know whether the next hours will bring your arrival. By now I'm really expecting a 'yes'. Oh, if only you don't disappoint me.

p.s. The *Wozzeck* première starts at 9.30 p.m. Vienna time.

(420)   Brussels, Sunday
                                                              28th February 1932

After writing the card at the hotel yesterday, I had to get into my tails quickly for the 100th performance of *Marouf*, then to a little reception for the composer with speeches and conversations, starting at 11.30, so that I got to bed late. That's why I didn't write more. But it's also because I was so unutterably depressed after your telegram that the whole Brussels excursion has become nearly futile for me. Apart from the professional side, which anyhow is a bit of a burden, our stay in Brussels would have been something words couldn't describe. If you had come, it would have been a firm and lovely memory: the city, the grand and solemn theatre, the wind-players, the food, the whole atmosphere—all this is past recovery, for now it's quite without substance for me.

If only I knew *why* you couldn't come. It can't have been the 400 Schillings. Nor the four or five days away from Vienna, or technical difficulties (passport, etc.)—what was it, what?

I had no rehearsal yesterday, only a talk with Thoren. So I went to the Beaux Arts gallery and had a good look at the primitives and Lucas Cranach, with just a glance at the rest. At the reception last night I met a lot of important and prominent people, also Madame de Thoren, a very charming woman, though extremely fat; must have been very pretty once, rather a doll-like beauty. Her three daughters (one married, one engaged, one in her 'teens) look very like father, but surprisingly almost Jewish. You can't imagine the *brilliance* of the opera performance. Oh, if you had only been there with me!

Your card gave me very great pleasure. At that time I still hoped you would come here. Now I don't enjoy anything any more, I just 'complete my sentence' of three more days.

At 8.40 Thursday evening I arrive at the West station ...

(421)   Sunday night,
                                                  28th February 1932

Another day gone. A sad day, for my Pferscherl is not coming, has let me down. I can't feel any other way about it, and that makes me twice as sad. Otherwise it's also a turning-point in my stay here: opening night tomorrow, rehearsal in the morning, next day final rehearsal of the *Chamber Concerto*; in the evening, performance. Things are getting serious! All the more as some fights can be expected over *Wozzeck*. Well, we shall see ...

Last night we had mushrooms on toast and lamb cutlets for dinner, and listened to a pleasant jazz band. In this beautiful land they also have fine beer and wonderful coffee, it's not exclusive to Munich and Vienna! The black pudding is supposed to be famous, too.

But what am I saying? I don't care a damn about all this. I've only adjusted my mind to these points, and to good quiet sleep in the hotel, because I'd painted myself so lovely a picture of these two or three days with you in these surroundings so new to you. All my new friends as well are deeply disappointed that you aren't coming. I've been showing your picture around everywhere for a long time. The warmth with which I'm treated has long been transferred to you. Everybody's mad about you, including Thoren and the Askenases, who would have written to you direct but felt too shy. They had already arranged a whole programme, ditto Collaer. Today the Milhauds have arrived.[1] ONLY YOU are missing—and for me that means everything's missing.

Your sad
Flohdi

[1] Darius Milhaud (b.1892), French composer, one of 'Les Six'.

VERY GREAT SUCCESS FLOHDI

(423)   Undated
                                                        (1st March 1932)
Everything went all right. So that's one thing well over, my
darling. You'll have had our card from the Opera Restaurant, with
Milhaud's signature among others. It felt like a big occasion, and
the packed house was in excited mood right from the start. Four
curtains after first act, six after second, and at the end, when I
appeared, a great ovation from the whole audience. Some opposition
too, but that's considered rather a good sign if anything. It was very
strenuous yesterday, though (rehearsal of the *Chamber Concerto*,
interview, etc.), and it's going on like that today: 10 a.m. interview,
photographer at 11, at 12 lunch at the Collaers with Milhaud, 1.30
final rehearsal, 5 p.m. visit to the Opera (saying good-bye, auto-
graphs, etc.), and then the concert in the evening.

Thank you for your letter. I still can't see why you wouldn't
come. I'd thought over my suggestion, and the 'dream', however
short, would have been worth it. These are my last greetings from
Brussels.

                                                           Your own

(424)   Berghof
                                                      (Undated, July 1932)
Well, my golden one, here I am again.[1] Didn't feel too well last
night (a bit 'steamy', and not really rested in the morning); I am
now quite all right again, as ready for work as ever. (During the
long drive I managed to work quite well in my head.) At Klagenfurt
I renewed the Yugoslav visa, and took the car to the garage. (1)
The springs need looking at, (2) it's already 120 miles over the
servicing mileage, (3) the spare tyre needs repairing. I'll pick it up
again in a few hours . . .

Now for a brief report: I left Deutsch-Landsberg at four o'clock.
To start with I was in such a confused state that I took the wrong

---

[1] The Bergs had been at Trahütten. Helene stayed on there with her aunt to
look after her sick brother Franz; Berg returned by car to the Berghof, having
had a bad attack of asthma at Trahütten.

turning three times—after receiving wrong directions from these idiotic rustics. In the end I found the right way to Schwanberg and Eibiswald: difficult mountain road, very steep, with stones and gutters. But our little car can manage anything! The scenery is magnificent—looking at it as objectively as I can in my present mood. The only bore is the four passport controls,[1] which take about an hour. But the part of the valley till Unterdrauburg—Völkermarkt—Klagenfurt is something quite specially to your taste, and I'm looking forward to doing it in your company. Owing to the long passport control, taking the wrong turnings, and leaving late, it was eight o'clock before I reached Klagenfurt. The prospect of having to cook myself something at the Berghof and not getting any beer induced me to stop for half an hour, and eat frankfurters with beer in the café. Then I jogged along at 20 m.p.h. to the Berghof, landing up there at 10.30. But the driving in fact took me only $4\frac{1}{2}$ to 5 hours—a splendid half-day excursion for us, if we repeat it.

I found quite a lot of mail: among it a photo of us (Casella, Malipiero,[2] Werfel and me in Almschi's garden). She's coming to Carinthia, by the way, at the end of August. The Böhms[3] arrive in Velden[4] the day after tomorrow.

Now to finish I can only say again and again: God bless you—I'm thinking of you with such love, such great love.

(425)   20th July 1932
An American publisher wants to publish some trifle I've written. (In these 'New Music' booklets, which come out every three months.) I think I'll give him 'With your dear hands'.[5] There must be a copy of it somewhere among my collected works in the bamboo fitment. Please find it so that you can give it me when we see each other again. I gather I'll get a few hundred Schillings from the song (50 to 100 dollars, which is 350 to 700 Schillings). Reich tried to lure me to Pörtschach to visit Stuckenschmidt,[6] who is leaving tomorrow. It might have been quite nice and certainly sensible, but I'm not

[1] On the Yugoslav border.
[2] Gian Francesco Malipiero (b.1882), Italian composer.
[3] Karl Böhm (b.1894), Austrian conductor.
[4] Summer resort on Lake Wörther in Carinthia.
[5] See footnote Letter 1.
[6] Hans Heinz Stuckenschmidt (b.1901), German music critic, who was staying at the summer resort of Pörtschach on Lake Wörther.

in the mood to talk to people. It was too much for me as it was, having to talk to Winter,[1] who had just arrived from Vienna and is going to the Kanzel for his summer holiday . . .

(426)   Undated
                                                                 (July 1932)
    No letter today. After eight days one single letter, that's not much. All of a sudden the most lovely summer weather has appeared . . . bathing so warm that even you would come in. Then there's the most beautifully cleaned little car awaiting you here, the radio working perfectly, and the flat freshly cleaned—only, fancy that, the 'phone is now out of order again. They're repairing the fault, but in case a telegram had arrived from you, they couldn't have 'phoned it through to me so far. Anyhow I'll enquire at the telegraph office in Villach, and go to the station at 7. Otherwise nothing new, and as I'm hoping you're already on your way here, I'm only writing this note. All the rest when we meet. Come, come, come to your

                                                                        Flea

(427)   Undated
                                                                 (July 1932)
    If all goes well, I'll arrive in Trahütten two hours after you receive this letter. Oh, I hope so much that all does go well . . .
    What a heat-wave! One would die here without the lake. Let's hope it'll be over by the time you arrive. Unfortunately I've got to go to Klagenfurt today to get the car greased. I went to the café in Villach yesterday afternoon (completely empty), and read the papers, including an outrageous article by Korngold attacking I.S.C.M. . . . In the evening I went to bed early. Slept well for the the first time in five nights, and apart from the tiresome mucous membranes am in quite good form today. Worked very hard this morning, had a splendid bathe, ate, rested a little (battle with the flies), and am now off to Klagenfurt . . .

[1] Hugo Winter, one of the directors of Universal Edition.

(428)   In the train to Carinthia,
                                       Friday, 4th November 1932[1]
What a day! Much too beautiful for me. Because (1) I don't look
out of the window. (2) When I do look out, I don't enjoy it, because
my head is too full of other things. (3) I'm sad that *you* aren't
seeing it. You wouldn't believe how the landscape has changed
during this last fortnight. Ten times as much colour in the countryside: summer colours plus autumn colours, multiplied by snow at
all heights and a sort of sheen over everything. In short, quite a
feast for you. I should be inconsolable at your missing it if I didn't
know you were feeling poorly. But perhaps you'll come on Tuesday,
and then we'll see the second 'Indian summer' together.
    The journey was all right so far, though tedious. I read the
papers, music magazines, etc., had lunch, then a nap. After Klagenfurt I'll go to the dining-car and drink some tea. Now and then the
road is visable, how familiar and friendly (but uncomfortable
compared to a train journey!). How I'm looking forward to seeing
you again—I hope in Klagenfurt.
    Kisses—

                                                    your own

(429)   Klagenfurt, 5th November 1932
    Please send an express letter so that I get something from you on
Sunday. I was met at Villach by Charly, Steffi and 'Awo-Awo',[2]
and dragged around for two hours, till I was at last allowed to sit
down. We then went to the Bank to fetch Wittek[3] who had meanwhile heard from the Regional Security Bank that they are expecting
me today, and would help me (really?). Eventually we limped off
there, discussed the house for another hour, and I changed Wittek's
initial pessimism into optimism. Dashed off to the station—with
the heavy coat in this heat! I'd sooner have walked without any
overcoat. You wouldn't believe how beautiful the Görlitz range
looked hanging down over Villach although just now, 9 a.m., it's

[1] Berg was on the way to Lake Wörther, to buy a villa, near Velden, which
had been neglected owing to its owner's financial ruin, and was therefore within
the composer's means. In this villa—the Waldhaus (House in the wood) in
Auen—he spent the summer months during the last years of his life, and the
winter months 1933-4, when he wrote large parts of *Lulu* and the Violin
Concerto.
[2] Nickname of Charly Berg's son Erich. (See footnote Letter 24.)
[3] Karl Wittek, bank manager in Villach, later the father-in-law of Berg's
nephew Erich.

still in thick mist. At 6.45 back again in the train, a dreadfully slow journey to Klagenfurt. Hotel Moser, nice room, which—as it has two beds—I would keep for you. It's very quiet. I slept splendidly, had breakfast at half past seven, washed and shaved. Dr Lifczis[1] arrived at five—I let him sleep till half past nine. Then we got going, bank, land register, consultations, etc. What else we'll be doing I don't know yet. Perhaps have another look over the Waldhaus. And now I send you a thousand 'landlordly' kisses in advance.

(430)   On the journey to Berlin,[2]
                                                21st January 1933

Afternoon. I've already got quite a large part of the journey over, and so far everything has been all right. No delays in spite of continuous snow. But now I must at last have a chat with my golden-headed one. First of all to say that I'm frantically looking forward to seeing you again. I know I simply had to make this journey and my stay in Berlin might even be a pleasant one, but all the same! I am already thinking of the return journey, picturing my restlessness and impatience as it gets nearer and nearer to Vienna . . .

Meanwhile I have nothing much to tell you. The journey has been comfortable so far. Up to the Czech border there were three of us in the compartment, then I was quite by myself for a while, till suddenly in Silesia we had eight people in it. I escaped to the dining-car, where I am sitting with a pot of strong tea and writing to you . . . In the morning I read the papers, then the music magazines (with a magnificent notice of the Ansermet concert), and finally Klenau's libretto,[3] which interested me a lot. Not a bad idea, but more an idea for a film. However, as they seem to want this sort of thing in the theatre too, or at least will accept it, he might have a success with it, providing he has had some musical ideas. Tell Klenau I enjoyed it, but don't say anything of my criticisms.

At lunch-time I greedily ate all the food you had prepared for me: chicken, cake, the whole 'production' perfect. I am already looking forward to my supper!

[1] Berg's lawyer, who arranged the legal side of the Waldhaus purchase.
[2] To be reconciled with Schoenberg, who seems to have been angry with him.
[3] Paul von Klenau based the libretto of his opera *Michael Kohlhaas* on a short story by Heinrich von Kleist (1777–1811). The work was performed, with no great success, at Stuttgart, later in the year.

Please ring up Charly and Almschi, and say good-bye to them for me . . . and keep thinking of what you'll give me for dinner on Wednesday, besides the whipped cream! Oh yes, and do eat my breakfast roll for these three days! . . .

(431)   Berlin, Sunday morning,
                                              22nd January 1933
   Well, my golden-headed one, as you will have seen from the telegram, I arrived here safely. Up to the last minute I hadn't really thought about seeing Berlin again. It was all the more of a surprise, and almost like a home-coming, if I hadn't been here on such a ticklish mission. The express went through the whole of Berlin, taking nearly an hour. What a city . . .
   As for the 'smartness' of the hotel, I needn't have worried. It's a second-class one, almost third-class. An old converted tenement between two houses, little corners everywhere, the lift put in later, the wooden staircase very steep. Compared to the Fürstenhof —it's no prince's court, more of a lower-middle-class court. I told a gentleman in the dining-car about the three hotels recommended to me. He lives nearby, knew the Eden and the Zoo Hotel, of course, but the Hessler was completely unknown to him, unpretentious as it is. Yet I have to pay 6 Marks[1] for the little room (including service). That's because of the position, of course, which is magnificent, particularly from my point of view. 5 to 7 minutes to Schoenberg, while from anywhere else I should have to travel by the underground, taking time and money. And after all, four nights[2] at 6 Marks each makes only 24 Marks. My health is excellent, the temperature outside is 3° below zero, and there's a bit of snow.
   And now, although the main purpose of my pilgrimage is only just starting, I am thinking already—as I've done all the time, come to that—of getting home. Please take care of yourself, put on the fire in the bathroom, and don't work too hard. Kisses.
                                              Your own

[1] About 14/-.
[2] Berg seems to have succeeded in 'making it up' with Schoenberg sooner than he expected; for he was able to return home only two days later.

397

(432)

My golden one,

We are eight in a compartment which is extremely narrow, so
that (what with the winter coats and fur coats hanging up) one
really can't move at all. On top of that, windows and doors are
hermetically closed: it must be about 25°C. here. At four I fled to
the dining-car, which was also crammed full—well, it's Saturday
afternoon and snowy weather. All this when I'm dreadfully tired
(was on my feet the whole morning), and yet can't sleep in this
squash. I'm even too lazy to read, let alone work, which I intended
to do. Hope the tea will refresh me. Nothing to tell you. I don't
talk to my fellow-passengers, so I just have to 'serve my time' this
first part of the journey.[2]

An hour later. We're approaching Salzburg. It's getting dark,
weather fine and clear. The tea did make me feel a bit fresher, and
I've been reading a music magazine. Time drags, though. I'll post
this letter in Salzburg so that you hear from me on Monday (even
if there's nothing of interest to hear). Don't worry if there should be
a break in the correspondence, Sunday will be to blame for that.
I'll write every day, please do that too, and give me your loving
thoughts. Look after yourself properly, for your own sake, and so
that you are completely well when I get home. A thousand kisses.

Your own

(433)

I arrived last night just before ten and went by bus to the hotel,
where much to my dismay a masked ball was just beginning—
extending all over the hotel. So I took 'my pint' instead in the
Café Luitpold nearby, only to find the same crazy carnival in full
progress there too, as it probably was on every square inch of Munich.
One thing has become clear to me: we can never on any account ally
ourselves with a people like this.[3] True it's a mixture of North

---

[1] On the way to Munich as juror at a meeting of the jury of the *Allgemeine
Deutsche Musikverein* (German General Music Society).

[2] The second part took Berg to Zurich.

[3] Four weeks before, Adolf Hitler had become Chancellor of Germany.
The *Anschluss* (Austro-German union) was vehemently discussed on all sides.
The Bavarian capital Munich had been proclaimed by Hitler 'Capital of the
Nazi movement'.

Germans and Austrians, but only a mixture of the disgusting traits of both races. They have none of the attractive qualities of Berliners or Viennese. In the end, when I left an hour later, I witnessed a brawl between a customer and the doorman of this 'Jewish café', although among all the thousands of people I haven't seen a single Jew—more's the pity . . .

In the hotel I spent a restless night, and now, at eight, I'm having breakfast in the hotel with some of your fruit-cake . . .

---

(434)   Munich, Monday morning,
                                           27th February 1933
First day over: strenuous. In the morning session, complete idiots and semi-idiots. I hadn't slept at all well, and had eaten a big breakfast served by Frau Hausegger and Frau Haas.[1] Consequently I parted with the others at lunch-time, they went to a restaurant and I to my hotel, to eat half a pound of fruit-cake and two pastries before lying down for an hour. A bit more rested, I had some black coffee and hurried back to the Odeon,[2] where we conferred till the evening. Result may not seem too cheering for my taste. Apart from Schoenberg, Webern and Pisk, the young composers I like can't be 'established'.

In the evening to the Opera House, The Bird-Seller.[3] Rather charming music, by the way, quite subtle and ingenious. Excellent production. Afterwards I was tired—and hungry. But now the sight-seeing guides started their efforts; I'll hardly be able to avoid them in future. Instead of going quickly to a restaurant, we had to walk for about twenty minutes to some places where 'Munich artists' used to gather fifty years ago, and where we were now the only customers. Of course I had to earn my dinner (still, it was a splendid one) by listening for hours to speeches and anecdotes. And there's already talk of ghastly visits to exhibitions and museums. I've got enough on just now with the sessions.

---

(435)   28th February 1933
. . . Sessions from half past nine on. Unfortunately not as successful

[1] Wives of the composers Siegmund von Hausegger (1872–1948) and Joseph Haas (1879–1960).
[2] Principal Munich concert hall, destroyed by bombing in 1945.
[3] Der Vögelhandler, well-known Viennese operetta by Karl Zeller (1842–1898).

399

as I'd hoped yesterday. The Nazis have to be considered so much that Schoenberg, for instance, drops out, also non-German names like Pisk and Jelinek, who in different circumstances would certainly have been chosen. But please, keep this very much under your hat, and don't mention it to anybody.

Went for lunch with the entire jury to the Court Theatre Restaurant, which you know. Afterwards the sessions continued ...

Arrived home after midnight, another carnival taking place, so there was no peace till the morning. Among other disturbances in the night there was the following 'joke'. About 3 a.m. I hear steps, and jump out of bed; look outside and my shoes are missing. Can still hear some merry-makers galloping down the stairs. The lift-boy happened to come up just then, and he called the boot-boy but they looked in the wrong places. Then when I set about the search myself —in trousers and overcoat—I found the shoes on the stairs between the second and third floor (I'm on the third floor). Satisfied but wide awake, I went back to bed. Wasn't it a 'scream'! Still, I had a chance to sleep on in the morning, as the session doesn't start till the afternoon.

Tomorrow lunch-time (Wednesday) or on Thursday morning at latest I am going to Zurich ... Today I am invited out to lunch, and perhaps to dinner too. At least I'll save money. All the better, for the German General Music Society are paying very handsomely, nearly 300 Schillings. The whole trip doesn't cost anything, except for time—and sleep. The train journey Vienna-Munich-Zurich-Vienna is about 150 Schillings, so there's another 150 Schillings left, which will do quite well for the seven days—as up to now I have paid for only one main meal ...

(436)   Wednesday morning,
                                                1st March 1933
... Dinner in one of the many hundred restaurants, where for the last six weeks they've been dancing and stamping all through the night.[1] You don't see or hear it any more, you become quite immune to it. The whole town and all its inhabitants are quite drowned in carnival din, masks and confetti. And on top of that the news of the Reichstag fire.[2] Dancing on a volcano!

[1] It was the time of the traditional 'Münchner Karneval'.
[2] In Berlin, on 27th February 1933.

400

(437)   Zurich, 2nd March 1933
Arrived in Zurich at three. The Alps in snow and Lake Constance
had flashed past me without my really noticing. I went straight to
the Music Academy, where I got a very friendly welcome from its
director . . .
How have I spent the boring half-day in Zurich? My visit to
the Academy lasted rather a long time, as we—that's to say the
director—talked endlessly of music, etc.; he expects 'harmony' in
this dissonant era, not dissonance; and yet he speaks of the Zurich
Wozzeck production as if it had taken place yesterday. After my
visit I returned to the hotel, where I revived myself, and killed time
until dinner. I took it in the hotel: cold meat plate. A jazz band is
playing, while some 'orgiastic' Swiss couples dance. What a lot
they are! In comparison with them the people of Munich might
come from Sodom and Gomorrah! It's eleven o'clock, the orgy has
finished: closing time in Switzerland. Good-night, my lovely one.
This time the day after tomorrow I'll be giving you the good-night
kiss in person—what joy to think of it! But one more horrible day in
Zurich lies ahead of me, and then 15 hours in a third-class compartment—still, it has been necessary . . .

(438)   Vienna, 10th April 1933[1]
If only I knew tonight how you were! I couldn't stop thinking of
it all day yesterday, you in the train, then arriving in Klagenfurt,
then tottering around all on your own. Felt sorry I wasn't more
insistent on your taking a taxi to the Waldhaus. I do wish I knew
you'd arrived safely, and whether you were facing your great task
with confidence, so that you'll manage it more easily than you'd
feared. It's certainly quite a big thing, but I believe now you're
there and actually meeting the different situations, you'll prove
yourself again, my angel of energy. I also think you're having good
weather, warmer than here. That's what the papers say, according
to my careful study of them yesterday . . .
In the morning an Italian journalist insisted on seeing me, but
hadn't much time. So I asked him to the café and had a talk with
him there. He represents three papers and a music magazine, wants
to write articles with photographs . . .

[1] Helene had gone to the Waldhaus to make it comfortable before Berg moved
in.

(439)   Tuesday, 11th April 1933
It's still not warm, 6° in the morning, and I'm very anxious about
how you are, with no heating, no hot meals, no good bed. I'm
waiting impatiently for your first news from the Waldhaus, about
how the building is getting on. Quite a lot must have been done by
now, and perhaps you can already begin to have some enjoyment
from the house, not just the garden.

Not much to report about myself. First day: after you left in the
morning, I worked till lunch on my last lecture at the 'Kurs'.[1]
Afternoon rest, dentist, then to U.E.: meeting with Křenek,
Wellesz and Stein about distribution of the Hertzka Foundation's
prizes.[2] K. and W. are also coming to Florence;[3] we're meeting in
Villach or in Bologna. Was home at eight, found Annerl in great
agitation: Sprintzerl[4] missing for hours. She had cleaned the bathroom all afternoon, and when she wanted to 'put him to bed', he
couldn't be found although she searched for a whole hour. I began
looking with a torch, and found him *behind* the silver cupboard,
on top of the straw basket which was squashed between cases and
boxes. I felt like calling the fire-brigade to dig him out, as I was afraid
if I moved the silver cupboard the whole thing would collapse and
bury Sprintzerl still fast asleep. But in the end I succeeded; and
now he's had a good sleep in his own cage, he's fresher than ever,
flying around me (I'm writing this in bed), hopping, eating, peering,
etc. I slept well too, have had breakfast, written this letter, and now
(8 a.m.) I am going to get up, as I've got an early appointment with
the dentist.

(440)   Vienna, 12th April 1933
Your two cards from the Waldhaus came yesterday. Perhaps I'll
have more news with the first post, then I can discuss things more
thoroughly. I keep thinking of you all the time, all by yourself in
those dismal surroundings, you poor thing.

Did a lot of 'phoning yesterday, including Almschi, who asked me

[1] Berg gave lessons in composition in a class at Frau Schwarzwald's school.
(See footnote Letter 200.)
[2] Emil Hertzka, head of Universal Edition, had died in May 1932. The
Foundation bearing his name was started by his widow in association with the
U.E.; it offered annual prizes to new composers.
[3] Berg was going as guest of honour to a music congress in Florence, on the
occasion of the first 'Maggio Musicale Fiorentino'.
[4] The Bergs' canary.

to come this afternoon with her to the (public) last rehearsal of Mahler's Eighth.[1] Holofernes[2] is acting as her escort tonight at the actual performance.

At lunch-time I went to U.E. to discuss precautionary measures at the Austrian Embassy in Berlin (Herr Winter has already begun them) to get an official declaration (!) that Křenek and I are *not* Jewish, etc. I heard that *Wozzeck* is to be produced in Buenos Aires, and they are asking about terms. Then to the concert, where I sat with Alma, and didn't really enjoy the performance too much. Bruno Walter's successes are certainly immense. He's hailed like a newly risen Saviour, *and* puts on the face of Christ on the Cross. Ostentatious joyful glorification by the 99 per cent Jews in the hall.

Your long letter has just arrived. I am rather in despair that Blufon[3] has let us down. I wish I could drive straight to the South Station to help you, but I've got the class[4] and can't put that off. How about my coming on Easter Sunday ? Perhaps we'll meet for a day or two at Villach (Park Hotel), and so have a little Easter excursion. Tuesday morning I can make my appearance at the Waldhaus and put everything in order in a further day or two, so that afterwards it will run smoothly—with or without you. Don't think it over too long, and send me a telegram. Kisses. The next ones, I hope, in Carinthia.

(441)   13th April 1933

In haste—just a note on my day yesterday. Morning at home, worked. Afternoon at U.E. Big final session of the Hertzka Foundation. Then with Webern to the café. London extremely anxious for him to conduct the middle movement of my *Lyric Suite*: although *he* is definitely against it. He wants to make it a direct prestige matter in London, and leave on the spot if there's the slightest opposition.[5]

Look after yourself *please*, and don't get worked up, everything at the Waldhaus will be all right. And agree to the arrival on Sunday of
Your Flohdi

---

[1] Under Bruno Walter.
[2] Nickname of Alma Mahler's friend, the Catholic priest Johannes Hollsteinter.
[3] The builder in charge of restoring the Waldhaus.
[4] See footnote Letter 439.
[5] Webern's third visit to London. He had already conducted for the B.B.C. in 1929 and 1932.

Well, that's not too good news your letter brought. It came at lunch-time today. Horrible, the way these workmen keep us hanging about, and how slack they are. I guessed that after my short stay there, and now you'll understand why I came home not very enthusiastic. I was almost too optimistic when I said, what had been done so far was splendid. Even that turns out to have been wrong. There is no water, and they have to dig a sewer. Where? Between lavatory and cesspool—or a new one? I really felt at the time one ought to stay on there, or they wouldn't finish things properly . . . The disgusting weather makes me terribly worried for your health. It's pouring here too and it's icy cold. Well, no possessions means a quiet life! I can see that even with our little car. I spent the whole morning at Ford's and in the workshop next to it. But now, by all forecasts, everything with the car is in a condition where nothing wrong can happen (touching wood twice). You will be very pleased with it. Even the keys work!

I feel quite a bit better today. Was hoarse last night, but my throat isn't nearly so sore this morning. And I don't think the drives in the Ford in this weather did me any harm either.

Hindemith concert last night, followed by dinner at Meissl and Schadn. I'm glad I was there (although it was boring). My presence was appreciated for what it was: a gesture of solidarity[1] from those few 'Aryans' *who are something*. I had a very good talk with Hindemith, and am extremely anxious you should meet them and they you. He's staying on here for quite a while. Otherwise the most horrible company at the dinner, though not many of them . . .

The little bird is in fine form. This morning he had a thorough bath, before breakfast. He was soaking afterwards so that I had to put on the bathroom stove and put the cage there. His foot doesn't seem to be hurting him any more . . .

6.15 p.m. Your telegram has just come. Quite clear but sounds rather unsatisfactory. Would so much like to be with you already, and if possible at the Waldhaus. If the weather weren't so horrible and I were quite fit, I would get in the car tomorrow morning (Saturday) and surprise you. But in this rain I couldn't drive faster than 20 to 30 miles an hour, and it would take me eight or nine hours. That might mean my arriving at the Waldhaus ill, which wouldn't be too nice for you.

[1] Against Hitler. The Third Reich boycotted Paul Hindemith (1895–1963)—although at that time the break was not yet complete. (See Letter 452.)

I must think up something else. The rain is bound to stop some time. But till then, for heaven's sake, put on the fire in one of the rooms at the Waldhaus, so that you can always retire to it when you feel cold; and send your loving thoughts to your very depressed and solicitous

Flea

(443)   20th April 1933

Two hours after your departure.[1] I hope it will be the last time you go to Carinthia by train on your own. I was in deep depression. This Waldhaus has so far caused you almost entirely annoyance, trouble, work and agitation. But once the horrible job of moving is over, and we're all settled out there, it'll be the end of this double or rather triple household (Trauttmannsdorffgasse, Maxingasse and Auen), which is just proving too much for us. I'm trying to get on top by thorough organization on all fronts! Spent this morning putting in order all the papers about Franzl,[2] the Waldhaus and Mama in seven files and four extra packets. I'm taking things rather easily today though, as I've still got some catarrh; and you must take good care of yourself too, I beg of you. It's quite enough that you've taken on yourself all the hardships of the journey and the supervision with all this starving and freezing! . . .

(444)   26th April 1933

Hope to get post from you soon. Meantime, here's a report on myself. Travel office in the morning. The train journey in Italy (frontier to Florence, 12 hours by express, and return) costs 28 Schillings. So I am coming on Friday[3] with Wellesz, who is going on to Udine. Afternoon I rested, then worked on my lecture for the class. Then a meeting at the A.K.M.,[4] had a bit of a talk with Marx,[5] and he had an afternoon snack—bread and cheese and salami, all eaten with his fingers! Met Klenau at the Café Westminster to say good-bye to him. He's leaving soon . . .

[1] After a short stay in Vienna, Helene had returned to the Waldhaus.
[2] Berg had become guardian to Helene's brother.
[3] To Carinthia, where Berg broke his journey to visit the Waldhaus.
[4] *Gesellschaft der Autoren, Komponisten und Musikverleger* (Society of Authors, Composers and Music-Publishers), the official Austrian Performing Right Society.
[5] Joseph Marx (1882–1965), Austrian composer, A. K. M. President.

(445)

In the train,[1]
Saturday morning,
29th April 1933

Here I am sitting in the train and freezing. Seems they don't heat the trains any more, nor is there a dining-car. Weather dull, and my thoughts are directed more to the past than the future—I'm thinking of Pferscherl and the Waldhaus, and have no idea what I'm trying to do down in Italy. At 9.30 Wellesz will be joining me, at noon Křenek. Reich will meet me. They all speak Italian, so at least I shan't be as helpless as I am now.

Only nice thing is that from the train I can follow the road we shall be taking when we drive to Venice in the not too distant future . . . I shall only be able to write short cards. Please do write yourself *every day*.

4.45 p.m.

In three quarters of an hour we'll be in Florence—thank the Lord Wellesz came in at Udine. It was icy cold till Venice. There we had to change with all our luggage. (The train goes on by the side of the new *autostrada*.) From Venice to Bologna in the dining-car: good Italian food, including artichokes, olives, parmesan cheese.

Bologna, last change, again with all the luggage. (Third-class in Italy has no through coaches.) On top of that it's crammed to overflowing, you really can't imagine. Big struggle needed to get a seat. No dining-car in the afternoon. No tea! And it's getting steamier all the time. I greedily ate some ice-cream they were selling on the platform. (In the morning one had been an ice-cream oneself, right up to the knees!) Why I inflict this on myself I can't imagine. Even the loveliest part of the journey, the Apennines, I prefer to see at the cinema: much more comfortable!

We haven't seen Křenek, though he may be on the train. Trying to meet somebody deliberately is hopeless.

Am already looking forward to Friday, no, Saturday, for I'm scared of the return journey. Write soon, my little Mouse from the Waldhaus,

to your Congress Coon

We saw each other yesterday for much too short a time. And I forgot to give you the keys of the flat!

[1] On his way to the International Music Congress in Florence.

(446)   Florence, Savoy Hotel,
                                              Sunday morning,
                                              30th April 1933

You just can't imagine the noise. For the first time I'm glad you didn't come with me on the trip. It lasts till 1 a.m., and at 7 it starts again. But not as in other big cities, where there's a regular buzz penetrating up to the fourth floor; here there's a whole chain of long-forgotten noises louder than one had ever dreamt, apart from the usual din of the streets. Besides the trams, motor horns (which they seem to blow just for fun), you get the noise of the pavement, tunes being whistled till you're crazy, a flood of shouting and singing, and suddenly fanfares blaring out like trumpets—etc., etc.

And yet, thanks to my ear-plugs, I slept well, and feel properly rested for the first time in three days. The *café complet* is on the bed (coffee is so good here, a small pot is quite enough), the bath is waiting . . .

(447)   Florence, 30th April 1933

Report continued in short interlude when I'm alone. Morning, festive opening of the congress. Really an occasion: the whole town is a camp of soldiers, military bands, flags, youth organizations, national costumes, processions, receptions in the street and in a splendid old hall with tapestries—and speeches there. Afterwards cold buffet and separate reception by the Duke of Aosta (representing his uncle the King), who talked to me very nicely.

Up to now those here include Richard Strauss with wife and son, the Milhauds, the Malipieros, Bartók, Kodály, Roussel (Paris), the Eberts,[1] Dr and Frau Aber,[2] Toch,[3] and many critics, like Bekker, Einstein and others I can't recall at the moment. After the first hubbub was over, the Milhauds, Malipieros, Křenek and I went for an hour's walk through the town, then to a little restaurant, where we had most interesting Italian food. Afterwards to the hotel for an hour's sleep. Then drank my Espresso outside, and went to the concert. New orchestra, very good, conductor moderate, lovely music: Beethoven's Seventh, the *Good Friday Music* and *Ibéria* by Debussy. The last piece was—booed! In Italy they are just discovering Richard Strauss. Not so surprising: a people whose primal

[1] Carl Ebert (b.1887), German-English opera producer.
[2] Dr Adolf Aber (1893–1960), German musicologist and music critic, later head of Novello & Co., the English music publishing firm.
[3] Ernst Toch (b.1887), Austrian composer.

instinct is for noise can't be as far advanced musically as a people with a primal instinct for melody or for rhythm. The most melodically-inclined people are the Austrians, whose primitive music (yodelling) is melodious. The people with the best rhythmic sense are the Russians perhaps, or the Hungarians.

You only have to hear a folk melody here. First condition, as loud as possible; second, rhythm; melody non-essential. Three or four notes are enough, taken up and down the scale.

1st May 1933

After the concert I met Křenek at a hotel. He, Reich and I ate in an interesting little restaurant. Lert[1] joined us—the man who wanted to produce *Wozzeck*. To bed at midnight, up at eight. Today is strenuous: three lectures, lunch with the Minister—so I don't know when I'll be able to write.

(448)   Florence, Monday afternoon,
                                                 1st May 1933

A little rest with Reich in a small outdoor café. It has been a strenuous day. Morning, first session; then lunch with the president of the congress, who owns a castle outside the town on one of the hills surrounding Florence. Of a classical magnificence you can't imagine. And the park you wind your way through as you drive up to the Palazzo! A car called for us. There were ten of us at the table, including Wellesz and the Malipieros. Food marvellous and interesting—remind me to tell you about it. From there straight to the second session, which lasted till six. The thing I find such a strain is continually talking English and French and trying to pick up some of the Italian as well.

2nd May 1933

After my little rest I went by myself to the hotel, as I'd heard one is entitled to full board there (no one knew this before). I got a superb dinner: fried sole, chicken, etc. If I'm not invited out, I'll eat here by myself from now on. Křenek and Wellesz live in another hotel, Reich in a *pension*. At 9 p.m. there was the third lecture session. One by Ebert, very interesting, with pictures of stage sets, and one by Rosbaud[2] (Frankfurt), who was to have played Schoen-

[1] See footnote Letter 303.
[2] Hans Rosbaud (b.1895), German conductor.

berg records, only the gramophone didn't work! Afterwards we sat outside with Frau Ebert and some other people from Berlin, drank a glass of beer and went home after midnight. To be continued Tuesday. Hope to find a little letter, then I'll write more.

An hour later
Nothing from Pferscherl, that's a bit hard ... It's beginning to get very hot here. But in the old *palazzi* where the sessions take place, it's cool. My sciatica's a bit better—though I'm rather scared of the journey home.

(449)   Florence, Wednesday
                                          morning, 3rd May 1933
Another day gone, and no letter. If none arrives today, I'll send a telegram. If there hadn't been two public holidays in between, I should be really cross. With you, instead of with the postal services!

Tuesday morning session, lunch alone at the hotel. Otherwise I spend a lot of time on 'propaganda'. Mainly with the Italian and French section, where some *Wozzeck* or other productions are most likely to materialize. For these purposes I decided to cut an unimportant lecture, and went for a little drive with some of the older Frenchmen. My share was 8 Schillings, and I didn't regret it. Enclosed a picture of the places we visited, thirteenth century—San Gimignano. From five to six a tea given to us by the Fascist musicians, then home to dress. Before that a lukewarm bath, as I was sweating, it's getting *so* hot here. The banquet—only for the invited composers, the press and the lecturers—was very nice. We ate at ten round tables in a wonderfully arranged hotel hall, all decorated with flowers.

Sitting at this table for guests of honour were, among others, Richard Strauss, Frau Busoni, and as the only Austrian your 'Flealet', next to an Indian with a turban.

Altogether, the appreciation I'm shown in this truly international circle gives me fresh courage. Which makes the Italian heat more bearable.

This heat is reason enough why one couldn't live here. Today, May 3rd, it's as hot as the hottest day in August. One goes to bed bathed in sweat. Windows as wide open as they'll go, but don't let in any coolness, only noise—second reason why I couldn't live here. To the Waldhaus, then. Despite all the glamour, glory and so-called entertainment, that's my only desire, to live in our Waldhaus . . .

(450)   Florence, Wednesday night,
                                                        3rd May 1933
Said I'd send a telegram in the afternoon if no letter arrived. Well, I haven't sent one, though there's been no letter. I returned to the hotel at night, and am waiting for the morning's post. If there's no letter *then*, I'll be quite clear something is wrong. I was depressed all day, convinced there must be a letter coming, and now I'm quite in despair, as you can imagine.

Well, here's my day in brief. Morning session, extremely interesting on sound films. The time is rapidly approaching when my ideas on that will become possible. Lunch alone at the hotel. Short rest. At 2 we went to Lucca in two huge buses, then on nearly to the sea, which you can see from a high pass; visit to the house where Puccini died.[1] Made a great impression. It's kept exactly as he left it on the last day he worked; only the bedroom has become the chapel! Back to Florence, where we arrived at 10 p.m., and sent a card to you from the restaurant. The excursion was madly strenuous, six hours in the bus, and not even specially rewarding.

Now, after midnight, I'll try to sleep, if the anxiety about your silence will let me.

PRAISE BE TO GOD

This morning, Thursday 4th May, your letter came at last, and all my nerviness, heart-thumping and despondency are gone.

Out of the letter steps my whole Swablunk, as she lives and breathes! Quickly to answer your questions. Your behaviour towards Almschi was absolutely right. She had left me in uncertainty too, although she knew my address all the time. As for the Waldhaus I've made notes of everything. It will all be done as you want and think fit.

Last sessions today. In the evening Ebert's opera production, and

[1] Berg's error—Puccini died at a nursing home in Brussels. The house Berg visited was Puccini's home at Torre del Lago on Lake Massaciucoli, between Viareggio and Pisa.

tomorrow, Friday, I'm off to Villach, where I arrive at midnight. Next day at eight in the Waldhaus, returning to Villach at lunchtime and on to Vienna, where I'll be arriving at 9.45 p.m. Saturday. Will you come to the station? I'll have to take a taxi in any case. So that's that, and now I don't think I'll write to you any more. Perhaps a card from Villach. Your letters of the 30th and 1st came today, on the 4th!

(451)   Vienna, 8th (?) May 1933
   The news of the progress at the Waldhaus makes me very happy—apart from the heavy work you're doing with washing the doors, etc. Painters finished, ditto floors, caretaker's flat, garage. Fine!
   Lunch at Wellesz's. We left at 4 o'clock, I was driving Hindemith back to his hotel. Just after we'd left Grinzing, there was a regular cloud-burst with thunder and hail, such as I've never had to face in the car before. Within seconds Hindemith in the dickey was like a drowned rat. Through the empty streets I shot back to town; it was like being in a storm at sea. No possibility of stopping or getting out, the only thing to do was treat it as a great joke and go on laughing about it till we arrived safe and sound. Made it all the more dreary and boring afterwards at Zsolnay's,[1] though. I should have been one of the first to leave, and was just about to, when Schuschnigg[2] turned up. So I stayed, and we talked politics for a whole hour, also about music, all taken quite lightly and between friends.
   I was almost happy getting home to dinner. Would have been completely happy if I could have told you all about it, talking and eating together . . .

(452)   Vienna, 15th May 1933,
                                                          morning
   I was at Almschi's yesterday morning. She invited me to a dinner on Thursday evening, which had evidently been arranged long ago (though it was kept quiet from me), with Furtwängler,[3] Schuschnigg,

[1] Paul Zsolnay, Viennese publisher, whom Alma Mahler's daughter Anna had married after her divorce from Ernst Křenek.
[2] Kurt von Schuschnigg (b. 1897), Austrian politician, Federal Chancellor at the time of Hitler's occupation of Austria in March 1938. At this time, 1933, he was Minister of Education.
[3] Wilhelm Furtwängler (1886–1954), German conductor.

General Wagner[1] and Perntner.[2] This seems to guarantee more intensive contact with the Ministry of Education. Pleasant as that is, I'm depressed at having to postpone coming to the Waldhaus. It's rather cold comfort telling myself that the spring weather will be there when I do come, that by then you will be ready with everything there, so that I shall disturb you much less with my 'moving in', and that my catarrh will be perfectly all right by then.

It will be very late on Thursday before I leave Almschi's, and I shan't be able to start on the drive till the early hours (even if I don't drink, as I intend not to); so I would rather start about midday on Friday, and drive as far as I can, to sleep somewhere half-way in a cheap hotel room (perhaps in Leoben), and come on to the Waldhaus on Saturday, arriving between one and three. Or would you prefer it if I don't start till Saturday in the early morning and we meet in Knittelfeld about one o'clock? I'm driving very nicely again, only I'm not used to driving fast. Even 40 m.p.h. seems horribly fast to me. So I shan't speed at all, and that's why I'm reckoning on eight or nine hours instead of five or six.

Saturday and Sunday we can then arrange everything we meant to a week earlier, including Berghof and the rest ... Anyhow, please let me know which you'd prefer: my arriving on Saturday between one and three, or our meeting at Knittelfeld at a quarter to one?

Second important thing. After my visit to Almschi I went to Wellesz's. During the meal Hindemith suddenly asked me:

'Why don't you come to us, to the Berlin Musikhochschule?

Me: ? ? ?

H.: 'Don't you want to?'

Me: 'Oh yes!'

H.: 'It could perhaps be arranged.'

Me: 'With the sort of music I write?'

H.: 'Why not?' (There are two vacancies at the moment, two old gentlemen are retiring.) 'I'll look into it, and I definitely think something could be done.'

What do you say? Even if we don't think of accepting such an offer (although it would be more feasible now than before, as S. is no longer in Berlin[3]), it would be a terrific triumph for me, and

[1] General Wagner, an Austrian politician, was an acquaintance of Alma Mahler's.

[2] Director of the Viennese State Academy of Music.

[3] Schoenberg had been dismissed from his post at the Berlin Musikhochschule by order of the new Nazi Ministry of Education.

something to play off against the Vienna government should they come out with an offer.[1]

Nobody must know anything yet about this Berlin offer, or rather the plan for it. Anyhow I'll meet Hindemith again on my own and perhaps discuss details. I get on quite well with him; he *is* the only serious composer at the Berlin Musikhochschule, firmly settled there, and with great influence, as everyone throughout Germany knows.

(453)   16th May 1933
... The Brahms Festival[2] is on now, I've been invited today for the opening and of course am going. Not to the concerts, which are sold out... Met yesterday the Hindemiths, and had dinner with them, which came about quite naturally; home at half past nine. Once more I had a very pleasant talk with him, so now we shall see. I've since heard that the German government has chosen Hindemith to reorganize the country's whole musical life. Also, the critic Strobel,[3] whom I got to know pretty well in Florence, made very intensive enquiries there of Reich as to whether I was definitely pure Aryan. And now I hear that Strobel and Hindemith are the best of friends.

(454)   17th May 1933
My Pferscherl,
    I was at U.E. yesterday morning. Then from 11.30 to 1 at the opening of the Brahms Festival. Miklas,[4] Dollfuss,[5] who got a special ovation, Schuschnigg, who read a prepared Brahms speech; but Furtwängler actually delivered the great address, which made me very depressed all day. It was a Nazi-inspired speech on *German* music, which, he implied, had found its last representative in Brahms. Without mentioning any names, he betrayed the whole of post-Brahmsian music, especially Mahler and the younger generation

---

[1] Berg hoped to receive a professorship at the Vienna State Academy of Music.
[2] On the centenary of Brahms's birth.
[3] Heinrich Strobel, German music critic, Hindemith's champion in the Third Reich.
[4] Wilhelm Miklas (1872–1956), Federal President of Austria from 1928–1938.
[5] Engelbert Dollfuss (1892–1934), Austrian Federal Chancellor, assassinated by the Nazis.

(like Hindemith). There was no reference at all to the Schoenberg circle as even existing.

It was horrible having to put up with all this and witness the frenzied enthusiasm of an idiotic audience. Idiotic not to realize how the Brahms *a cappella* choral songs which followed made nonsense of Furtwängler's tendentious twaddle.

(455)   18th May 1933

I've been extremely shocked by all the troubles which have beset you this last week. By the unreliability of everybody there, on whose help you and I had counted, and who let you down because of their dances and such like. By the bad workmanship, meaning everything will now have to be done twice, and the postponement of all jobs and deliveries for half-days, days, even weeks! By the weather yesterday in Velden, rain, cold, and your own drudgery and chores in the house, carrying buckets, etc. By your not eating and probably eating the wrong things at that, etc., etc., and all the other things I can just picture, such as no lights, no lavatory, no water, privations you're taking on alone for weeks . . .

(456)   Waldhaus, 22nd February 1934

An hour and a half without you,[1] and I already feel such emptiness that I just have to write to you. From tomorrow on, I believe, I'll be so looking forward to seeing you again that I shall find peace for work[2] and develop a daily routine. But today I feel sad and have to keep thinking of the deeper purpose of your journey. I tell myself it will bring you on to a level of health where first, all disturbances from head to toe will cease, and secondly, you won't suffer from universal every-day illnesses like 'flu as if they were terrible diseases. In fact that you should take delight in your dear body, just as I enjoy it with my own (far less dear) body.

After leaving the station I went shopping, and now I'm sitting in the café, reading the papers, which are quite optimistic, and writing to my just-as-lonely Pferscherl . . .

---

[1] Helene Berg had gone to Hof Gastein to take the waters.
[2] Berg was working on *Lulu* at this time.

414

(457)   Friday afternoon,
                                              23rd February 1934

About twenty-four hours ago you left here, and it feels an age!
Meanwhile you'll have had my yesterday's letter from Villach. I
left there at seven and in the evening listened to Radio Munich.
Another, rather more pleasant *Gauführer* spoke—with effusive
friendliness—about all the advantages of a reconcilation between
Austria and Germany. Not a single word of hate. Then there was
some music from the 'Führer's native land': very clever, for it was
real Austrian music. This morning I listened to the news from
Vienna: the Italians are shocked about Habicht,[1] 'that chattering
little Führer', his criminal provocations and monstrous threats.
Our own government seems to be remaining quite cool.

The weather is marvellous. In the morning 2° of frost, the lake
even more beautifully frozen (like silk). No sign of our robin,
although I looked out several times, but lots of titmice, among them
a bluetit. Worked hard in the morning, then lunch. Now, after
short rest, am dealing with correspondence. Almschi's letter
enclosed, will please you as much as it did me; answer her as you
feel. I'm replying to her today, saying I have sent her letter on to
you, and also sending her Rufer's article, of which I received two
copies today. Then I told her that in case we should have to clear
out of here (though I consider this quite out of the question) we
would think of the Casa Mahler[2] as our first refuge. I suggest that
she stops for one night with us, so that we can talk it over. We
would fetch her at Velden at three, and she can then go on to Venice
the next day. Perhaps she'll do it. By the time she comes, you'll be
already here. (I'll write her that, too.)

The 150 Schillings[3] the Performing Right Society sent me
yesterday were for performances in England in the first half of 1933.
Rather fine, eh? And what are you doing, my Schnudoa. Write to
me a lot. You have more time than I have, and the separation will
be easier to bear, the long days will pass quicker, if each of us has a
letter from the other every day, And—love me!

                                              Your own

---

[1] Theo Habicht, member of the German Reichstag, appointed by Hitler as
Inspector of the Austrian Nazi Party.
[2] Alma Mahler's house in Venice.
[3] About £7.

415

(458)   Saturday, 24th February 1934

Thanks a million for the card, I've been waiting for it so eagerly. Thank the Lord your journey hasn't been for nothing. I have obeyed all my orders, and don't drink a drop of either coffee or tea. It doesn't do me any harm at that; at fifty I look like a fifteen-year-old (!) and feel as full of energy as a five-year-old.

Yesterday afternoon I received the honorific commission from an Auen farmer to write and set to music a four-line motto for his Choral Society. I've got two lines already:

> Auen Village sweet and kind
> Can gladly look up my behind.

After a good night's sleep, work in the morning went better than yesterday. Saw the robin on the tree, very chirpy. Try to find Station 500 (*Parsifal* bells), and if you get it, think of me sitting by my wireless and listening too—just as if you were sitting at my side, my golden one.

(459)   Sunday morning, still in bed,
                                          25th February 1934

Waiting for breakfast (the birdies have had theirs already).

Am sending this card to avoid a break in my letters because of the Sunday. Was in Klagenfurt yesterday; very lonely without you there. By asking around, I got the impression of complete indifference about the 28th.[1] Radio Moscow however, is pouring out abuse in German against the government, and so is Czechoslovakia. By the way, Radio Munich is on 450, not 500, I made a mistake yesterday. Hope to hear from you, my golden one. A Sunday kiss from

                                                          Flea

(460)   Sunday afternoon,
                                          25th February 1934

Haven't had such joy for a long time as this morning with your lovely letter. That's how I like it, and that's how I get the inner peace which alone makes me capable of work. But for heaven's sake ask for a different room, which won't be as hot as the one where we stayed. Are there others staying there? And what else goes on in

---

[1] The date when the referendum took place on whether Carinthia should remain a part of Austria.

Hof Gastein? Just tell me everything, every little detail. A letter like that is a ray of sunshine in a bleak, tormenting day. Tormenting because I spent the whole morning going over and over a short passage, as if I were under a spell. And in the end I made no progress, so that now I'm very depressed over it.

But the day brought other cheering news besides your letter. First of all, Schoenberg[1] sent me a letter from the Washington Library, which wants my address, as they are interested in buying the original score of *Wozzeck*.[2] 'Hope something comes of it,' Schoenberg remarks. So do I!

Then there was a letter from Fräulein Herlinger,[3] saying *Der Wein* was played brilliantly and that the orchestra applauded like anything—which couldn't be heard in the broadcast, alas. Kolisch writes that he played the *Lyric Suite* again in Paris yesterday, and in the spring is going to play it at the Austrian Embassy in London ... Reich informs me that Gombrich[4] will play the *Adagio* from my *Chamber Concerto* on Radio Paris on March 16th. Finally, you'll be interested in Auntie's letter, which I enclose.

This morning the weather was once more marvellously clear, at —2°. Then it became overcast, and I was afraid it was going to snow. Now, in the afternoon, it's sunnier again, so that I can write on the veranda. Later on I'll take the letter to Velden, so that it won't lie around till tomorrow afternoon. Then I'll go on working, to get out of the depression caused by this morning's 'blockage'. I've seen the robin often: he flew up to your window, where there is always some food for him. Lots of other birds clustering round too ...

(461)   Monday, 26th February 1934
Your nice card again gave me great pleasure. So the whole expedition is going to turn out a success after all. The baths will be good for you, I'm sure, and I'll gladly bear my loneliness here even

---

[1] Schoenberg emigrated from Germany in the summer of 1933. He travelled via France to the United States, and at first made his living as a teacher of composition in Boston and New York.

[2] The Library of Congress in Washington bought the three volumes of the original score. Berg had to hand over half the sale price to Universal Edition. Schoenberg had acted as his intermediary in the negotiations.

[3] Ruženka Herlinger, the Prague soprano, for whom Berg had composed *Der Wein*.

[4] Dea Gombrich (b. 1905), the violinist and sister of E.H. Gombrich, the art historian.

after the 28th if you are going to have more baths. I can just picture you in the water.

Yesterday afternoon I was in Velden to post the letters. On my way home I met the bus, put the car nicely on the verge, let the bus pass, and then couldn't move the car. It was so icy I had to put on a chain, then another, and even a third, before I was at last able to drive on, in a rage. Got to bed nice and early, and up early this morning for work, which today went very well. Reich's metronome (which he borrowed) came in the post—praise be. I wasn't at all sure about the metronome figures. Now I'm sitting in the Park Café, Villach writing this and picturing you bustling round the shops!

I actually rode in on the bus today. Not expensive—3 Schillings return—and I'm saving the car, which has been nicely cleaned. The road is even more horrible than it was five days ago. And I'm forced to walk home in the evening, which is good, because otherwise I wouldn't get any exercise at all. You are so right, this is the most important thing of all. If I can somehow manage it, what with work and correspondence, I very much want to have an hour or two's walk every day. But till now I've never got beyond wanting! Still, I feel wonderfully fit.

Politically there's nothing new. Everybody here is full of quiet confidence, and it really looks as if everything will stay quiet, for the moment anyhow. Mainly because of the Italian-Hungarian-Austrian alliance, which is growing firmer all the time . . .

(462)   (Undated,
                                                        27th February 1934)
To make the most of my time in Villach, I had a haircut. Quite a change trying to put my cap on afterwards: but I'm afraid it hasn't made me any handsomer! As I intend to have it cut again in another nine months or so, I got the following hair-style (only possible under a cap!)

I'm afraid we're in for some bad weather, but never mind as long as Pferscherl is with me.

(463) (Undated,
28th February? 1934)

Thanks for your nice letter of Tuesday. First of all: break off the baths, my golden one. Let me tell you that, as one who has stopped all baths from August till June, and so hasn't any hallucinations—who only composes music. But composing music is really nothing more than having hallucinations. Sometimes I feel just like that when I'm still half asleep. But anyhow I'm well, and you don't have to worry about *me*. Kisses.

Your own

(464) (Undated,
28th February 1934)

My Schnudoa,

I can inform you today of a most interesting, not to say gratifying letter:

Dear Herr Berg,
We would like to let you know that our efforts to take over the London transmission of *Wozzeck* for Geneva have been successful, and that it will be broadcast possibly by Radio Sottens (Suisse Romande). Everything has been prepared in London as far as possible, and if the performance is good, good future prospects may be hoped for, in particular a production of the opera at Covent Garden next year.[1]

What about Soma,[2] eh? You tell me he's in Paris. I was very sorry to hear about it: one friend less in Vienna. And as unpleasant things are all one hears from there (Vienna), I'd really like to get right away from the place. If at all possible, first production of *Lulu not* in Vienna—you're right . . .

The walk home from Velden was rather strenuous, although I had a stick. The months-old snow has now turned into a soft slush you have to trudge through very laboriously. On top of that, it

---

[1] Letter from U.E. dated 26th February 1934.
[2] Soma Morgenstern, a Jewish poet and intimate friend of the Bergs, had left Austria owing to the political situation.

419

began to rain. Still, it did me some good, for I arrived home with a terrific thirst (a thirst for beer, at that) and ready for a terrific sleep. In consequence I worked well all morning today. No unpleasant post disturbed me. On the contrary, your little letter revived my joy in life and work—so I've come back again to Schnudoa, whom I hug and kiss in a frenzy of love!

(465)   (Undated,
                                              1st March 1934?)
Went for a walk, a short one this time. Worked in the morning as per normal. Besides beastly letters from Antschi and Auntie, a pleasant one from Stein: the *Fragments* are to be done in Madrid, and a delightful letter enclosing a magnificent review from the Geneva critic, Mooser (after the performance of the *Fragments* in Geneva on the 14th). At the end it says in the French review: 'The concert ended with *Death and Transfiguration*. I cannot refrain from expressing my antipathy to its melodramatic quality and its light sentimentality, which made an even more painful effect when set beside *Wozzeck*.' I like *Death and Transfiguration* myself, but I couldn't help being pleased by this sentence, with which I must now close or I'll miss the post . . .

(466)   (Undated,
                                              1st March? 1934)
This is a sad day. No letter from Schnudoa, so I am left hanging in the air, and all my joy in life, and work, vanishes abruptly. In Velden yesterday afternoon I found an important express letter: Jalowetz is to conduct in Paris the Adagio from the *Chamber Concerto*, which Gombrich[1] will play. Suits me well, as I am afraid of French conductors . . .
    When I got back home, I worked till dinner, listened to the radio (political news, saying nothing much) and Mahler's First—saying a great deal—under Bruno Walter in Prague. Got through a lot of work this morning.

(467)   Friday, 2nd March 1934
My golden one,
    A nice letter came from you again this morning, so my outlook

[1] See footnote Letter 460.

is brighter, despite the thick mist outside . . . I went for a good long walk, worked again on getting home, and at 8.30—the *Lyric Suite*. You can't imagine what pleasure the thought gives me that you too are sitting in front of a loudspeaker. This in itself is almost a complete removal of our separation. Still—how I'm looking forward to the literal removal of it. Kisses.

(468)   (Undated,
                                        Saturday, 3rd March 1934)
   I'll pass over the unpleasant stuff to come to the pleasant: Reich's letter (which you might keep, please), and then still pleasanter, your letter . . . I haven't seen the robin since the thaw started. But the canaries sit huddled together when their cage is uncovered in the morning.

(469)   4th March 1934
   Am posting this card Sunday morning, hoping it will reach you soon enough to avoid any break in your mail from me. It's only a note between getting up and starting work, on the way between bed and piano, where the desk stands, inviting me to chat with you, which I would much rather do than get Alwa killed by the Negro.[1] Temperature outside is zero, thick fog, so that one can only *hear* the trains taking the farmers to Villach this morning—for the parade before Dollfuss. Will continue in the afternoon, for now just this card and two paper kisses.

(470)   Monday, 5th March 1934
. . . Fine that Almschi is stopping with us. We can discuss all the practical details. I'll write her a picture postcard to tell her how delighted I am to hear she's coming.
   Weather dull, but not unpleasant, plus 5°. Yesterday afternoon, I took the letter to the post office, then walked back on the main road, from Velden to the factory opposite us, and back again. Did some good work while walking. Wrote a bit of music when I got home. Then dinner, then listened to the *Lyric Suite*. Excellent transmission. Very thrilled by the fine words of introduction, the wonderful performance and the terrific applause. Hope you too could enjoy it. Will go on later today . . .

[1] *Lulu*, Act III.

... At 8.15 introductory speech, then the works by Mozart, Bloch, Berg, Strauss—and an interval (with a sports report), so that the *Fragments* will be over by 9.45, and you will be able to hear them.

And now, my golden one, I keep studying the railway time-table, wondering whether I could manage a trip over to you for a day. What do you think? It would be wonderful, wouldn't it! I could stay in Gastein from 10.30 till 2.30 or even till 6. Say yes, and I'll do it straight away. Countless kisses.

(471)   6th March 1934

Now I know! 'The Voice of the Blood' from the newspaper *Der Angriff*:[1] 'anyone of Nordic blood, or with enough left of the Nordic inheritance not only physically but above all mentally and spiritually, will for ever remain an enemy of the big Stores.'

I am disconsolate that you didn't hear the *Lyric Suite*, or, presumably, the *Fragments* on the same station. I listened yesterday, and got an even better reception than the day before. Very clear and pure and even too loud, so that I had to turn the volume down at some points. It was also quite a decent performance, and a very musical, pleasant-sounding voice. Big applause again, and I was very pleased with the fine introductory speech. My *pieces* were discussed by the speaker in detail as the main item of the concert. Now, my golden one, the next broadcast, which Geneva is taking over from London, will be on the 14th (tomorrow week), and you'll be listening to it with me, I expect: the whole of *Wozzeck*. Two days later, it'll be from Paris with Gombrich. I also heard today that at the *Biennale*[2] the Kolisch Quartet will be playing the *Lyric Suite*, which reassured me like anything; so glad it's not being done by some Italian quartet society.

The article by Korngold is good, almost pleasant—but Vienna still remains Vienna! Now Rosé is again performing a new string quartet by a young composer, and everything else here is all the same, whether the colours are black, red, brown or black and yellow.[3] I'm getting more and more worried about Austria and Germany.

[1] Goebbels's Berlin daily newspaper.
[2] In Venice.
[3] The colours of the different political parties in Austria: Christian-Socialists, Socialists, National-Socialists, Monarchists.

It's snowing in Gastein, is it? Incredible! Here the last snow is thawing. I'm again sitting in the sun on the veranda—no overcoat! Yes, I do have a wash now and then, and shave every third or forth day! Robin invisible; but another bird comes, a lovely little titmouse, nearly black and white. What do you think of Smaragda's letter, which I enclose, with some comments at the side? Please answer it from Hof Gastein, and the questions that concern me as I've indicated. Oh, my golden one, how I'm longing for you! I wonder whether I'll get the word to come to you. And then—when do *you* mean to come? How many baths have you taken?

I worked well this morning. Now I'm going to drive to the post office. Outside, spring is at the door, and soon, let's hope, my golden-haired girl will be there too.

(472)   7th March 1934
... How horrified I am at Vienna ... *Karl V*[1] has been cancelled for political reasons! This will give us a lot to talk about, won't it! And when I write that last sentence, I picture the glorious moment when we are sitting together first in the car, then in the green room, and doing all our talking; then listening together from nine o'clock on—*how I'm looking forward to it.* I shan't easily get over your not having been able to listen (with me) to the *Lyric Suite* and the *Fragments*, when the reception was so good.

Now I know you'll be here for sure on the 14th, I'm full of joyful anticipation. In fact, I'm happy altogether which I have not been the whole time till now ...

(473)   Waldhaus, 8th March 1934
No letter arrived today, I'm sad! Perhaps this afternoon. Haven't much to tell you either. Yesterday afternoon Velden, post office. This morning work, and now correspondence. A lot of it again, unfortunately: Stein, six pages on business; Ansermet, Dent ... Weather dull, around zero. There are still some people, quite crazy, walking across the lake. But still no rain or snow, which I'm glad about because of the roads. The birds only come *en passant*, although they always find some food, of course. Robin has quite

---

[1] Křenek's opera *Karl V* had been accepted for its first performance at the Vienna Opera and rehearsals had started. Then the première was cancelled for political reasons.

vanished, but we've got a substitute now, a very light, silvery-whitish-grey little bird about as big as a small titmouse, only slimmer and more graceful, with a smooth black head. Really lovely, but so shy. A beauty, almost exotic.

Gerhart Hauptmann in his memoirs says of his youth: 'Even though my position was near to socialism, I never felt myself to be a Social Democrat.' How wonderfully simple an expression of his point of view, which would also do for me.

Can't think of anything else for today, and so, although I've not washed or shaved or cleaned my teeth yet, I dare (from afar!) to kiss my golden one right on her little mouth.

Your own

(474)   Waldhaus, 9th March 1934
And no letter today either. Do you post your letters later now? I only got your card yesterday in Velden. I was glad of that after an anxious morning. Today is gloriously fine again, and I keep on thinking: this would be something for Pferscherl. But patience, patience—it soon will be. I'm really counting the days. Worked well in the bus on the way over. (Haven't much feeling really for the character of the Countess Geschwitz,[1] though I must respect her. I find her harder to set to music than all the rest of Lulu's 'satellites' put together. But now at last it looks as though I've found the right notes for both her closing stanzas.)

This morning's mail brought only a letter from Reich with two cuttings enclosed (please keep them).

Stein will probably make the piano score. He also writes about a concert performance of *Lulu*, and I replied that I would rather wait till after the German première. In the friendly foreign countries (USA, England, Holland, Belgium, France, Czechoslovakia) the concert performances may start straight away. The *hostile* foreign countries (Austria) can wait! . . .

Oh, how much we shall have to talk about. Things to tell each other, too, but even more than that, to bring up all we have been thinking about and thinking right through in our loneliness.

Also: spring is coming! By then our little road to the Waldhaus will be dry. At the moment I have to splash through it at speed. Wonder if Almschi will really come. Would be very nice if she did.

[1] In *Lulu*.

424

We'd let the two[1] of them have our own room just for the one night. Did you think over my idea of coming here by express? There I am, back at our reunion—but then the anticipation of it is what I'm living on just now. *How* I'm longing for it. Before then you'll get four more letters. Frenzied kisses

from
. the Flea

(475)   Waldhaus, Saturday afternoon,
                                        10th March 1934
You are right, my golden one, to long for the Waldhaus and this heaven-blessed region. After three most horrible days, there's now magnificent sunshine. I'm sitting on the veranda (where it's 15°), writing this to my silver pheasant, looking forward madly to when she will again be quietly sunning her plumage. And she'll be able to do it for months—till we look for the shade of the other veranda, only to go back into the sun in the autumn, returning to the world laden with a heavy score. Think of these eight months, with their beauty for us to appreciate to the full. By thinking of that, you will be able to stick out a few more days at Hof Gastein. If you can't, just leave for here at any time. A card will be enough, saying 'Come at once to Villach', where there will be a blissful embrace. If it only concerned me, I would send you a wire this very day, saying 'Come at once'. But when I remember that every single medicinal bath you take will probably guarantee you a week more of well-being, then I don't mind biting into the sour apple of loneliness, which is twice as palpable here in the lonely woods. Even if one goes to Klagenfurt, as I did yesterday, it's a dreadfully dull business on one's own . . . Went to the cinema instead of the café. Interesting newsreel and a magnificent travel film about Canada, Chicago, and the Niagara Falls. Indescribably grand, this America.

Well then, my golden one, if you can't bear it any more, make an end. Otherwise comfort yourself with the inescapable glory of the Waldhaus, which you will enjoy even more when you're quite fit again. What joy for *me* when you do come.

(476)   Waldhaus, 11th March 1934,
                                        Sunday afternoon
Today's post put me into a nasty dilemma. A card from Erich

1 Alma Mahler had married Franz Werfel, her third husband.

425

Kleiber, saying 'it's absolutely imperative in all our interests that I should get the authentic libretto of *Lulu* from you as soon as possible.'

I can't postpone this till I've finished the score. So I have to sit down immediately and type out about fifty to a hundred pages. For lots of it I'll first have to find a satisfactory version, but still won't have the final version for the printed libretto, as I don't want to finalize that till all the music is written; there may be one or two changes, etc. Do the work twice over, in fact. Well, I'd better sleep on it. Today and tomorrow I'll go on composing. Have to get some typing paper anyhow. Am rather worried about it all, but won't cross the bridge till I come to it. And perhaps with my inspiration flagging a bit, a little break like this before the final spurt might prove quite beneficial! I am just turning on the radio, searching for music, and lo and behold, the great aria from *Turandot*. Pferscherl would enjoy that . . .

(477)   Undated
                                                    (11th March 1934)

. . . Would like to fetch you at Villach, if possible meeting the express at 5.10. I don't want you to change trains by yourself with the heavy case, perhaps even feeling rushed if the train is late. And when we at last get home, you mustn't suppose we'll be able to *rest*, even when lying down, with so much to talk about! For I've also got something important, interesting and long-winded to tell *you*, something that's just cropped up now; only, because it's such a long-winded business, I don't really feel like putting it all in writing.

Altogether I think my idea is best, that you should take the express to Villach. The lovely drive up here would be much jollier for us both and more worthy of your coming! As it will be rather late in the evening of the 14th (the concert on the radio doesn't start till 9 o'clock, and will end about half-past eleven or twelve), it would be a terribly strenuous day for you if you started in the early morning. But this way, (1) you'll get another bath at Gastein in the morning, (2) can rest for hours after it, (3) eat at the normal time and catch the train at 2.30, (4) relax and have a siesta in the train, (5) have a shorter train, (6) a pleasanter time to arrive at Villach; and you'll be rested when you come to the Waldhaus. We'll chat and caress there, and then after a few hours the concert . . .

(478)   Monday, 22nd March 1934

These are glorious letters if we write only about our reunion and everything connected with it. I'm typing this so that you can read it better and to get myself into training . . .

I'll be at the station in Velden. That's all settled, my golden one, and all that remains—is the joyful anticipation. Alas, the joy is slightly clouded by the fact that I shall have to type like mad during these next few days.

Yesterday was a typical dull Sunday. Late afternoon I drove to Velden to post letters and drink a black coffee. This morning I worked, and got to a good point in the score before the break in composing. Then I told Kleiber the libretto would be done and wrote this last-but-one letter to Pferscherl.

Enough, my swan. Soon you will be floating here into your Flohdi's arms.

With Pferscherl the spring arrives at last. The ice on the lake is shattered right in the middle.

(479)   Waldhaus
                                 (Undated, July? 1934)

My dearest Pferscherl,

Just a note so that you hear something from me the first day[1] (same old words, every time we are separated). Hope you had a good journey, arrived safely and had a good night. Please write me a card—in case you haven't already. News bulletin was completely reassuring. The post brought the expected from Washington.[2]

Tell everybody we don't yet know who will be conducting in Venice.[3] Please ask Reich whether we have to do anything about the 70 per cent railway reduction or whether we can get it even after the beginning of the festival. I'll see him anyhow on Friday in Velden. In case you already know something definite about our journey and hotel, tell him that too.

It wasn't till after you left that I noticed you hadn't taken the

---

[1] Helene had gone to Vienna in connection with her brother, Franz.

[2] The money paid by the Washington Congress Library for the original manuscript of *Wozzeck*.

[3] The Biennale of Music in Venice was to include the *Three Fragments* from *Wozzeck*. Owing to Nazi pressure the performance was cancelled, and Berg's appointment to the Committee of Honour was withdrawn. He protested successfully: his name was put back on the list, his music performed.

carrying strap with you and *had* taken your *old* umbrella . . . Please ask Křenek whether they are coming to Venice.

Countless kisses
from
the Flea

(480)

Friday afternoon
27th July 1934

My Pferscherl,

What terrible days these are.[1] If only you were here. It's very hot, perhaps even hotter than Vienna, but the cloudless sky and summer peace over lake and wood are magnificent. The house is lovely and cool if one is careful. On the veranda, for instance, it's 27° in the shade, in the sun, 35° while it's only 17° in the house itself. Wonder what it's like in Vienna. You write of the tropical heat. Are you having a bad time with it? I do feel sorry for you. Of all the hot days, you have to be in Vienna for the two or three hottest in the whole year. The lake is pleasantly warm, you could enjoy a bathe in it. Hope you'll be coming soon! Don't let the house renovation make you stay an hour longer in Vienna than you have to for Franz's sake. Don't worry about the renovation at all. Very anxious to hear how Franz is, I can't quite make it out from your two cards. As I haven't had a telegram, I presume you won't be arriving today. What about tomorrow??!! Oh, it would be lovely. I feel very like 'phoning you to find out what's happening.

I could weep to think of you missing these wonderful days here. Otherwise I'm working hard. Slept well, breakfast at six, work all morning. Meanwhile your express card arrived, which I answered at once, and an hour later the post brought your second card, from which I took it that one of the keys I sent you must be the right one . . .

Heinsheimer told me that Philadelphia is performing operas again this year, and that they will have *Wozzeck* in their repertoire. Thank heavens foreign countries are beginning to move . . .

---

[1] On the 25th July the Austrian Federal Chancellor, Dollfuss, was assassinated by the Nazis, and for some time it looked as if the Nazis would assume power in Austria. Part of this letter seems to be in code, as Berg was very anxious for Helene to get out of Vienna and to return.

(481)   (Undated,
                                       7th October 1935?)

My Schnudoa,

Half of the first day is over.[1] In the morning I worked hard. The sun came late, which meant only a short stay on the veranda. But this afternoon I've been for a magnificent bus ride. You can't imagine the glaze of this 100 per cent-friendly-dreamy-day. I have never seen the lake so beautiful! What luck for us that at this blackest of times[2] we have been granted such light.

Now (still afternoon) I'm sitting in the café. Have read all the papers, then wrote the more important letters: U.E., and Wiesengrund.[3] I told him the truth, and asked about the sale of the orchestral score of the *Lyric Suite* and English pupils, etc., etc. Perhaps he can think of a way of helping me.

News: Fey receives the highest order and an important economic post, Drexel is pensioned off![4] Somebody I know quite well came into the café just now, an art historian from Vienna, whom I met several times at Zsolnay's, etc., but I can't remember his name. We had a very good and intensive talk, and that's why this letter got interrupted. Now the bus is starting back, so I'll finish in haste with heaps of kisses

from
the Flea

(482)   (Undated,
                                     8th October 1935)

Interesting mail: Jalowetz about the Prague performance.[5] In some ways very reassuring for me, in case—which God forbid—we can't get *Lulu* produced anywhere but in Prague. A card from Auntie, who would like to know the date you arrive in Vienna; and

[1] After staying at the Waldhaus all summer, the Bergs were now returning to Vienna, so Helene had gone ahead to get the flat ready in Trauttmannsdorffgasse.

[2] The political and economic situation of Austria was deteriorating.

[3] Berg's financial position had worsened owing to the Nazi boycott of his works. He turned for possible help to his pupil, Dr Theodor Wiesengrund-Adorno.

[4] Two Austrian politicians of the day.

[5] The *Lulu Symphony*, a suite of five symphonic pieces from the still incomplete *Lulu* score, had been first performed at Berlin on 30th November 1934 under Erich Kleiber. It was now played at the I.S.C.M. Festival in Prague. Berg planned to be present, but had to give up the idea owing to the abscess (contracted in August 1935), which led to his death in December.

an invitation to the Hagenbund[1] at last. I would be glad if you could go (1) for social reasons, (2) you'll see Zsolnay there, (3) because the sculptor is very interesting. So try to make it: Friday, five o'clock, Hagenbund. Perhaps you can give somebody the enclosed tickets to the Szigeti concert. One of the finest violinists, although he is not a Jew![2]

(483)   Wednesday, 9th October 1935
   A dull, cloudy day. Yesterday it was lovely, and I made the most of it. Walked in the sunshine to Velden, and back to the Waldhaus, sun still shining. I managed it splendidly, no damage but five blisters on the sole of my feet! In between I had been to Villach, there by train, back by bus . . .
   Slept well, started work early—interrupted by the post coming: Hanna Schwarz (she's singing tomorrow on the radio); the French concert agency, pressing me for the *Piano Sonata* and the *Pieces for Clarinet and Piano*; the new Nirenstein Gallery wants to have a look at the Schoenberg and Gerstl portraits,[3] which they think I've got. Finally, and most important: an invitation to a Fashion-Show tea. I don't think you'll be able (or willing) to go, mainly because you haven't the clothes; still, I'll let *you* decide, as one can't just ignore it. So do as you feel with the printed reply-card—perhaps ask Almschi's advice. Anyhow I'm sending you straight away the 6 Schillings for the ticket, which is also enclosed. Goes against the grain, but we can't give society even the slightest chance to put us in the wrong. If you write as from here saying that unfortunately you won't be in Vienna, it will at least show we've not been mean . . .
   There might now be a short break in my letters, as there is a big public holiday tomorrow (plebiscite), which puts the post out of action too. The postman won't be coming to the Waldhaus tomorrow (Thursday) either, so I shan't have anything from you till Friday. Hope you're *well*. For heaven's sake don't work too hard. We want to have a few more lovely days here, and for that you must be without any aches and pains or other troubles. Countless kisses
                                                            from
                                                         the Flea

[1] Association of Viennese artists, which arranged exhibitions.
[2] Joseph Szigeti (b. 1892), Hungarian violinist.
[3] Of Berg by Schoenberg (who was also an accomplished painter) and the Viennese artist Richard Gerstl.

National holiday, so no mail, much to my irritation, as I shan't know for 48 or 72 hours how you are ... Not much to report about myself. Took a bus to Klagenfurt and settled the mortgage business. Am now paying only 620 Schillings a half-year instead of 1,050, a great relief. To have some exercise (despite the blisters on my foot, which make every step agony!) I went to the art exhibition (only the portrait of a child stuck out), then walked through Klagenfurt, where I was struck by some delightful new parts, for instance the Schiller Park and the Goethe Park. Then I went to the café to read the papers, including foreign ones—so full of interest for us just now. Home by bus, back there at six, worked a bit, listened to the radio ...

Slept well, started work early, good progress. While walking I think over new composition plans. Otherwise I'm already rather on edge today, not having heard from you for so long. Are you eating properly? Hope you didn't starve on your journey.

Love me!

(485)   11th October 1935

Today I'm sure I'll get news from Pferscherl—and high time too!
Wonder how your work in the flat is progressing, what you've been
doing in Vienna, who you've been seeing, etc. I'll give this letter
to the postman when he comes, as I don't think I shall go out this
afternoon. The blisters on my foot hurt too much, and for some
time I've been fed up with Carinthian city life—after going to
Klagenfurt again yesterday. Though of course it was rather magnificent there. All the flags out, really lovely, people in their national
costumes, heaps of different groups and organizations: from children
right to the World War veterans with their medals. I was only there
for an hour or two in the afternoon, but the Zoys[1] went off at 5 a.m.,
making a terrific clatter, and in the evening they were so late, I
didn't even hear them come home.

Yesterday morning, while working on the score, I listened in to
the celebrations for the Carinthian plebiscite. A great deal of
speechifying. In the evening I listened to Hanna Schwarz: not bad,
but not all that good either. So that's all. Now I'll wait for the
postman, and just scribble a few lines in reply.

Thanks for card and letter. So much to say, I had better not make
the postman wait. Please: take care of yourself, and do buy yourself
those throat pastilles. I shall follow all your instructions, just as you
write. A thousand kisses

from
Your own

(486)   Friday, 11th October 1935,
                                                          midday

Your letter made me feel rather out of sorts, because of the
physical strain, which you're really not up to, and because of the
various things you told me: Almschi, Carola, that you're not going
to the Kolisch concert, evidently not to the Hagenbund either, and
that all this will be going on for several days. Still, by the time you
get this letter (by the same post, I expect, as the one I gave the
postman this morning), you'll be over the worst, I hope, and thinking of coming home, where it will again be tremendously *gemütlich*.
As the first rehearsal[2] doesn't take place till the 29th November, we
are not even *obliged* to leave here for a fortnight or more—we can

[1] The caretakers of the Waldhaus.
[2] For the first performance of the *Lulu Symphony* in Vienna.

432

stay on, if the weather is nice. If I hear in your next letter that you aren't travelling on Sunday, I'll write an express letter tomorrow, which you'll get on Sunday. Have you had all my letters? I've written every day . . .

Lili Claus writes, and claims pretty convincingly, that she would be absolutely right for singing the part of Lulu.[1] But so far nothing has happened about Prague (praise be). Have you heard anything definite by any chance? For instance, whether Dr Eger[2] was there. Here too the weather is a bit changeable, but quite fine and pleasantly mild. Be sure to let me know when you're coming so that I can get in the food.

They've just announced brilliant sunshine for tomorrow, Saturday. Who'd have thought it after the break in the weather in the west. And you, my poor thing, will be bathed in sweat.

Enough, my golden one! As I shan't leave the house today because of my foot, I'll be working all day long, quite slowly and steadily, without any rush . . .

(487)   Saturday, 12th October 1935
Great disappointment, nothing from you today. Hope these are my last lines, or perhaps they won't even reach you, in case you're arriving tomorrow, Sunday. I hope, too, that I'll know in good time when you're coming. The caretaker's wife is going to the post office this afternoon, perhaps there'll be something there for me. I can't walk that far because of my leg. I can sit at my desk again today; perhaps tomorrow I'll be able to get about normally. I don't mind telling you that it's[3] been pretty wretched. Last time I was in Klagenfurt, it was so bad I could hardly get back from the cinema to the main square. Quickly to bed when I got home, the leg raised, and put on an antiphlogistin poultice. All day in bed yesterday, changing the poultices continually. Today I'm quite all right keeping the leg down. Don't know exactly what the trouble was. Of the various blisters on both feet all but one subsided normally. There was just that one spot of inflammation right at the ball of the foot. It

[1] Lili Claus, Viennese soprano, sang the part at the concert on 11th December 1935.
[2] The German opera in Prague, under its excellent director, Dr Paul Eger, was trying to secure the world premiere of *Lulu*; but Berg was still hoping for a *première* at one of the leading German opera houses—or at the Vienna State Opera.
[3] See Postscript page 435.

AB–DD   433

hurt like anything, so that I thought another abscess was developing or something like that, and that in the end it would have to be lanced. Thank the Lord, nothing like it, and only the lesson: Never again go for a long walk! This last experience and the one before with the wasp's sting may be a bit of divine guidance—or warning!

So I'm again sitting at home today, while outside there's the most glorious, tempting, autumn weather. Hope it will go on like this for quite a long time so that you can enjoy it too.

Otherwise: work, radio, work, radio—and at night *Winetou*.[1] Food: mostly smoked meat! . . .

See you soon, my golden one . . .

Did you tell Almschi how enthusiastic we were about Werfel's book of poems?

(488)   Sunday, 13th October 1935

Just so that you get one more letter from me, my Pferscherl, I'll give it to Frau Zoy, as she's just off to the post office. Yesterday, after returning from Klagenfurt, I worked on the score for about two more hours, had a splendid supper (remains), listened to Mozart's *Requiem*, and slept well. (No pressure on my chest.) This morning early to work, the weather is dull, no mist. The lake is flowing in the wrong direction! Looks to me as if the weather is getting worse.

A thousand kisses from

                                                            the Flea

---

[1] Famous German boys' book by Karl May (1842–1912).

POSTSCRIPT

Four weeks after his last letter to Helene—on Tuesday, 12th November—Alban Berg returned to Vienna. 'Things are not going well for me,' he wrote to Schoenberg.[1] 'Not *financially*, as I seem unable to maintain my present standard of living, including the Waldhaus. (Yet I can't make up my mind to sell the place, where in two years I did *more* work than in the previous ten.) Nor with my *health*, because for months I have been having boils ... They began shortly after I finished the Violin Concerto[2] with a horrible carbuncle resulting from an insect sting ... Finally things are bad *morally*— which won't surprise you, coming from someone who suddenly discovered he was no longer a native of his own country, and was therefore homeless ...'

On Wednesday 11th December, the *Lulu Symphony*, after many performances abroad, had its Viennese première. Berg—feverish and exhausted—listened for the first time to its actual sound. 'It was to be the last time that any music reached his ear,' Willi Reich reports. 'On 14th December, in severe pain, he looked through the piano score of the Violin Concerto. On 16th December the pains suddenly subsided; the abscess seemed to have burst inwardly, causing general blood poisoning.'

Two emergency operations at the Rudolfspital (Vienna III) and a blood transfusion brought only temporary relief. On Sunday 22nd the heart grew weaker. As he woke up next morning Alban Berg said calmly: 'Today's the 23rd—it will be a decisive day.'

He died on Tuesday, 24th December, at fifteen minutes past one in the morning. Anna Mahler, 'Gucki', prepared the death-mask. It showed a countenance of peace, tranquillity and unearthly beauty.

The City of Vienna gave Alban Berg a memorial grave; in the early afternoon of 28th December he was buried in the Hietzing cemetery.

On the same day, Frau Berg received a letter from Gerhart

---

[1] Letter of 30th November, quoted in Willi Reich's *Alban Berg: Leben und Werk* (Atlantis Verlag, Zurich 1963, Thames and Hudson, London, 1965), which is also the source of the following three paragraphs.
[2] On 11th August.

Hauptmann. In seven lines the great poet expressed his own feelings and the feelings of all the world of art.

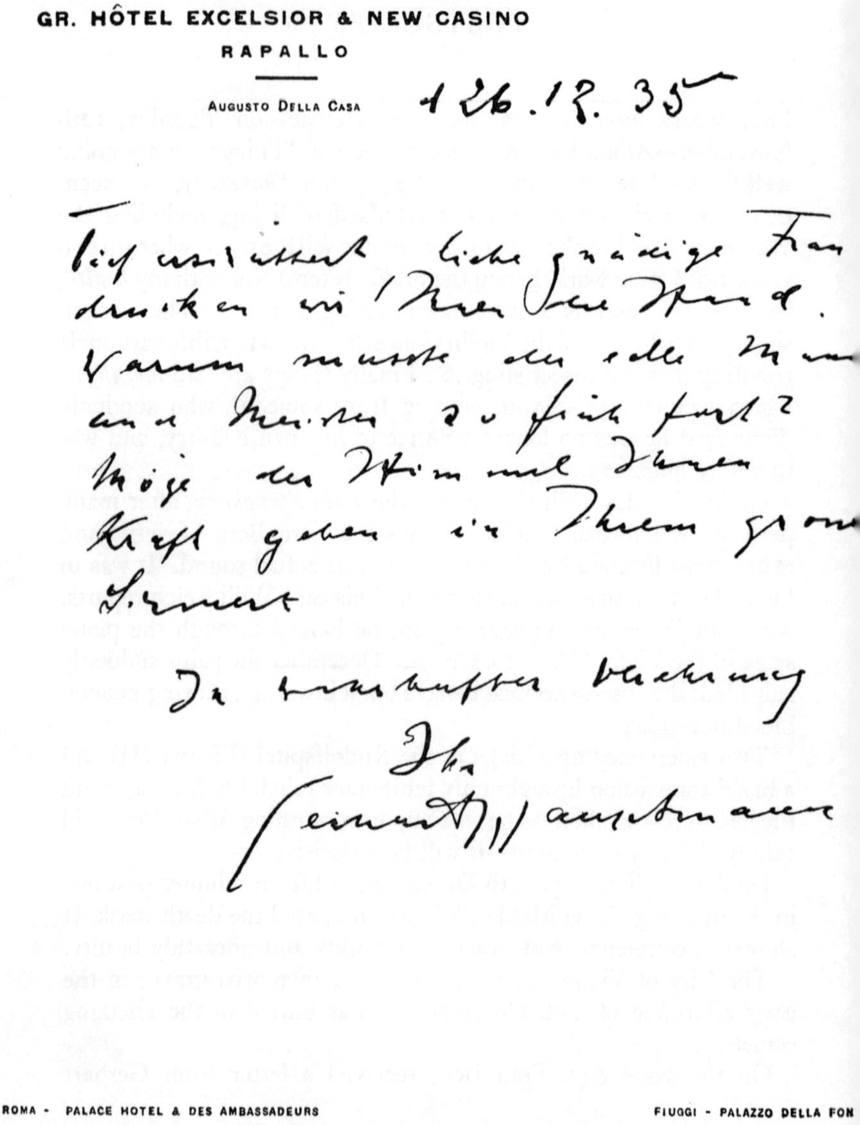
GR. HÔTEL EXCELSIOR & NEW CASINO
RAPALLO
AUGUSTO DELLA CASA

1 26.12.35

Tief erschüttert liebe gnädige Frau drücken wir Ihnen die Hand.
Warum musste der edle Mann und Meister so früh fort?
Möge der Himmel Ihnen Kraft geben in Ihrem grossen Schmerz

In verehrungsvoller Bewunderung
Ihr
Gerhart Hauptmann

ROMA - PALACE HOTEL & DES AMBASSADEURS   FIUGGI - PALAZZO DELLA FON

'Deeply shaken, dear gracious lady, we press your hand
Why had so noble a man and master to take his leave so early?
May Heaven give you strength in your great sorrow.
In sincere admiration,
Yours
Gerhart Hauptmann'

Willi Reich in his obituary voiced the emotions of Berg's friends and pupils: 'Thanks, a thousand times thanks for every moment lived with us and for us, for every smile of his bright yet so enigmatic features, for every note of his unprecedentedly intense and noble work.'

The Violin Concerto was given its first performance (under Scherchen) at the I.S.C.M. Festival at Barcelona in April 1936; performances in London (Webern), Vienna (Klemperer), Paris (Münch) and Boston (Koussevitzky) followed—always with Louis Krasner as soloist. The world première of *Lulu* with the Turkish soprano Nuri Hadzic in the title role took place in Zurich on 2nd June 1937.

Austria had in the meantime entered the last stage of its free existence: on 11th March 1938 the Nazis occupied the country. They regarded all music of the Schoenberg school as 'cultural Bolshevism' and 'degenerate art', and blacklisted it. Webern was forbidden to teach or lecture, and had to earn his living as proofreader in a Viennese publishing house. During the war a member of the Berg family suggested to Helene that since Berg was of Aryan extraction she should petition to Baldur von Schirach, Hitler's governor in Vienna, who could procure performances of his works in Germany. Here is Helene Berg's answer:

Waldhaus,
1st January 1942

Dear brother-in-law,

Thank you for your letter, and for the suggestion, I'm sure well-meant, which, however, I can only reject. Alban Berg's art belongs to the eternal beauties of the divine and spiritual world. I could never bring myself to do anything not in accord with *his* beliefs: this man of utter integrity who *never* compromised in artistic matters. It would seem to me only a profanation to have him 'taken up' by people who are completely alien to his works and must remain so.

Alban can wait with confidence till this Hell on earth has ceased to rage. His time will come, a better time, I am convinced.

Perhaps you will say that the performances might make my life easier. This I admit. But it is unthinkable for me to buy advantages by 'a sin against the Holy Ghost'. My life's sole remaining

437

purpose is to watch over his legacy and preserve its purity. What else is left for me in this world estranged from God!

All greetings to you and yours,

Helene

As the Hell on earth ceased to rage, Berg's time did come: his once scanty following had grown into a vast enthusiastic community of global dimensions. *Wozzeck*, *Lulu*, the Lyric Suite, the Three Pieces for Orchestra, the Chamber Concerto and the Violin Concerto had established him as one of the great composers of the twentieth century.

One by one the voices of his friends fell silent too. Zemlinsky died in 1942 in New York; Webern in 1945 in Mittersill, a small town not far from Salzburg (where he was accidentally shot by a U.S. soldier); Schoenberg in 1951 in Los Angeles; Kleiber in 1956 in Zurich; Stein in 1958 in London; and Alma Mahler in 1964 in Hollywood.

Helene Berg became the faithful, high-principled guardian of her husband's work. As tribute to him, she dedicated the proceeds from his works to an Alban Berg Foundation for the Furthering of Young Composers. She continued to live in the old flat; the master's working room remained in exactly the condition it was when he left it. In 1961 the municipality of Vienna affixed a memorial plaque outside Trauttmannsdorffgasse No. 27.

In the Preface to his edition of Mozart's letters[1] the late Eric Blom says: 'Once the man is known more intimately than he can be before a reading of his own words, one cannot fail to penetrate several layers deeper into his works . . . some profit will be his: he, as well as his work, will be loved the more by those who have come to know him more intimately through these pages.' When Helene Berg, a generation after her husband's death, decided to publish his letters to her, this was precisely what she aimed at: to make him more intimately known through his own words, so that his works will be the more loved. Her collection (Albert Langen Georg Müller Verlag, Munich 1965) included 569 letters. As several of them seemed rather repetitive in their content, more concerned with the Bergs' family circle or long-forgotten Viennese affairs than with Berg himself—and therefore of less interest to the English reader—it was considered expedient to reduce the present volume

[1] Penguin Books, 1956.

438

to 488 items. The same motive prompted any abbreviations within the remaining letters—always marked by an ellipsis.

Pet names, expressions of love and affection, the usage of the German '*Du*' (Thou), local idioms and Berg's stylistic idiosyncrasies —so near the poetry of Hugo von Hofmannsthal and the prose of Karl Kraus—have presented the usual problems of translation. It is hoped that they have been solved, while preserving the baroque peculiarities of the original.

The editor offers his deep and sincere thanks: to Frau Helene Berg for all her help and kindness: to Dr Franz Willnauer who furnished several footnotes; to Dr Herbert Fleissner and Dr Joachim Schondorff of Langen-Müller, Munich who have amicably made available their wide practical knowledge; to Messrs. Donald Mitchell and Charles Ford of Faber and Faber, London for their valuable expertise; to Eric and Blanche Glass, two trusted old friends who brilliantly carried out the most complicated contractual negotiations; and to Mrs Betty Marshall who took great pains preparing the typescript.

Finally grateful acknowledgements are made to my friend Oliver Coburn. His advice and co-operation in linguistic matters were of immeasurable value, while his patience and intelligent zeal were weighty factors in the fulfilment of a responsible, beautiful and exciting task.

B.G.

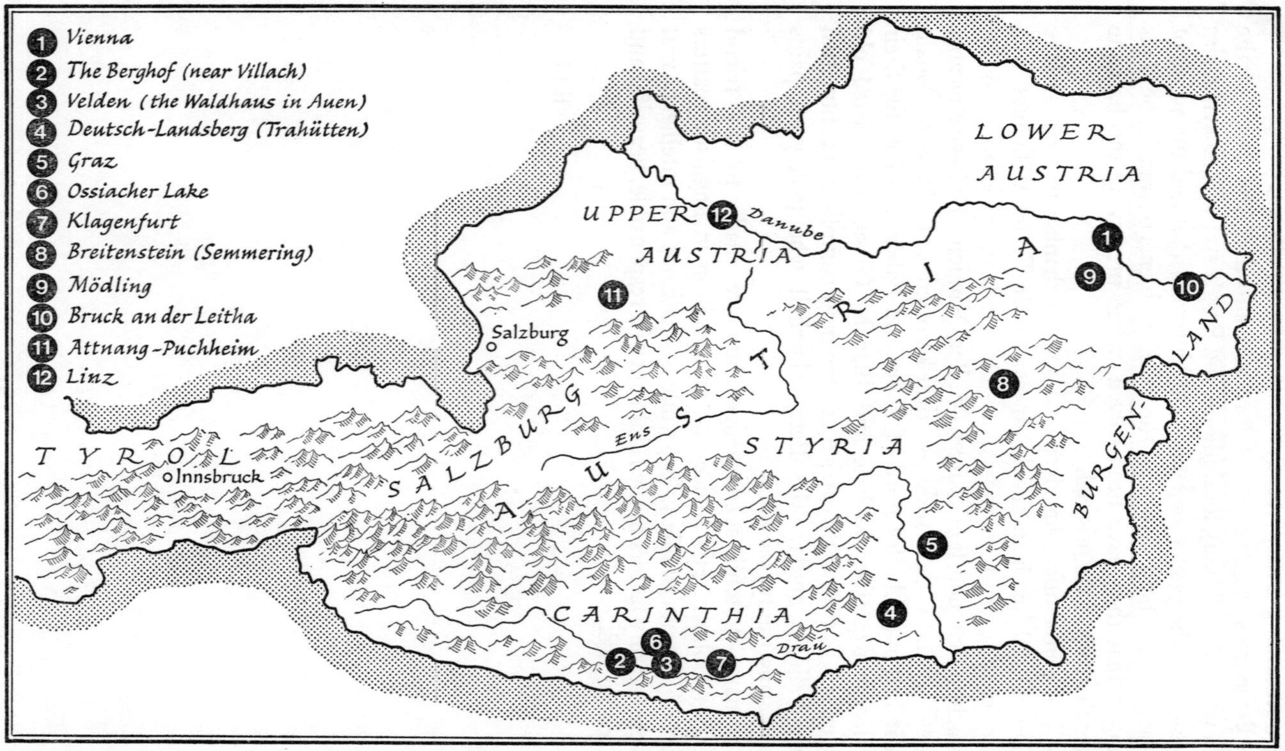

Austria

Key:
1. Vienna
2. The Berghof (near Villach)
3. Velden (the Waldhaus in Auen)
4. Deutsch-Landsberg (Trahütten)
5. Graz
6. Ossiacher Lake
7. Klagenfurt
8. Breitenstein (Semmering)
9. Mödling
10. Bruck an der Leitha
11. Attnang-Puchheim
12. Linz

LOWER AUSTRIA

BURGENLAND

STYRIA

CARINTHIA

UPPER AUSTRIA

SALZBURG

TYROL

Danube

Drau

Ens

Salzburg

Innsbruck

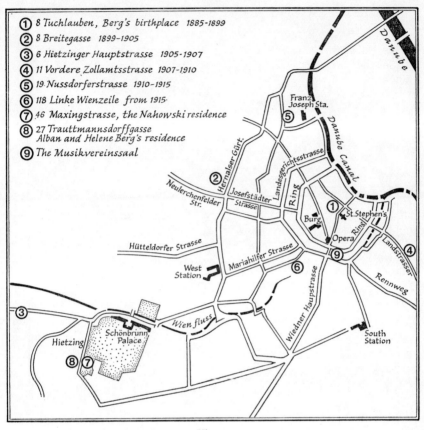

① 8 Tuchlauben, Berg's birthplace 1885-1899
② 8 Breitegasse 1899-1905
③ 6 Hietzinger Hauptstrasse 1905-1907
④ 11 Vordere Zollamtsstrasse 1907-1910
⑤ 19 Nussdorferstrasse 1910-1915
⑥ 118 Linke Wienzeile from 1915
⑦ 46 Maxingstrasse, the Nahowski residence
⑧ 27 Trauttmannsdorffgasse
   Alban and Helene Berg's residence
⑨ The Musikvereinssaal

Vienna

INDEX

Aber, Dr Adolf, 407
Aber, Frau, 407
Accordion: Berg research on, 280, 282, 289; player virtuoso, 352
Acknowledgments, 439
Adler, Dr Alfred, 283, 335
Alban Berg Foundation, 438
Allgemeine Deutsche Musikverein, 398 n. 1
Almschi, 162 n. 2, 179, passim; *see also* Mahler, Alma
Also One, (Vischer), 35
Altenberg, Peter, 25, 33-4, 75, 94, 122, 159 n.
Alwin, Karl, 329, 332
Anbruch, 219, 281 n. 2
And Pippa Dances, (Hauptmann), 89-90, 368
Andreae, Volkmar, 234, 361
Annerl, *see* Nahowski, Anna and Lebert, Anna
Ansermet, Ernst, 379-80, 396, 423
Antschi, Annerl, *see* Nahowski, Anna, and Lebert, Anna
Aosta, Duke of, 407
Apocalypse, (Kraus), 80 n. 3
Apostel, Hans Erich, 158 n. 2, 300, 304, 371
Ariane et Barbe-Bleu, (Dukas), 89
Arnim, Bettina von, 218
Arravantinos, Panos, 354
Art of Fugue, (Bach), 361-2
Askenases, The, 384-91
Association, The, 250, 254-5, 260, 263, 266, 285
Asthmatics cannot be diabetics, 369
Auch Einer (Vischer), 35-6
Auffenberg, General Moritz von, 166 n. 2
Auftakt, 337

Bach, Dr J., 285
Bach, Johann Sebastian, 121, 141

Bachrich (conductor), 216, 219, 231
Bahr, Hermann, 27, 85 n. 1, 233
Bahr-Mildenburg, Anna, 85 n. 1, 86
Balzac, Honoré de, 61, 68, 180, 280 n. 4
Bartók, Béla, 302, 323, 407
Baudelaire, Charles Pierre, 380 n.
Becker, Paul, 326
Beethoven, Ludwig, 25, 74, 218, 225, 232
'Beethoven's Disease of the Ear', (Loos), 219-20
Beethoven's family, 110
Beethoven—Variations for two pianos (Reger), 246
Bekker (critic), 407
Berg, Alban; abscess leads to death, 429 n. 5; accomplished painter, 66 n. 1; admiration for Zemlinsky, 338; advertising, no pupils from, 304; Amsterdam, 152-4; Bayreuth, 82-4; Berlin, 152 n. 1, 341-54, 365-7, 396-7; Brussels, 382-92; Cambridge, 376-8; Duisberg, 367-8; Florence, 406-11; Frankfurt, 294-6; Leningrad, 354-60; London, 373-6, 378-9; Munich, 132-5, 397-400; Nuremberg, 84; Prague, 135-42, 149-52, 336-41; Salzburg, 322-8; Venice, 41-2, 95-7; Zurich, 360-2, 379-81, 400-1 Analyses Mahler Symphony, 219; annoyed with father-in-law, 221; anti-Hitler, 404 n.; anti-Nazi, 398; asthma, 65, 66 n. 2, 67, 70-1, 160, 165-6, 190, 196, 204, 279, 287, 392 n.; auditions pianists, 51; Aryan descent, inquiries about, 413; barrack square, 183-4; blistered feet, 430-3; bodily frailty, 60; boils, complains of, 435; buys Waldhaus, 395 n. 1, 396; canon for Schoenberg,

Berg, Alban—(*cont.*)

369; career, fifteen-year standstill, 318; clerical work at War Ministry, 190 n. 1; composition 'seething inside me', 158; composition lessons at Schwarzwald's school, 402 n. 1, 403, 405; copyright problems, 310; critical of Helene's economizing, 373; critical of Wagner, 336; death of mother, 300 n. 3; defends music as a profession, 107–8; denies indigence, 250; depressed mood, 35, 43, 170, 188, 184, 252, 355, 405, 417; dislike of Hohenberg, 72; ecstatic at rehearsal, 298; eight-minute meeting with Helene, 45; emergency operations, 435; enjoys Schoenberg's approval, 219; enlists, 178–84; exacting military training, 184–92; exemption efforts by Schoenberg, 234–5; fears economies on *Wozzeck*, 346; finances, Nazis impair, 429; financial problems, 435; food costs, 224, 226; foot inflamed, 433–4; Freud consulted on asthma, 335 n.; front-page news, 345; grandfather a baron, 110; guardian to Helene's brother, 405 n. 2; Helene's visit forbidden, 92; helps Schoenberg professionally, 206–8; homosexuality, attitude to, 110; hygienic corset, 363; ill health, 28, 33, 36–8, 46, 60–2, 65–7, 70, 109, 160, 194–6, 204, 238–9, 279, 287, 392 n. 435; in gallery, recognized, 368; interprets Mahler's Ninth, 147; introductory lecture for *Wozzeck*, 372 n. 3; invited to join Berlin Musikhochschule, 412–13; irritability, 39, 160; I.S.C.M. juror, 373 n. 2; juror with German General Music Society, 398 n. 1; 'kid', Helene's references, 23, 25; leave delayed by Spanish 'flu, 226–7; leg trouble, 433–5; letter to Helene's father, 106–11; living in chains, 234; Mahler concert in Munich, 132 n.; marriage, 115 n. 1, 123; medically exempt from army,

35; medicine list, 66; military transport displeases, 185; misgivings at *Wozzeck* rehearsals, 347; money preoccupations, 244; moods and sulks, reproached for, 33; Nazi boycott of, 429 n. 3; neck pain, 186, 194; 'never compromised in artistic manners', 437; New Year's Eve alone, 176–8; nicknames for Helene, 121 n. 3; office routine bores, 230; only one suit, 323; on sick parade, 186; opposes psychoanalysis for Helene, 335–6; outburst against Viennese operetta, 177 n.; ovation for, 380, 392; passed medically fit, 179; photographer, 135 n. 1, 157; physical breakdown from over-strain, 188 n.; picture in Brussels evening paper, 388; politics disturbs, 422; portrait by Schoenberg, 430; posthumous reputation grows, 438; property manager, 49 n. 1, 141–8; pupils of, 140 n. 1, 150, 158; radio lecture names, 382; reaction to war, 170, 177–8; reasons with Helene's father, 106; red roses from Helene, 31, rejects low-salary job, 350 n.; resents Schoenberg's tutorial attitude, 306–7; retort to Pfitzner criticism, 344 n. 3; return to Berghof, 363 n. 6; reverts to Catholicism, 180 n. 3; sails with others but alone, 22; Schoenberg reconciliation, 396 n. 2, 397 n. 2; seeks official non-Jewish declaration, 403; sees meaning in number 23, 150 n. 3, 206, 223, 288, 386–7, 435; sets verses to music, 19 n. 1; Shaw, judgment of, 237; sketches, 134, 149, 157, 163, 173, 175, 215, 217, 258, 279, 282, 314, 332, 418, 431; stamina low, 179; steward at Berghof, 251–67; stops train, fined, 374–5; successful protest stops cancellation, 427 n. 3; suicide, reference to, 23; their first kiss, 30; three lost war years, 224; throat infection, 194–5; troubled by Webern's visits, 292–3;

448

Miklas, Wilhelm, 413
Mildenburg, Anna Bahr-, 85 n. 1, 86, 161
Milhaud, Darius, 26 n., 391–2, 407
'Minneleide', 20 n. 1
Mitzi, 315
Moissi, Alexander, 211
Moll, Carl, 197 n. 3, 319
Moll, Frau, 197 n. 3
Molnar, Ferenc, 364 n. 2, 365
Mooser (critic), 420
Mopinka, 337 n. 1, 341–3
Morgenstern, Christian, 205
Morgenstern, Soma, 419 n. 2
Mozart, Wolfgang, 35, 140, 422
Muller, Dr, 297, 386 n. 1
Muller, Stephanie, 386, 390
Münch, 437
Musical Courier, 159 n.
Musical Impotence of Hans Pfitzner's New Aesthetics (Berg), 344 n. 1
Music and stewardship incompatible, 255
Musik, 316–17, 321
Mutzi, 314, 319

Nahowski, Anna, 28–30, 32, 47, 54, 65, 76–7, 89, 91, 92 n., 99, 106–7, 109, 115 n. 2, 117–19, 141, 162, 182 n. 2; *see also* Lebert, Anna
Nahowski, Anna (*née* Novak), 53 n. 2, 82, 89, 113, 115–16, 131, 162, 191, 199, 205, 209, 214, 294, 299, 309, 363
Nahowski, Franz, 36 n. 1, 51, passim; ignores Berg letter, 111 n. 1; Protestantism a consent condition, 180 n. 3
Nakowski, Franz Joseph, 38, 309, 370–2, 392 n. 427 n. 1,428; schizophrenia, 214 n. 1; worsening condition, 370 n. 2, 372
Natural Affinities (Goethe), 24
Nazis: Berg dislikes Munich carnivals, 398–400; blacklist Schoenberg school, 437; boycott Berg music, 429 n. 3; election successes, 370; forbid Webern to teach, 437; 'Hell on earth', 437; impair Berg's in-

come, 429; occupy Austria, 437; propaganda ignores moderns, 413–414; Schoenberg's 'degenerate art', 437
Neisser, Arthur, 236 n.
Neue Freie Presse, 165, 291–2
Neumann, František, 338
New Aesthetics of Musical Impotence, The, (Pfitzner), 344 n. 1
New piano works, request for, 321
Nietzsche, Friedrich, 27, 37–8, 72, 90
Nightingale, The, 31 n.
Nilius (conductor), 323
Ninth Symphony (Mahler), 90, 220, 249, 302; Schoenberg plans analysis, 220

Oestvig, Karl Aagard, 297, 392, 332
Olympia (film), 364–5
Opera première, politics cancels, 423
Oppenheimer, Max, 55, 72, 95
Orchestral score, tedium of revising, 312,
Ostrčil, Otokar, 338 n. 1

Přihody Lišky Bistroušky (Janáček), 340 n. 4
Palestrina (Pfitzner), 343
Palmström (Morgenstern), 205
Pandora's Box (Wedekind), 25 n. 2
Panzer, Dr, 216, 371
Pappenheim, Herr, 321, 330
Pappenheim, Marie, 200, 212, 231–2, 247, 321, 330
Parsifal (Wagner), 24, 77, 81–6, 89–90
Påsk (Strindberg), 59 n.
Passacaglia (Webern), 303, 318
Paul, Jean, 84
Peace, 218
Pella, Pau, 318
Pelléas and Mélisande (Schoenberg), 135 n. 2, 138–9, 141, 152 n. 1, 264–5, 303
Pepi (housekeeper), 141
Performance cancelled, then restored, 427 n.
Performing Right Society remittance, 415
Perntner, 412

451

Pfitzner, Hans, 20 n. 1, 25, 230, 343
Physiology of Marriage (Balzac), 61
Piano Sonata (Berg), 111 n. 2, 159,
    249 n 2, 296, 321, 430
Piccaver, Alfred, 232, 233 n. 1
Pieces for Clarinet wanted by Hertzka,
    318, 430
Pieces for Orchestra (Berg), 248, 303,
    307–8, 318, 321, 373
Pieces for Orchestra (Schoenberg), 223
Pierot Lunaire (Schoenberg), 145
Pilzer, Dr, 299, 313
Pippa, (Haputmann), 89–90, 368
Pisk, Paul Amadeus, 246, 399–400
Ploderer, Dr Rudolf, 186–8, 191, 216,
    266, 308–9, 313
Ploderer, Frau, 248
Polgar, Alfred, 283
Pollak (court councillor), 134
Pollak, Egon, 381
Polnauer, Dr Josef, 140, 161, 200, 219,
    238, 290, 292, 321–2, 326, 333, 341
Pongracz, Danka, 209–10
Pongracz, Major-General Arthur,
    209–10
Popper, Josef, 40 n. 2
Possessed, The, 156
Poverty all round, 246
President boxes insulter's ears, 159 n.
Private Life of Helen of Troy, The,
    (Erskine), 363
Professorship, hopes of government,
    413
Protestantism condition of marriage,
    180 n. 3
Psychoanalysis, crazy confidence trick
    of, 335
Puccini, Giacomo, 72, 410

Quartet (Berg), 255, 277, 287, 303–4,
    307, 323–8, 337; wanted by
    Hertzka, 318
Quartet (Křenek), 327–8
Quartet (Schoenberg), 307, 334
Quartet (Webern), 306–7
Quartet (Zemlinsky), 362

Ragtime (Stravinsky), 275
Rankl, Karl, 213 n. 2, 333

Raoul (rival), 20–1, 33, 35, 38, 68
Raphael, 41
Ratz, Erwin, 216, 219, 231, 283
Ravel, Maurice, 169, 255, 265, 296
Realist's Fantasies, A, (Popper), 40
Redemption (Tolstoy), 211 n. 1
Reger, Max, 246, 249
Reich, Dr Willi, 150 n. 3, 158 n. 2,
    286, 371, 378, 387, 393, 406, 413,
    417–8, 421, 424, 427, 435
Reichstag fire: 'Dancing on a vol-
    cano', 400
Reichwein, Leopold, 330
Reigen (Berg), 162
Reinhart, Hans, 379 n. 2, 380
Reinhart, Werner, 379 n. 2, 380
Rembrandt, van Rijn, 35
Requiem (Mozart), 434
Réti, Rudolph, 246, 248
Reversion to Catholicism, 180
Reznicek, Ernst Nikolaus, 367–9
Ridi, R., 42, 62
Rienzi (Wagner), 336
Rilke, Rainer Maria, 26 n
Ring of the Nibelungs (Wagner), 63
Ritter, Julie, 23
Rittersbach, 226
Roller, Alfred, 47 n. 4, 329
Rosbaud, Hans, 408
Rosé, Arnold, 152 n. 2, 219, 422
Rose from the Love-Garden, The,
    (Pfitzner), 20 n. 1
Rosegger, Peter, 150, 165, 168–9, 179,
    191
Rose of Stamboul (Fall), 241
Rosmersholm (Ibsen), 91
Rottenberg, Ludwig, 295
'Round', (Berg), 162 n. 1
Roussel, 407
Rovelli, Dr Bruno, 65 n.
Rufer, Josef, 213 n. 2, 290–1, 326–7,
    350, 352, 415

Salome (Wilde), 24 n. 1
Salzburg success for Quartet, 326–7
Salzgeber, Barness, 62, 71
Satie, 275
Scandal, famous **V**iennese musical,
    159 n.

452

Schalek, Alice, 203–4
Schalk, Franz, 245
Scherchen, Hermann, 287, 303, 327, 337 n. 2, 361–2, 373, 388, 437
Schiller, Friedrich von, 37, 48 n.
Schillings, Max von, 344, 350, 351 n. 352
Schinko, First Lieutenant, 223
Schirach, Baldur von, 437
Schirmer, 307
Schlafend trägt man mich (Berg), 198
Schmedes, Erik, 86
Schmid, Frau (Josef's mother), 322, 324, 366
Schmid, Josef, 140, 203, 220, 245, 282, 286, 289, 292–3, 322 n. 3, 324, 327–8, 343–4, 346, 350, 352, 354
Schmidt, Franz, 245
Schnabel, Thomas, 284 n. 3, 285
Schnitzler, Arthur, 309 n. 1
Schoenberg, Arnold, 29 n. 1, passim; accomplished painter, 430 n. 3; anti-Semitism involves, 290–3; Berg writes about financial problems, 435; book on harmony, 287; cantankerous mood, 330; circle, Nazis ignore, 414; critical of Berg's efforts, 315; death, 438; directs master composition class, 366 n. 3; dismissed from Berlin Musikhochschule, 412 n. 3; emigrates to USA, 417 n. 1; faults Chamber Concerto passages, 306; finances sound, 304; financial distress, 211; military exemption withdrawn, 210; money problems eased, 223; Nazis and, 400; physically unfit for army, 213 n. 2, pupils, concert by, 31 n., 51 n., school, 'cultural Bolshevism', 437; terrific superiority, 216; twelve-note composition, 310 n. 1
Schoenberg, Georg (Gorgel), 240, 304
Schoenberg, Heinrich, 290 n. 1
Schoenberg, Mathilde (*née* Zemlinsky), 137, 150, 182, 191, 214, 231, 234, 238, 241–2, 246, 277, 290, 292, 303, 309–10, 321
Schoenberg, Trude, (*m.* Felix Greissle), 214, 216, 223, 231, 246, 264, 321; son for, 321 n. 1
Schopenhauer, Arthur, 37–8
Schreker, Franz, 210, 219, 231–2, 346–8, 350, 377 n.
Schuh (Berghof bailiff), 253
Schumann, Elizabeth, 329 n. 3, 332
Schuschnigg, Kurt von, 411 n. 2, 413
Schützendorf, Leo, 343–4, 349–50
Schwarz, Hanna, 430, 432
Schwarzwald, Dr Eugenie, 203 n. 2, 210–11, 402 n. 1
Scriabin, Alexander, 169
Second Symphony (Mahler), 132 n, 135, 186
Segantini, Giovanni, 232
Seidlhofer, Bruno, 312
Seligmann, Frau, 295
Seligmann, Walter Herbert, 295 n. 1, 346
Seminar for Composition, 213
Seraglio (Mozart), 233 n. 1
Seraphita (Balzac), 180 n. 1
Seven Early Songs (Berg), 31 n., 36 n. 4, 79 n. 2, 365
Seventh Symphony (Beethoven, 407
Seventh Symphony (Mahler), 231, 248
Sex Question, The, (Forell), 136
Sezession (Viennese art form), 29
Shaw, G. Bernard, 237
Shops display Berg music, 323
Sieben Frühe Lieder (Berg), 26 n., 31 n.
Siegfried (Wagner), 47, 81 n. 2
Siegfried Idyll (Wagner), 305
Siegl (soprano), 161
Simplicissimus, 86, 93
Six Little Pieces (Schoenberg), 264 n.
Six Orchestral Pieces (Webern), 159 n.
Six Songs with Orchestra (Schoenberg), 149 n.
Sixth Symphony (Mahler), 248
Skoda (industrialist), 206
Slezak, Leo, 364
Society for Private Concerts, 213 n. 2, 225 n. 2, 235, 276, 284, 287, 289, 304
Society of Authors, Composers and Music-Publishers (A.K.M.), 405 n. 4

453

158 n. 1, 161 n. 2, 317–8, 377, 438;
contract with Hertzka signed, 318;
dedication copy for Schoenberg,
318
Tiefland (D'Albert), 101
Toccata (Busoni), 275
Toch, Ernst, 407
Tolstoy, Leo, 211
Toni (Bergs' housekeeper), 157–8,
190–1, 204–5, 249, 275, 278, 283,
306
Torch, The, 78 n. 2; *see also Die Fackel*
Torquato Tasso (Goethe), 24 n. 2
Tote Stadt, Die (Korngold), 295
Traumgekrönt (Rilke), 26 n, 31 n.
Traumgörg (Zemlinsky), 203
Traviata, 297
Trio (Webern), 362
Tristan und Isolde (Wagner), 24, 78
n. 1, 136, 138
Turandot, 426
Turnau, Josef, 332
Twelve-note composition (Hauer),
333 n. 1
Twelve-note composition, (Schoen-
berg), 310 n. 1
'Twelve Variations on an original
theme' (Berg), 51 n.

Und Pippa Tanzt (Hauptmann), 89
n. 2, 368 n. 2
Uproar at concert, 159 n.

Valkyrie, The (Wagner), 231 n. 3
Variations and Fugue on a theme by
Beethoven (Reger), 246 n. 2
Vaugouin, Carl, 371
Vera Violetta (Eysler), 39
Verdi, Novel of the Opera, (Werfel),
333 n. 2
Verklärte Nacht, 265
Viebeg, Ernst, 316 n.
Viennese Court Opera, 20 n. 3
Viertel, Berthold, 222 n., 290
Violin Concerto (Berg), 198 n. 2, 395
n. 1, 435, 437–8
Violin Concerto (Mendelssohn), 151
Violin Pieces (Webern), 275

Violin Sonata in E minor (Pfitzner),
230
Violin Sonata (Reger), 249
Von Heute auf Morgen (Schoenberg)
369 n. 4
Vossiche Zeitung, 340, 350

Wagner, Cosima, 86
Wagner, General, (Austrian politi-
cian), 412
Wagner, Richard, 23, 37–8, 42 n. 1,
63, 72, 74 n. 1, 77, 80–1, 83, 85–6,
89–90, 102, 136, 194, 351; antiquated music, 336
Wagner, Siegfried, 85–6
Waldhaus: bad workmanship, 414;
bought, 395 n. 1, 396; thoughts of
selling, 435; workmen delay restora-
tions, 403–4
Walter, Bruno, 132 n., 248, 403 n. 1,
420
Waltz Dream, A, (Dorman), 283 n. 4
Waltz Dream (Oscar Strauss), 43
Watza (Berg's pupil), 304
Watznauer, Hermann, 183
Webern, Anton, 26 n., 72, 95, 137–40,
passim; accidentally shot dead,
438; angina, 150; becomes proofreader, 437; different light on,
241–2; greatest conductor since
Mahler, 301, 303–5; in disfavour,
235; London seeks, 403; people
unfair to, 320; quarrel with Schoen-
berg patched, 246 n. 1; shockingly
ill, 220
Webern, Frau, 140, 216, 222, 240–2,
278, 281, 330
Wedekind, Frank, 25, 362 n. 3
Wedekind, Frau, 366, 368
Weidemann, Herman, 86
Weinberger, Joseph, 310, 313
Weingartner, Felix von, 47 n. 5, 176,
245
Weininger, Otto, 27
Weisengrund-Adorno, Dr Theodor,
429 n. 3
Weissmann, Adolph, 323, 325–6
Wellesz, Egon, 246, 402, 405–6, 408,
411–12